QUALITY MANAGEMENT
IN URBAN TOURISM

International Western Geographical Series

editorial address

Harold D. Foster, Ph.D.
Department of Geography
University of Victoria
Victoria, British Columbia
Canada

Since publication began in 1970 the Western Geographical Series (now the Canadian and the International Western Geographical Series) has been generously supported by the Leon and Thea Koerner Foundation, the Social Science Federation of Canada, the National Centre for Atmospheric Research, the International Geographical Union Congress, the University of Victoria, the Natural Sciences Engineering Research Council of Canada, the Institute of the North American West, the University of Regina, the Potash and Phosphate Institute of Canada, the Saskatchewan Agriculture and Food Department, and the B.C. Ministry of Health and Ministry Responsible for Seniors.

QUALITY MANAGEMENT IN URBAN TOURISM

edited by

PETER E. MURPHY

JOHN WILEY & SONS

CHICHESTER • NEW YORK • WEINHEIM • BRISBANE • TORONTO • SINGAPORE

Other Wiley Editorial Offices

John Wiley & Sons, Inc., 605 Third Avenue,
New York, NY 10158-0012, USA

VCH Verlagsgesellschaft mbH, Pappelallee 3,
D-69469 Weinheim, Germany

Jacaranda Wiley Ltd, 33 Park Road, Milton,
Queensland 4064, Australia

John Wiley & Sons (Asia) Pte Ltd, 2 Clementi Loop #02-01,
Jin Xing Distripark, Singapore 129809

John Wiley & Sons (Canada) Ltd, 22 Worcester Road,
Rexdale, Ontario M9W 1L1, Canada

Library of Congress Cataloging-in-Publication Data

A catalogue record for this book is available from the Library of Congress

British Library Cataloguing in Publication Data

A catalogue record for this book is available from the British Library

ISBN 0-471-97099-9

Produced from camera-ready-copy supplied by the editor,
Printed and bound in Great Britain by Bookcraft (Bath) Ltd,
This book is printed on acid-free paper responsibly manufactured from sustainable
forestation, for which at least two trees are planted for each one used for paper production.

Contents

The Contributors vii

Acknowledgements xi

Preface xi

SECTION 1:   MANAGEMENT ISSUES

1   Quality Management in Urban Tourism 1
    Peter E. Murphy

2   Seasonality in Tourism: Problems and Measurement 9
    R. Butler and B. Mao

3   Urban Tourism Development in the
    Modern Canadian City: A Review 25
    Michael J. Broadway

4   Impacts of Inner City Tourism Projects: The Case of
    The International Convention Centre, Birmingham, U.K. 41
    Jane Lutz and Chris Ryan

5   Competition and the Resort Community:
    Towards an Understanding of Residents' Needs 55
    Alison M. Gill

6   Special Events Legacy:
    The 1984 Louisiana World's Fair in New Orleans 67
    Frédéric Dimanche

7   Mega-Events And Their Legacies 75
    C. Michael Hall

SECTION 2:   COMMERCIALIZING HERITAGE AND CULTURE

8   The Politics of Heritage Tourism: Place, Power and the
    Representation of Values in the Urban Context 91
    C. Michael Hall

9   Urban Tourism and the Performing Arts 103
    Howard L. Hughes

10 Collusion, Collision or Challenge?:
Indigenous Tourism and Cultural Experience in
British Columbia, Canada 115
   Heather Norris Nicholson

11 Linking Heritage and Tourism in an Asian City:
The Case of Yogyakarta, Indonesia 137
   Geoffrey Wall

12 An Institution in Transition: The Royal
British Columbia Museum's Futures Project 149
   Bill Barkley

13 Biltmore Estate and the Business of Historic Preservation 157
   W.A.V. Cecil

SECTION 3: MANAGEMENT PARTNERSHIPS

14 Creating Value for Visitors to Urban Destinations 169
   K. Michael Haywood

15 Improving The Tourist's Experience: Quality
Management Applied To Tourist Destinations 183
   Albert Postma and Andrew K. Jenkins

16 'Visioning' for Sustainable Tourism Development:
Community-based Collaborations 199
   Tazim B. Jamal and Donald Getz

17 Attraction Land Use Management in Disney Theme Parks:
Balancing Business and Environment 221
   Peter E. Murphy

18 Researching Tourism Partnership Organizations:
From Practice to Theory to Methodology 235
   Philip E. Long

19 Botanical Garden and Satisfaction of the Tourist:
An Exploratory Measurement of the Experience 253
   Laurent Bourdeau, Sylvie Paradis, and Simon Nyeck

AUTHOR INDEX 265

SUBJECT INDEX 275

The Contributors

Bill Barkley completed his undergraduate and graduate degrees at the University of British Columbia and the University of Victoria. He taught high school and college biology in British Columbia for 4 years and worked as a wildlife biologist for the Canadian Wildlife Service for 10 years. He has been Executive Director of the Royal British Columbia Museum for 12 years

Laurent Bourdeau is professor of Marketing at Université de Moncton, New Brunswick, Canada. He has taught Services Marketing and Tourism for six years. Now, Professor Bourdeau is teaching ethics in Marketing and Methodology. His present research interests span hedonic experience and the linkages between emotions, memorization and orientation.

Michael Broadway is associate professor and chair, Department of Geography, State University of New York at Geneseo. His research interests include: recent changes in the social and economic composition of Canadian inner cities, urban tourism, and community development issues among small towns in the Great Plains and Prairies.

Richard Butler is a professor of Geography at the University of Western Ontario, London, Canada. He was born in England, and earned degrees in Geography at Nottingham (B.A.) and Glasgow (Ph.D.) Universities before moving to Canada in 1967. His main research interests include the process of tourism development and the resulting impacts, with particular reference to islands and peripheral locations. He has travelled and conducted research in the Canadian Arctic, the South Pacific, the Caribbean, Australia and Western Europe. His publications include books on tourism research, sustainable tourism, and tourism and indigenous peoples, and many articles and chapters in tourism and leisure volumes. He is past president of the Canadian Association for Leisure Studies and current president of the International Academy for the Study of Tourism.

William Amherst Vanderbilt Cecil is president of The Biltmore Company, which owns and operates Biltmore Estate in Asheville, North Carolina. Cecil was chairman of the board and founder of the Historic House Association of America and past president of the Asheville Area Chamber of Commerce, and was founding chairman of the Asheville/Buncombe County Tourism Development Authority. A graduate of Harvard University, Cecil was formerly a representative of Chase Manhattan Bank of New York City in Washington, D.C. and was an officer with Chase in the International Department in New York.

Frédéric Dimanche joined the School of Hotel, Restaurant, and Tourism Administration at the University of New Orleans in 1991, after completing his Ph.D. degree from the University of Oregon. His research interests are in the areas of tourism marketing, consumer behaviour, and tourism impacts.

Donald Getz is a professor in Tourism and Hospitality Management at the University of Calgary. He received his doctorate in Social Sciences (Geography) from the University of Edinburgh, his M.A. from Carleton University (Geography), and a Bachelor of Environmental Studies (Urban and Regional Planning) from the University of Waterloo. He specializes in event management and event tourism, tourism and recreation planning and impact evaluation. His most recent book, *Event Management and Event Tourism*, is being published in late 1996.

Alison M. Gill is an associate professor with a joint appointment in the Department of Geography and the School of Resource and Environmental Management at Simon Fraser University. She joined the faculty in 1984, after completing her Ph.D. degree at the University of Manitoba. She teaches several courses relating to tourism including, community tourism planning, a course which reflects her primary research interests. Dr. Gill's recent tourism research has focused on mountain resort communities and the role of tourism in community economic development.

C. Michael Hall is director of the Centre for Tourism and Leisure Policy Research at the University of Canberra, Australia. His teaching and research interests are varied and include tourism planning and development, tourism and politics, arts, culture and heritage tourism, events, visitor management, environmental history, and resource management.

Michael Haywood is director and professor, School of Hotel and Food Administration, University of Guelph, Guelph, Ontario, Canada. He has published widely on topics related to the management of hospitality and tourism enterprises, and serves on the editorial board of six industry journals. He is a fellow of the Hotel, Catering and Institutional Management Association and the International Academy of Hospitality Research. In 1992, Michael received the John Wiley and Sons Award in recognition of lifetime contributions to outstanding scholarship and research in hospitality and tourism.

Howard L. Hughes is professor of Tourism Management at Manchester Metropolitan University, UK. He gained his Bachelor's and Master's degrees in economics from the University of Wales and Leeds University respectively, and was awarded his Ph.D. by the City University, London, for research into the tourism dimensions of a UK opera company. Author of a specialist economics textbook, *Economics for Hotel and Catering Students*, published in 1986 and now in its second edition, he has also written over 30 published papers on aspects of the hotel and tourism industries.

Tazim B. Jamal is a Ph.D. candidate in Tourism and Hospitality Management at the University of Calgary. Her main area of study is destination management and planning, with special interest in cross-sectoral collaborative planning and tourism in developing countries.

Andrew Jenkins joined the Hotel Management School Leeuwarden in 1989 after graduating with a Master of Science degree in Tourism from the University of Strathclyde and having worked as researcher and assistant lecturer at the School of Planning, Oxford Polytechnic (now Brookes University, Oxford). He teaches courses in tourism and is also a member of the staff team of the M.A. International Leisure and Tourism Studies. Activities now include curriculum development and teaching for the Leisure Management School, the Hotel Management School and the International School of Hospitality Management, Leeuwarden.

Philip Long is a senior lecturer in Tourism Management at the Centre for Tourism, Sheffield Hallam University. Before embarking on an academic career, Philip worked in the tourism industry, including two years in Zimbabwe. His current research interests include the study of partnerships for tourism development, the subject of the chapter in this volume and, the relationships between arts/culture and tourism.

Jane Lutz is a lecturer in the Centre for Urban and Regional Studies in the School of Public Policy at the University of Birmingham, UK. She has practitioner experience within a city marketing organization, and a background in education and public health research. Her current research interests are in urban tourism, tourism partnerships and health and tourism.

Baodi Mao recently completed his doctorate in Geography at the University of Western Ontario, London, Canada, and is currently studying in the Richard Ivey School of Business at the University of Western Ontario. He was born in the People's Republic of China, and completed degrees at Xinjiang University (B.Sc.) and Chinese Academy of Sciences (M.A.), as well as being a visiting scholar at Texas Tech University, before beginning his doctorate in Canada in 1991. He was an assistant professor in the Chinese Academy of Sciences, and has worked as a consultant in the private sector in Canada. His publications include books on regional development and a number of articles and chapters on tourism and development. His research interests in tourism include the effects of political partition and restrictions on travel between nations, and the nature and dimensions of seasonal and spatial patterns in tourism.

Peter Murphy is Head of Tourism Programs in the Faculty of Business at the University of Victoria and Adjunct Professor in Geography. He has been engaged in tourism research for the past 20 years, during which time he has published over 50 academic articles and three books. His major book, *Tourism: A Community Approach*, has been acclaimed widely and translated into Japanese. He has received two major awards for his work in tourism, the Roy Wolfe Award for tourism research in 1992, and election into the prestigious (75 members worldwide) International Academy for the Study of Tourism in 1995. His focus has been community participation in the development of local tourism, involving the concept of sustainable development from both an environmental and business perspective. His research and input helped in the creation of Tourism Victoria, where he has served on the Executive Board, and he has facilitated in the development of its constitution and business plan.

Heather Norris Nicholson is senior lecturer in Geography at the University College of Ripon and York St John (University of Leeds, UK). Her teaching includes courses on Canadian Studies, cultural geography, heritage studies and development issues. She has research interests in areas of tourism, cultural identity and historical geography. She is an active member of the British Association of Canadian Studies and traces her West Coast interests to long-established family connections.

Simon Nyeck is professor of Marketing at Université Laval, Ste-Foy, Québec, Canada. His research interests include consumer behaviour and tourism.

Sylvie Paradis is professor of Marketing at Université de Québec à Montréal, Québec, Canada. Her area of specialization is Methodology and Tourism.

Albert Postma joined the Leisure Management School Leeuwarden in 1988, after completing his study in Human Geography at the University of Groningen and working as a research co-ordinator and manager in information and automatization in the municipality of Leeuwarden. He teaches courses in Geography, Spatial Planning, Research, Statistics and SPSS, is member of the staff team of the MA International Leisure and Tourism Studies (a joint venture with the University of North London), and works as project manager and consultant at the Institute for Service Management, the research and consultancy department of the faculty.

Chris Ryan was formerly head of the Tourism and Recreation Research Unit at Nottingham Business School, UK. He has taught in universities in the UK, Canada, and New Zealand. He is author of six books, including *Recreational Tourism* (1991) and *Researching Tourism Satisfaction* (1995), is on the editorial board of four academic journals, and the author of over 70 articles and papers. In 1996 he was undertaking research in New Zealand on behalf of regional and national tourism organizations while based at Massey University, Palmerston North.

Geoffrey Wall is Professor of Geography in the Faculty of Environmental Studies, University of Waterloo, where he holds a cross-appointment with the Department of Recreation and Leisure Studies. He is interested in the impacts of tourism, particularly the consequences of different types of tourism for destinations. He has undertaken a number of investigations of tourism in Indonesia and provided input on tourism in the formulation of a sustainable development strategy for Bali.

Series Editor's Acknowledgements

In the early summer of 1995 the University established the Western Geographical Press. Negotiations were conducted with both John Wiley and Sons, Ltd. and UBC Press. As a result, the Western Geographical Series was split into two components. The International Western Geographical Series is edited under the auspices of Western Geographical Press, and published and distributed by John Wiley and Sons, Ltd. The Canadian Western Geographical Series is published by the Western Geographical Press but distributed by UBC press. This is the second volume of the International Western Geographical Series.

Several members of the Department of Geography, University of Victoria cooperated to ensure the successful publication of this volume. Special thanks are due to members of the technical services division. Diane Macdonald undertook the very demanding task of typesetting. Cartographic work was performed by Ken Josephson, who also designed the cover. Their dedication and hard work is greatly appreciated.

University of Victoria
Victoria, B.C., Canada
20th July 1996

Harold D. Foster
Series Editor
Western Geographical Press

Preface and Editor's Acknowledgements

The topic of "Quality Management in Urban Tourism" was conceived, over several discussions with colleagues in the Faculty of Business, as an area of tourism to which social and management science research could contribute. It was noted that our home base of Victoria is one of the foremost tourist destinations in Canada, yet there was little in the research literature to guide us or the industry in proposing appropriate management strategies. The topic of destination research and management is just beginning to emerge as a significant subfield within tourism studies, so most of the publications in this area are more descriptive than prescriptive to this point. In an attempt to move the subject of destination management forward it was decided to issue a call for conference papers and this produced a significant and successful conference that was held in Victoria, B.C. in November 1994.

The full title of the conference was "Quality Management in Urban Tourism: Balancing Business and Environment". This reflected the twin purposes of the conference. First, to focus on ways to develop a quality product and experience for the tourists. Second, to acknowledge that these products and experiences involved significant externalities, such as people's homes and quality of life. Therefore, quality management was viewed from the perspective of balancing the needs of industry with the needs of local residents and the physical environment.

To put such a conference topic together took teamwork, which in itself reflected the approach that is needed to produce quality urban destinations. The universal nature of the topic brought forward submissions from a variety of social science and business disciplines, all with a common interest in and commitment to seeing more appropriate use being made of tourism destination settings. No progress would be made in such areas unless government and the industry were appreciative of the opportunities and responsibilities. Thus it was reassuring to receive considerable support for this conference from both the government, represented by the provincial and federal levels, and the tourism industry of Victoria in the form of sponsorships and active participation. To put on a successful conference required the cooperation and support of our faculty, staff and students, who devoted many hours to ensuring every aspect functioned smoothly and that we were able to demonstrate what we were preaching—quality management. To provide the personal touch and hospitality required the ultimate teamwork of a supportive wife. I shall be forever grateful for the significant contributions made by my wife Susan, who helped with the driving, the catering, the accommodations, and made everyone feel welcome and at home.

Given the success of the conference, with its 58 papers, 163 delegates from 16 different countries and the positive reaction that was generated, it was only natural to seek a means of recording the evidence and thoughts of this event in a more permanent form. We are fortunate that the University of Victoria's Geography department has developed a fine series of geographic publications and showed an interest in publishing the results of this conference. We are grateful to Dr. Harold Foster for putting us in touch with John Wiley and for taking on the responsibility of senior editorship.

The papers produced in this volume were originally presented at the "Quality Management in Urban Tourism" conference, but each has been revised in response to the conference feedback and the views of referees. The selection process involved a double blind review of the submitted papers, with those which were successful being put together in logical groupings.

It is hoped that the readers of this book will find the topics and approaches advocated as useful and relevant as did the original conference delegates. The collection is a good cross-section of the conference papers and is intended to build on the recent publications in this growing area of tourism research. We will have achieved our overall objective if the contents generate further research and thoughtful action in this significant and sensitive area of tourism management.

Plate 1 Butchart Gardens—the Italian Garden in Spring
(photo courtesy of The Butchart Gardens Ltd.) ➡

SECTION 1
MANAGEMENT ISSUES

Quality Management in Urban Tourism

Peter E. Murphy

Tourism Programs,
Faculty of Business, University of Victoria

INTRODUCTION

Academic interest in the urban tourism domain has long trailed the significance of this activity to the industry and host destinations, but in recent years there has been an increase in the academic study of this phenomenon. In parts of the world, like Europe, associated with traditional seaside resorts, historic cities, and centres of culture and learning, urban tourism has become a major trip purpose. Pearce(1989: 58) cites a European survey that showed 52 percent of the respondents had spent holidays at the seaside, of which a good portion would take place in traditional seaside resort destinations, and a further 19 percent in towns. Such statistics are likely to have underestimated the contribution of urban places to the European vacation experience since the touring component was not captured in these figures, and use of the word town may have led some urban areas, like villages, to be discounted. Despite the fact that in the social sciences urban centres are placed on a continuum, ranging from metropolis to hamlet. Even in parts of the world more associated with the outdoors, such as North America, urban tourism has become either an important trip purpose in its own right or in association with some of the outdoor recreation pursuits. Surveys of overseas traveller market awareness by the U.S. and Canada revealed that nine of the most frequently mentioned locations in the U.S. were cities and in Canada six out of eight were cities. In addition, many of those surveyed had visited cities during their previous visits to North America (Market Facts of Canada, 1989). Despite the high profile of these urban tourism statistics and their subsequent impact on the economic and social well-being of visited communities, few academics have examined this tourism niche or analysed the problems and opportunities it presents. So few, in fact, that Ashworth in 1989 was forced to conclude "In 60 years of urban spatial modelling tourism is ignored, rendered invisible by its very ubiquity" (Ashworth, 1989: 34).

Ashworth (1989) made this judgement on the basis of a "double neglect". He contended that not only has tourism neglected its urban context, but urban studies have failed also to observe the importance of tourism activity to city life. Possible reasons given for this include the ubiquitous and invisible nature of tourist economic exchanges, since tourists are served by facilities which also cater to residents and there is no convenient Standard Industrial Classification (S.I.C.) to separate out the overall economic contribution of tourism's output. Furthermore, tourists themselves and their motivation are difficult to identify within complex urban-economic systems. There is no uniform definition of a tourist or visitor, and a person may act as a tourist one day and be a business person, family member or student the next. Despite these difficulties in measuring the size and impact of tourism within urban areas the impact of its increased presence is undeniable. More communities are experiencing the crowds and pressures on their infrastructure as tourism increases in volume and spreads to new areas, whether these be large cities or rural villages. Within tourist destinations, more individual businesses recognize the growing importance of tourism spending to the success or survival of their operations, including peripheral operations like museums, galleries and parks.

Fortunately, since Ashworth's remarks there has been an upsurge in urban tourism research and publication. Ashworth contributed to this development himself with the publication of two key texts in 1990. *The Tourist Historic City* (Ashworth and Tunbridge, 1990) revealed the growing links between heritage and tourism in European cities; links that brought both benefits and problems, which would require delicate planning and management if the two were to co-exist in a mutually beneficial manner. This theme was present also in *Selling the City: Marketing Approaches to Public Sector Urban Planning* (Ashworth and Voogd, 1990), where the difficulties and rewards in treating the city, including its non-business elements, as a single tourist product are examined. That urban places have become tourist products is apparent on the demand side, where Urry's *The Tourist Gaze* (Urry, 1990: 3) identifies the tourist gaze or focus as being "directed to features of landscape and *townscape* which separate them off from everyday experience" (author's emphasis) and on the supply side, with the introduction of marketing texts to guide the business development of such a phenomenon (Heath and Wall, 1992; Kotler et al., 1993).

Like most newly developing research and management areas, this surge of interest in the urban tourism domain has demonstrated a wide range of viewpoints and potential ramifications, which need to be integrated into a meaningful conceptual framework that can lead to more integrative analysis and pragmatic management solutions. In this respect, the area has been well served by two recent publications which have attempted to address the patterns and implications of urban tourism from a social science perspective. Law's (1993) book *Urban Tourism: Attracting Visitors to Large Cities* is a synthesis of research into urban tourism, with an emphasis on the demand aspect and larger urban areas. This was followed by Page's (1995) *Urban Tourism* text, which was built around the central concept of tourist experiences, using an interdisciplinary systems approach to examine ways to "optimise visitor satisfaction" (Page, 1995: 233). As part of this process Page goes beyond a synthesis of papers and trends to introduce the potential contribution of management sciences, specifically in the areas of planning, business management and marketing. Among the concepts he introduces are service quality (Parasuraman et al., 1985) and quality management (Haywood and Muller, 1988).

Page reinforces the need to examine business principles if society is to successfully manage a business function, such as urban tourism. The focus on consumer expectations regarding the anticipated tourism experience is a logical place to start, but in the urban tourism domain there is more than one category of client. In addition to the tourists, who can have a wide variety of interests and expectations, there are the hosts, who can be either directly or indirectly involved with providing the tourist experience. Those indirectly involved are local residents not employed in the industry but whose tax contributions have helped to provide much of the infrastructure and some of the attractions used by the industry, and whose attitude to the industry and tourists can affect the product delivery. Thus, in this industry one needs to ensure that both internal and external environments of the management process are considered.

MANAGEMENT AND URBAN TOURISM

Management is a process businesses undertake to achieve organizational performance (Ivancevich et al., 1991: 3), and for tourism such organizational performance must include consideration of the internal and external environment. The four functions of management common to individual businesses: planning, organization, leading, and controlling are all pursued within a destination setting that involves consideration of external relations with other tourist businesses, through the process of inter-organizational relationships (Selin and Beason, 1991), and with the community at large (Murphy, 1985). *Planning* is the initial activity of management, and for a tourism business to succeed in an urban setting it will need to work with others to increase the attractiveness of the destination. Many tourism businesses believe they need to sell their destination before they can sell their individual offerings. This can be achieved by increasing the competitive advantage of the whole product matrix, so that individual businesses may benefit from the increased profile and trade. The *organization* needed to achieve planning goals will undoubtedly be assisted by the creation of a destination association, to coordinate functions and assist in the development of cooperative marketing. In British Columbia several destination associations have the right to collect a local hotel tax, the revenue from which is used to promote the entire destination. *Leading* or motivating staff to achieve planning objectives benefits also from local support organizations and external recognition. This is a key function of some destination associations in British Columbia which are responsible for operating a "Super Host" educational program and provide public recognition of excellent service. *Controlling* through the establishment of standards and information is another area where support organizations have a role to play. Governments and industry associations are setting standards, such as industry certification, and some destination associations generate local tourist statistics to guide the destination and individual business development.

Generally, management texts have focused on manufacturing situations, leading to an emphasis on the internal environment and the transformation process of increasing value, but in a service industry, such as tourism, the key element is customer satisfaction and the quality of people and product interactions a tourist experiences during a journey. This has led service companies to establish quality management strategies that are based on the consumer being both a consumer and a co-producer of the experience (Normann, 1991). Since tourism involves a series of individual experiences businesses are attempting to ensure each is a positive "moment of truth" (Carlzon, 1987). However, the tourism business does not always operate within a controlled and private business environment. In many instances the interactions and their moments of truth will occur in public places and in public facilities, such as museums and parks. Therefore, tourism management needs to place greater emphasis than usual on managing these moments of truth and quality experiences in the broader context of an external environment.

The external environment consists of those factors which affect a firm or organization's activities from outside their boundaries. Factors commonly associated with this classification include the labour force, legal considerations, unions, stockholders, competition, customers, technology and society (Gordon et al., 1990). While this is an inclusive list, terms such as society need further expansion and exposure in tourism, because as Murphy (1980: 1) has stated: "Tourism is an industry which uses the community as a resource, sells it as a product, and in the process affects the lives of everyone". Therefore, in tourism the society component should be expanded into at least two basic elements, those social and physical features which give individual communities their distinctiveness or "sense of place". Examination of these features will reflect the state of relations between tourism and its host community in two directions. First, from an industry perspective it can demonstrate how successfully it is developing and marketing the distinctive geographic and social characteristics of its host community—differentiation strategies that are being emphasized in competitive advantage strategies (Porter, 1985). Second, from a community perspective it can indicate whether such strategies are in harmony or in conflict with community aspirations.

This book, based on papers presented at the conference "Quality Management in Urban Tourism: Balancing Business and Environment" held at the University of Victoria, British Columbia in November 1994, is an attempt to direct research and planning along the path of providing service quality both internally within a business or industry environment and externally within the social and physical environment of its setting. It builds on the work of Page and others by combining the internal business environment thrust for quality tourist experiences with the need to work closely with external environmental forces of the host community. Therefore, it examines the interactive relationships between tourism and urban areas from the viewpoint of customer and host satisfaction; aiming to illustrate some successful synergistic strategies that may be adopted elsewhere.

STRUCTURE OF TEXT

The book is divided into three sections. The first sets the scene into today's urban tourism domain, by examining management issues that are occurring around the world with regard to recent urban tourism developments. The second looks specifically at the implications of commercializing heritage and culture, with contributions from two major practitioners in these areas. The third focuses on management concepts that have been used in places to balance industry and community needs to bring about more successful partnerships.

The *management issues* in urban tourism can be divided into generic and more site specific cases, all with implications for tourism management at large. In a generic sense authors explore traditional problems, such as the difficulties caused by seasonality (Butler and Mao); the continual redevelopment of inner cities, which now includes a tourism component in most cases (Broadway); and the need to balance industry with resident needs as urban areas attempt to make themselves more competitive in the global tourism business. As part of these general processes we witness specific product developments that are being studied and copied by an increasing number of urban centres. One attempt to even out the seasonal variability and to stimulate downtown renewal has been the development of conference centres. Lutz and Ryan report on the record of the Birmingham International Conference Centre in these and other regards. Hall and Dimanche explore the success of another agent of downtown revival, the mega-event. Hall considers such events do improve the image and awareness of urban destinations, but he doubts whether they have lasting tourism impacts. Dimanche, however, feels that such a judgement may be premature. Examining the impact of a recognized mega-event failure, he notes that 10 years after the bankrupt Louisiana World's Fair closed its doors prematurely one can now see positive results emerging from its financial wreckage.

Discussion of *heritage and cultural commercial links* with tourism starts with the scene setting chapter from Hall, followed by chapters examining various elements of the heritage-cultural tourism market, and ending with two case studies. Hall notes that what is preserved and placed on show is often a political decision, but in the process this has helped to retain the place identity of different societies. Hughes' chapter demonstrates the importance of tourism to the performing arts, but that the performing arts generally play a secondary role in attracting and holding visitors. Consequently, if the performing arts are to build on this relationship, more needs to be done to strengthen their position within the urban product mix. Two chapters deal with the difficulties and opportunities in introducing non-Western culture to the tourism market. In North America interest in indigenous cultures and crafts is booming, so Nicholson's appraisal of this process in British Columbia is opportune and highly relevant to smaller urban areas. She reminds us that the emergence of this indigenous-led tourism is more than a business venture; it is tied to the wider goals of sociopolitical recognition, broader economic development, and cultural recovery. Likewise, in Indonesia, Wall notes a variety of objectives that are tied to the early stirrings of cultural tourism, and the need for management to move beyond a purely site related focus to a broader socioeconomic thrust, one which helps to develop an image that is acceptable to visitors and residents alike.

Two case studies, related by their respective CEOs, deal with successful cultural-heritage tourism products, where that success has been built on tough decisions and hard work. Barkley's account of the Royal British Columbia Museum's "future project" illustrates how a successful public facility, with over a million visitors a year, needs to reassess its future and the role of tourism when its traditional funding source begins to diminish. The development of a five year business plan involved consultation with a wide range of stakeholders and a plan that has led to a more open access museum that includes a definite tourism component. In the case of the Vanderbilt's Biltmore Estate, which is owned and operated by William Cecil, the issue was one of holding on to the property and earning sufficient revenue to help preserve this stately family home. In a frank and informative manner Cecil outlines the decision-making process and experiences that have turned this private home into a premier tourist attraction. However, he notes that all this may be self-defeating. As he reinvests profits into the preservation of his home and grounds, death duties associated with the current tax legislation continue to rise. This will make it more difficult for his heirs to retain the estate as a heritage unit, in the form that was planned and laid out by the original architect and landscape designers.

The *management partnerships* section starts with an introduction of Total Quality Management (TQM) as a viable business strategy to help cities create value for both visitors and residents and as a guide to more effective marketing strategies. Haywood outlines the TQM paradigm, illustrating how its principles can be extended to an urban tourism situation. This is followed by an example of its successful adoption by a hospitality company and how Rochester, New York has used this approach in transforming both its optics industry and community into a successful community endeavour. Postma and Jenkins examine TQM's potential from the perspective of improving the quality and relevance of destination marketing. They report on a marketing monitoring system that has been developed for the three northern provinces of the Netherlands that includes TQM elements such as consumer and product profiles, mismatch analysis, empowerment, and co-production with the tourists.

A common concern among conference speakers was the establishment of sustainable urban tourism, sustainable from the perspective of the community at large and individual businesses. Jamal and Getz focused on this management goal by studying how a variety of destinations integrated sustainable tourism development into their community vision statements. They found vision exercises came about because of the need to manage growth and that these collaborative mechanisms helped to raise awareness and fostered better understanding between stakeholders. Murphy examines how one company has attempted to create sustainable business practices through careful planning and site preparation, and in the process has developed a benchmark model which has been copied extensively and taken to other cultures. The success of the Disney theme parks has been built on their attention to quality and detail which has helped to make them one of the most enduring tourist products in the world, but their success may have created a sense of over-confidence which has led to problems in Europe and may do so in Florida.

All of the above strategies require inter-organizational collaboration and have the goal of producing visitor satisfaction. Long explores the prospects of increasing effective partnerships via inter-organizational relations. These relationships are sorely needed in such a fragmented industry, operating in a complex and multifunctional domain. Long provides examples of the process from the United Kingdom and calls for further development in this area to build on its potential. Bordeau et al. examine the nature of consumer satisfaction and its links to expectancy theory, via an empirical analysis of Montreal's Botanical Gardens. In this case they found significant predictors of satisfaction to be the facilities offered and the ambience of the site; but a larger contribution is the demonstration that satisfaction components can be isolated and measured, thereby allowing businesses to build on this type of information to improve future tourist experiences and levels of satisfaction.

SUMMARY

These papers represent only the beginning of an exciting era in the planning and management of urban tourism. They reflect the growing awareness of the significance of tourism in the urban domain and the need to ensure this form of economic activity combines with other activities and community aspirations to produce an industry that is beneficial to everyone. To achieve this goal, social science is moving beyond classification and model building to embrace business and planning principles to guide development of the world's largest industry within the socially sensitive, economically changing, and physically limited confines of human habitation. It is hoped that these papers, and the conference call to which they were in response, will generate further analysis and utilization of management tools to bring out the best in tourism and its host communities.

REFERENCES

Ashworth, G.J. (1989). Urban tourism: An imbalance in attention. In C. Cooper (Ed.), *Progress in tourism and hospitality management*, Volume 1, (pp. 35-54). London: Belhaven.

Ashworth, G.J., and Tunbridge, J.E. (1990). *The tourist historic city*. London: Belhaven.

Ashworth, G.J., and Voogd, H. (1990). *Selling the city: Marketing approaches to public sector urban planning*. London: Belhaven.

Carlzon, J. (1987). *Moments of truth: New strategies for today's customer-driven economy*. New York: Harper & Row.

Gordon, J.R., Mondy, R.W., Sharplin, A., and Premeaux, S.R. (1990). *Management and organizational behavior*. Boston: Allyn and Bacon.

Haywood, K.M., and Muller, T.E. (1988). The urban tourist experience: Evaluating satisfaction. *Hospitality Education and Research Journal*, 12(2), 453-459.

Heath, E., and Wall, G. (1992). *Marketing tourism destinations.* New York: John Wiley & Sons.

Ivancevich, J.M., Donelly, J.H., Gibson, J.L., Collins, J.R., and Nielsen, N.A. (1991). *Canadian management: Principles and functions.* Boston: Irwin.

Kotler, P., Haider, D.H., and Rein, I. (1993). *Marketing places: attracting investment, industry and tourism to cities, states and nations.* New York: Free Press.

Law, C.M. (1993). *Urban tourism: Attracting visitors to large cities.* London: Mansell.

Market Facts of Canada (1989). *Pleasure travel markets to North America: United Kingdom, France, West Germany and Japan Highlights Report.* Ottawa: Tourism Canada.

Murphy, P.E. (1980). Tourism management in host communities. *Canadian Geographer,* 24(1), 1-2.

Murphy, P.E. (1985). *Tourism: A community approach.* London: Methuen.

Normann, R. (1991) *Service management* (Second Edition). New York: John Wiley & Sons.

Page, S. (1995). *Urban tourism.* London: Routledge.

Parasuraman, A., Zeithmal, V.A., and Berry, L.L. (1985). A conceptual model of service quality and its implications for future research. *Journal of Marketing,* 49(4), 41-50.

Pearce, D. (1989). *Tourism today: A geographical analysis.* Harlow, U.K.: Longman.

Porter, M.E. (1985). *Competitive advantage: Creating and sustaining superior performance.* New York: Free Press.

Selin, S., and Beason, K. (1991). Inter-organizational relations in tourism. *Annals of Tourism Research,* 18(3), 639-652.

Urry, J. (1990). *The tourist gaze.* London: Sage Publications.

Seasonality in Tourism: Problems and Measurement

2

R. Butler and B. Mao

Department of Geography, University of Western Ontario

INTRODUCTION

Seasonality is one of the most characteristic features of tourism, however, there has been relatively little research on this topic which has meant that problems exist in understanding the basic causes of seasonality. Seasonality is generally viewed in the literature as a major problem in tourism, often seen as the reason for difficulty in gaining access to capital, for staffing problems, and for uneconomic returns on investment. As a result, a large number of agencies have endeavoured to reduce seasonality, generally with limited success. The one area of tourism in which seasonality is felt to be of less significance is urban tourism, despite little empirical research to justify this conclusion. This chapter examines the origin, nature, and mechanisms of seasonality and its various dimensions and measurements, in order to better understand the phenomenon and its occurrence, both generally and in urban areas in particular. A brief review of literature on seasonality in tourism is followed by a discussion of the fundamental mechanism of tourism seasonality and the dimensions and patterns of tourism seasonality. Following this is an examination of patterns of seasonality in urban areas and a short commentary on policy implications.

The limited literature on seasonality in tourism has several foci, including the relationship of seasonality to demand and visitation; seasonality in specific locations; the economic effects of seasonality, including employment; and attempts to mitigate the level of seasonality. Little of this literature deals with concepts or theory (Hartmann, 1986), or with definitions, causes, or problems of measurement, although limited attention has been paid to seasonal variations in types of visitors (see, for example, Bonn et al., 1992; Calantone and Jotindar, 1984; Spotts and Mahoney, 1993; and Usyal et al., 1994).

The most comprehensive study of seasonality is by BarOn (1975), who examined 16 countries over a period of 17 years. However, most references to seasonality occur either as brief discussions in books on tourism (for example, Cooper et al., 1993; Murphy, 1985; Pearce, 1989; Shaw and Williams, 1994; and Witt and Buckley, 1991) or in articles which have other primary foci (Bonn et al., 1992, Hannigan, 1980; Kemper et al., 1983; Ronkainen, 1983).

Research on seasonality in specific locations has most commonly been linked to the impacts and effects of seasonality in those places (Belisle and Hoy, 1980; Dieke, 1991; Drakatos, 1987; Donatos and Zairis, 1991; Netherlands, 1991) or on employment (Clarke, 1981) or under-utilization of infrastructure (Van der Werff, 1980). Only in a very few cases has there been discussion of the environmental effects of seasonality (Mathieson and Wall, 1982; Mitchell and Murphy, 1991; Murphy, 1985).

INFLUENCING FACTORS AND THE MECHANISM OF SEASONALITY IN TOURISM

Seasonality refers here to a temporal variance in the phenomena of tourism activities, and also has a spatial component. It may be expressed in terms of dimensions of such elements as numbers of visitors, expenditure of visitors, accommodation occupancy rate, traffic flows, employment, and admissions to attractions. It is generally accepted that seasonality has two basic origins, "natural" seasonality, and "institutionalized" seasonality (BarOn, 1975; Hartmann, 1986). The first relates to regular temporal variations in natural phenomena, such as climate (temperature, rainfall, sunlight, snowfall). The second relates to traditional, sometimes legislated, temporal vacations and holidays. Despite its apparently simple origins, seasonality is a complicated phenomenon, involving not only physical, economic, and social variables in both origin and destination regions, but also an interaction process between factors and between origin and destination regions (Figure 2.1).

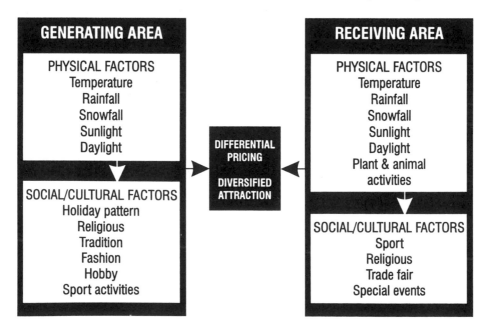

Figure 2.1   Factors of seasonality in tourism.

Seasonal Factors in Origin Areas

There are two factors that affect the temporal fluctuation of the generation of tourism. First, the seasonal changes in physical conditions (temperature, precipitation, sunshine, and daylight), which influence people's decision when to travel. People have developed a relatively fixed travel tradition in response to changes in weather and, not surprisingly, most countries generate most tourism in the warm and dry seasons, when most people desire to travel.

Second, the temporal patterns of work and leisure, often the result of religious, cultural, ethnic, and social factors, or legislation, determine the seasonal variations in tourism. The most common form of such institutionalized seasonality is the public holiday, frequently based on religious holy days, days of pagan significance, and the occurrence of natural features, for example, solstices. Public holidays, formally single days, used to have only minimal influence on tourism, but since the early nineteenth century, social reforms related to the industrial revolution have seen holidays expanded into weekends and breaks of longer duration, assuming increasing relevance for tourism and long distance travel.

The most significant manifestations of this factor are school holidays and industrial vacations. The summer school holiday continues to dominate the tourist industry in much of the world (Netherlands, 1991), and means that the major time when holidays can be taken without children missing school is during the summer recess. Coupled with this is the fact that, in most countries, summer is the period of better weather. Thus people not only desire to go on vacation then, but they have to go then for institutional reasons also. In addition, given that the bulk of world tourism is still generated by western industrial countries, which were the first to enshrine summer school holidays in legislation, tourist seasonality became essentially a western concept, as Hartmann (1986) suggests.

As the concept of holidays with pay became a part of nineteenth century social reforms, particularly in urban industrial areas, such holidays were often tied to summer school vacations. In some urban centres whole industries, and even most economic operations in the community would close for a one or two week period.

Social pressures and fashion in a society also play an important role in generating seasonal patterns, and in many societies there developed a traditional season for taking holidays. The privileged elite often divided their years into specific "seasons", during each of which it was considered socially necessary to participate in certain activities and be in certain locations, such as taking waters at spas, socializing in appropriate centres (Nash, 1979), or hunting on country estates.

Recent years have seen the establishment of "seasons" for specific sports and hobbies which may also influence the seasonal pattern of tourism generation. Some of these "seasons", such as those for skiing or wildlife watching, may be closely related to physical phenomena such as climate, and there may be only a limited time to participate in an activity. Some urban-centred sports, such as commercial baseball, football, and ice hockey, may have developed their own "sport seasons" which, especially when they are played in indoor facilities, become seasonal for traditional and economic reasons, and not because of necessity.

Seasonal Factors in Receiving areas

Destinations also have two seasonal factors. The most important one is related to regular temporal variations in natural phenomena, particularly those associated with climate, which may determine the nature and characteristics of the attraction, and thus lay the foundation for the "tourism season". Except for equatorial areas, most regions have a seasonal variation in terms of temperature, precipitation, and sunlight, which in turn affects the basic attributes of the tourism destination. Most tourism activities require a set of unique natural conditions which are deemed as optimal for tourist satisfaction (Mieczkowski, 1990).

The temporal fluctuations of physical conditions vary in different locations, as does the seasonal pattern of tourism, in particular where the destination's attraction is related to landscape and outdoor activity. For example, the Mediterranean has water-oriented resorts which require a comfortable temperature and plenty of sunlight to attract visitors, thus summer is the main vacation season. For Caribbean countries, summer is the off-season and winter is the high season, primarily because of the relative location of this region to its major markets and the climatic differences between them, which are at their maximum in the winter. In general, seasonal differences are more marked in high latitudes than in equatorial locations. Natural seasonality has been regarded as stable and unchangeable, although recently some researchers have suggested that the greenhouse effect and subsequent climatic change will have impacts on tourism in mid-latitudes, such as shortening the skiing season in Ontario (Wall, 1993).

Secondly, the temporal distribution of religious, cultural, ethnic, and social events and activities in destination areas also profoundly influence the numbers and nature of incoming tourists. Some of the best examples of this phenomenon occur in sports. Multi-annual events, such as the Olympic Games, World Cup (of soccer), and world championships of other sports, attract thousands of visitors to the urban locations of these events for short periods in specific seasons. In North America, annual events in football (Superbowl) and baseball (World Series) also attract many sport fans to the events' locations, normally major urban centres, and create unique seasonal travel patterns.

Annual religious events also influence the seasonal pattern of tourism. Each year around one million Muslims over the world travel to Mecca for pilgrimage during the Haj and, the effects of unrest notwithstanding, traditionally many Christian tourists have travelled to Bethlehem and other holy sites at Christmas and Easter. Moreover, other regular events such as trade fairs, art exhibitions, concert series, and other cultural activities can also be factors causing seasonal variations in visitation to destinations.

Interaction Between Source Areas and Destinations

While it may be generally accepted that the above factors in both generating and receiving areas influence seasonality in tourism, merely identifying these factors does not explain the nature of seasonality, because those factors do not act independently, but are interrelated and interdependent, and more importantly, they interact with each other. In fact, this type of interaction between factors and between origin areas and destination areas has resulted in two industry responses: diversified (multiple) attractions and seasonalized pricing, which actively impact on the original seasonal pattern.

The diversified (multiple) attractions approach is a process whereby destinations create attractions or events in order to spread tourism visitation more evenly over a year. Hallmark Events and Festivals, built around a major theme, attempt to attract tourists to fill what may be seasonally under-utilized facilities (Getz, 1991). Many of these have been established in urban centres, such as Mardi Gras in New Orleans, Winter Carnival in Quebec City, and the Snow Festival in Sapporo, Japan, as well as a host of smaller, more local events (Butler and Smale, 1991). In addition, those destinations with the appropriate physical conditions, such as Banff (Alberta) and Whistler (British Columbia), increasingly market themselves as year-round resorts, offering traditional summer and winter activities, and other attractions in spring and fall.

Seasonalized pricing is another common practice in the tourism industry, which relates to the fact that tourism essentially is a price elastic product. Discounted transportation fares and accommodation rates appear to increase the incentive to travel. As a result, seasonalized pricing is practised widely to improve the off-season performance. For example, during the Caribbean off-season (April 15 to December 1), accommodation prices drop significantly to a level of 35 to 70 percent of high season (winter) prices (Mieczkowski, 1990). This action has considerable impacts on the seasonal pattern of the market.

Modelling the Mechanism of Tourism Seasonality

From the above analysis, we can argue that tourism seasonality is both an attribute and a process. The fundamental pattern is the result of three attributes and their interaction: the seasonal generating process, the seasonal receiving process, and the modifying process. The generating process, in particular institutionalized holidays and traditions, shapes the basic temporal pattern of markets. The receiving process, especially temporal fluctuations of climatic conditions, shapes the attraction of the "tourism season" at the destination, and the conditions the tourist activities require for satisfaction. A modifying process is developed as a result of interaction between origin and destination, and competition between destinations. Diversified attractions and seasonalized pricing will strongly affect the previous two processes and thus influence the seasonal pattern of visitation. Figure 2.2 displays the relationships between these three processes.

Theoretically there are two major combinations of these processes:

(1) *where the seasonal pattern of the origin region matches that of the destination region* —thus, the seasonality experienced at the destination may be very marked. Often, aggressive pricing and a diversified marketing strategy based on increased attractions may be developed to compensate for this. This may

increase arrivals in the off-season, but it is not very likely to reduce the peak season. Most destinations within Western Europe and North America belong to this type.

(2) *Where the patterns of seasonality in the generating region and the destination region are the reverse of one another*—which means that the destination may not have a very defined high season because the effects are cancelled out. To increase visitation, such a destination may develop new markets whose seasonal patterns match those of the destination, or create new attractions or events to match the existing markets. Travel between North America and the Caribbean region is an example of this.

Figure 2.2   The mechanism of tourism seasonality.

DIMENSIONS OF SEASONALITY

Forms of Seasonality

There are a number of forms of seasonality as a result of the interaction of the processes and attributes discussed above. For the purposes of discussion they can be characterized in three basic forms.

1. *One-peak seasonality*—which is characterized by one very significant peak tourism season, generally three to four months in duration, usually in summer. Examples are 'Medsun' countries: Spain, Portugal, Greece, and Cyprus.

2. *Two-peak seasonality*—in which there are two tourism seasons or peaks in a year, often a traditional summer one and a shorter, perhaps three month, winter one. For example, the mountainous parts of Europe and North America enjoy two seasons—summer and winter: The Alps, Scandinavia, the Rockies.

3. *Non-peak seasonality*—which tends to be found primarily in urban states and centres, where the major attractions (heritage, architecture, shopping and services) are non-seasonal in nature, and especially where such centres are major gateways and transportation hubs for international tourists. Even in urban centres, however, tourism may be affected by seasonality of demand in the origin areas. Singapore and Hong Kong are examples of this type of pattern.

SPATIAL DIMENSIONS OF SEASONALITY—URBAN AREAS

It is clear that although seasonality may be an almost universal characteristic of tourism, it varies considerably from location to location. Climatic seasonality is much less marked the closer one gets to the Equator, but even in Equatorial destinations tourism may be seasonal because of seasonal factors (both climatic and institutionalized) in tourist origin areas as noted earlier. It is also clear that the degree of seasonality varies within destination countries and perhaps regions, reflecting in part the variety of physical conditions and the nature of the attractions. Little is known, however, as to whether seasonality also varies with respect to the human characteristics of regions and countries.

Of particular relevance to this discussion is the fact that there has been little investigation as to whether seasonality varies between urban and non-urban tourist destinations and urban and non-urban tourist origin regions. Murphy (1985: 79) has noted that large cities such as London have a less seasonal pattern of tourism than do more conventional tourist resorts, although he does not expand to any degree on this idea. This perception is found also in publications by the World Tourism Organization (W.T.O.), which comments that "Tourist destinations supported by large urban centres, while having high points of activity, have more continuous operation throughout the year because they depend upon a more diversified demand" (W.T.O., 1984: 43). These statements are among the few that discuss seasonality in the context of urban centres specifically, and which suggest there may be an appreciable difference in seasonality patterns between tourism in urban and rural destinations. There have been other brief discussions which also suggest that the degree of seasonality varies with the relative location of destinations within their country or major region. Snepenger et al. (1990) point out that the seasonality of tourist visitation to Alaska was almost 10 percent higher in the more remote interior than in coastal areas (which, although not heavily urbanized, do contain a higher proportion of urban development than the interior). Yacoumis (1980) argued that it was necessary to analyse seasonality at three levels (national, regional, and sectoral) because of considerable variations he noted in the seasonality ratio on a spatial basis in tourism in Sri Lanka. Butler (1973) also identified considerable variations in seasonality in the pattern of tourism between central and peripheral locations in the Highlands and Islands of Scotland. The link between seasonality and spatial pattern has also been commented on by Shaw and Williams (1994: 195) who state "temporal polarization has the effect of reinforcing spatial polarization".

Little of this discussion examines the relationship between the degree of urban development of an origin or destination region and the pattern of seasonal demand and visitation in tourism. One may argue that it would be highly appropriate for urban-focused tourist destinations to experience a less seasonal pattern of visitation than more rural destinations for several reasons. The pattern of tourist visitation to most destinations is rarely accurately broken down between what may be defined as "pleasure tourists" and "business tourists", particularly if the source of information on tourist numbers is hotel or accommodation occupancy. Surveys of tourists at a national level may separate business, pleasure, visiting friends and relatives (VFR), and other types of tourists, but this is rarely done at a destination level. Business travel is traditionally year round, with brief periods of lower visitation during major holiday periods such as Christmas, and occasionally the summer holidays. Major urban centres, therefore, will experience continuous business tourism throughout the year, and any variations in that pattern are probably the exact opposite to the pattern of visitation of pleasure and VFR tourists, who tend to come during conventional holiday periods. This complementarity of pattern is found also at the weekly scale, where business travel declines at weekends, while pleasure and VFR traffic is heaviest at these times. While it is not claimed that there is no business tourist traffic to rural or non-urban areas, such traffic as there is is small in comparison to pleasure tourism in these areas, and therefore has a smaller moderating effect on the seasonal fluctuations.

A second factor is that the attractions which are found in urban areas for tourists are generally less dependent on climatic conditions for their attractiveness and are, therefore, less vulnerable to natural seasonality. Attractions such as museums, heritage buildings, art galleries, restaurants, theatres, and shops are all primarily indoor facilities, and operate under climatically controlled conditions. In some major cities, for example Montreal and Toronto, it is possible to move around the downtown area completely underground, using subway transportation and visiting malls and facilities connected by subterranean walkways (Hopkins, 1995). In other urban centres the enclosure of recreation and tourist facilities is a particular selling point of shopping malls, with one of the best examples being the West Edmonton Mall, where major leisure facilities are enclosed and shielded from the elements, thus offering shoppers and visitors access to a range of opportunities, despite at times exterior inclement climatic conditions (Butler, 1991; Jackson, 1991). The seasonal pattern of use of these facilities by visitors to the Mall varies with the origin of the visitors, with local residents visiting the Mall more to use the recreational and leisure facilities in the winter, and distant tourists being more frequent in the summer (Hopkins, 1991), however, it would appear that these seasonal variations to a large extent cancel themselves out and are dwarfed by the primarily non-seasonal conventional shopping pattern in the Mall.

A third consideration is the fact that such attractions are not "natural", in the sense of being outdoors and related directly to the exterior environment. This means that their visitor attractions can be offered at any time throughout the year, and specific offerings can be targeted to particular time periods. As with festivals and special events, organizers and providers of such attractions can schedule specific events, shows, concerts, and exhibitions at what are conventional "low season" times, and thus attract visitors throughout the year. This is often done also in order to be able to serve and attract local residents who may otherwise be on holiday themselves at peak vacation times.

Unlike the situation in the more remote locations, access to urban destinations is normally assured throughout the year. Even in the worst climatic conditions, most major urban centres remain accessible and linked to other areas, unlike more peripheral locations, where transportation links may be tenuous in the best of conditions. Finally, by virtue of being central places or regional gateways, many urban destinations have a wide range of frequently offered transportation links. Visits may, therefore, only involve a short period of time for the travel component, due to extensive carrier schedules allowing a wider market to have access to these centres, and to be able to visit them for shorter periods of time. The time and financial costs, as well as logistical difficulties involved are likely to be much lower for visitors to such areas than to peripheral or remote locations. This can, and often does translate into a greater number of visits, and possibly a higher frequency of visitation, both of which work against seasonal peaking.

Some initial research on the levels of seasonality in a variety of destinations would appear to support the above points. Table 2.1 shows an index of seasonality for a range of destinations at the national scale. The index is a simple measure of temporal variation of visitation, and is derived from the ratio of the level of visitation in the peak month to the level of visitation in the month with the lowest total number of visitors. Because of the data used, no differentiation among visitors could be made between business, pleasure, VFR or other types of tourists. The data indicate significant variations in the levels of seasonality as defined by the index, and those destinations which are most urban, in particular Hong Kong and Singapore, are those destinations which display the lowest levels of seasonality. The variation in levels of seasonality displayed in Table 2.1 is extremely large, from a little over parity (no seasonality) to a ratio of over 12 to 1, but even then, some patterns are marked by other factors. It may be noted that "winter" destinations also tend to have visitation in the summer low season made up primarily of returning residents on VFR trips, for example from Canada to Caribbean destinations. The southern Pacific destinations are affected by seasonality in their northern hemisphere market regions which is the opposite to their own, thus reducing rather than accentuating the pattern of seasonality they experience. The index used is a very simplistic one, and further research needs to be carried out at a sub-national level, and between types of tourists and their motivations for travel, before one is able to make any more detailed comments.

Table 2.1   Seasonality in International Tourism, Selected Countries

Type	Place	Ratio	Date
"Summer"	Greece	1:14.5	1989 (visitors)
	Cyprus	1:11.8	1991 (visitors)
	Majorca	1:8.1	1986 (air arrivals)
"Mixed"	Germany	1:2.5	1986 (bednights)
	Austria	1:2.0	1985 (visitors)
"Winter"	Bahamas	1:2.2	1990 (visitors)
	Barbados	1:1.5	1989 (visitors)
"Pacific"	Fiji	1:1.6	1986 (visitors)
	Japan	1:1.5	1991 (visitors)
	China	1:1.5	1988 (visitors)
	Tahiti	1:1.4	1988 (visitors)
"Urban"	Hong Kong	1:1.15	1990 (occupancy)
	Singapore	1:1.17	1989 (occupancy)

Source: Economist Intelligence Unit, various dates.

Some data on seasonality in tourism are available at a provincial and sub-provincial level in Canada, and they are illustrated in Table 2.2. The data are only available for a limited time period and reflect occupancy of accommodation units in tourist regions across the province of Ontario (Ministry of Tourism and Recreation, 1988). Table 2.2 contains data on selected regions of the province and types of accommodation, although for the purposes of illustration, only those regions which best portray the extremes of urbanized and non-urbanized regions are included. The urbanized regions are Metropolitan Toronto, the City of Ottawa, and South Western Ontario. The least urbanized areas are portrayed by The James Bay Frontier, and Algoma/Kinniwabi. Complete data on a monthly basis exist for six years, 1982-1987, and the average peak and low months over this period have been used in the calculation of the seasonality indices. The accommodation categories can be taken to reflect, to a limited degree, aspects of urbanization. Hotels in particular are most associated with urban centres, motels with both urban and rural areas, while cabins, lodges and resorts are almost all found in rural and remote areas in Ontario. The hotel category displays the lowest level of seasonality, and the cottages/cabins the highest, even when taking into account the fact that many cottages/cabins and resorts/lodges close completely in the off-season. The pattern which emerges is not as clear as that portrayed in Table 2.1, however, the least seasonal of all regions is the major metropolitan region centred on Toronto. The lower-than-anticipated levels of seasonality in some of the more remote and less urbanized regions may be due to a year round pattern of business and administrative travellers. These visitors inevitably have to utilize accommodation because of the remoteness of these regions from their origins. The numbers of these visitors is often sufficiently high to counteract the relatively low total numbers of pleasure tourists. As well, in many peripheral regions much accommodation is closed during the off-season, thus resulting in higher occupancy levels for those properties remaining open. In certain areas, such as major urban centres, almost all accommodation establishments remain open year round. Additional research is required on these data to determine what other patterns can be identified, and whether the period for which these data are available is representative of longer term trends and patterns.

Table 2.2   Occupancy Seasonality in Ontario, 1982-1987

Accommodation Sector	Minimum Monthly Average 1982-87	Maximum Monthly Average 1982-87	Ratio 1:2
Hotels	41.7	80.0	1:1.9
Motels	35.3	77.5	1:2.2
Cottages/Cabins	25.3	89.9	1:3.6
Resorts/Lodges	27.2	81.3	1:3.0
Regional			
Metropolitan Toronto	45.8	84.3	1:1.8
Ottawa	41.0	79.0	1:1.9
South Western Ontario	38.5	70.7	1:1.8
Algoma	27.3	81.3	1:3.0
James Bay	38.5	79.5	1:2.1
Provincial Average	39.3	79.7	1:2.0

Source: Ministry of Tourism and Recreation (1988)

It would appear clear, however, that as anticipated, the pattern of seasonality is less marked in the more urbanized destinations than in the more remote and peripheral ones. In the case of the sub-provincial data, the peripheral regions, while possibly receiving business and administrative visitors as noted, will not receive any appreciable convention or conference traffic, and because of generally low numbers of local residents, relatively little VFR traffic also.

POLICY IMPLICATIONS AND CONCLUSIONS

As noted briefly at the beginning, there have been very considerable efforts made by all sectors of tourism to reduce the seasonal aspects of tourism. BarOn (1975) devotes a large proportion of his comprehensive study to discussing methods for reducing the seasonal pattern of tourism. There have been a rather limited number of approaches to reducing seasonality, including attempts to lengthen the main season, establish additional seasons, use tax incentives, stagger holidays, and, as noted earlier, diversify markets, apply differential pricing and provide off-season activities such as festivals and conferences (Butler and Smale, 1991; Sutcliffe and Sinclair, 1980; Witt et al., 1991).

Seasonality has remained a difficult phenomenon to overcome, despite intensive efforts, which suggests that the problem is more complex than is often thought. Most efforts to reduce seasonality in demand have concentrated upon the destination areas rather than the consumer, for example, the attempts to diversify the market and vary prices as noted above. In general these attempts have not been very successful in reducing seasonality, although they have quite often been successful in increasing visitor numbers in the off-peak seasons. The reason the level of seasonality has not been appreciably reduced is that, in many cases, the efforts which have increased the number of off-peak visitors have also increased the numbers of peak season visitors (Netherlands, 1991). The most successful attempts to overcome the peaking problem would appear to be have been made in those countries with well-established tourism industries which have begun to feel the effects of overall declining visitation in specific destinations, often older urban holiday resorts. While such urban centres have rarely been able to restore visitor numbers to earlier levels, they have often been successful at attracting off-peak visitation for short stays. This pattern would appear to be not uncommon, and most shifts in seasonality which have occurred have done so because of an increase in additional holidays, rather than from changes in the time at which the primary holiday has been taken.

The long term nature of seasonality in tourism would suggest that its causes are complex and unlikely to be significantly changed by adjustments in one particular variable. While destinations, especially urban ones, may be able to increase overall visitation, and even off-peak visitation, they are rarely able to achieve this on a selective basis. More effort needs to be paid to examining and identifying the underlying causes of seasonal fluctuations in visitation in the tourist origin areas and addressing these, rather than continuing to modify attractions and features in the destination areas. The one element which has had some effect on producing a less seasonal pattern of visitation is the occurrence of time-sharing developments in destinations which are at least moderately attractive for visitation at all or most times of the year, for example, Arizona and Florida, in mountain resorts such as those in British Columbia, Alberta, Colorado and Utah in North America, and in Portugal, Spain and other Mediterranean destinations in Europe. In this sort of development, property owners have purchased weeks throughout the year except for a very short maintenance period, usually in the lowest season, and it is in the owners' interests to use their time allotments. Periods in traditional low seasons are normally priced lower than peak times, and the use patterns of such developments are less seasonal than is the case in traditional resorts (Butler, 1985). In the urban context such development is likely only to a very limited degree, and then only in specific centres which are attractive to tourism, for example, San Francisco, Miami and London.

This discussion has focused particularly on the topic of seasonality in tourism, and aspects of this phenomenon in urban settings. Urban areas have been suggested to be less prone to seasonality in visitation than less central destinations for a number of reasons. In general, they have a greater and more varied series of attractions than other destinations, and many of these are less dependent upon climatic or physical factors for their attractiveness. Indeed, they may be attractive for visitation when other destinations are not attractive because of climate. As urban areas tend to be centres of cultural diversity, their range of heritage and cultural features similarly tends to be wider than many other locations. In terms of strategies adopted, major accommodation units in many urban centres have traditionally offered reductions in prices for use during the non-business or high season periods, especially at weekends and during other holiday periods, and thus have long been trying to reduce short term seasonality. Urban areas may be prone to long term fluctuations, especially if they are capable of attracting the occasional event such as major sports events or trade fairs. All urban areas, however, still remain prone to seasonal fluctuations in visitation because of seasonal fluctuations in demand based in the origin regions. Until there are significant changes made in the origins of the demand, for example through the introduction of year-round school operation and the disappearance of the universal long summer school holiday, changes in seasonality are likely to be minor. Such fundamental changes as year-round schooling are likely to arouse considerable opposition based on limited experience because of difficulties in implementation and may not be seen for a long time in the future except in limited areas. The aging of the population may, through time, cause some changes in seasonal patterns of visitation to many areas, as the more elderly population has considerably more freedom in when vacations can be scheduled.

The previous discussion has revealed the lack of theory and concepts on this subject, and the absence of detailed empirical research. There can be little doubt that seasonality represents a problem, in both origin and destination regions, to maximizing the efficient operation of tourism facilities and infrastructure, and results in excess capacity for most of the year. However, the advantages to destination areas of one or more off-seasons which may provide periods for recuperation and restoration, thus allowing residents to prepare for the next tourist season, has remained unstudied, although not unnoticed (Murphy, 1985).

As noted earlier, very little research has been reported in the literature on the causes of seasonality. The nature of the relationship between seasonality and the motivation of visitors is not known, and issues such as whether dissatisfaction with conditions in the origin region or desire for the attractions of the destination play a greater role in shaping the seasonal patterns of tourism is also a mystery. It is not known whether tourists travel in peak season because they want to, because they have to, or because of inertia. While seasonality in visitation to urban destinations may be less marked than that experienced by peripheral destinations, it still remains an issue worthy of more detailed investigation and conceptual development.

REFERENCES

BarOn, R.V. (1975). *Seasonality in tourism*. London: Economist Intelligence Unit.

Belisle, F., and Hoy, D. (1980). The perceived impact of tourism by residents: A case study in Santa Marta, Colombia. *Annals of Tourism Research*, 7(1), 83-101.

Bonn, M.A., Furr, H.L., and Uysal, M. (1992). Seasonal variation of coastal resort visitors: Hilton Head Island. *Journal of Travel Research*, 31(1), 50-56.

Butler, R.W. (1991). West Edmonton Mall as a tourist attraction. *The Canadian Geographer*, 35(3), 287-295.

Butler, R.W. (1985). Timesharing: The implications of an alternative to the conventional cottage. *Loisir et Societe*, 8(2), 769-780.

Butler, R.W. (1973). The tourism industry of the Highlands and islands. Ph.D. thesis, Department of Geography, Glasgow University, Glasgow.

Butler, R.W., and Smale, B.J.A. (1991). Geographic perspectives on festivals in Ontario. *Journal of Applied Recreation Research*, 16(1), 3-23.

Calantone, R.J., and Jotindar, J.S.S. (1984). Seasonal segmentation of the tourist market using a benefit segmentation framework. *Journal of Travel Research*, 23(2), 14-24.

Clarke, A. (1981). Coastal development in France: Tourism as a tool for regional development. *Annals of Tourism Research*, 8(3), 447-461.

Cooper, C., Fletcher, J., Gilbert, D., and Wanhill, S. (1993). *Tourism: Principles and practice*. London: Pitman Publishing.

Dieke, P. (1991). Policies for tourism development in Kenya. *Annals of Tourism Research*, 18(2), 269-294.

Donatos, G., and Zairis, P. (1991). Seasonality of foreign tourism in the Greek island of Crete. *Annals of Tourism Research*, 18(3), 515-519.

Drakatos, C.G. (1987). Seasonal concentration of tourism in Greece. *Annals of Tourism Research*, 14(4), 582-586.

Getz, D. (1991). *Festivals and special events*. New York: Von Nostrand Reinhold.

Hannigan, J.A. (1980). Reservations cancelled: Consumer complaints in the tourist industry. *Annals of Tourism Research*, 7(3), 364-384.

Hartmann, R. (1986). Tourism, seasonality and social change. *Leisure Studies*, 5(1), 25-33.

Hopkins, J.S.P. (1995, in press). Excavating Toronto's underground streets: In search of equitable rights, rules and revenue. In J. Caulfield and L. Peake (Eds.), *Critical perspectives in Canadian urbanism*. Toronto: University of Toronto.

Hopkins, J.S.P. (1991). West Edmonton Mall as a centre for social interaction. *The Canadian Geographer*, 35(3), 268-279.

Jackson, E.E. (1991). Shopping and leisure: Implications of West Edmonton Mall for shopping and leisure. *The Canadian Geographer*, 35(3), 280-287.

Kemper, R., Roberts, J., and Goodwin, D. (1983). Tourism as a cultural domain: The case of Taos, New Mexico. *Annals of Tourism Research*, 10(1), 149-172.

Mathieson, A., and Wall, G. (1982). *Tourism: Economic, physical and social impacts*. London and New York: Longman.

Mieczkowski, Z. (1990). *World trends in tourism and recreation*. New York: P. Lang. p. 195

Ministry of Tourism and Recreation. (1988). *Ontario occupancy monitor*. Toronto.

Mitchell, L.S., and Murphy, P. (1991). Geography and tourism. *Annals of Tourism Research*, 18(1), 57-50.

Murphy, P.E. (1985). *Tourism: A community approach*. New York and London: Methuen.

Nash, D. (1979). The rise and fall of an aristocratic culture, Nice: 1763-1936. *Annals of Tourism Research*, 7(1), 61-75.

Netherlands: Ministerie van Economische Zak. (1991). *Improving seasonal spread of tourism*. Rotterdam: Netherlands Ministerie van Economische Zak.

Pearce, D.G. (1989). *Tourist development*. Harlow: Longman Scientific and Technical.

Ronkainen, I. (1983). The Conference on Security and Cooperation in Europe: Its impact on tourism. *Annals of Tourism Research*, 10(3), 415-426.

Shaw, G., and Williams, A.M. (1994). *Critical issues in tourism*. Oxford: Blackwell.

Snepenger, D., Houser, B, and Snepenger, M. (1990). Seasonality of demand. *Annals of Tourism Research*, 17(4), 628-630.

Spotts, D.M., and Mahoney, E.M. (1993). Understanding the Fall tourist. *Journal of Travel Research*, 32(2), 3-15.

Sutcliffe, C.M.S., and Sinclair, M.T. (1980). The measurement of seasonality within the tourist industry: An application to tourist arrivals in Spain. *Applied Economics*, 12(4), 429-441.

Usyal, M., Fesenmaier, D.R., O'Leary, J.T. (1994). Geographic and seasonal variation in the concentration of travel in the United States. *Journal of Travel Research*, 32(3), 61-64.

Van der Werff, P. (1980). Polarizing implications of the Pescaia tourism industry. *Annals of Tourism Research*, 7(2), 197-223.

Wall, G. (1993). Tourism alternatives in an era of global climatic change. In V.L. Smith and W.R. Eadington (Eds.), *Tourism alternatives* (pp. 194-215). Philadelphia: University of Pennsylvania Press.

Witt, S., Brooke, M.Z., and Buckley, P.J. (1991). *The management of international tourism*. London: Unwin Hyman.

World Tourism Organization (1984). *World tourism statistics*. Madrid: World Tourism Organization.

Yacoumis, J. (1980). Tackling seasonality: The case of Sri Lanka. *Tourism Management* 1(2), 84-98.

Plate 2 Downtown Osoyoos
(photo courtesy of The Province of British Columbia) ➡

Urban Tourism Development in the Modern Canadian City: A Review

3

Michael J. Broadway

Department of Geography, SUNY Geneseo

Despite the obvious importance of cities as tourist destinations, researchers largely neglected studying urban tourism until the late 1980s (Ashworth, 1989), due to the inherent difficulty in identifying tourist and non-tourist use of urban facilities as well as the wide variation in size, function and age of urban areas. Urban tourism research since then has focused primarily upon developing spatial models of the 'tourist city', the behaviour of urban tourists and the role of tourism in urban regeneration, with most studies being completed in European or American cities (Law, 1993; Page, 1995). A small number of studies have been completed in Canadian cities, but they are largely ideographic in nature and focus on such diverse topics as: planning for tourists (Murphy, 1980), visitor attitudes towards attractions (Murphy, 1992; Wall and Sinnott, 1980), cultural tourism and festivals (Wall and Knapper, 1981; Getz, 1993), the distribution of restaurants (Gazillo, 1981; Smith, 1983) and hotels (Wall, Dudycha & Hutchinson, 1985; Broadway, 1993). This chapter broadens the scope of these earlier studies by viewing tourism as a means of promoting urban economic development.

Tourism is one of Canada's fastest growing industries and city and provincial governments have viewed the industry as a means of job creation and source of tax revenue. The first Canadian city to embrace this strategy, in the age of mass tourism, was Montréal. Beginning in the 1960s the city embarked upon an ambitious effort to attract tourists by: hosting a World's Fair, the Summer Olympics, constructing several museums, a convention centre and opening a Casino. But despite the widespread adoption of tourism as a means of promoting urban economic development in Canada, there is little research that examines the effectiveness of such a strategy. The purpose of this chapter is to critically examine the role of tourism in Canadian cities by: (1) explaining the rationale behind development of tourism in cities, (2) identifying the factors affecting the demand for urban tourism, (3) describing the role of tourism in transforming the urban landscape, and (4) discussing the principal marketing techniques used by cities to attract tourists. In accomplishing these tasks, a systematic approach which emphasizes publicly funded efforts toward tourist development in Canada's largest cities is adopted. The study concludes with some suggestions to guide future research.

CITIES AND TOURIST DEVELOPMENT

Canadian cities have always attracted visitors. Today, people travel to a city to undertake business, see friends or relatives, shop, see a play, visit a museum, attend a sporting event. But it is only recently that tourism has been widely adopted as a means of promoting urban economic development (Law, 1992; Owen, 1990; Hall, 1987; English Tourist Board, 1980, 1983; Judd and Collins, 1979). This use of tourism has been prompted, in part, by technological and structural economic changes which have adversely affected cities. Declines in manufacturing employment have produced abandoned factories and high levels of unemployment in the inner city areas of old industrial cities, while changes in transportation have brought about the demise of old port and railyard facilities and resulted in acres of derelict land. In response, local politicians, policy makers and business groups have looked to tourism as a means of urban regeneration.

Although many jobs in the tourist sector (e.g., food and beverage) are low paying and often part-time in nature, governments favour tourist development due to the industry's above average employment growth and ability to absorb unskilled labour. At the national level, between 1984 and 1991, the number employed in tourism related industries increased by over 20 percent, while the comparable figure for all industries was just 13 percent (Tourism Canada, 1992). Tourists provide economic benefits to cities in the form of increased expenditures and tax revenues. In metropolitan Toronto, visitors to the area in 1990 spent over $5.5 billion on tourist related items. This, in turn, produced over $1.4 billion in taxes, with 8 percent of this amount going to municipalities, 30 percent to the province and 62 percent to the federal government (Peat Marwick Stevenson and Kellogg, 1992: 91).

Montréal was among the first cities to utilize tourism to boost its local economy in the post World War II period. By the late 1960s, Toronto had eclipsed Montréal to become Canada's leading financial and manufacturing centre, and in an effort to offset this situation Montréal's Mayor Drapeau sought to make the city a leading tourist destination (Whelan, 1991). During the 1960s the Mayor presided over the preservation of Vieux Montréal, the staging of the 1967 World's Fair (Expo 67) and the capture of major league baseball's first franchise outside the United States —the Montréal Expos (Lanken, 1986). In subsequent decades the city hosted the 1976 Summer Olympics and constructed a new convention centre, the Palais des Congrès, in 1983. Drapeau's efforts to boost tourism proved extremely successful in the short term. Expo 67, for example, spawned new hotel construction and attracted 50 million visitors. But, these schemes were extremely costly; nearly twenty years after hosting the Olympics the city is still paying for the Games.

Montréal has continued to pursue an urban tourism strategy in the wake of continued job losses in manufacturing and a federal commission's economic development recommendations (Levine, 1989). In preparation for celebrating the city's 350th anniversary in 1992, a total of nearly half a billion dollars was invested in new or expanded tourist attractions (L'Office des Congrès et du Tourisme du Grand Montréal, 1992), while Loto Québec spent nearly $100 million to transform the French pavillon at the Expo 67 site into a Casino (MacIsaac, 1994). Despite Montréal's sustained efforts at developing an urban tourism product there has been little research to identify the beneficiaries of this investment. No consideration has been given to determining whether workers who lost their jobs through plant closures have obtained employment in the tourism sector. Alternatively, there has been no assessment of the degree to which the private sector has benefited from these investments.

Despite the gaps in knowledge concerning tourism's effectiveness in dealing with structural economic change, Canadian cities have added to their attractions. Toronto, for example, since the late 1960s has witnessed the construction of the Ontario Science Centre, Ontario Place, Metro Toronto Zoo, CN Tower and Skydome. In some cases, the hosting of a tourist mega-event such as the Olympic Games or World's Fair and the opportunity to market the city to a wide audience have provided the impetus for developing a city's tourist product.

Calgary attempted to use the 1988 Winter Olympics as a means of attracting new investment to the city and broadening its economic base beyond its function as the corporate centre of Canada's petroleum industry. According to the proponents of this strategy, Calgary's hosting the Games would "legitimize" the city as a tourist destination and leave it with a legacy of tourist attractions (Ritchie, 1990). Two years earlier Vancouver hosted the 1986 World's Fair, Expo 86. As a result of staging this event the city widened its market as a tourist destination (Lee, 1987), and was left with a new domed sports stadium, mass transit system, convention centre and cruise ship terminal. In sum, cities now compete to attract tourists in the same manner they compete to attract other businesses through the provision of infrastructure and promoting a positive image of the community. But little consideration has been given to the implications of this strategy, namely whether cities are products to be sold. Moreover, there is little research to indicate that, beyond the short term economic boost associated with hosting a World's Fair or Olympic Games, these developments are an effective long-term strategy in dealing with the problems associated with structural economic change (see Chapter 7 for further discussion of this point — editor).

THE DEMAND FOR URBAN TOURISM

Since the early 1980s most cities experienced an increase in their number of visitors, followed by a decline and recovery in the early 1990s. In Montréal it is estimated that the 5.7 million tourists who visited the city in 1992 surpassed the 1990 total by 100,000; however, this total is still below the 1988 figure of 5.9 million (Research and Development Department of the Greater Montréal Convention and Tourism Bureau, 1993: 7-8). Montréal's recent experience is similar to most other Canadian cities and reflects the cyclical nature of the national economy and in particular the 1990-92 recession, which had the effect of depressing the demand for tourism. The majority of tourists to Canadian cities come from within the country, with the largest single source being the province in which the city is situated. In the late 1980s, Québec, for example, provided approximately 38 percent of Montréal's tourists (Research and Development Department of the Greater Montréal Convention and Tourism Bureau, 1993: 7). In smaller and less well-known cities the importance of the province as a supplier of tourists increases. Prior to the 1988 Winter Olympics in Calgary, over 75 percent of the city's overnight visitors were from Alberta (Regional Planning Services, Calgary Regional Planning Commission, 1989: 5), while 85 percent of Edmonton's visitors in 1990 were from Alberta (Alberta Tourism, Parks and Recreation, 1991). Thus, a key determinant of the demand for urban tourism is the overall health of a city's regional economy, and this factor increases in importance for smaller and less well-known cities.

Despite the recent downturn in the number of urban tourists, cities have in fact increased their share of Canada's tourism market. This increase is the product of changing consumer tastes, demographics and household structure. The increase in two income households and the associated difficulty of coordinating the traditional two week vacation block together has meant that many households have resorted to shorter vacations. These short breaks are usually spread out over a year and are often associated with a city visit. Tourists may stay with friends or relatives or take advantage of reduced accommodation rates that hotels offer over weekends (Peat Marwick Stevenson and Kellogg, 1992: 20-21).

The aging of the population has also increased the demand for urban vacations, with baby boomers aged 35-54 years having the greatest propensity to travel. This well-educated group is associated with looking for more authentic and educational components to their vacations in the form of heritage or cultural tourism (Regional Planning Services, Calgary Regional Planning Commission, 1990: 5-6). A cultural vacation might involve spending time in a city, sampling the local cuisine, attending the theatre or local film, jazz or folk music festival. Among American visitors to Canada these factors have combined to increase the number of city tourists by 25 percent between 1985-1989 (Tourism Canada, 1994: 8).

Although cities have increased their share of Canada's tourist product, the competition for tourists between cities is increasing as more attractions are continually being added to the marketplace. As a result, cities have attempted to widen their market beyond North America by hosting such mega-events as the Olympics or World's Fair, with the hope that these events will increase the numbers of future tourists and international awareness of the host city. Despite the numbers of overseas visitors to cities being relatively small, when compared with domestic or American tourists, they are highly valued because of their larger expenditures. In metropolitan Toronto an estimated 807,000 overseas visitors spent $805 million in 1990, compared with $553 million spent by 2.3 million U.S. visitors, most of whom just spent the day in the area (Peat Marwick Stevenson and Kellogg, 1992: 9-10). These data clearly indicate the importance of the overseas market in any urban tourist promotion strategy. However, as the following section illustrates, the principal beneficiaries of cities' increasing emphasis on tourist development have been those citizens who have been able to be involved with new tourist attractions in revitalized or restored portions of inner city areas.

TOURISM AND URBAN REGENERATION

Increases in ship size, the development of container technology and changing patterns of trade have resulted in the widespread abandonment of port facilities. Portions of these areas have, in turn, been transformed by the federal government into major tourist attractions in Québec City, Montréal, Toronto, Vancouver and Halifax (Ashworth and Tunbridge, 1990; Desfor, Goldrick and Merrens, 1988; Tunbridge, 1988). North Market wharf in Saint John was revitalized into Market Square with the assistance of a private developer and all three major levels of government —an integrated commercial civic complex that includes a Festival marketplace, convention centre, first class hotel and library! After its completion the project was credited with: boosting tourism to the city, attracting private investment to the downtown and improving residents' level of satisfaction with living in Saint John (Schuyler and Ircha, 1987).

With the declining importance of the railway as a means of shipping freight and passenger transportation, railway yards close to city centres have become highly valued properties and sources of tourist oriented developments. Toronto's Skydome, a 50,000 seat sports stadium with a retractable roof, hotel and restaurants, was constructed in the late 1980s by the Ontario government on abandoned rail yards between downtown and Lake Ontario. Earlier in the decade, the federal and B.C. provincial governments funded the construction of B.C. Place, a 60,000 seat domed sports stadium, on rail yards east of Vancouver's city centre; while old rail facilities in Winnipeg have become the site for the Forks urban renewal project and National Historic Site at the junction of the Red and Assiniboine rivers.

Decaying or abandoned structures of historic significance in city centres have provided another opportunity for cities to develop tourist attractions. In the early 1960s much of Old Montréal was falling into disrepair; the city responded by establishing the Viger Commission to oversee the restoration of buildings and adding nineteenth century style lampposts and cobblestones; while the province declared a 95 acre area bounded by McGill, Notre-Dame, Berri and de la Commune Streets as an historical site, containing many of the city's historic tourist attractions. Across the continent, Vancouver's original town site of Granville, later known as Gastown, has become a major tourist attraction due, in part, to its designation as an historic site by the provincial government and city efforts to enhance its historic appeal by reconstructing cobblestone streets and providing antique lamp standards (Klenke, 1975).

The quintessential tourist-historic city is, of course, Québec City, whose 325 acre old town area was added to UNESCO's list of World Heritage sites in 1985 (Leahy, 1986/7). The city's old stone buildings, narrow winding streets, churches, monuments and statues provide tourists with a sense of history that is unique to North American cities. Government efforts at developing the tourist historic city can be traced to 1963 when the city created an historic district, within the city's walls, to protect many of the remaining old buildings (Ashworth and Tunbridge, 1990: 207). At the end of the decade, the provincial Ministry of Cultural Affairs began the rehabilitation of Place-Royale, the site of Champlain's original settlement along the waterfront. The successful restoration of this area led to the renovation of buildings along rue Petit-Champlain, the city's oldest street, and many other structures in the Quartier du Petit-Champlain area (Leahy, 1986/7: 14-16). Today, many of the buildings serve tourists with an array of boutiques, art galleries and restaurants.

In Ottawa, the National Capital Commission (NCC) is credited with being the catalyst for the revitalization of historic Sussex Drive which connects Parliament with the residences of the Prime Minister and Governor General. Beginning in the early 1960s, the NCC rehabilitated many of the old limestone buildings along the eastern edge of the street, and in the process displaced many of the older commercial functions and replaced them with up-scale boutiques, restaurants and pubs. These facilities serve many of the tourists who visit the National Gallery, War Museum and Mint along Sussex Drive. This revitalization effort was furthered in the late 1970s when the city of Ottawa restored the Byward Market building immediately east of Sussex Drive. The success of the restoration project has, in turn, attracted private developers who have restored additional buildings in the area and turned them into wine bars, pubs and restaurants (Tunbridge, 1992).

Most restoration projects result in improving the urban fabric of cities and widening the recreational opportunities for city residents. However, there is little research to indicate who uses these new facilities, whether any persons were displaced by the developments and, more generally, whether these projects have brought prosperity to the inner city. Nor has there been much attention given to the increasing homogeneity of revitalized inner-city tourist attractions with their familiar Festival Marketplaces and whether tourists will continue to be attracted to such landscapes. These and other issues relating to an urban tourism research agenda will be addressed in the concluding section of this chapter.

From an economic development perspective, cities need to develop their export capacity and, in the case of tourism, this means attracting outside visitors who will generate new jobs by spending money on accommodations and other tourist related activities. The following section examines some of the principal strategies used by cities to attract tourists: cultural tourism, sports tourism and conventions.

CULTURAL TOURISM

Cultural tourism deals with visits to the historical, artistic, scientific or lifestyle/heritage attractions of a community (LORD Cultural Resources Planning and Management, 1993: 11). In recent years, this form of tourism has been widely used by city planners as a means of urban regeneration (Griffiths, 1993; Bianchini, 1991). This strategy has received support from commercial and financial corporations that believe by sponsoring or promoting a cultural event their public image will be enhanced, while at the same time attracting potential new customers. Cities are interested in attracting cultural tourists because of their high spending patterns.

Among Canadians travelling in Ontario, the average reported expenditure per person trip in 1990 was about $95; for cultural event attendees the corresponding figure was $214! (LORD Cultural Resources Planning and Management, 1993: 40).

In utilizing cultural tourism to attract visitors, cities have developed three distinct products—events, lifestyle/heritage, and institutional. Since the 1960s, governments have made major investments in cultural institutions. The Toronto area, for example, has witnessed the expansion of the Art Gallery of Ontario and Royal Ontario Museum, the construction of Roy Thomson Hall, the North York Performing Arts Centre, Ontario Science Centre, O'Keefe Centre and Harbourfront arts complex. Smaller cities have benefited from similar investments. Edmonton's Citadel Theatre, constructed in 1976, is Canada's largest theatre complex, while an old power plant in Regina's Wascana Park was recently renovated to house the Saskatchewan Science Centre. The potential of these public investments to attract tourists can be seen in Toronto where 60 percent of visitors to the Ontario Science Centre are from out-of-province (LORD Cultural Resources Planning and Management, 1993: 31).

Administrators of *institutional* attractions have increasingly looked to special exhibitions, known as "blockbusters," as a means of boosting visitation. The impact of such a strategy is well illustrated by the Tutankhamen exhibition at the Art Gallery of Ontario. Between November 1st and December 31, 1979, 800,000 people visited the exhibit, 18.6 percent of whom came from outside Toronto, stayed overnight and spent $11 million in the city. Total visitor expenditure associated with the exhibition was estimated at over $20 million (Wall and Purdon, 1985).

Of much less significance, in terms of public investment, are those attractions associated with a city's *lifestyle/heritage,* such as its ethnic enclaves. Tourists interested in visiting such areas are usually attracted by differences in landscape, language, customs and cuisine. Chinatowns in Vancouver, Toronto and Victoria are, for example, an important component of each city's tourist product, while Canada's diverse immigrant population has become an "attraction" at Toronto's Kensington Market and Montréal's boulevard St. Laurent. Cities rarely market such areas as attractions and as such there are no data to indicate the number of tourists that visit such areas or their contribution to local economies.

Special events in the form of *festivals, fairs and exhibitions* have become an increasingly popular means for cities to boost tourism. They range in size and scale from one time events like Montréal's Expo 67, which drew 50 million visitors, to annual events like the Canadian National Exhibition in Toronto, which attracts approximately 2 million persons, and Edmonton's Folk Music Festival, which averaged 45,000 attendees in the early 1990s. In an effort to broaden the appeal of such events and increase the tourist season, most cities host a variety of festivals throughout the year. Music, comedy and film festivals are commonly held during the summer, and winter is celebrated by such events as Québec City's Carnaval d'Hiver, while spring is celebrated in Ottawa with its May Tulip festival. The impact of these events upon a city's tourist industry depends upon attendance and the number of outside visitors. The annual 10 day Calgary Stampede in the late

1980s generated an annual revenue of $60 million based upon attendance of over 1 million people (Getz, 1993: 148). By contrast, a study of seven Edmonton Festivals in 1988 found that although total attendance exceeded the Calgary Stampede, the events only generated $45 million in tourist revenue (Saxby, Payne and Cook, n.d.). This difference is attributable to the fact that nonresidents exceed residents in tourist expenditures, and, in the case of Edmonton, only 11 percent of festival attendees were from out-of-town compared with 30 percent for the Stampede.

SPORTS TOURISM

Spectator sports have become integral components of most cities' tourism and economic development strategies (Johnson, 1991; Euchner, 1993). Cities compete to host international, national and provincial championships as well as major and minor league franchises, because of their perceived economic benefits. These include improvements in infrastructure, increases in tourism and enhancement of the city's image (Marshall Macklin Monaghan Limited in association with Christopher Lang and Associates Ltd., 1993). One study estimated that Toronto's new NBA basketball team would raise an estimated $347 million a year from out-of-town basketball fans (Chianello, 1992), while the 16 day Pan-Am Games, to be hosted by Winnipeg in 1999, have been estimated at creating $179 million in economic activity for the city (Taylor, 1994). Although these claims are controversial, cities with the assistance of the provincial and federal governments have invested millions of dollars to support one-time sporting events like the Olympics and the subsequent use of a stadium by a sports franchise. In hockey, the Calgary Flames use the Saddledome, which was built for the 1988 Winter Olympics, and, in the Canadian Football League, the Edmonton Eskimos use Commonwealth Stadium, which was constructed for the 1978 Commonwealth Games.

The benefits to be gained from sports tourism depend upon the size of the event, its duration, and the number of outside visitors. The 1990 Molson CART Indy Race in Vancouver attracted 169,000 spectators, 35,000 of whom were from out-of-town along with 2,000 staffers; together, these two groups spent an estimated $12.4 million on tourist related expenditures during the three day event (Tourism Vancouver, 1990). By contrast, a preliminary study of the 1994 Victoria Commonwealth Games estimated that visitors would spend $32 million during the 10 day event and that the city would benefit from obtaining a television audience of over 300 million persons and 130 hours of broadcasting (Coopers & Lybrand, 1990). This type of exposure has proven to be an effective method of increasing the short-term awareness of a host city and broadening its image (Ritchie and Smith, 1991), although there is no research evidence to indicate that awareness of a destination will necessarily result in a visit.

Hosting a sports mega-event can produce unintended consequences. In Montréal, the high cost of the 1976 Summer Olympics forced the postponement of needed city housing, environmental and public transportation projects, as well as reductions in social service budgets (Kidd, 1981), while the construction of facilities related to the 1978 Edmonton Commonwealth Games led a consultant to predict that an estimated 6,000 persons would be displaced from their homes (Chivers, 1976). These experiences have created scepticism among community groups about plans to host similar events. In Toronto, one of the leading opposition groups to the city's plans to host the 1996 Summer Olympics was an organization entitled 'Bread not Circuses', which argued that government funds should be directed towards meeting the needs of the local population and not an elite group of athletes and outside spectators.

The economic importance that cities attach to the presence of a major league franchise is well illustrated by the so-called "small market teams" in the National Hockey League (Houston and Shoalts, 1994). Team owners argue that they need increased revenues to meet players' salary demands, either from gate receipts from a larger stadium with skyboxes and other premium seating (Winnipeg and Québec City), or a new lease at the existing stadium where the team currently plays (Edmonton and Calgary). In response, the cities of Edmonton and Calgary have renegotiated leases with their hockey teams, while in Québec City the team owner and government officials were unable to come to an agreement concerning a new stadium and the team was sold to a franchise based in Denver, Colorado. In an effort to keep the Jets in Winnipeg, provincial and city leaders commissioned several studies to demonstrate the economic importance of the team to the city and Manitoba. Besides the jobs created and the expenditures associated with the operation of the hockey club, it was estimated that, over the course of a season, 57,000 visiting fans spent $6.2 million in the city (The Interim Steering Committee Inc., 1993: 7-10). The presence of the team also created "exceptional international media exposure" to potential investors and visitors (The Interim Steering Committee Inc., 1993: 12). But despite these findings and the public sector's willingness to support the team, the Jets' owner announced in May 1995 that the team was for sale and that it would in all likelihood be moving to the United States (Roberts, 1995). Studies of the economic effects of sports teams are highly controversial, since there is little scholarly evidence to indicate that the net economic impact of a team can actually be determined (Johnson, 1986), neither is there any evidence to support the view that constructing a stadium boosts an area's economy (Baade and Dye, 1990). Nevertheless, sports tourism remains an important component of most cities' tourist marketing strategies.

CONVENTIONS

Hosting meetings is another means by which cities attempt to attract visitors. Convention attendees who stay overnight are particularly sought because of their high spending patterns. A 1989 study of meeting attendees in Greater Vancouver found that the average total expenditure per party was $1,120, while total expenditures in 1989 for all attendees was estimated at between $121 million and $243 million (Pannell, Kerr Forster: Campbell Goodell Consultants Limited, 1990: D31). These expenditures, in turn, support employees throughout the hospitality industry and boost local tax receipts. In response to this perceived economic bonanza, governments throughout North America have built convention centres and expanded exhibition space. Convention centres in Montréal and Toronto that opened in the early 1980s are now undergoing expansions in order to attract the largest conventions.

The largest proportion of conventions come from the province in which the city is situated (Table 3.1), which means that attendance is largely dependent upon the health of the local economy. In Toronto the number of conventions hosted by the city declined from a peak of 975 in 1989 to 710 in 1991, while attendance peaked at 749,000 in 1989 and dropped to 555,000 the following year (Peat Marwick Stevenson Kellogg, 1992: 33). These declines reflect the severe recession that hit Ontario in the early 1990s. Cities have made an effort to lessen their dependency upon local markets by attracting conventions from the United States and other countries. A survey of meeting planners for British Columbia's Ministry of Tourism found that 47 percent of planners in Western Canada had brought a meeting to the province, compared with just 5 percent for planners in the Western United States (Pannell Kerr Forster: Campbell Goodell Consultants, 1990: C7). This difference, according to a consultant's report, represents "the greatest potential for increasing the size of the meeting and convention market" in British Columbia (Pannell Kerr Forster: Campbell Goodell Consultants, 1990: E9). Some cities already attract a significant proportion of international conventions. Montréal has successfully marketed itself as an "international city," attracting 16 percent of its conventions from outside North America in 1992, while the comparable figure for the Metro Toronto Convention Centre was just 5 percent (Table 3.1).

Table 3.1   Convention delegate sources—Montréal[1] and Toronto[2] (percent)

Delegate Source	Montréal	Delegate Source	Toronto
Québec	38	Ontario	40
Rest of Canada	26	Rest of Canada	20
United States	20	United States	5
International	16	International	5
TOTAL	100		100

[1] Data refer to 1992.
[2] Data refer to usage of Metro Toronto Convention Centre various years.

Sources: Research and Development Department of the Greater Montréal Convention and Tourism Bureau, *The State of Tourism in Montréal*, Montréal, 1993; Peat Marwick Stevenson & Kellogg, *Competitive Tourism Development Strategy for Metropolitan Toronto Volume II —Background Report*, Toronto, 1992

SUMMARY AND SUGGESTIONS FOR FUTURE RESEARCH

Canadian cities now compete against each other to attract tourists in the same manner they compete to attract other businesses, by engaging in marketing activities, creating images, and constructing infrastructure. Over the past 30 years cities have added museums, sports stadia, convention centres and festival-type marketplaces to their list of attractions, with many such efforts being related to city centre revitalization. These investments have reshaped the urban fabric, and tourist landscapes have emerged. The largest single source of tourists is provided by the province in which the city is situated. The size of this market leaves the tourist industry dependent upon the health of local economies. In an effort to lessen this dependency and remove some of the fluctuations associated with the cyclical nature of the economy, cities have widened their marketing efforts to include foreign countries, most notably by the hosting of mega-events.

Much of the research cited in this chapter focuses upon short-term impacts such as the numbers of visitors to a particular event and their economic impact, but little attention has been given to assessing the long-term effectiveness of an urban tourism development strategy or analysing the overall beneficiaries of revitalization projects. For example, while Montréal's Old Port area attracts an estimated four million visitors a year, little is known about their origin and socioeconomic profile or the private sector beneficiaries. Clearly, given the enormous expenditures of public funds associated with such projects, there is a need to identify who benefits from them. In appraising tourism as a means of inner city regeneration, research needs to focus on determining: the types of jobs created (part-time, full-time, or seasonal), wage levels, location of the work force, gender make-up, and whether area residents were displaced by the projects. More generally, are these projects an effective means of providing employment opportunities for inner city residents displaced by economic restructuring, or are they another means of encouraging conspicuous consumption among an already affluent segment of society?

The commodification of the city has meant that a city's image is 'sold' to potential tourists and investors. Research indicates that an effective means of increasing destination awareness and broadening or creating a new image for a city, albeit for a short period, is to host a mega-event. But there is little evidence to link such events with future tourist visitation to a city, in part due to the difficulty of relating a person's decision to visit a destination with a single event that happened in the past. Nevertheless, as community groups show increasing scepticism towards the hosting of mega-events, there is an obvious need to identify their long-term economic benefits.

Tourists are increasingly important to the urban economies of Canadian cities, but as cities look to tourism to solve some of their economic development problems, they need to be mindful of adopting a long-term strategy. A successful tourist development plan is highly dependent upon offering new products, but many cities appear to be content with a major one-time investment, such as a waterfront redevelopment project or convention centre, which means that over time tourist visitation will almost inevitably decrease unless there is complementary and continuous private investment. Moreover, many of these projects have borrowed their designs from such successful attractions as Baltimore's Inner Harbor, with the net result that there is an increasing homogeneity to the urban tourist landscape. This, in turn, will almost inevitably result in further declines in tourist visitation as tourists see little that is unique in such attractions.

Tourism can play a significant role in a community's development if it is part of a long range strategy that focuses upon a city's unique characteristics. This means that a community must have an appealing, believable, simple, and distinctive image that differentiates it from other destinations (Kotler et al., 1993). This image can be conveyed to potential tourists in the form of a slogan (Toronto's "There's no place like it on earth"), visual symbol (Calgary's skyline against the backdrop of the Rocky mountains), or series of events (Edmonton Canada's Festival City). Communities must also address the issue of quality and the tourist experience, since a positive experience may result in visitors promoting the destination to friends and relatives. However, promoting a place and re-imaging a city is not a panacea for urban problems; these have to be addressed as part of an overall development strategy. Researchers can assist in the formulation of such a strategy by ensuring that the benefits of tourist development are shared among all community residents and visitors.

ACKNOWLEDGEMENTS

This research was funded by a Canadian Studies Faculty Research Grant, Canadian Embassy, Washington, D.C. The author is grateful for comments provided by two anonymous reviewers and the assistance of the following persons: Pierre Bellerose, Fran Blackman, Ellen Cole, Margot Inches, Nancy Klos, and Mebbie Pidner.

REFERENCES

Alberta Tourism, Parks and Recreation (1991). *1990 Alberta non-resident travel exit survey*. Edmonton.

Ashworth, G.J. (1989). Urban tourism—An imbalance in attention. In C. Cooper (Ed.), *Progress in tourism, recreation and hospitality management*, Vol. 1 (pp. 33-54). London: Belhaven.

Ashworth, G.J., and Tunbridge, J.E. (1990). *The tourist historic city*. London: Belhaven.

Baade, R.A., and Dye, R.F. (1990). The impact of stadiums and professional sports on metropolitan area development. *Growth and Change*, 21, 1-14.

Bianchini, F. (1991). Urban renaissance? The arts and the urban regeneration process. In S. MacGregor and B. Pimlotts (Eds.), *Tackling the inner cities: the 1980s reviewed, prospects for the 1990s* (pp. 215-250). Oxford: Clarendon Press.

Broadway, M.J. (1993). Montréal's changing tourist landscape. *Canadian Journal of Urban Research*, 2, 30-48.

Chianello, J. (1992). NBA spinoffs put at $347 million. *Financial Post*, October 12.

Chivers, B. (1976). Friendly games: Edmonton's Olympic alternative. In J. Lorimer and E. Ross (Eds.), *The City book* (pp. 183-189). Toronto: Lorimer.

Coopers & Lybrand (1990). *Victoria Commonwealth Games Society, estimated economic impact of the 1994 Commonwealth Games.* Vancouver.

Desfor, G., Goldrick, M., and Merrens, R. (1988). Redevelopment on the North American water-frontier: The case of Toronto. In B.S. Hoyle, D. Pinder and M.S. Husain (Eds.), *Revitalising the waterfront: International dimensions of dockland redevelopment* (pp. 92-113). London: Belhaven.

English Tourist Board. (1980). *Tourism and the inner city.* London.

English Tourist Board. (1983). *Tourism and urban regeneration.* London.

Euchner, C.C. (1993). *Playing the field: why sports teams move and cities fight to keep them.* Baltimore: Johns Hopkins University Press.

Gazillo, S. (1981). The evolution of restaurants and bars in Vieux-Québec since 1900. *Cahiers de Geographie du Québec*, 25, 101-18.

Getz, D. (1993). Case study: Marketing the Calgary exhibition and stampede. *Festival Management and Event Tourism,* 1, 147-156.

Griffiths, R. (1993). The politics of cultural policy in urban regeneration strategies. *Policy and Politics,* 21(1), 39-46.

Hall, P. (1987). Urban development and the future of tourism. *Tourism Management,* 8, 129-30.

Houston, W., and Shoalts, D. (1994). Canadian cities play on thin ice. *Toronto Globe and Mail,* January 4.

Interim Steering Committee. (1993). *Report on the preservation of NHL hockey in Winnipeg.* Winnipeg.

Johnson, A.T. (1986). Economic and policy implications of hosting sports franchises: Lessons from Baltimore. *Urban Affairs Quarterly,* 21, 423-424.

Johnson, A.T. (1991). Local government, minor league baseball and economic development strategies. *Economic Development Quarterly,* 5, 313-324.

Judd, D.R., and Collins, M. (1979). The case of tourism: Political coalitions and redevelopment in central cities. In G. Tobin (Ed.), *The changing structure of the city* (pp. 177-199). Beverly Hills: Sage.

Kidd, B. (1981). *The political economy of sport.* Vanier City, Ottawa: Canadian Association for Health Physical Education and Recreation.

Klenke, M. (1975). *Gastown economic study. Commercial rehabilitation and revitalization of Gastown historic site.* Vancouver: Vancouver City Planning Department.

Kotler, P., Haider, D.H., and Rein, I. (1993). *Marketing places: Attracting investment, industry and tourism to cities, states and nations.* New York: Free Press.

Lanken, D. (1986). Drapeau's Montréal: great moments, great monuments. *Canadian Geographic,* 106(4), 10-23.

Law, C. (1992). Urban tourism and its contribution to economic regeneration. *Urban Studies,* 29, 599-618.

Law, C. (1993). *Urban tourism: Attracting visitors to large cities.* London: Mansell.

Leahy, G.W. (1986-7). Québec: Our city of World Heritage renown. *Canadian Geographic,* 106(6), 8-21.

Lee, J. (1987). The impact of Expo '86 on British Columbia markets. In P. Williams, J. Hall, and M. Hunter (Eds.), *Tourism where is the client?* Conference papers of Travel and Tourism Research Association, Canada Chapter.

Levine, M.V. (1989). Urban redevelopment in a global economy: The cases of Montréal and Baltimore. In R.V. Knight and G. Gappert (Eds.), *Cities in a global society* (pp. 141-52). Beverly Hills: Sage.

LORD Cultural Resources Planning and Management Inc. (1993). *Ontario's Cultural Tourism Product.* Toronto.

MacIsaac, M. (1994). Winner take nothing. *Canadian Business, 67*(5), 36-42.

Marshall Macklin Monaghan Limited in association with Christopher Lang and Associates Ltd. (1993). *Spectator sporting activities in Canada from a tourism perspective.* Ottawa: Industry Science and Technology Canada.

Murphy, P.E. (1980). Tourism management using land use planning and landscape design: The Victoria experience. *Canadian Geographer, 24,* 60-71.

Murphy, P.E. (1992). Urban tourism and visitor behavior. *American Behavioral Scientist, 36,* 200-211.

L'Office des Congrès et du Tourisme du Grand Montréal (1992). Les attraits et événements. *L'indicateur touristique, 2*(1), 6.

Owen, C. (1990). Tourism and urban regeneration. *Cities, 7,* 194-201.

Page, S. (1995). *Urban tourism.* London: Routledge.

Pannell Kerr Forster, Campbell Goodell Consultants Limited (1990). *British Columbia meeting market study.*

Peat Marwick Stevenson and Kellogg (1992). *Competitive tourism development strategy for metropolitan Toronto, volume II.* Toronto.

Regional Planning Services, Calgary Regional Planning Commission (1989). *Prospect: The region's tourism market.* Calgary.

Regional Planning Services, Calgary Regional Planning Commission (1990). *Prospect 1990: Tourism in the next decade.* Calgary.

Research and Development Department of the Greater Montréal Convention and Tourism Bureau (1993). *The state of tourism in Montréal 1992 report.* Montréal.

Ritchie, J.R. Brent (1990). Promoting Calgary through the Olympics. In S.H. Fine (Ed.), *Social marketing: Promoting the causes of public and nonprofit agencies* (pp. 258-274). Needham Heights, MA: Allyn and Bacon.

Ritchie, J.R. Brent, and Smith, B.H. (1991). The impact of a mega-event on host region awareness: A longitudinal study. *Journal of Travel Research, 30*(1), 3-9.

Roberts, D. (1995). Jets' sale ends bailout bid. *Toronto Globe and Mail,* May 4.

Saxby Payne and Cook Inc. (n.d.). *Edmonton summer festivals 1988 market study.* Edmonton.

Schuyler, G., and Ircha, M. (1987). Market square: Downtown economic revival. *Plan Canada, 26* (March), 16-22.

Smith, S.L.J. (1983). Restaurants and dining out, geography of a tourism business. *Annals of Tourism Research, 10,* 515-549.

Taylor, S. (1994). Games mean big business for Winnipeg. *Winnipeg Free Press,* July 31.

Tourism Canada (1992). *Tourism related employment in Canada.* Industry Science and Technology Canada.

Tourism Canada (1994). *Packages featuring selected canadian cities: Calgary, Halifax, Ottawa, Québec City, Regina, Victoria, Winnipeg, state of the product and development opportunities, the United States market.* Industry Science and Technology Canada.

Tourism Vancouver (1990). *Tourism economic impact analysis 1990 Molson Indy Vancouver.* Vancouver.

Tunbridge, J. (1988). Policy convergence on the waterfront? A comparative assessment of North American revitalization strategies. In B.S. Hoyle, D. Pinder and M.S. Husain (Eds.), *Revitalizing the waterfront: International dimensions of dockland redevelopment* (pp. 67-91). London: Belhaven.

Tunbridge, J.E. (1992). Farmers, festival markets: The case of Byward Market, Ottawa. *Canadian Geographer, 36,* 280-285.

Wall, G., and Sinnott, J. (1980). Urban recreational and cultural facilities as tourist attractions. *Canadian Geographer, 24,* 50-59.

Wall, G., and Knapper, C. (1981). *Tutankhamen in Toronto.* Department of Geography Publication Series, No. 17. University of Waterloo, Waterloo.

Wall, G., Dudycha, D., and Hutchinson, J. (1985). Point pattern analysis of accommodation in Toronto. *Annals of Tourism Research, 12,* 603-18.

Wall, G., and Purdon, M. (1985). *The economic impact of the arts in Ontario.* Toronto: Ontario Arts Council.

Whelan, R.K. (1991). The politics of urban redevelopment in Montréal: Regime change from Drapeau to Doré. *Québec Studies, 12,* 155-69.

Plate 3 (overleaf - top) The City of Vancouver
(photo courtesy of The Province of British Columbia) ➡

Plate 4 (overleaf - bottom) A cruise ship under Lions Gate Bridge
(photo courtesy of The Province of British Columbia) ➡

Impacts of Inner City Tourism Projects: The Case of The International Convention Centre, Birmingham, U.K.

Jane Lutz

Centre for Urban and Regional Studies, University of Birmingham

Chris Ryan

Nottingham Business School, Nottingham Trent University

INTRODUCTION

The city of Birmingham, located in the West Midlands region, is the UK's second city, with a population of just under one million. Long regarded as the centre of the country's industrial heartland, it has recently had to confront considerable economic challenges. It has actively pursued tourism development as a significant strand in its urban regeneration strategy and has a string of accolades to confirm the quality of new flagship developments, notably its International Convention Centre (ICC) which opened in 1991. Perhaps unsurprisingly, it has also attracted the attention of urban policy analysts (Loftman and Nevin, 1992) who have argued that significant opportunity costs have arisen from it.

This chapter begins by looking at why Birmingham developed a policy of urban tourism development and outlines the subsequent strategy adopted. It describes the facilities that were created within the complex and traces the convention centre's linkages to wider city centre planned change. The impacts of the ICC are evaluated by drawing upon published research. Finally, an attempt is made to consider the ICC's wider achievements in relation to the opportunities and constraints the city faces.

THE UK CONTEXT

Economic Challenges and Policy Responses

In the early 1980s, faced with recession, but also a growing level of domestic and overseas tourism, both central and local government turned to tourism as one means of generating economic growth. Tourism was also perceived as a vehicle for the promotion of small business enterprise, much in vogue, politically, at that time as another potential growth point within the economy. The decline in the inner cities of the UK stimulated a range of urban regeneration policy initiatives under both Labour and Conservative governments (Lewis, 1992). What was new as the 1980s progressed was the increasing importance attached to tourism as one possible generator of employment, albeit often in association with retail and property development and linked to wider cultural revitalization policies.

Birmingham

The need for economic regeneration in Birmingham can be simply illustrated. In the period 1971-1984, Birmingham lost more than half of its manufacturing jobs —a decline from by far the largest source of employment in the city at 295,000 jobs in 1971 to only 130,00 in 1984. The city became aware that it needed to respond to global restructuring which involved new competitors and demanded new economic strategies. The city's 1985 economic strategy declared that, although aid to manufacturing was its main focus, there was a need to develop new sectors in order to broaden the city's economic base. Business tourism was identified as a new service sector to be supported. For instance, the city had reaped considerable economic rewards from its earlier investment in the National Exhibition Centre (NEC) on the city fringes. It was confident that there was continued employment growth potential from the development of additional tourism facilities.

Also, the encouragement of tourism was seen as being especially congruent with the strong commitment, within the economic strategy, to environmental improvements within the city. These were seen as vital to enhancing the city's image and attracting inward investment. Thus the development of the ICC, a major new facility (see Figure 4.1) in an identified employment growth area and in the new service sector, on a city centre site offering the promise of environmental improvement can be seen as a significant strand in the city's overall economic strategy.

The new ICC was central to the re-imaging of the city. It would be tangible evidence of its transition from a grey industrial provincial city with a dull and declining central business district to a post-modern city with a thriving new heart.

THE INTERNATIONAL CONVENTION CENTRE

As already noted, the city council had underwritten development of the NEC in the 1970s and controlled in NEC Ltd. a profit-making company that was well established in the exhibitions business. In the early 1980s it was looking to expand and add a conference facility to complement the existing business. Following a feasibility study in 1983, Birmingham decided to promote the UK's first international convention centre. The site chosen was Broad Street in the city centre, where

Figure 4.1   The International Convention Centre (with classic car exhibition in Centenary Square).

spin-off benefits attracting investment and new activity could be maximized. The Broad Street Redevelopment Area (BSRA) defined in 1984 identified adjoining sites for the convention centre and a Hyatt Regency Hotel, together with a further larger area for other related developments. The city council owned some of the redevelopment area. Compulsory purchase of the remainder was promoted in 1984 alongside an outline planning application. In 1987, following extensive public consultation, the city council issued a development brief for a substantial part of the total area and invited private sector proposals for a National Indoor Arena (NIA) and a festival marketplace complex, which came to be known as Brindley Place.

Thus, the ICC is the centrepiece of a larger complex (see Figure 4.2). The convention centre itself is comprised of 11 halls on a 6.7 acre site. Hall 2 is widely recognized to be Britain's finest Symphony Hall and is the home of the City of Birmingham Symphony Orchestra. There is a central pedestrian mall through the convention centre with small cafés, banking and business facilities, and a few small shops. This mall links Centenary Square in the front of the building to canalside open space and towpath areas at the core of the BSRA. The Square is a major new civic open space which also functions as an outdoor exhibition and event area.

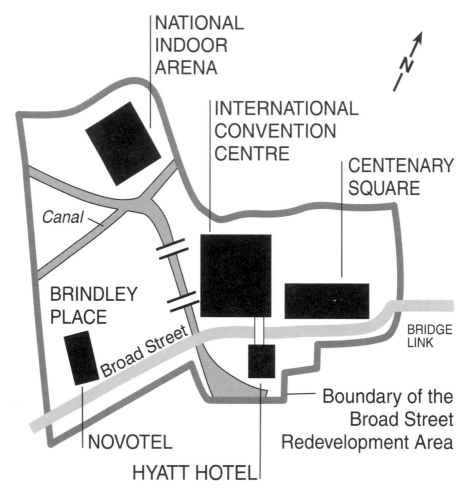

Figure 4.2   The International Convention Centre and related developments in the Broad Street Redevelopment area.

Environmental Impacts

A review of city council documents (Birmingham City Council, 1989; Birmingham City Council, 1993; Upton, 1991; Wright, 1994) reveals the catalytic role the ICC has had in stimulating new thinking about planned physical changes within the city. The definition of the BSRA, which came to be known as the Convention Centre Quarter, started a process whereby a bland and uniform city centre came to be rethought as a more varied collection of discrete and distinctive quarters. Thus, a new map of a differentiated central area emerged, with a central business core, defined by the inner ring road, surrounded by a Jewellery Quarter and a Chinese and Entertainment Quarter. The development of the ICC and its associated facilities has added a Convention Centre Quarter to this structure.

The physical location of the ICC on the edge of the Central Business District means that there has always been a focus on linkages between the two areas. For instance, major road works accompanied the construction of the ICC. These involved lowering the inner ring road so that the cars now go under the people. Pedestrians can now walk from the city centre to the ICC by way of a ground level bridge over the ring road and through the newly created public open space, Centenary Square. The restrictive and pedestrian-hostile concrete collar of the Inner Ring Road has been effectively and importantly breached (Figure 4.3).

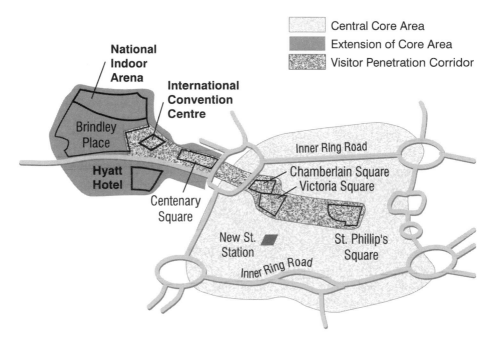

Figure 4.3   The International Convention Centre and Birmingham City Centre: new linkages.

This initial experience of pedestrianization and the creation of links through new squares of public open space was to be replicated in New Street, the city's major shopping street, and in the creation of a dramatically improved Victoria Square within the city centre. It also stimulated the removal of dank pedestrian underpasses and the creation of improved surface crossings at other key points of the inner ring road.

The development of the ICC can be seen as a mechanism whereby a provincial UK city was prompted to look outside itself and draw inspiration from US regeneration models (Wright, 1994: 1) much in vogue at the time. It also can be seen as an attempt to re-invent its city centre as a place imbued with an European ambience. With its new boulevards and new quality squares it could compare itself with other continental European cities. The physical evidence is now in place to show the dramatic environmental improvements that have followed the ICC's construction.

Social and Economic Impacts

The International Convention Centre and its related developments consumed large amounts of money, much of it from public funds. The convention centre was originally predicted to cost £91.2 million, but by 1991 the actual cost was reported as £160 million (Upton, 1994: 64). Funding came mainly from stock issues by NEC Ltd. and a grant of £49.75 million from the European Community. Private sector funds have also accompanied the development. Apart from the Hyatt Regency, four other new hotels have been built within walking distance of the ICC, adding over 800 new bed spaces. The Brindleyplace development scheme adjoining the ICC is estimated to represent private investment of around £300 million (Birmingham City Council, 1993: 2).

This investment was intended to stimulate activity and create demonstrable benefits to the city, both in terms of increased visitor expenditure and new employment. What is known about the scale of the impacts generated by the development? In 1993, NEC Ltd. commissioned the consultants KPMG Peat Marwick (KPMG Peat Marwick, 1993) to undertake the first economic impact assessment of the ICC and its related Symphony Hall (SH) and National Indoor Arena (NIA), as well as the NEC.

Part of the rationale underpinning the support for the ICC was that it would create a new business tourism market and draw in staying international visitors. The KPMG study revealed that the ICC was the most successful venue in attracting the highest proportion, 18 percent, of its visitors from overseas, the percentages at the NIA and the NEC being 1 percent and 3 percent respectively (KPMG Peat Marwick 1993: 27). The ICC (with its Symphony Hall) was also the venue which generated the highest proportion of staying visitors, as demonstrated in Table 4.1. Overnight visitors at the ICC also tended to stay in paid accommodation as indicated in Table 4.2.

Table 4.1   Categories of users at Birmingham venues (in percent)

	Daytrippers	*Staying Visitors*
ICC	37.5	62.5
NIA	63.0	37.0
NEC	91.3	8.7

Source: KPMG Peat Marwick, (1993: 28).

Table 4.2   Use of accommodation by visitors to Birmingham venues (in percent)

	Hotels	*Guest Houses*	*B&B*	*Other*
ICC	52.7	0.6	0.6	8.1
NIA	21.7	2.2	2.4	4.8
NEC	2.2	0.2	0.1	0.3

Source: KPMG Peat Marwick (1993: 29).

The final estimate of the income multiplier for the ICC was 0.42, and the employment multiplier 0.41. Hence, the net additional economic impact of the visitor expenditure on the West Midlands regional economy was estimated to be £27.72 million in 1993—£66 million from the estimated visitor spending at the ICC, multiplied by 0.42 (KPMG Peat Marwick, 1993: 8). Highly focused regional multipliers tend to be low because of the high leakages, but those of the ICC would, at first sight, appear somewhat lower than might be hoped for when compared with tourism multipliers calculated for small regions, for example see Murphy (1985). However, it must be noted that most of the studies quoted by Murphy and others relate to rural or less densely populated areas, while highly specific urban areas can have high initial leakages but subsequently such leakages are returned to the area through its role as, for example, a retail centre (Ryan, 1996).

Apart from the expenditure multiplier, what is known about the employment generated by the ICC? For the West Midlands region as a whole the study reported that the ICC had created 2,700 full time equivalent jobs, 1,093 of these being in Birmingham (KPMG Peat Marwick, 1993: 45).

The earlier Loftman and Nevin (1992) study was noticeably less generous in its appraisal of the ICC's power to create jobs. Unconvinced by the strength of the trickle down economic theory related to the mainly US tourism related inner city regeneration schemes, and taking a social equity perspective, these authors argued that inner city residents gained very little from the project. Their work claimed that there had been significant opportunity costs related to the resourcing of the ICC and suggested that allocations of monies for housing and education had been adversely affected by commitments made to the development of inner city prestige projects like the ICC. They noted: "The direct impact of the financing of the prestige projects on the capital programme of the council's housing has been substantial" (Loftman and Nevin, 1992: 117-118), and again, with reference to the City's underspending on housing and education as judged by Central Government criteria: "This underspend was shifted to support the capital programme of other projects such as the prestige projects and economic development generally" (Loftman and Nevin, 1992: 123-124)

Their study focused on the period when the ICC was under construction and immediately after its opening. Using different methodology from the KPMG survey and focusing on whether jobs were filled by inner city residents, they reported that only 7 percent of permanent jobs had gone to residents living in nearby deprived areas. Their allegations were hotly disputed at the time by the city council in the local press and the City leader said the study was based upon "selective quotations and one-sided evidence" combined with an inappropriate methodology and incorrect data (Bell, 1992: 2).

Although the city council's reaction to Loftman and Nevin's report criticizing the number and quality of jobs that local people had gained was dismissive, it too had identified that the nature of tourism jobs was less than ideal. A 1987 tourism policy document noted "tourism makes a major contribution to job creation", but adds, in parentheses, "that the quality of employment is often a source for concern" (Birmingham City Council, 1987: 8). The same document signalled the need to invest in providing appropriate training to accompany the inner city tourism developments.

One impact of the ICC is the development of the UK's first customized Hotel Academy, which was set up in purpose built premises attached to the Novotel Hotel adjacent to the ICC. The ICC can therefore be seen as having clear linkages with a significant new training initiative, proposed initially by the city council, but developed later in collaboration with local employers and the quasi-autonomous agency, the Training and Enterprise Council.

Difficulties with Monitoring

The problems of measuring the impacts of tourism are well documented and the ICC presents yet another illustration of this complexity. The ICC's integration with wider planned city centre change can be seen as a strength, as is evidenced by the noted environmental improvements. It also, however, creates a problem in terms of disaggregating its economic benefits. The interconnectedness of the project and the problems of using direct jobs as performance indicators has been acknowledged: "The prime objective was to provide the city with some of the economic infrastructure it needs in the shift being forced by global economic change towards a different kind of economic role. The direct jobs were a bonus." (Wenban-Smith, 1992: letters page).

A Change in Mood?

It is a truism to state that the 1990s are significantly different from the 1980s in that there is scepticism about the economic growth promised by large property development schemes. In Birmingham, this mood change was compounded by a change in leadership within the city's ruling Labour Party. Interviewed shortly after her election, the new leader, Councillor Stewart, signalled that the city council's attitudes towards continuing investment in the city centre had changed. She gave a much more sober appraisal of tourism's contribution, which, while recognizing the "ravishing" nature of the city centre, criticized the nature of the jobs created as being "low pay, short-term, non-union jobs" (Cohen, 1993: 11).

Councillor Stewart's concern, not only about the quality of employment, but also about the above-expected capital costs and the continuing annual losses of the ICC, has not, however, been accompanied by a withdrawal of support for the ICC. A comparison of the 1987 tourism action plan and the 1994 tourism strategy reveals that tourism is now perceived to be highly integrated within the city's development strategy. The need to consider the tourism implications in day-to-day planning is also flagged in this document, viz: "Members and officers should therefore always consider the wider implications for the City's Tourism potential when taking decisions on new developments" (Birmingham City Council 1994: 3). A more critical and focused attitude towards research into, support for, and evaluation of tourism development is also evident in the same document.

Another indication of the closer connections between tourism and economic development is evident in the changes that have occurred in the body with responsibility for City tourism, the Birmingham Convention and Visitor Bureau (BCVB). As a result of a review of its functions in 1992, the BCVB was subsumed into a more focused Birmingham Marketing Partnership which would have a more explicit role in the promotion of the city for inward investment (Smith, 1993: 13). Previously the BCVB had a much narrower remit to promote the city for tourism purposes.

Lessons to be Learnt

Evidence from the Department of the Environment (1990), and indeed from Birmingham's own initial experience from the National Exhibition Centre, does not indicate that major projects inevitably fail expectation. What perhaps they do indicate is just how costly it is to produce jobs, and that in this sense major tourism projects are little different from the manufacturing industry in that millions of pounds of capital expenditure are required to produce a few hundred jobs. Inner city areas pose real problems for employment generation in that, almost by definition, residents have a low skill base.

Critics of Birmingham's policies must not overlook that the city had followed conventional wisdom in planning its development. Law (1993: 23-26) notes that successful urban renewal programs have the following features:

a)   an emphasis on economic policies;
b)   an emphasis on obtaining private investment;
c)   public sector investment in the infrastructure;
d)   public sector 'anchors'—museums or convention centres;
e)   an emphasis on property development;
f)   a focus on the city centre;
g)   public-private sector partnership;
h)   semi-autonomous public agencies;
i)   flagship projects; and
j)   image.

Birmingham did all of these things. Its unemployment is currently 15.1 percent (Birmingham Economic Information Centre, 1995), the sixth highest of the metropolitan areas in the UK. If, therefore, in spite of following the formula of success described by Law, Birmingham cannot yet report significantly increased employment, especially in relation to direct jobs to inner city residents, and more impressive multipliers, what factors have deterred success?

In the case of Birmingham, several factors can be identified. These include:

a)   a recession in the property market;

b)   locational features favouring peripheral development;

c)   the political relationship with central government;

d)   increased competition from other cities; and

e)   lack of viable alternative policies.

As the public sector showed the necessary commitment to redeveloping Birmingham, was there a failure on the part of the private sector? A key part of the plan associated with the ICC was the rebuilding associated with the neighbouring Brindleyplace. This scheme, modelled on the festival marketplace concept, was a mixture of retail, leisure and office space. The collapse of the property market meant that it had repeated changes in ownership and it lay derelict until September 1993, over two years after the opening of the ICC (Construction News, 1993).

A second problem the city had to encounter was a drift away from the centre towards the NEC and Birmingham International Airport which created powerful magnets for new businesses. The availability of land is a key factor, and hence, unlike the NEC, the ICC faced all the difficulties involved in constructing a major development in a built-up area, and the costs associated with such work.

A third problem was the relationship of Birmingham with a central government that in the 1980s was characterized by policies of capping local government expenditure. One example of this troublesome relationship was the failure of central government to provide funds to support Birmingham's proposed integrated light rail public transport system which was designed to complement the city centre environmental improvements (Wright, 1994: 3)

A fourth problem was that the policies being adopted by Birmingham were also being adopted by other cities. As the competition for retailers, property developments, service, and manufacturing industries increased between these cities, so, too, did they become increasingly alike. Judd (1994: 25), in a United States context, notes that:

> *Such a stance often means that cities become driven by a vision of regeneration that is not entirely their own invention. Cities exist in a complex political environment shaped by economic changes, national policies, the action of other cities, and, in the case of tourism, a well organized industry. The manner in which inter-urban competition in the United States is conducted, however, dictates the cities must compete, they must be as generous as their competitors in providing subsidies,*

and they must adopt every new variation on a theme that comes along.
The result is the production of a remarkably standardized tourism space
from one city to the next.

The same, too, is true of British cities, and indeed Ryan (1991: 140) commented upon the very uniformity of architectural style associated with waterfront developments. One outcome was that throughout Europe new, similar convention centres grew in 'second tier' cities, offering comparable facilities. In such circumstances the ability to charge premium rates for footloose international symposia becomes very limited.

A Post Modernist Response?

It can also be argued that such City projects are part of a contemporary process which has been variously described as post-Fordism, de-constructionism or post-modernism. In an age of uncertainty, de-industrialization, and doubts concerning identity, new identities are sought based upon symbols which are consumed as avidly as actual consumer goods. Cities, too, may be part of this process. Birmingham had possessed, until the late 1960s, an image and a confidence based upon its metal and car industries, with a proud civic reputation dating from the 1880s. In the 1980s, it had found itself with a crisis of confidence, the demise of past certainties, and a fear of being relegated to a 'second division' of cities far from the sources of power in a growing European Union. Under such circumstances, symbols of progress are important in a reversal of decline, and, arguably, it is a function of the public sector to provide these, just as, in the 1880s, progress was recorded by municipally owned water, sewage, and gas companies with public participation in health, housing, and education. Hence, the case of Birmingham and similar cities can be perceived as evidence of a municipal post-modernism where convention centres, the rediscovery of meeting places and marketplaces, and investment in aesthetics, become the means of seeking identity even when, paradoxically, the adoption of similar policies by others diminishes the uniqueness of any one city.

SUMMARY

The critics of Birmingham's policies must also answer the question, what was the city to do? To state the obvious, local authorities cannot directly enter manufacturing. The options open to local councils such as Birmingham, when faced with persistent unemployment, are limited, and recreation, leisure, and tourism as economic growth sectors must, therefore, play a significant part in local public sector revival policies.

The ICC is a major asset with which to compete in the international conference market. Additionally, the subsequent changes within the city centre that it generated have led to a dramatically altered and improved environment with far reaching consequences. The city has demonstrated that it has the ability to undertake a massive 'makeover' and create a new city centre mosaic with places for new economic functions, new public open spaces, and a refocusing on the needs of pedestrians rather than cars.

Landry and Bianchini (1995) argue that creativity and innovation will be the hallmarks of successful cities of the future. It was noted earlier that a key challenge will be to avoid 'serial monotony' and develop distinctive city environments. The case of Birmingham is interesting in that it illustrates a move from the initial development of 'green belt'/open fields, as demonstrated by the building of the NEC and its supporting road structures, to reinvestment in the city centre. Writers such as Hough have argued that there is a need for a continuing dynamic process of wider, healthier city change. He notes:

> . . . . the diversity principle deals with health. If health, in an environmental sense, can be described as the ability to withstand stress, then diversity may also imply health. In the context of the city, diversity has biological and social relevance. Quality of life implies, among other things, being able to choose between one environment and another, and between one place and another. A city that has places for foxes, owls, geese, natural woodlands, regenerating fields and urban wilderness is more interesting . . . . Cities also need hard urban places, busy plazas and markets, noisy as well as (quiet) places, cultivated landscapes, and formal gardens (Hough, 1990: 17).

Arguably, the developments in Birmingham City Centre, of which the ICC, Brindleyplace, and the new public open spaces are part, have sought to reinvigorate Birmingham's centre. Perhaps the next stage in the evolution of urban planning will be the intrusion of green spaces, thereby completing the retreat from devouring green peripheries to a policy of introducing pockets of countryside into the heart of the city.

ACKNOWLEDGEMENTS

The authors gratefully acknowledge Joanne Pearcy, Nottingham Trent University, without whose help this study would not have started. Thanks are also due to Bob Prosser who gave helpful guidance on the text and illustrations.

REFERENCES

Bell, D. (1992). City fury over Gloss attack. *Evening Mail*, October 21.

Birmingham City Council (1987). *Action programme for tourism.* Birmingham.

Birmingham City Development Department (1987). *City centre strategy.* Birmingham City Council.

Birmingham City Council (1989). *The highbury initiative.*

Birmingham City Council (1993). *Broad Street redevelopment area fact pack.*

Birmingham City Council (1994). *Finance and management (Promotions and Public Relations) Sub-Committee.*

Birmingham Economic Information Centre (1995). *Birmingham Labour Market Bulletin.* April.

Cohen, B. (1993). Renaissance that never was. *Independent on Sunday,* 10 October, p. 11.

Construction News (1993). *Argent rescues Brindleyplace.* July 15.

Department of the Environment (1990). *Tourism in the inner city: An evaluation of grant assisted tourism projects.* London: HMSO

Evening Mail (1994). City set to lose £7.2 million in Centre. October 10, p. 10.

Hough, M. (1990). Formed in natural process—A definition of the Green City. In D. Gordon (Ed.), *Green cities—ecologically sound approaches to urban space.* Montreal and New York: Black Rose Books.

Judd, D. (1994). Promoting tourism in American cities—A comparative analysis. Paper presented at Urban Tourism and City Trips Conference, April 28-29, Rotterdam.

KPMG Peat Marwick (1993). The *economic impact of the International Convention Centre, the National Indoor Arena, Symphony Hall and the National Exhibition Centre on Birmingham and the West Midlands.*

Landry, C., and Bianchini, F. (1995). *The creative city.* London: Demos.

Law, C. (1993). *Urban tourism.* London: Mansell.

Lewis, N. (1992). *Inner city regeneration: The demise of regional and local government.* Buckingham: Open University.

Loftman, P., and Nevin, B. (1992). Urban regeneration and social equity. Research Paper No. 8. Faculty of the Built Environment: University of Central England.

Murphy, P. (1985). *Tourism: A community approach.* London: Methuen.

Ryan, C. (1991). *Recreational tourism: A social science perspective.* London: Routledge.

Ryan, C. (1996). Economic impacts of events in Palmerston North, New Zealand - work in progress.

Smith, P. (1993). The Hanna Report. *The Birmingham Post,* August 5, p. 13.

Upton, C. (1991). *The past, present and future: A commemorative book for the opening of the International Convention Centre.* Birmingham: Birmingham City Council.

Wenban-Smith, A. (1992). New economic role for centre. *The Planner,* 947, Letters Page.

Wright, G. (1994). Giving the streets back to the people. Introductory Paper, Local Authorities Pedestrian Planning Group Conference, Birmingham, July 1.

Plate 5 The Inner Harbour, Victoria
(photo courtesy of The Province of British Columbia) ➡

Competition and the Resort Community: Towards an Understanding of Residents' Needs

5

Alison M. Gill

Department of Geography, Simon Fraser University

INTRODUCTION

The need for resorts to remain competitive has frequently led to tourist-related development at the expense of both the physical and social needs of resident populations. It is now widely acknowledged that resorts must address the needs of the resident population if they are to avoid the negative repercussions associated with exceeding the social carrying capacity of the community (O'Reilly, 1986). However, few tourism communities have resolved the problems of how to successfully control and manage the balance between tourists and residents in a resort setting. In part this reflects the economic forces of tourism development which make local control difficult and, in part, it reflects the lack of understanding of the distinctive social system of tourism-dependent communities.

Increasingly, as notions of sustainability shift planning and development strategies from traditional top-down processes to bottom-up ones, the role of "the community" in finding solutions to its own problems is greatly increased. The underlying thesis of this chapter is that a clearer conceptualization of the structure and processes within the community tourism system will ultimately assist in more effective management practices which will balance the needs of both resident and tourist groups. The chapter begins with a definition of "community" that seems especially appropriate for understanding processes of interaction and change in tourism communities. This is an ecological definition, proposed by the sociologist Roland Warren, which centres on the concept of competition (Warren, 1977). This idea is then elaborated upon using examples from Whistler, British Columbia, a planned four-season resort which during the past few years has been forced to deal with the needs and concerns of an emergent local community. The growth management strategy adopted in Whistler offers useful guidelines for resort management.

DEFINITIONS OF COMMUNITY

There are many definitions of community. Some are based solely on social networks and interactions between people, whereas others suggest that local sentiment and attachment to place is the identifying element (Hillery, 1955; McMillan and Chavis, 1986). A definition of community that seems especially appropriate to the study of tourist communities, where growth and change are central characteristics, is that of Roland Warren. He defines "community" as:

> . . . . an aggregation of people competing for space. The shape of the community, as well as its activities are characterized by differential use of space and by various processes according to which one type of people and/or type of social function succeeds another in the ebb and flow of structural change in a competitive situation. People are bound together not by sentiment but by utilitarian considerations, cooperating through their mutual interdependence caused by the division of labor, but at the same time, competing in matters of common desire but scarce satisfactions (Warren, 1977: 208).

This definition is based on ecological principles that conceptualize change as an outcome of competition. This is appealing because tourism communities are generally dynamic by nature. When tourism is introduced into a community, whether as a planned element of economic restructuring or as the result of external demand forces, the changes to the social, economic and political structures of communities are significant and often rapid. Further, even when tourism becomes established, change is a constant because of economic forces that result in communities competing with one another for market share.

A first step in understanding the community tourism system is to recognize the distinctiveness of such places from other types of community. A fundamental difference between tourist places and other communities is that residents compete with tourists for basic community resources such as space and facilities. There is an essential dichotomy between residents who view the community as their home and a place to live and the tourist who views the community as a resource that is commodified and consumed. While generalizations can be made, it must be emphasized that each situation is context-specific and contingent factors will vary from place to place. A second distinguishing characteristic of tourist-dependent communities is the type of stakeholder groups within the community. Both residents and tourists can be further segmented into subgroups who compete with one another in various ways because of differing needs and attitudes. Resident subgroups may include categories such as permanent residents, transient residents, and second-home owners. In the next section, these concepts of community are elaborated with reference to the case study of Whistler, British Columbia. A brief overview of the development of Whistler is first presented as context for this discussion.

THE EVOLUTION OF WHISTLER, BRITISH COLUMBIA

Whistler, British Columbia is located 120 kilometres north of Vancouver. A small resident community has existed in this location since around 1915 when the community of Alta Lake developed. In the 1960s and early 1970s, the community expanded from a few seasonal summer lodges and cabins to an unorganized winter community centred at the base of the early downhill ski development on Whistler Mountain (now called Whistler Creekside). Whistler Resort is a new planned community that formally came into existence with the creation of a provincial government act in 1975 giving it status as a "Resort Municipality". With Municipality status and both private and public investment, a planned village centre was developed with ski-in/ski-out access from both Whistler and Blackcomb Mountains (each operated by a separate ski corporation). The first phase of this development was completed by 1980, but the recession led to financial crisis necessitating a large scale and controversial bailout by the provincial government and subsequent financial and organizational restructuring of the land company. Nevertheless, Whistler has grown and flourished. Rapid development occurred especially during the latter part of the 1980s when the Blackcomb Ski Corporation exercised its development rights in the Benchlands area adjacent to its ski lifts and engaged in extensive condominium and hotel development. Having attained international recognition as a ski resort, the focus in the last few years has been to extend tourism throughout the year with an emphasis on summer recreational activities, and conventions and events during shoulder seasons. A second major phase of village centre development (Village North) is currently in progress and when complete, within the next 10 to 15 years, will contribute to a doubling in the bed base of the community to around 52,500 bed units.

Concurrent with the most recent development has been the emergence of residents' concerns about development and the role of the resort as a community. In response to these concerns, development of community facilities as well as an attempt to involve residents in the planning process mark a new direction in management of the resort.

DISAGGREGATING THE RESORT COMMUNITY

A dichotomous distinction was made above between residents and tourists as competing users of a resort community. Much of the research on the social impact of tourism explores differences in attitude between these two groups (e.g. Smith, 1977; Lui and Var, 1986; Long et al., 1990). However, in order to understand the nature of competition, one needs to go further in disaggregating this population. The need to recognize different "publics" rather than a homogeneous "public" has been acknowledged in recent work on public involvement in decision making (Davies et al., 1989; Simmons, 1994). In a similar vein, market research increasingly identifies very specific tourism market segments.

A general differentiation, commonly recognized by residents in many resort communities, distinguishes people in the community on the basis of temporal differences in their use of the community. At its most general level this would include: i) permanent residents; ii) second home owners; iii) seasonal workers; and iv) tourists. Each group has a different temporal attachment to the community as well as differing spatial behaviours and patterns of resource use. Examples from Whistler illustrate these differences in the context of Warren's definition of community.

The permanent resident population in Whistler is about 4,000 and there are around 5,000 second-home owners. In addition, there are about 2,000 seasonal workers in the peak winter season. The number of winter skier visits exceeds 1.5 million and there are 650,000 summer visitors. Permanent residents can be further differentiated by length of residence. There has been an increase of 121 percent in the permanent resident population since 1986, thus short and mid-term residents outnumber long-term residents. A recent housing survey by the Resort Municipality identified 24 percent of the respondents as short-term residents (under 2 years and planning to leave in less than one year); 53 percent as midterm residents (from 2 to 5 years of residence, or less than two years but with no plans to leave within a year), and 23 percent as "long-term residents" (more than five years) (Resort Municipality of Whistler, 1992). Competition associated with length of residence often relates to differences in attitude towards development and competition for power to control such decisions. It is not uncommon for longer term residents to be displaced, choosing to eventually leave the community if growth and change is too great and larger numbers of newcomers gain control (Williamson, 1992).

The relationship of resident to tourism industry is another basis for differentiating community subgroups. While some residents are employees in the tourism industry or community service sector, others have a dual role as resident entrepreneurs (e.g. Williams et al., 1988). Most residents have chosen to live in the community primarily because of lifestyle (Gill, 1991). Finding ways to support themselves in the community results in development of many entrepreneurial activities, not only in tourist-related businesses such as retailing, but also in various, often home-based, consulting and small business ventures. The resident entrepreneurs are often the most politically active in the community, perhaps due to their vested interests as both residents and business people. This group tends to form local coalitions to lobby their position, for example, through the Chamber of Commerce. In Whistler, all tourist-related businesses must belong to the Whistler Resort Association, the main marketing and central accommodation reservation agency.

In some settings, second home owners form a substantial portion of the community's tax payers. While often not involved politically or socially in community affairs, they could potentially, where they have voting rights, be effectively organized to swing votes. While often supporting improvements to the recreational amenities, they may oppose development if it encroaches on their sense of place. In Whistler there are 4,800 second home properties. These absentee property owners represent 82 percent of the total number of property owners in Whistler. A recent provincial government attempt to exclude nonresidents from voting in municipal elections has been overturned. This community group of second home owners more than any other stimulates competition for an essential resource—space and housing. Such competition translates into rising real estate values.

Indeed, the most pressing problem in many tourism communities is affordable housing for residents. The group most seriously impacted is the seasonal workers. This group is usually young, receives low pay and is frequently nonunionized. In Whistler, there are about 2,000 seasonal employees during the peak winter season, including a large contingent of Australian workers who are in Canada on temporary work visas. These temporary residents are detached both socially and politically from the community. In some cases these temporary workers, as well as other service sector workers, especially those with families, cannot afford to live in the tourist community. The housing market is not linked to labour force demand as it is in most communities, but is driven by the external demands of the tourism and second home market.

In Whistler, the cheapest market-priced three-bedroom family home sells for about $250,000. While not excessive by Vancouver standards, the problem is one of choice. There are no nearby cheaper suburbs, as in the city. Displacement to more distant communities is evident as the ripple of housing costs spreads out from the tourist centre. In Squamish, 50 kilometres to the south, where there is older housing stock as well as new developments, the average single-family home costs approximately $170,000. Pemberton, 35 kilometres to the north, is experiencing a housing boom as demand for affordable housing by Whistler employees stimulates development in this small community. New three-bedroom town houses are selling there for $142,000. Displacement of workers to other communities seriously undermines the sense of community and associated community functions.

For seasonal workers during the winter, the situation is especially acute as many rental costs are substantially increased during winter months when tourists compete with workers for rental accommodation. The solutions for many have been either to endure overcrowding in Whistler or commute from other communities. Recently, however, in response to the magnitude of the affordable housing problem, the Municipality has introduced measures to ensure that developers provide employee housing.

COMPETITION BETWEEN RESIDENTS AND TOURISTS

Territorial Competition

To understand the three-way relationship between the tourist, the community, and the resident, the work of environmental psychologists on territorial behaviour is informative, although most work on territoriality deals with crowding in city environments, and there is an absence of such work in tourist settings. A comprehensive definition offered by Altman states:

> *Territorial behavior is a self/other boundary regulation mechanism that involves personalization of or marking of a place or object and communicates that is owned by a person or group. Personalization and ownership are designed to regulate social interaction and to help satisfy various social and psychological motives. Defense responses may occur sometimes when territorial boundaries are violated* (Altman, 1977: 107).

Residents of resorts, just as residents in any town, view the community in which they live as their "home community" and thus, their sense of place and attachment is strong. Indeed, the term "tourist invasion" is sometimes used to suggest the negative aspects of intrusion by tourists into "foreign" territory. The tourist's experience of place is often mediated by marketing devices that create an image of the place. In a resort context, this image is most frequently one which portrays the place and its amenities as being solely for the pleasure of the tourist. The tourist purchases the right of ownership to this place for a limited period of time.

There are different levels of territorial occupancy: primary, secondary, and public territory. Certainly, at the centre of this is the primary territory of the home. There are many anecdotal stories of how tourists, perhaps through ignorance, fail to read the territorial markers and peer in windows or walk through private gardens. But such intrusions by tourists are less common than intrusions into community spaces. As essentially public spaces these places are frequently socially rather than physically defined as being for local use. While the tourist may innocently encroach upon these territories, such action engenders resentment. Territorial markers might not be clear—especially if there are cultural differences between resident and tourist. The way in which tourists behave with respect to their time/space activities also distinguishes them from residents and may be a cause of underlying friction. Whereas residents often must maintain work schedules, tourists are in leisure mode thus they may, for example, drive slowly along the highway while sightseeing or occupy scarce restaurant space for an overly long period of time.

Responses to open-ended questions concerning adaptive behaviour, in a survey of Whistler residents conducted in 1991, suggest that while residents do not generally feel negatively towards tourists, they acknowledge that tourist activities do affect the ways in which they conduct their lives (Gill, 1991). Many engage in various forms of avoidance behaviour, primarily with respect to the timing of activities. They tend to avoid the Village centre on weekends and holidays. While they must share such retail outlets as the pharmacy and liquor store with tourists they are selective about the times they shop. Most residents shop at the main grocery store outside the Village centre. During the ski season they ski during the week and avoid banks, service stations, and the post office in the later afternoon. While residents make use of many of the tourist amenities, certain pubs, restaurants, and night clubs are perceived as local haunts. They never, except of necessity, travel to Vancouver on Friday or Sunday evenings.

Resource Allocation

Competition for resources between tourism interests and all categories of resident is most evident with respect to the allocation of funds for community facility development. Local governments in resorts are faced with the dilemma of ensuring that the needs of the tourism industry are adequately met in order that the resort can remain competitive with other places. This requires considerable public expenditure on high quality infrastructure that can accommodate peak demands (e.g. sewers). Aesthetic considerations such as landscaping, underground parking, and appropriate building designs are also costly. While these costs can be recouped from commercial developments, the cost of providing community facilities places a heavy financial burden on the local government. In Whistler, until a new municipal government was elected in 1991, little if any attention was given to community needs—there was no community or recreation centre, no affordable housing policy, no high school or day care, and limited medical, religious, and library services. Growth was essentially developer-driven with the rationale that it was necessary to establish a critical mass of tourism-related development in order to ensure the long-term viability of the resort. While necessitated by the financial crisis of the early 1980s, the transformation of the planned community centre into a conference centre which could generate income is often cited as an extreme example of how community needs were sacrificed in favour of tourism development in the early stages of development in Whistler. Whistler has now achieved international recognition as a resort and is ranked as one of the top ski resorts in North America, as well as being consistently the first choice of the Japanese ski market. This now solidly established reputation, and the recognition that a strong community is an essential component of the overall resort product, has led to significant changes in the community during the last two years. Such facilities as a new community centre, an ice arena, public transit system and day care centre have all recently been established and forthcoming projects include a high school, a swimming pool, and new medical facilities.

IMPLICATIONS FOR RESORT MANAGEMENT

The challenge for resort managers is to balance the needs of tourists and residents in an environment of constant change. A critical element in an era of sustainable development policy is to engage residents in the process of decision-making. To date, most community-based efforts to assess residents' responses to tourism change are related to specific development projects or are sporadic endeavours associated with updating community plans. Ongoing social monitoring and continuous input into planning decisions is rare. However, some resort communities in North America (e.g. Aspen, Colorado; Lake Tahoe, Nevada) are turning to growth management practices as a guide to appropriate development (Gill and Williams, 1994). In 1988, Whistler also officially adopted a growth management approach. In essence, growth management is a systematic impact management strategy that calls for an integrated sharing of ideas between citizens and managers (Innes, 1992). The greatest challenge to growth management planning is to reconcile different systems of value that exist concerning desired conditions. Indeed, the tasks of coordination and consensus-building are at the heart of the growth management process (Innes, 1993). The process therefore mediates the normal forces of competition that Warren (1977) suggests generate community change by replacing competition with cooperation.

In the Resort Municipality of Whistler (RMOW), the mayor and council are democratically elected and, as in all municipalities, are responsible for providing services and community infrastructure as well as approving planning decisions. A Comprehensive Development Plan (CDP) acts as a strategic planning guide for the community and influences the content of the more detailed development regulations expressed in the Official Community Plan (OCP) and its related zoning bylaws. Prior to the introduction of a growth management policy in the 1988 CDP, the primary goal guiding development in Whistler was to achieve a level of development that would ensure a viable position in the international mountain resort destination market. Priority was placed on attracting investment to develop infrastructure and facilities serving tourists' needs—a reflection of the stage of development reached at that time. By 1988, the resort had evolved from that stage and the challenge was shifted to achieving a more balanced approach to serve both residents' and tourists' needs. While some development of tourist facilities was seen as necessary, there was recognition in the CDP that "too much or inappropriate development can erode the resort and limit its success" (Resort Municipality of Whistler, 1988).

By 1990, while public meetings had been held as a component of the ongoing planning process in the municipality, there were few opportunities for members of the community to express their growing concerns over development issues. This situation was exacerbated by the lack of a community centre or other suitable building in which the residents could meet as a community. While large public meetings were held in the Conference Centre, this well-appointed facility was designed to serve visitor rather than resident needs, and availability and cost of the facility limited its accessibility to residents. While, depending on the issue, some public meetings attracted several hundred participants, the opportunity to voice an opinion at such an event was constrained by problems inherent to the public meeting process, such as over-representation by organized lobby groups, and the widespread reluctance of many individuals to engage in public speaking. The growing frustration of residents in their attempts to voice opinions on development issues was reflected by the increasing number of letters and opinion articles that appeared in the local newspaper.

Community involvement lies at the heart of the growth management approach that underlies the development policy in Whistler. There has been a commitment to growth management procedures at a policy level since 1988. An initial attempt to facilitate the involvement of residents in community development issues through an alternative form of public participation occurred in 1990. Small group "living room meetings" were held permitting dialogue between individuals from various subgroups of the community and providing a non-intimidating setting for discussion of development issues. The focus on residents' community needs articulated during these meetings was reinforced in the subsequent local election. The election of a council sympathetic to these community concerns paved the way for implementation of many of the expressed needs. In 1992 a questionnaire survey offered all residents the opportunity to express their needs and preferences for future development. The results of this survey, and several other studies on issues such as affordable housing, recreational needs, heritage, transportation, and environmental quality, provided information used in the revision of the OCP in 1993.

The commitment to growth management was reinforced and more clearly articulated in the revision of the OCP in 1993. Notably, a commitment was made to a comprehensive community and resort monitoring system. Data collection for this monitoring program began in 1994 and covered aspects of land use and development, environment, commercial and social elements, infrastructure and transportation, and market demand (see Table 5.1).

With reference to public involvement, which as noted above is central to the notion of growth management, the establishment of an annual community forum, the "Whistler Symposium", was also recommended. This is designed as an opportunity for citizens to be informed of community change and discuss issues of growth. While this is now in its second year, its role as an instrument of communication has yet to be established. Traditional public meetings have continued to be the principal method of public involvement and no further living room meetings have been held. This suggests that, while in principle the resort is committed to growth management, implementing a system which truly integrates citizens and managers in the decision process will require continuing commitment.

CONCLUSIONS

Tourist towns are different from other types of communities, with a distinctive set of stakeholders who value and use the place in different ways each competing for space and resources. Understanding the relationship between place and each of these groups and how best to accommodate conflicting uses and values is a central issue in successfully planning and managing such places. While the overall notion of competition is useful in understanding the dynamics of place and the nature of change, the specifics are locality-dependent, thus, each community must ascertain the nature of their stakeholder groups in order to ensure that they are adequately represented in decision-making. In Whistler, it has recently been recognized that there is a diversity of views concerning growth and development. Setting strict limits to growth in terms of a maximum bed-limit development has been replaced by a growth management approach based on an iterative process driven by the desires of the community. While mechanisms for monitoring the impact of growth and ensuring that all members of the community are adequately represented in decision-making still need further refinement, the imbalance between tourists' and residents' needs in the community has been reduced dramatically in the past year as Whistler begins to resolve the dilemma of being simultaneously a resort and a

Table 5.1   Elements of monitoring system,
                Resort Municipality of Whistler, 1994.

Category	*Indicator*
Land Use/Development	inventory of residential/commercial development
	construction activity
	hotel accommodation
	resort-related development and other land use changes in Highway 99 corridor
Environment	water system quality
	wastewater effluent quality
	air quality
	vegetation cover
	lakes and river quality
Commercial/Social	population
	school enrolment
	health unit statistics
	unemployment
	crime, traffic violations
	community satisfaction survey
	selected community/recreational facility usage
Infrastructure/Transportation	water system - remaining capacity
	sewer system - remaining capacity
	Highway 99 volumes
	transit system ridership
	BC Rail passenger volumes
Market	hotel occupancy, hotel rates
	skier volumes
	conference delegate volumes
	golf-green fees
	visitor satisfaction surveys
	residential sales prices

Source: RMOW, Planning Department

strong resident community. A growth management approach is designed to acknowledge the competing forces within a community, but in doing so effects a paradigm shift from one in which competition drives the system—as suggested in Warren's definition—to one in which conflicts and change must be negotiated.

REFERENCES

Altman, I. (1977). *The environment and social behavior*. Monterey, California: Brooks/Cole.

Davies, D., Allen, L., and Cosenza, R. (1989). Segmenting local residents by their attitudes, interests, and opinions towards tourism. *Journal of Travel Research*, 27(2), 2-8.

Gill, A.M. (1991). *Final report, Whistler residents' survey, 1991*. Unpublished report for Resort Municipality of Whistler, British Columbia.

Gill, A.M., and Williams, P.W. (1994). Managing growth in mountain tourism communities. *Tourism Management*, 15, 212-220.

Hillery, G.A. Jr. (1955). Definitions of community: areas of agreement. *Rural Sociology*, 20, 111-123.

Innes, J.E. (1992). Group processes and the social construction of growth management. *Journal of the American Planning Association*, 58, 440-453.

Innes, J.E. (1993). Implementing state growth management in the United States: Strategies for coordination. In J.M. Stein (Ed.), *Growth management: The planning challenge of the 1990s* (pp. 18-47). Newbury Park, California: Sage Publications.

Long, P.T., Perdue, R.R., and Allen, L. (1990). Rural resident tourism perceptions and attitudes by community level of tourism. *Journal of Travel Research*, 28(3), 3-9.

Liu, J., and Var, T. (1986). Resident attitudes towards tourism impact in Hawaii. *Annals of Tourism Research*, 13, 193-214.

McMillan, D.W., and Chavis, D.M. (1986). Sense of community: A definition and theory. *Journal of Community Psychology*, 14, 40-52.

O'Reilly, A.M. (1986). Tourism carrying capacity. *Tourism Management*, 7, 254-258.

Resort Municipality of Whistler (1988). *Comprehensive Development Plan*, RMOW, Whistler.

Resort Municipality of Whistler (1992). *Affordable housing study*. Planning Department, RMOW, Whistler, British Columbia.

Simmons, D.G. (1994). Community participation in tourism planning. *Tourism Management*, 15, 98-108.

Smith, V.L. (Ed.) (1977). *Hosts and guests: The anthropology of tourism*. Philadelphia: University of Pennsylvania Press.

Warren, R.L. (1977). *Social change and human purpose*. Chicago: Rand McNally.

Williams, A.M., Shaw, G., and Greenwood, J. (1988). From tourist to tourism entrepreneur, from consumption to production: evidence from Cornwall, England. *Environment and Planning A*, 21, 1639-1653.

Williamson, D. (1992). Which came first the community or the resort? In A. Gill and R. Hartmann, (Eds.), *Mountain resort development: Proceedings of the Vail Conference* (pp. 22-26). Burnaby, British Columbia: Centre for Tourism Policy and Research, Simon Fraser University.

Plate 6 Whistler Village
(photo courtesy of The Province of British Columbia) ➡

Special Events Legacy: The 1984 Louisiana World's Fair in New Orleans

Frédéric Dimanche

School of Hotel, Restaurant, and Tourism Administration
College of Business Administration, University of New Orleans

The city of New Orleans celebrated the opening of the 1984 World's Fair with an excitement reminiscent of Mardi Gras and with great expectations about the economic benefits of this large scale event. Six months later, the city closed the fair in a mood similar to that of a jazz funeral. The Fair had proven to be a financial disaster and was generally considered to be a failure due to negative publicity in the media and too optimistic attendance forecasts. Indeed, an examination of the short term impacts indicates that the Fair failed to reach its attendance and economic impact goals. Hall has warned that "the use of events to attract tourists should not be separated from the broader scope of tourism development" (Hall, 1992: 173). Therefore, understanding how special events will affect tourism development and the future of a destination requires longitudinal studies. However, a perusal of the special event literature reveals a lack of long-term impact studies. Considering long-term impacts can shed some light on the true benefits generated by mega-events such as the Louisiana World's Fair. This chapter uses a theoretical framework that involves a diverse and long-term evaluation approach so as to examine the impact of a mega-event, the 1984 Louisiana World's Fair (LWF), on the city of New Orleans.

MEGA-EVENTS

Getz (1991) reviewed the various conditions that are required for a special event to earn the "mega" prefix. He indicated factors such as the economic effect that results from the event, the volume of visitors attending during the event, the cost involved in organizing the event, and the prestige and reputation that are derived from getting the event. The worldwide publicity created by the event was also mentioned. The limitations of these factors appear to reside in the fact that they are bound to the time frame of the event—that is, the short-term impact. However, Getz concluded that, more than any measure, the definition of a mega-event has to do with the "relative significance of an event" (Getz, 1991: 47). In fact, the true significance of a mega-event might only appear and be understood in the long run.

"Mega-events are short-term events with long-term consequences for the cities that stage them" (Roche, 1994: 1). The long-term significance of hallmark events must be evaluated because their multiple impacts cannot be fully understood in the short-term. This aspect is apparent in another definition: A mega-event or hallmark event is a "major one-time or recurring event of limited duration, developed primarily to enhance the awareness, appeal, and profitability of a tourism destination in the short and/or long-term" (Ritchie, 1984: 2).

Because of the very large investments that are necessary to stage a mega-event such as Olympic Games or World's Fairs, the short-term economic return is likely to be negative. Since the first world's fair was organized, only a few have achieved an operating profit, whereas most have made huge losses (Walker and Chacko, 1987). Much research has been conducted on the short-term impact of special events, while few researchers have considered a long-term perspective in their evaluation studies. Therefore, one needs to examine the long-term impacts and the legacy of a mega-event so as to adequately evaluate its true performance and significance.

According to the criteria indicated above, the LWF certainly was a failure. To quote Getz, who may have thought about the LWF in writing the following, "A world's fair of enormous cost and prestige that attracted only a handful of tourists to the site would be a partial failure" (Getz, 1991). Although not a handful, only 7.3 million visitors came, short of the 11 million predicted, leading the private group that staged the Fair to file for bankruptcy a week before the exposition ended. However, 10 years later, the legacy of the LWF becomes apparent and shows that the event has had a tremendous long-term impact on the New Orleans community and the local tourism industry.

CONCEPTUAL FRAMEWORK

Because of the diversity of mega-events, it is impossible to generalize about the impacts they have (Law, 1993:98). In fact, it may be more accurate to say that the impossibility to elaborate about the legacy of events is due to the lack of a standard method of impact measurement. Ideally, data should be collected to reflect the long-term impacts *as well as* the short-term impacts of a World's Fair. The variables that should be used to measure the success of an event include visitor satisfaction, resident satisfaction, visitor expenditures, economic impact data (costs and benefits), inward investment, regeneration of urban neighbourhoods, image of the destination, improvement of the touristic infrastructure, and overall growth of tourism. Unfortunately, as in this case study, such information is rarely available because no research plans are generally made prior to an event.

In order to examine the long-term legacy of a special event, a framework that will allow researchers and tourism managers to contemplate the breadth of impacts, both short- and long-term, is suggested. A model was recently designed to assess the impact of a mega-event on international tourism (Kang and Perdue, 1994). This marketing model demonstrates the "linkages by which a mega-event may produce long-term impacts on international travel to the host country" (Kang and Perdue, 1994: 208). According to the model, the initial short-term impacts include: (1) increased tourist participation; (2) infrastructure and service quality improvements; (3) increased media coverage; and (4) increased tourism promotion. This model is here adapted to reflect the LWF situation and an additional fifth dimension is presented: the impact the event had on the local community (Figure 6.1).

Figure 6.1   Impact of the 1984 World's Fair on New Orleans tourism.

The impact of the LWF consists of a combination of the above-mentioned effects that resulted in increased travel to New Orleans and growth of the tourism industry. The following section evaluates and summarizes each of those effects, then considers their global effect on the city after a 10 year span.

IMPACT OF THE LWF ON NEW ORLEANS TOURISM

Increased Number of Tourists

A mega-event is supposed to boost visitation to the community that hosts it. This is often the primary measure of a special event's success. Before the Fair, the LWF organizers felt confident about the popular success of the event. They thought that if Knoxville, a city that is not well known as a tourist attraction, could draw 11 million people for its world's fair, New Orleans with its existing reputation and appeal could easily be as successful (Walker and Chacko, 1987). The LWF attracted 83,111 visitors on opening day, but failed to reach its overall goal of 11 million visitors. The Fair did produce a significant visitation increase but it was not enough to warrant its economic success. In fact, it was reported that two of every three visitors who attended the Fair already lived in Louisiana, resulting in little economic input for the state. Like many other fairs and mega-events such as the Olympic Games, the LWF resulted in a loss. Its corporate backers lost more than $50 million, and the state of Louisiana lost another $25 million. In addition, several local businesses had to file for bankruptcy when their small business investments did not yield any profit.

Reasons for that loss abound and can be summarized by the following:

- *Poor management* (Walker and Chacko, 1987): (1) spending over budget; (2) under-financing; (3) mismanagement of funds; (4) since it was a private venture, the books were not available for audit; (5) lack of sponsorship.

- *Poor marketing*: (1) unrealistic forecasting; (2) inadequate marketing budget; (3) inadequate planning (a marketing director was hired only 15 months before the opening); (4) poorly executed marketing plan (the marketing director was fired two weeks after the opening); (5) poor public relations efforts resulting in poor publicity; (6) failure to recognize the competitive impact of another mega-event taking place the same summer, the Los Angeles Summer Olympic Games.

- An additional point needs to be made so as to explain the LWF's failure: *the impact of politics*. Politics are paramount to hallmark events but the account of the relationship between events and politics has been limited in the tourism literature (for a treatment of tourism and politics, see Hall, 1994 and chapters 7 and 8 in this volume). The LWF presents an example of the impact political battles can have on a hallmark event:

  > *When the Republicans captured the Senate and the Presidency in 1980, Louisiana lost a lot of clout . . . . Within the Reagan administration, there was a faction that wanted to dump the Louisiana fair altogether as a boondoggle put together by Democrats . . . . The fair was held, but virtually without federal participation. In contrast to the 1992 Knoxville fair, which drew more than $300 million in indirect federal support (for road and street improvements) and a $50 million federal pavilion, New Orleans got a scant $10 million pavilion. The President did not visit the Fair, making it the only world's fair in history to go unattended by the chief executive of the sponsoring country . . . . No matter how badly planned or promoted it was, no matter how the press handled the fair, it would have been reckoned a success if it had drawn the usual federal largesse. Without that benefit, it was doomed to appear a failure* (Esolen, 1987).

The influence of politics on tourism development (particularly mega-events) has largely been understudied by tourism researchers (Hall, 1994). Nonetheless, as shown by the LWF, politics are very significant in the decision to host special events and in their ultimate success. Mega-event research has to go beyond the study of economic effects and develop an effort to examine the political causes and production processes that lead cities to consider hosting special events (Roche, 1994: 2).

Improvement of the Touristic Infrastructure

The most apparent benefits of the LWF reside in the addition of infrastructure that allowed tourism to grow in New Orleans in following years. Three major changes must be considered. First, in the four years preceding the fair, a large number of first class hotel rooms were added; second, a quality convention centre was built; and third, a festival marketplace was created in one of the fair's buildings. These major improvements to the New Orleans product mix created the foundation for what is now one of the leading urban tourism destinations in the USA. The improvements are described more fully below:

- In preparation for the Fair, the city experienced a 'hotel boom.' Between 1981 and 1984, an additional 10,000 hotel rooms brought the total available to about 26,000. The list of new hotels and additional rooms built for the Fair included: Sheraton, Hotel Intercontinental, Hilton Riverside, the Westin, Le Méridien, the Windsor Court, and the Holiday Inn Plaza. These major hotels now represent the backbone of the hospitality industry in New Orleans, and since the Fair, no new hotel was opened until 1994. The building boom cannot be entirely attributed to the Fair. Other factors, such as the growth of the local oil and gas industry in the late 1970s and the promise of the convention centre, also played significant roles in attracting hospitality investors to New Orleans. The Fair was expected to boost occupancy rates in the new hotels' first year of operation, while the convention centre would assure long-term demand. Occupancy rates were quite respectable for 1984, but the industry suffered in the following years, because it took time for the increase in supply to be matched by an increase in demand. In fact, it took nearly 10 years for the hospitality industry to experience the high occupancy rates of 1984 again (Figure 6.2).

- The New Orleans convention centre, while not built specifically for the Fair, did become its centrepiece and hosted several pavilions. It held its first convention in 1985, and since then it has been a favourite facility for meeting and trade show planners because of its size and its location. The centre is located along the Mississippi river, just a short walk away from the major downtown hotels, and today it helps generate a total economic impact estimated at $1.9 billion. The convention centre already has been expanded once, and a third phase is soon to be developed.

- Next to the convention centre, another significant change in the tourism product mix resulted from the Fair. The Riverwalk, a large, linear tourist-oriented shopping centre, opened alongside the river in one of the Fair's buildings. This festival marketplace is now one of New Orleans' top tourist attractions. It offers open access to the river, that is directly connected to the convention centre.

The impact of the added infrastructure could not be evaluated immediately after the fair. Only after a 10 year period was New Orleans able to realize how it benefited from the public and private investments made in preparation for the Fair.

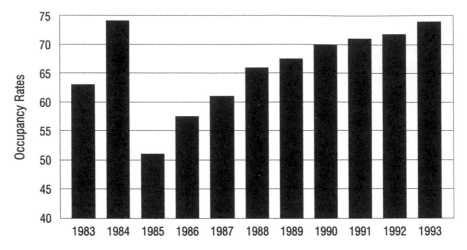

Figure 6.2 Hotel occupancy rates in New Orleans from 1983 to 1993 (Source: New Orleans Hotel-Motel Association).

Community Benefits

Tourism and special events should also benefit the communities that host them. The importance of considering the community as part of the tourism marketing mix is well known (Haywood, 1990). Residents' perceptions of tourism and their support of tourism development are more likely to be positive when they can perceive some benefits issued from tourism, resulting in quality of life improvements. The LWF created residents' satisfaction, improved an urban neighbourhood, and gave the river back to the residents.

First, New Orleans residents did enjoy the Fair despite the negative publicity that surrounded it in the media. Local fair goers were excited about this mega-event and supported it. The entertainment was world-class and most residents who attended the festivities still share fond memories of the fair, as reported in a local newspaper (Pope, 1994).

The LWF, whose theme was The World of Rivers, did provide an opportunity for New Orleans to regain access to the Mississippi, which had been kept behind port facilities until then. In addition, the Fair provided the impetus necessary to revive an urban neighbourhood that was a desolate industrial area into a popular place to live and work. Old warehouses were converted into apartment buildings, art galleries, restaurants, and shops. Preservation efforts helped keep the area as a "historic district." The LWF allowed New Orleans residents to rediscover their river and to find pride in a new and exciting urban residential area.

Because of the renewed interest in the river front that the Fair generated, the Aquarium of the Americas and Woldenberg Park were later created. These two attractions are now satisfying tourists and residents alike. A new form of recreational and touristic activity is now being developed in the same river front area: namely, casino gambling.

Increased Media Coverage

One of the main impacts of a mega-event is for a community to enjoy extensive media coverage. Worldwide publicity often starts years before the opening of the event, such as for the Olympic Games. The media usually offer the community staging a mega-event positive publicity that should result in a stronger image and increased awareness for the destination. Unfortunately, in the case of the LWF, not only was the publicity limited, but it was also negative. The local media were critical of the Fair, and their reservations were echoed by national and international media. The Fair's marketing strategies were poor and did not generate the publicity that the event deserved. However, New Orleans became a renewed tourism destination because of the Fair's infrastructure legacy, and increasingly enjoyed positive media coverage in the following years.

Increased Tourist Promotion

As stated earlier, the Fair's marketing strategies, including public relations and advertising, were not adequate and therefore did not have the impact that was needed or expected. Nonetheless, the Fair's legacy was a first class convention centre and a set of international hotels that the Convention and Visitors Bureau has aggressively used to promote the city as a premier convention destination. Unfortunately, the exact promotion expenditure figures for the past 12 years were not made available to this researcher by the CVB.

CONCLUSIONS

Although the LWF had to file for bankruptcy and failed to live up to the short-term economic expectations, we now realize, 10 years later, that it greatly helped shape today's tourism industry and economy in New Orleans and led to the revitalization of the Warehouse district, a rundown urban neighbourhood that may not have become attractive and popular otherwise. In addition, the LWF gave the river back to the city, and a festival retail centre was developed on the waterfront. Indeed, the legacy of the Fair has proven to be very positive to the city of New Orleans as it laid the foundation for a successful urban tourist destination. Long-term goals, such as redeveloping the warehouse district and opening up the city to the Mississippi riverfront, were achieved. In addition, secondary benefits proved to be essential to the city's tourism industry. The Fair gave the first opportunity for the New Orleans Convention Centre to operate and the city is now one of the premier convention destinations in North America. Also, the city experienced a hotel building boom in preparation for the Fair, giving the city the hotel capacity it has today.

The convention centre and hotel combination, born out of the Fair, has proved to be a winning strategy for the local tourism industry, as hotel occupancy rates grew steadily from 52 percent in 1985 to 74 percent in 1993. Also, the New Orleans

Convention and Visitors Bureau has increased and improved its promotion of the city. This has resulted in widespread economic benefits for the city as well as the state for the 10 years following the Fair. Only now do we see construction of new hotel rooms in New Orleans, as a new form of tourism attraction, casino gambling, and a planned extension of the convention centre promise to take the city to another level of tourism development.

Mega-events such as the LWF can be thought of as spring boards that will allow a local tourism industry to reach a new potential and a community to be rejuvenated. Because of the large investments that are usually necessary in planning for and operating a mega-event, the benefits are not likely to appear soon after the event. A hallmark event should be part of a long-term planning and development strategy whose effects can only be felt and evaluated over time. Early planning and vision for a mega-event can lead to long-term benefits for a destination, even though short-term economic gains may be disappointing. It must be mentioned that a research strategy allowing the study of multiple impacts must be planned before the event itself. A multi-method research approach (Brewer and Hunter, 1989) seems to be most appropriate for the study of phenomena as complex as mega-events and their impacts, and the theoretical framework presented here and adapted from Kang and Perdue (1994) is recommended. Policy makers and government officials are encouraged to make mandatory the collection of short- and long-term impact data that detailed the costs as well as the benefits associated with hosting a mega-event.

REFERENCES

Brewer, J., and Hunter, A. (1989). *Multimethod research: A synthesis of styles*. Newbury Park, CA: Sage.

Esolen, G. (1987). Residual effects. In J. Pailet (Ed.), *The World's Fair*, pp. 85-87. New Orleans: A Gallery for Fine Photography.

Getz, D. (1991). *Festivals, special events, and tourism*. New York: Van Nostrand Reinhold.

Hall, M. (1992). *Hallmark tourist events: Impacts, management, and planning*. London: Belhaven Press.

Hall, C.M. (1994). *Tourism and politics: Policy, power and place*. New York: Wiley.

Haywood, K.M. (1990). Revising and implementing the marketing concept as it applies to tourism. *Tourism Management*, 11(3), 195-205.

Kang, Y.-S., and Perdue, R. (1994). Long-term impact of a mega-event on international tourism to the host country: A conceptual model and the case of the 1988 Seoul Olympics. *Journal of International Consumer Marketing*, 6(3/4), 205-225.

Law, C.M. (1993). *Urban tourism: Attracting visitors to large cities*. London: Mansell.

Pope, J. (1994). Feelings on '84 fair are mixed. *The Times Picayune*, May 12, A1-A8.

Ritchie, J.R.B. (1984). Assessing the impact of Hallmark events: Conceptual and research issues. *Journal of Travel Research*, 23(Summer), 2-11.

Roche, M. (1994). Mega-events and urban policy. *Annals of Tourism Research*, 21, 1-19.

Walker, J.R., and Chacko, H. (1987, December). World expositions: An endangered species? Paper presented at the *World Hospitality Congress*, Boston.

Mega-Events
And Their Legacies

7

C. Michael Hall

Tourism and Services Management,
Victoria University of Wellington, New Zealand

> *... the question arises as to whether or not there should be some form of*
> *public life or culture, accessible to all local citizens of the city; and if so,*
> *how this can be stimulated by local policies. This last question is par-*
> *ticularly relevant in local politics. Is the city a product to be sold on the*
> *tourism market and/or as a location in which to invest money? Or is a*
> *city a place to live, where people can express themselves, even if it is in*
> *terms of resistance to, rather than rejoicing in, the dominant culture?*
> (Bramham, Henry, Mommaas, and van der Poel, 1989: 4).

INTRODUCTION

Mega tourist events, otherwise referred to as hallmark or special events, are
major fairs, festivals, expositions, cultural, and sporting events which are held on
either a regular or a one-off basis (Hall, 1992). Mega-events have assumed a key
role in urban and regional tourism marketing and promotion strategies, their primary function being to provide the host community with an opportunity to secure
high prominence in the tourism market place. Nations, regions, cities, and corporations have used events to promote a favourable image in the international tourist
and business marketplace (Ashworth and Goodall, 1988). Mega-events are also
extremely significant not just because of their visitor component, but because they
may leave behind legacies which will have an impact on the host community far
greater than the period in which the event took place. When asked as to the 'most
likely legacy' of the Victoria Commonwealth Games, a readers' poll in *Monday*
Magazine ranked debt, new pool, higher taxes, increased tourism, and higher real
estate prices as being the Games' legacies (McCaw, 1994). Such an assessment may
well be quite astute. Mega-events such as the Olympic Games or World's Fairs
have been associated with large-scale public expenditure, the construction of facilities and infrastructure, and the redevelopment and revitalization of urban areas
which may have substantial impacts on local communities. According to Law
(1993: 107), the mega-event, "acts as a catalyst for change by persuading people to
work together around a common objective and as fast track for obtaining extra
finance and getting building projects off the drawing board. This is not without its

problems, since some would argue that it gives priority to development issues over those of welfare. The physical aspect of this strategy is that it has been linked with inner city regeneration and in particular with that of the city centre."

This chapter examines the legacies of mega-events and the reasons for their hosting and development. Specific attention is paid to the role of mega-events in urban revitalization projects and urban re-imaging strategies. However, mega-events may also play a role in urban place promotion and redevelopment to the detriment of certain groups in society.

THE NATURE OF MEGA-EVENTS

Event tourism is developing as a substantial area of research within the field of tourism studies. Event tourism has been defined 'as the systematic planning, development and marketing of festivals and special events as tourist attraction, catalysts, and image builders' (Getz and Wicks, 1993: 2). The primary function of the mega or hallmark tourist event is to provide the host location or region with an opportunity to secure a position of prominence in the tourism market for a short, well defined, period of time. The standard definition of hallmark events is provided by Ritchie (1984: 2) who defined such events as, "Major one-time or recurring events of limited duration, developed primarily to enhance the awareness, appeal and profitability of a tourism destination in the short and/or long term. Such events rely for their success on uniqueness, status, or timely significance to create interest and attract attention."

Large-scale tourist events are, therefore, not a continuous or seasonal phenomenon. Indeed, in many cases the events are a strategic response to the problems that seasonal variations in demand pose for the tourist industry (Ritchie and Beliveau, 1974). In addition, events may assume a major function of highlighting the attractiveness of a destination to an extent which more permanent tourist attractions may not be able to achieve. Ritchie (1984: 2) understood hallmark events to be major events which have an "ability to focus national and international attention on the destination". Similarly, Burns and Mules noted the importance of scale in "special events", "... sometimes called a 'Hallmark' event..." which are "events that are expected to generate large external benefits, or where the external benefits are so widely distributed and the event costs are so substantial that they are funded, either partially or wholly, with public monies" (1986: 6,7). Burns and Mules (1986) identified four key characteristics of special events:

1. The major demand generated by the Special Event is, for the most part, not the demand for the event itself but demand for a range of related services, typically accommodation, food, transport and entertainment.

2. This demand is condensed into a relatively short period of time, from a single day to a few weeks and, as services cannot be produced ahead of time and stored, this leads to the typical 'peaking' problems experienced in the main service industries mentioned.

3. 'Peaking' influences both the level and the distribution of benefits received.

4. The net impact of redirecting local funds towards Special Events is relatively small; the major benefits arise from the attraction of new funds from outside the region by way of the export of goods and services, especially services.

Mega-events may be defined separately to that of hallmark events. Ritchie and Hu's (1987) categorization of a 'mega-event' corresponds to Ritchie's earlier definition of hallmark events, while the 1987 Congress of the Association Internationale d'Experts Scientifiques du Tourisme resolved that mega-events could be defined in three different ways: by volume (1 million visits), by a money measure (Can. $500 million, DM 750 million, FFr 2,500 million), and in psychological terms (by reputation: "Must see", "*Muss miterlebt werden*", "*Il faut absolument voir*") (Marris, 1987: 3). Nevertheless, while substantial disagreement remains over the definition of mega-events, it is apparent that several key and related factors occur in the study of large-scale events: redevelopment, imaging and place promotion, and their impacts.

HALLMARK EVENTS AS A REDEVELOPMENT STRATEGY

The hosting of hallmark events is often deliberately exploited in an attempt to "rejuvenate" or redevelop urban areas through the construction and development of new infrastructure, including road and rail networks, airports, sewage, and housing. This has been used to revitalize inner-city locations that are regarded by government, municipalities, and business interests as requiring renewal.

World's Fairs and the Olympic Games in particular have been used to provide a boost to urban development projects. For example, the majority of bids for the 1996 and 2000 Summer Olympics involved substantial investment in new capital and infrastructure, such as transport facilities, quite separate to that of sports facilities. Indeed, Hughes (Hughes, 1993: 157,159) observed that "the Olympics may be of particular significance in relation to the 'inner city' problems that beset many urban areas of Europe and N[orth] America" and noted that Manchester's bid for the 2000 Summer Olympics were "seen as a possible contribution to solving some of [the city's] inner city problems".

The commonly-held perspective of many government authorities of the social benefits of using events as a component of city renewal programs is presented by Hillman (1986: 4): "As center city revitalization continues to be viewed as a major ingredient of economic development, the questions of enlivening public spaces and extending usage of downtowns after 5 o'clock have become critical issues . . . . Events are a proven animator capable of turning barren spaces into bustling places."

World's Fairs have long been used for urban development. Indeed, since its World's Fair of 1962, Seattle has been described as "the city of renewal" (Peters, 1982). Although international fairs and expositions have always been closely connected to the interests of local business elites, it was not until 1962 that they were consistently used to redevelop rundown city areas and attract private and public investment. In the case of Seattle, the Fair was used to develop 50 acres of a publicly owned "blighted" area. The 1968 San Antonio World's Fair was explicitly connected to a federal and locally funded inner-city renewal program which acquired 147 acres of "substandard housing" for the Fair site (Peters, 1982). According to Montgomery (1986: 85): "The two things fit beautifully: the urban renewal process provided the vehicle that made possible the land assembly and clearance necessary to get the fair up on time; at the same time the fair provided impetus that picked up the pace of public development action." Similar hopes were expressed for the 1974 Spokane Expo which was used as a means "to squeeze a revitalization program that would have ordinarily taken 20 years into an intensive five-year effort" (Yake, 1974: 55). The reasons for using Expo for redevelopment were explained by King Cole, President of the Spokane Expo: "If it seems a complicated route to urban renewal, it was necessary. This city had a sort of resentment of its downtown area . . . . Three times in the past, the city voters have turned out city councils that ran for office on a platform of downtown renewal . . . . But when we started pushing the idea of a world fair, which would bring about downtown renewal incidentally, citizens bought the idea" (in Olds, 1988: 40). World's Fairs in both Vancouver, Canada (1986), and Brisbane, Australia (1988), have also been used to redevelop waterfront areas for housing and urban leisure space, and the attraction of tourists.

Maritime-themed festivals, such as the Adelaide Port Dragon Boat Festival in Adelaide, South Australia, have been utilized to assist in urban renewal strategies. Indeed, Prosser (1993: 125) noted that "event tourism has been embraced enthusiastically in Adelaide as a response to 'deindustrialization' which has eroded its traditional economic base". In the case of the Port of Adelaide, people's perceptions of the area had to be altered in order to meet redevelopment objectives. "To increase the area's attractiveness to potential investors, residents and visitors, the image of a working port, with its associated noise, dirt and smell has to be altered to that of a lighter, cleaner, social environment with a strong maritime history" (Mules, 1993: 65). According to Mules, in the case of the Dragon Boat Festival, "The intention was to bring people to the area and have it seen in a festive, leisure-based manner. This is part of the process of altering the public's mind-association of the area being synonymous with a working port. However, in addition to this long term objective, the event also has the characteristic of bringing visitors and their spending power to the area . . . . Thus the spending which the event brings to the area either immediately or subsequently is also an important ingredient in the redevelopment strategy" (1993: 65).

Olympic Games, although primarily a sporting event, have also been utilized to redevelop rundown areas and to provide a justification for the development of new infrastructure, such as urban transit systems, highway construction, airport redevelopment, and housing (Hall, 1992). For example, Melbourne and Toronto's bids for the 1996 Olympic Games, to be hosted by Atlanta, both featured massive urban waterfront redevelopment schemes as part of their bid plans, while Sydney's 2000 Olympic Games is a major component and justification for a massive redevelopment of the city's waterfront.

HALLMARK EVENTS AND RE-IMAGING STRATEGIES

The revitalization of downtown areas through the creation of new tourism and leisure spaces is regarded by some commentators as being indicative of a crisis of the local state in which the importance of welfare functions are lessened (e.g. Henry and Bramham, 1986). However, in a broader context the current use of tourism to re-image the city may also be seen as a response by urban growth coalitions and elites to the globalization of capital and the changing nature of the role of the state in society (Hall, 1994). As Harvey (1989) noted, imaging a city through the organization of spectacular urban space by, for example, hosting a hallmark event, is a mechanism for attracting capital and people (of the right sort) in a period of intense inter-urban competition and urban entrepreneurialism. Indeed, an improved image seems to be one of the most significant legacies of the Calgary 1988 Winter Olympic Games: "In the end, declares Art Smith [co-chair of the Calgary Economic Development Authority], the prime Olympic legacy may be the casting aside of Calgary's age-old reputation as an outpost. 'People will know us as not just a western frontier town, but as a metropolitan, sophisticated city' " (Martin, 1988: 31, quoted in Mount and Leroux, 1994: 15).

The principal aims of urban imaging strategies are to attract tourism expenditure, to generate employment in the tourist industry, to foster positive images for potential investors in the region, often by 're-imaging' previous negative perceptions (e.g. the attempted transformation of the image of Sheffield from an 'industrial' to a 'modern' city through the hosting of the World Student Games), and to provide an urban environment which will attract and retain the interest of professionals and white-collar workers (Roche, 1992, 1994; Hall, 1994). Urban imaging processes are characterized by some or all of the following: the development of a critical mass of visitor attractions and facilities, including new buildings/prestige centres; hallmark events; development of urban tourism strategies and policies often associated with new or renewed organization and development of city marketing; and development of leisure and cultural services and projects to support the marketing and tourism effort (Hall, 1994).

In the case of the Olympic Movement and Olympic cities, the environment has now become a key part of the imaging process. Sydney, following the lead of Lillehammer, focused on the environment as a key element in its bidding strategy. In its August 1993, news release as to "why Sydney would stage a great Olympics in 2000", the Sydney Olympics 2000 Bid Limited (SOB) argued that Sydney is "Pioneering environmentalism for the Olympics. Throughout Sydney's Olympic plan, from venue and residential construction to event management, the highest environmental principles are applied. Sydney's Olympic Village design, prepared in collaboration with Greenpeace, foreshadows the sustainable city of the 21st century" (Sydney Olympics 2000 Bid Limited, 1993a: 2).

According to SOB, the guidelines developed for the bid, which address five major global environmental concerns (global warming, ozone depletion, biodiversity, pollution, and resource depletion), "would make Sydney's Olympic Plan a prime example of ecologically sustainable development in the 21st century", and "integrate the latest technologies with tried and tested measures into a coordinated environmental protection plan for a summer Olympic Games" (1993b: 2). Specific examples of these environmental guidelines, supported by Greenpeace which was involved in their development (Greenpeace Australia, 1993; Sydney Olympics 2000 Bid Limited, 1993b), include:

- In athletes' Village design, Sydney will use solar power, water recycling, and public transport. It will also design buildings which require no air conditioning and fridges will contain no ozone destroying gases.

- In new sporting facilities, Sydney will use recyclable building materials, energy-efficient systems, and water recycling.

- In event management, Sydney will use electronic mail to reduce the need for paper, have multi-use tickets (for events, transport, food), and will minimize the amount of food packaging.

- Companies tendering for a contract will have to satisfy the environment guidelines as laid down by the Organizing Committee for the Sydney Olympic Games, should the Bid be successful.

The greening of the Sydney Olympic bid has been seen as a positive in terms of Australia marketing its environmental technology to other countries bidding in the future, while Ms. Karla Bell, who left Greenpeace in May 1994 to work as a consultant, has been appointed to the new International Olympic Committee/United Nations Environment Program Working Party on the environmental standards for future Olympic Games (Foreshaw, 1994). However, debate is now growing over whether the green games is just a marketing and imaging ploy rather than a substantial contribution to the issues facing sustainable development in Australia. Indeed, it is not surprising that the Games have been seen by the former Premier of New South Wales as "the best marketing exercise ever undertaken in Australia" (Greiner, 1994: 13).

Although urban areas have long attracted tourists, it is only since the 1970s that cities and regions have consciously sought to develop, image, and promote themselves in order to increase the influx of tourists. As noted above, tourism has been perceived as a mechanism to regenerate urban areas through the creation of an attractive urban environment. This process appears almost universal in Western society. Such a situation led Harvey (Harvey, 1988) to ask "How many museums, cultural centres, convention and exhibition halls, hotels, marinas, shopping malls, waterfront developments can we stand?" Similarly, Urry (1990: 119) observed that "in recent years almost every town and city in Britain has been producing mixed development waterfront schemes in which tourist appeal is one element". Mommaas and van der Poel (1989: 263) go so far as to argue that the development of a more economically-oriented city development policy style, aimed at the revitalization of the city, has lead to "projects, developed in public-private partnerships, [which] are meant not for the integration of disadvantaged groups within society, but for servicing the pleasures of the well-to-do."

In many cities the nature of the urban core is changing. Although the commercial functions of central business districts are still important, "the entire urban core is presently looked upon as a recreational environment and as a tourism resource" (Jansen-Verbeke, 1989: 233). The ramifications of such an approach are far reaching, particularly in the way in which cities and places are now perceived, by some, as products to be sold and promoted. As Bramham et al. (1989: 9) observed, "it is no longer unusual to see the city as a tourist product, although on the level of local policy this may still be more an expression of certain political ideas than a coherent policy with practical consequences". Indeed, the imaging of the city in order to attract the middle class employment market and the associated focus on the economic benefits of tourism has "reinforced the idea of the city as a kind of commodity to be marketed" (Mommaas and van der Poel, 1989: 264).

THE IMPACTS OF MEGA-EVENTS

The post-industrial urban environment associated with contemporary hallmark events often has a major impact on the socioeconomic groups that occupy the inner-city areas or deindustrialized areas designated for renewal. The creation of a "desirable" middle-class environment invariably leads to increased rates and rents, and is accompanied by a corresponding breakdown in community structure, including ethnicity, as families and individuals are forced to relocate (Hall, 1995). Moreover, the people who are often most impacted by hallmark events are typically those who are least able to form community groups and protect their interests. This tends to lead to a situation in which residents are forced to relocate because of their economic circumstances. In the case of the Vancouver Expo, 600 tenants were evicted including long-term, low-income residents from hotels near the Expo site (Olds, 1988). Similarly, the 1987 America's Cup and the 1988 Brisbane Expo also led to substantial resident dislocation (Day, 1988; Hall, 1989a, 1989b, 1992). However, the eviction of tenants due to the hosting of hallmark events is not isolated to Western nations. For example, the Asian Coalition for Housing Rights noted that South Korea's preparations for the 1988 Olympic Games led to the "rehabilitation" and "beautification" of numerous areas in Seoul whereby "many communities were evicted from sites, simply because they were next to the path along which the Olympic torch was to be carried and the public authorities did not want these communities to be visible to the reporters and television cameras following the path of the torch" (Asian Coalition for Housing Rights, 1989: 92).

In examining the hosting of large-scale hallmark events and associated redevelopments, the preponderance of political and economic benefits of the hallmark event to local growth coalitions appear to outweigh the costs to the less politically organized segments of the host community, usually the poor. As Jon Muller, evicted following the impacts of the Vancouver Exposition on Downtown Eastside, Vancouver, stated, "I'm not going to move unless they force me out. I'm not a piece of garbage. I've been here three years and don't mind if they raise the rent, but I won't move . . . . Once you get used to a place, it's like a pair of shoes, they're comfortable. Even if they get worn out, you still put your old shoes on. This hotel to me is home. You go to the beer parlour, you know everybody . . . I like this place, but what they've done—it's inhuman" (in Olds, 1989: 49).

Hallmark events are typically dependent on the large outlay of public monies that may be associated not only with hosting but also with bidding for such events. As Bonnemaison (1990: 25) commented, "most commonly a city wanting to up-grade its infrastructure or its political image will use a large-scale event as a tool to generate funds from higher levels of government and corporations". However, despite the substantial costs and benefits of hallmark events, their net contribution to local communities, through the study of social and environmental effects as well as economic impacts, is rarely calculated. Indeed, there are substantial pressures operating against such evaluation (Crompton and Mckay, 1994). As Hiller (1989: 127) noted in the case of the 1988 Calgary Winter Olympics, 'The overarching com-pelling rationale of preparation for the Olympics in general tended to minimize opposition and controversy thereby supporting capital cost expenditures.' Why does this happen?

A mixture of coercion and co-option centred around maintenance of real estate values, assumptions regarding employment and investment generation, and an assumption that growth is automatically good, has led to the creation of local growth coalitions in many urban centres. "Coercion arises either through interplace com-petition for capital investment and employment (accede to the capitalist's demands or go out of business; create a 'good business climate' or lose jobs) or more simply, through the direct political repression and oppression of dissident voices (from cutting off media access to the more violent tactics of the construction Mafia's in many of the world's cities)" (Harvey, 1993: 9).

In the case of the Sydney Olympic bid, the former Premier, Nick Greiner, ar-gued that 'The secret of the success was undoubtedly the creation of a community of interest, not only in Sydney, but across the nation, unprecedented in our peace-time history' (1994: 13). The description of a 'community of interest' is extremely apt, as such a phrase indicates the role of the interests of growth coalitions in mega-event proposals. In particular, the Sydney media played a critical role in creating the climate for the bid. As Greiner stated: "Early in 1991, I invited senior media representatives to the premier's office, told them frankly that a bid could not suc-ceed if the media played their normal 'knocking role' and that I was not prepared to commit the taxpayers' money unless I had their support. Both News Ltd. and Fairfax subsequently went out of their way to ensure the bid received fair, perhaps even favourable, treatment. The electronic media also joined in the sense of com-munity purpose (1994: 13).

Greiner's statement begs the question of "which community?". Certainly, the lack of adequate social impact assessment prior to the Games' bid indicates the failure of growth coalitions to recognize that there may well be negative impacts on some sections of the community. Those most impacted are clearly the ones least able to affect the policy making and planning processes surrounding the Games.

The lack of debate surrounding the Olympics will have substantial implications for the long term economic and social development of Sydney and New South Wales. For example, the New South Wales Government has also been taken to task over its handling of the deal for the construction of the Airport Link rail project. Disregarding its own 1990 guidelines for private sector participation in public sector infrastructure projects which recommend competitive bidding, the project has gone to the private sector without tender with Professor Bob Walker of the University of New South Wales suggesting that "the Government, in its haste to finalize the 2000 Olympics-related deal, has been outsmarted, at a heavy cost to the taxpayer" (Sydney Morning Herald, 1994: 14). According to Professor Walker, the deal means that the private sector consortium is insulated from inflation risk and stands to earn a prospective real rate of return in the range of 21 to 25 percent over a 30 year period. After contributing most of the finance and bearing most of the operating risk, the government would earn a return of only 2 percent per annum. As Professor Walker states "it seems absurd that annual budget allocations for cash expenditures require parliamentary scrutiny and approval, while major contracts involving the alienation of revenue streams and financial commitments stretching over 30 years can be handled in secret by executive government" (Sydney Morning Herald, 1994: 14).

The stifling of opposition to mega-events may be more overt than the creation of a "community of interest". For example, in the case of the Formula One Grand Prix to be hosted in Melbourne in 1996, an event which has already produced substantial community protest including a rally by more than 10,000 people, the Victorian Government's grand prix bill extinguished "substantive" rights of appeal. The bill granted indemnity to the grand prix from court action by residents or businesses who believe that they are entitled to compensation. This led the Vice-president of the Victorian Council of Liberties to tell a hearing of the Scrutiny of Acts and Regulations Committee that elements of the grand prix bill were "abhorrent" (Henry, 1994: 4).

In the society of the spectacle illustrated by the hosting of mega-events the "carnival mask" of re-imaging may conceal the history of struggle over place and space. Inner city space, therefore, becomes a space of conspicuous consumption, celebrating commodities rather than civic values (Debord, 1973; Harvey, 1990).

The new inner city space of leisure consumption is reflective not only of particular values, but also of particular interests. The 'new' civic values reflect those of the local growth coalitions which influence urban redevelopment and planning processes. As Mommaas and van der Poel observed, "local policy has increasingly sought to stimulate the mixture of economic enterprise, culture and leisure, attempting in this manner to attract the new economic elite to the city" (Mommaas and van der Poel, 1989: 267). However, in focusing on one set of economic and social interests, other community interests, particularly those of traditional inner-city residents, are increasingly neglected, "because urban policy has adopted and legitimated the profiles and potentials of the lifestyle of this new economic elite, thereby also legitimating the economic dimensions involved (the acceptance of making leisure, culture, and welfare strategies and criteria), the interests of those not having the opportunity to emulate the new economic elite in its pleasures fail to be considered" (Mommaas and van der Poel, 1989: 267).

The creation of a "bourgeois playground" (Mommaas and van der Poel, 1989: 263) in the name of economic progress may create considerable tension in the urban policy-making environment. For example, the integration of tourism functions in the inner city may contest with traditionally different functions such as residential areas, such as in the case of the Melbourne Formula One Grand Prix, the track for which is being constructed in an inner-city park.

The redevelopment of the inner city in terms of visitor attractiveness can lead to the transformation of the community-based organization of local spaces and populations into an individual, or family-based organization, or what Castells (1983) has characterized as the "disconnection of people from spatial forms". The implications of the transformation of the core of many cities for lower socioeconomic groups is amplified by the reallocation of local state resources from social welfare to imaging functions, because at the same time that the inner city is being promoted and developed as a leisure resource, public spending on social programs, such as subsidized housing, has been decreasing (Mommaas and van der Poel, 1989).

CONCLUSIONS

The hosting of mega-events and their role in urban imaging strategies cannot be separated from the crisis of the local state in Western Europe and North America. The crisis of the local state is bound up in a crisis of legitimacy in which certain groups in society, particularly the powerless and disadvantaged in the inner cities, have become disenchanted with the existing political arrangements which have failed to deliver needed social, economic, and infrastructural improvements in inner city areas. In addition, it may be asked whether city centres, the focal point of the new urban tourism, are gaining resources at the expense of the interests of those in the suburbs? A second crisis is what may be termed a "fiscal crisis" in which "the central state is attempting to revitalize private industry by reducing expenditure on social consumption, and therefore reducing grant aid to local government which is responsible for many such services, while local government, deprived of such income and with a declining tax base (as the local economy suffers), is faced with increasing demands both for welfare services and for local economic development" (Henry and Bramham, 1986: 190).

The two crises are intimately related and may be regarded as two sides of the same coin, with the reallocation of scarce financial resources only serving to exacerbate the frustration of certain groups in society to achieve desired social and welfare ends. However, while many civic governments claim that through the development of visitor attractions they will also be encouraging employment and investment, it should be recognized that many of the jobs do not go to those who were most affected by such developments in the first place because they often do not have the requisite skills or, if they do gain employment, it will often be at the most unskilled and menial levels.

A mega-event may improve the image of a destination (Ritchie and Smith, 1991). However, whether this can be turned into a sustained increase in visitor numbers and investment is highly debatable (Mount and Leroux, 1994). As Hughes (1993: 162) has argued, tourism "can only be a component of an overall strategy for urban regeneration rather than a major force in its own right. Tourism associated with the Olympics, given its short-term nature, provides even less direct opportunity for urban regeneration. The hopes of regeneration lie largely in the belief that inward investment in other industries and increased long-term tourist flows will result. The prospect is based on improvements to the environment and infrastructure and a generally enhanced image or awareness of an area. The case for this has, however, not yet been demonstrated".

Indeed, Hughes went on to note that the hosting of a mega-event, such as the Olympics, may even disturb "the 'normal' development of tourism and other activity", with the possibility that they be "a distraction from the pursuit of a more fundamental development strategy that will ensure long-term sustainable growth" (1993: 162). Appropriately scaled and planned events can revitalize, redevelop, and re-image communities and destinations. However, mega-events generally only serve a narrow range of interests, with their hosting having the potential to be but a chimera in the search for sustainable forms of tourism development.

ACKNOWLEDGEMENTS

The author would like to acknowledge provision of a grant from the Australian Research Council, and the assistance of Nicolle Lavelle, Vanessa O'Sullivan, and Kirsty Scott in the preparation of this chapter.

REFERENCES

Ashworth, G., and Goodall, B. (1988). Tourist images: Marketing considerations. In B. Goodall and G. Ashworth (Eds.), *Marketing in the tourism industry: The promotion of destination regions* (pp. 213-238). London: Routledge.

Asian Coalition for Housing Rights (1989). Evictions in Seoul, South Korea. *Environment and Urbanization* 1, 89-94.

Bonnemaison, S. (1990). City policies and cyclical event. In *Celebrations urban spaces transformed, Design Quarterly 147* (pp. 24-32). Cambridge: Massachusets Institute of Technology for the Walker Art Center.

Bramham, P., Henry, I., Mommaas, H., and van der Poel, H. (1989). Introduction. In P. Bramham, I. Henry, H. Mommaas, and H. van der Poel, (Eds.), *Leisure and urban processes: critical studies of leisure policy in Western European cities* (pp. 1-13). London and New York: Routledge.

Burns, J.P.A., and Mules, T.J. (1986). A framework for the analysis of major special events. In J.P.A. Burns, J.H. Hatch, and T.J. Mules (Eds.), *The Adelaide Grand Prix: The impact of a special event* (pp. 172-185). Adelaide: The Centre for South Australian Economic Studies.

Castells, M. (1983). Crisis, planning, and the quality of life: Managing the new historical relationships between space and society. *Environment and Planning D, Society and Space*, 1, 3-21.

Crompton, J.L., and Mckay, S.L. (1994). Measuring the economic impact of festivals and events: Some myths, misapplications and ethical dilemmas. *Festival Management and Event Tourism*, 2(1), 33-43.

Day, P. (1988). *The big party syndrome: A study of the impact of special events and inner urban change in Brisbane.* St. Lucia: Department of Social Work, University of Queensland.

Debord, G. (1973). *Society of the Spectacle.* Detroit: Black and Red.

Foreshaw, J. (1994). Olympic green good as gold for environment firms. *The Weekend Australian*, 24-25 September, 1994, 13.

Getz, D., and Wicks, B. (1993). Editorial. *Festival Management and Event Tourism*, 1(1), 1-4.

Greenpeace Australia (1993). *Press release: Greenpeace calls on International Olympic Committee to adopt environmental criteria for Games.* Balmain: Greenpeace Australia, 23 March.

Greiner, N. (1994). Inside running on Olympic bid. *The Australian*, 19 September, 1994, 13.

Hall, C.M. (1989a). Hallmark events and the planning process. In G.J. Syme, B.J. Shaw, D.M. Fenton, and W.S. Mueller (Eds.), *The planning and evaluation of hallmark events* (pp. 20-39). Aldershot: Avebury.

Hall, C.M. (1989b). The politics of hallmark events. In G.J. Syme, B.J. Shaw, D.M. Fenton and W.S. Mueller (Eds.), *The planning and evaluation of hallmark events* (pp. 219-241). Aldershot: Avebury.

Hall, C.M. (1992). *Hallmark tourist events: Impacts, management and planning.* London: Belhaven.

Hall, C.M. (1994). *Tourism and politics: Policy, power and place.* Chichester: John Wiley & Sons Ltd.

Hall, C.M. (1995). *Introduction to tourism in Australia: Impacts, planning and development*, 2nd ed. South Melbourne: Longman Australia.

Harvey, D. (1988). Voodoo cities. *New Statesman and Society*, 30 September, 1988, 33-35.

Harvey, D. (1989). *The condition of postmodernity: An enquiry into the origins of cultural change.* Oxford: Basil Blackwell.

Harvey, D. (1990). Between space and time: Reflections on the geographical imagination. *Annals of the Association of American Geographers*, 80(3), 418-434.

Harvey, D. (1993) From space to place and back again: Reflections on the condition of postmodernity. In J. Bird, B. Curtis, T. Putnam, G. Robertson, and L. Tickner (Eds.), *Mapping the futures: Local cultures, global change* (pp. 3-29). London and New York: Routledge.

Henry, I., and Bramham, P. (1986). Leisure, the local state and social order. *Leisure Studies*, 5, 189-209.

Henry, S. (1994). Grand prix bill branded 'abhorrent'. *Australian*, 28 September, 1994, 4.

Hiller, H.H. (1989). Impact and image: The convergence of urban factors in preparing for the 1988 Calgary Winter Olympics. In G.J. Syme, B.J. Shaw, D.M. Fenton, and W.S. Mueller (Eds.), *The planning and evaluation of hallmark events* (pp. 119-131). Aldershot: Avebury.

Hillman, S. (1986). Special events as a tool for tourism development. *Special Events Report*, 5(16), 4-5.

Hughes, H.L. (1993). Olympic tourism and urban regeneration. *Festival Management and Event Tourism*, 1(4), 157-162.

Jansen-Verbeke, M. (1989). Inner cities and urban tourism in the Netherlands: New challenges for local authorities. In P. Bramham, I. Henry, H. Mommaas, and H. van der Poel (Eds.), *Leisure and urban processes: Critical studies of leisure policy in Western European cities* (pp. 233-253). London and New York: Routledge.

Law, C.M. (1993). *Urban tourism: Attracting visitors to large cities.* London: Mansell.

Marris, T. (1987). The role and impact of mega-events and attractions on regional and national tourism development: Resolutions. *Revue de Tourisme*, 4, 3-10.

McCaw, F. (1994). Best of Victoria 1994: Monday readers' poll. *Monday Magazine*, 30 June-6 July, 20.

Mommaas, H., and van der Poel, H. (1989). Changes in economy, politics and lifestyles: An essay on the restructuring of urban leisure. In P. Bramham, I. Henry, H. Mommaas, and H. van der Poel (Eds.), *Leisure and urban processes: Critical studies of leisure policy in Western European cities* (pp. 254-76). London and New York: Routledge.

Montgomery, R. (1986). Hemisfair 68: Prologue to renewal. *Architectural Forum*, October, 85-88.

Mount, J., and Leroux, C. (1994). Assessing the effects of a mega-event: A retrospective study of the impact of the Olympic Games on the Calgary business sector. *Festival Management and Event Tourism*, 2(1), 15-23.

Mules, T. (1993). A special event as part of an urban renewal strategy. *Festival Management and Event Tourism*, 1(2), 65-67.

Olds, K. (1988). *Planning for the housing impacts of a hallmark event: A case study of Expo 1986*, unpublished MA thesis. Vancouver: School of Community and Regional Planning, University of British Columbia.

Olds, K. (1989). Mass evictions in Vancouver: The human toll of Expo '86. *Canadian Housing*, 6(1), 49-53.

Peters, J. (1982). After the fair: What expos have done for their cities. *Planning*, 18(7), 13-19.

Prosser, G. (1993). Mansell meets Mozart: Event tourism in Adelaide, South Australia. *Festival Management and Event Tourism*, 1(3), 125-130.

Ritchie, J.R.B. (1984). Assessing the impact of hallmark events: Conceptual and research issues. *Journal of Travel Research*, 23(1), 2-11.

Ritchie, J.R.B., and Beliveau, D. (1974). Hallmark events: An evaluation of a strategic response to seasonality in the travel market. *Journal of Travel Research*, 14(Fall), 14-20.

Ritchie, J.R.B., and Hu, Y. (1987). The role and impact of mega-events and attractions on national and regional tourism: A conceptual and methodological overview, Paper presented at the 37th Annual Congress of the International Association of Scientific Experts in Tourism (AIEST), Calgary, Canada.

Ritchie, J.R.B., and Smith, B.H. (1991). The impact of a mega-event on host region awareness: A longitudinal study. *Journal of Travel Research*, 30(1), 3-10.

Roche, M. (1992). Mega-events and micro-modernization: On the sociology of the new urban tourism. *British Journal of Sociology*, 43(4), 563-600.

Roche, M. (1994). Mega-events and urban policy. *Annals of Tourism Research*, 21(1), 1-19.

Sydney Morning Herald (1994). Editorial. Taken for a ride to the airport. *Sydney Morning Herald*, 22 September, 1994, 14.

Sydney Olympics 2000 Bid Ltd. (1993a). *News release: Why Sydney would stage a great Olympics in 2000*. Sydney: Sydney Olympics 2000 Bid Ltd.

Sydney Olympics 2000 Bid Ltd. (1993b). *News Release: Sydney's plans for an environmental Olympics in 2000*. Sydney: Sydney Olympics 2000 Bid Ltd.

Urry, J. (1990). *The tourist gaze: Leisure and travel in contemporary societies*. London: Sage Publications.

Yake, G.A. (1974). Expo 74 sparks city's downtown renewal. *The American City*, November, 55-56.

Plate 7 The town of Nelson
(photo courtesy of The Province of British Columbia) ➜

SECTION 2
COMMERCIALIZING HERITAGE AND CULTURE

The Politics of Heritage Tourism: Place, Power and the Representation of Values in the Urban Context

8

C. Michael Hall

Tourism and Services Management,
Victoria University of Wellington, New Zealand

INTRODUCTION

Heritage represents the things that we want to keep. Heritage is the things of value which are inherited. If the value is personal we speak of family or personal heritage, if the value is communal or national we speak of "our" heritage. More often than not, heritage is thought of in terms of acknowledged cultural values. For example, a residence is not usually deemed as heritage unless it can be seen as part of the symbolic property of the wider culture or community, as an element of that culture's or community's identity (Hall and McArthur, 1992, 1993, 1996). As the Wellington City Art Gallery (1991) recognized: "The linkage of heritage and identity is significant. References to heritage typically propose a common cultural heritage. Distinguished old buildings are spoken of as being part of 'our' heritage. It is suggested that 'we' metaphorically own them and that their preservation is important because they are part of our identity. But who is the we?"

The issue of the 'we' in heritage serves as the focus of this chapter. Heritage is not a value free concept. By its very definition, heritage is concerned with the preservation, maintenance and representation of values. Heritage values may well be highly contested or, in some cases, may even be uncontested yet still reflect the inability or failure of certain groups in a community to have its interests revealed in heritage conservation and representation. Therefore, heritage management is inextricably linked to broader political questions of values, interests and control.

This chapter is divided into three main sections. The first section discusses the nature of power and its relevance to an understanding of the politics of heritage. The second section highlights the political nature of heritage management and representation with particular reference to the urban situation. The concluding section stresses the importance of political analysis on heritage studies and calls for the need for greater attention to this area in heritage management and urban heritage tourism.

POLITICS AND POWER

The study of politics is inexorably the study of power. Politics is about power, who gets what, where, how, and why (Lasswell, 1936). Decisions affecting heritage policy, the nature of government involvement in heritage management and tourism, the structure of agencies responsible for heritage conservation and management, the role of heritage in tourism development, and the identification, management and representation of heritage within communities all emerge from a political process. This process involves the values of actors (individuals, interest groups, and public and private organizations) in a struggle for power. "One chooses among values and among policies at one and the same time" (Lindblom, 1959: 82). Similarly, Simmons et al. (1974: 457) noted that "It is value choice, implicit and explicit, which orders the priorities of government and determines the commitment of resources within the public jurisdiction".

Politics denotes the struggle over scarce resources, the domination of one group over another, and the potential exercise of state control. Heritage tourism studies, as with mainstream tourism research, has either neglected or ignored the inherently political nature of their subject. However, in recent years, the political issues associated with heritage representation have increasingly come into focus, particularly with respect to indigenous peoples and control of their heritage. Nevertheless, with few exceptions, questions regarding the political dimensions of heritage tourism and place and the power of certain interests within a community to dominate over other interests have not received the attention they deserve (Hewison, 1987; Hollinshead, 1992; Hall, 1994; Hall and Jenkins, 1995). As Thrift and Forbes (1983: 247) declared, "any satisfactory account of politics and the political must contain the element of human conflict; of groups of human beings in constant struggle with each other over resources and ideas about the distribution of resources".

Politics is essentially about power. The study of power arrangements is, therefore, vital in the analysis of the political dimensions of tourism because power governs "the interplay of individuals, organizations, and agencies influencing, or trying to influence the direction of policy" (Lyden, Shipman and Kroll, 1969: 6). Within the processes of tourism development and heritage management, certain issues may be suppressed, relationships between parties altered, or inaction may be the order of the day. "All forms of political organization have a bias in favour of the exploitation of some kinds of conflict, and the suppression of others, because organization is the mobilization of bias. Some issues are organized into politics while some others are organized out" (Schattsneider, 1960: 71). Those who benefit from tourism development and/or from a particular representation of heritage may well be placed in a preferred position to defend and promote their interests.

The very notion of "power", one of the cornerstones of political analysis, is an "essentially contested" concept (Gallie, 1955-56). Power may be conceptualized as "all forms of successful control by A over B—that is, of A securing B's compliance" (Lukes, 1974: 17). The use of the concept of power is inextricably linked to a given set of value assumptions which predetermine the range of its empirical application.

Lukes constructed a typology of power and related concepts in an effort to clarify their meaning and relationship (Table 8.1).

Table 8.1   Typology of power and related concepts.

Concept	Meaning
Authority	B complies because he recognizes that A's command is reasonable in term of his own values, either because its content is legitimate and reasonable or because it has been arrived at through a legitimate and reasonable procedure
Coercion	Exists where A secures B's compliance by the threat of deprivation where there is a conflict over values or course of action between A and B
Force	A achieves his objectives in the face of B's non-compliance
Influence	Exists where A, without resorting to either a tacit or overt threat of severe deprivation, causes B to change his course of action
Manipulation	Is an 'aspect' or sub-concept of force (and distant from coercion, power, influence and authority) since here compliance is forthcoming in the absence of recognition on the compiler's part either of the source or the exact nature of demand upon him
Power	All forms of successful control by A over B—that is, of A securing B's compliance

Sources: Bachrach and Baratz,1970: 24, 28, 30, 34; Lukes, 1974: 17.

Lukes (1974) identified three different approaches, or dimensions, in the analysis of power, each focusing on different aspects of the decision-making process: a one-dimensional view emphasizing observable, overt behaviour, conflict, and decision-making; a two-dimensional view which recognizes decisions and non-decisions, observable (overt or covert) conflict, and which represents a qualified critique of the behavioural stance of the one-dimensional view; and a third dimensional view which focuses on decision-making and control over the political agenda (not necessarily through decisions), and which recognizes observable (overt or covert) and latent conflict. The third dimension of power bears significant parallels with the work of Foucault (1972) on power. However, the agency exerting power is located locally in the work of Lukes and globally in the writings of Foucault.

Each of the three dimensions arise out of, and operates within, a particular political perspective as the concept of power is "ineradicably value-dependent" (Lukes, 1974: 26). For example, a pluralist conception of the tourism policy-making process, such as that which underlies the notion of community-based tourism planning (Murphy, 1985, 1988; Haywood, 1988), will focus on different aspects of the decision-making process, than structuralist conceptions of politics which highlight social relations within the consumption of tourist-services (Urry, 1990a, 1990b; Britton, 1991). As Britton (1991: 475) recognized, "we need a theorization that explicitly recognizes, and unveils, tourism as a predominantly capitalistically organized activity driven by the inherent and defining social dynamics of that system, with its attendant production, social, and ideological relations. An analysis of how the tourism production system markets and packages people is a lesson in the political economy of the social construction of 'reality' and social construction of place, whether from the point of view of visitors and host communities, tourism capital (and the 'culture industry'), or the state—with its diverse involvement in the system".

However, given the need to understand the dominant groups and ideologies operating within the political and administrative system which surrounds heritage tourism, it seems reasonable to assume that the use of a wide conception of power, capable of identifying decisions, non-decisions and community political structure, will provide the most benefit in the analysis of the political dimensions of tourism (Hall, 1994; Hall and Jenkins, 1995).

Political issues have an organizational aspect. Therefore, research on heritage tourism's political dimensions needs to connect the substance of policy, that is, the general focus on data, with the process of policy making including the relationship between power, structure and ideology. There are "politically imposed limitations upon the scope of decision-making", such that "decision-making activities are channelled and directed by the process of non-decision-making" (Crenson, 1971: 178). As Crenson recognized, pluralism is "no guarantee of political openness or popular sovereignty", and "neither the study of [overt] decision-making" nor the existence of "visible diversity" will tell us anything about "those groups and issues which may have been shut out of a town's political life" (1971: 181). Studies of the political aspects of heritage tourism should therefore attempt to understand not only the politically imposed limitations upon the scope of decision-making and heritage representation, but also the political framework within which the research process itself takes place (Hall, 1994).

THE POLITICS OF HERITAGE

Throughout the world, heritage and tourism have become inextricably linked. Tourism is used as an economic justification for the preservation of heritage, although tourism also serves to preserve artefacts and folklife in the gaze of the tourist (Hewison, 1987; Boniface and Fowler, 1993; Hall and McArthur, 1993, 1996). Therefore, the identification, management, and representation of heritage will have substantial implications for both collective and individual identity and, hence, for the creation of political and social realities.

As noted above, the exercise of power may take several forms. Several examples can be provided as to the overtly political nature of heritage tourism. In some

cases, and particularly in the former state socialist nations of East
itage was utilized as a source of political legitimacy. For exam;
Nallbani, "Any visit to [Albania's] museums is . . . still prefaced/justified by q
tations from Enver Hoxha emphasizing the need to treasure and learn from past
Albanian material culture. Onufri [a sixteenth-century icon painter], for example,
is linked with the 'anti-Ottoman resistance of the Albanian people' " (Hall, 1991a:
270). Heritage can, therefore, serve a direct, observable, ideological function. For
example, in Red Square, the former Soviet Union's most popular tourist attraction,
was the embalmed remains of Lenin, while the hundredth anniversary of Mao's
birth provided a focal point for celebrations which aimed to reinforce the legitimacy of the current Chinese leadership (Hall and McArthur, 1992).

History is also the ground for contested space in Western nations. For example, the decision by the Walt Disney Company not to proceed with its plans for an
historical theme park at Manassas, Virginia, site of the Bull Run American Civil
War site, was as much opposed on cultural concerns as it was on environmental
grounds. "A broad coalition of historians, politicians and pundits argued that the
project would trivialize the country's history, and insisted that Mickey Mouse had
no place in such momentous events as the abolition of slavery or the carnage of the
Civil War" (Macintyre, 1994: 16).

Heritage is clearly related to issues of identity. In the former state socialist
nations, heritage has played an important part in the formulation of post-commu-
nist identities. As Hall (1991b: 284) observed, "The immediate past state-socialist
period has quickly become the source of a new heritage industry". The relics of
the communist period have become relegated to the foundries or to the backs of
museums or have become political tourist curiosities. History is being re-written
and re-presented again in order to both attract foreign tourists and to forge new
national identities by reference to a pre-communist past.

Heritage is, therefore, a flexible concept which indicates selective reinterpretations of the past. The history which is part of the fund of knowledge or the ideology of nation, state, community, or movement is not necessarily what has actually
been preserved by popular memory, but what has been selected, written, pictured,
popularized, and institutionalized by those with the power to do so. Heritage is
made by the winners. Heritage therefore represents the power of the winners.

Heritage tourism is an essential element in the representation of the winners'
view of history. Communities reconstruct the past and reinterpret the present within
the context of tourism development. Particular ideologies represent themselves to
the gaze of the tourist through museums, historic houses, historic monuments and
markers, guided tours, public spaces, heritage precincts, and tourist landscapes.
The gaze of the tourist is not value neutral, and the representation of heritage may
act to legitimate current social and political structures. As Norkunas (1993: 5) recognized, "The public would accept as 'true' history that is written, exhibited, or
otherwise publicly sanctioned. What is often less obvious to the public is that the
writing or the exhibition itself is reflective of a particular ideology". Similarly,
Papson (1981: 225) commented: "Tourism depends on preconceived definitions of

place and people. These definitions are created by the marketing arm of government and of private enterprise in order to induce the tourist to visit a specific area ... government and private enterprise not only redefine social reality but also recreate it to fit those definitions. This process is both interactive and dialectical. To the extent that this process takes place, the category of everyday life is annihilated".

In most Western cities, positive imaging, and heritage as an important component of such imaging, is a primary focus of governance. The outcome has been described as "the city as theme park" in which the architecture of the inner-city utilizes historic facades "from a spuriously appropriated past" to generate consumption within an atmosphere of nostalgia and display. "The result is that the preservation of the physical remnants of the historical city has superseded attention to the human ecologies that produced and inhabit them" (Sorkin, 1992: xiv).

THE URBAN CONTEXT

Tourism redefines social and political realities. Advertising and visitation creates images of place which then also creates expectancies on the part of the visitor and which, in turn, may reinforce representations of place. Destinations may, therefore, become caught in a tourist gaze from which they cannot readily escape unless they are willing to abandon their status as a destination. "Policies which are used to attract tourists, lengthen their stay, and increase their expenditures also function to redefine social realities. As definitions are imposed from without, the sociocultural reality which arises out of everyday life becomes further consumed" (Papson, 1981: 233). Tourism development, marketing, routing, and zoning affects notions of place. The organization of history in tourist settings transforms the cultural and historical life of communities and, hence, transform place itself.

Monterey, California provides a valuable example of the political nature of heritage. Monterey has a substantial heritage tourism industry based on the historic significance of the region in terms of United States expansionism, and a literary and industrial heritage in the form of Cannery Row, made famous by Steinbeck, and Fisherman's Wharf.

Different tourist landscapes, such as those in Monterey, whether historic or commercial, can be read as distinct cultural texts, a kind of outdoor museum which display the artefacts of a community and society. Each of these tourist cultural texts reveal certain ideological assumptions and power relationships that underly the tourist environment as a form of cultural production. Indeed, Norkunas (1993: 10) notes that the "ideology of the powerful is systematically embedded in the institutions and public texts of tourism and history".

The rich and complex ethnic history of Monterey is almost completely absent in the "official" historic tours and the residences available for public viewing. In Monterey, as in many parts of the world, heritage is presented in the form of the houses of the aristocracy or elite. Historically significant houses are also highlighted from this perspective. History is "flattened" or conflicting histories suppressed, thereby creating a simplified, generalized image which is consumed by the visitor. "This synopsis of the past into a digestible touristic presentation eliminates any discussion of conflict; it concentrates instead on a sense of resolution. Opposed events and ideologies are collapsed into statements about the forward movement and rightness of history" (Norkunas, 1993: 36). However, this occurs with little or no overt conflict over heritage representation. Heritage is not contested in the public sphere. Despite there being "democratic" institutions and channels for the representation of diversity, conflicts and issues are ignored in the public history of Monterey. Therefore, what gets reproduced "is the image of elite Americans of European descent who control, and have always controlled the destiny of the city . . . public history texts as well as tourist texts are involved in a form of dominance, a hegemonic discourse about the past that legitimates the ideology and power of present groups" (Norkunas, 1993: 26).

The recent industrial past has also been de-emphasized in the heritage product of Monterey. As in many Western urban centres, economic restructuring within the new global economy has led to the demise of many industrial operations, such as canning. The industrial waterfront has now become a leisure space combining shopping and entertainment with residential and tourist development. Industrial heritage is typically an essential component of waterfront redevelopment. Heritage precincts are established which tell the reader the economic significance of the area, not of the lives of those who contributed to wealth generation. Narratives of labour, class, and ethnicity are typically replaced by romance and nostalgia. Overt conflicts, whether between ethnic groups, classes, or, more particularly, in terms of industrial and labour disputes, are either ignored or glossed over in "official" tourist histories. The overt conflict of the past has been reinterpreted by local elites to create a new history in which heritage takes a linear, conflict-free form. In the case of Monterey, the past is reinterpreted through the physical transformation of the canneries. "Reinterpreting the past has allowed the city to effectively erase from the record the industrial era and the working class culture it engendered. Commentary on the industrial era remains only in the form of touristic interpretations of the literature of John Steinbeck" (Norkunas, 1993: 50-51).

The Monterey experience is repeated time and time again throughout the Western World. From Victoria and Vancouver in British Columbia to Liverpool and the London Docklands in the United Kingdom, and from Hobart and Sydney in Australia to Auckland and Wellington in New Zealand, the urban heritage waterfront has been developed as a means of rejuvenating inner-city areas and of solving urban problems such as the environment and overcrowding. However, the political dimensions of heritage representation and the simplification of place have been little considered. As Boyer (1992: 199) observed, "in both the tourist industry and historic preservation, there seems to be an attempt (not wholly successful) to unify and heighten the sense of the present by emphasizing the break with the past and with tradition, or to justify a particular aspect of the present by emphasizing a related aspect of the past. In the reconstructed seaport, do we concentrate on the ingenuity of the mechanics or the exoticness of the imports, on the wealth of the merchants or the poverty that led seamen to indenture themselves? Everything is significant. Museums, historic zones, and city tableaux present highly particular stagings of the past".

URBAN HERITAGE TOURISM AS THE POLITICS OF PLACE

The creation and representation of place is a social process. Urban heritage tourism is explicitly related to notions of place. "There is no better stage set for the spectacle of capital than a recycled mercantile area" (Boyer, 1992: 201). Urban heritage conservation, particularly the ubiquitous waterfront redevelopment schemes, is interconnected to the power relationships that exist within and outside a community. However, within such relationships it is apparent that the heritage of the losers is often lost or, at least, under-represented. The past becomes a sanitized pastiche of its former self as the sights, sounds, and smells of the old waterfront are banished, and retailers have a diminished relationship with a maritime past. The preservation of historic waterfronts and the creation of festival marketplaces occur merely as props for larger enterprises within the context of contemporary patterns of consumption. As Boyer (1992: 203) noted, with respect to New York's South Street Seaport which had set out to evoke the Fulton Fish Market, "Only the removal of the fish from the fish market finally made the 'historic' tableau commercially viable".

Heritage, as with place, is a social construct. However, the vast majority of heritage tourism research has failed to identify the political dimensions of the social process(es) by which heritage and place are constructed. Heritage is a major component of interplace competition. Nevertheless, it is somewhat ironic that the very places which have sought to differentiate themselves have ended up looking the same, what may be described as serial monotony or the serial replication of homogeneity (Boyer, 1988; Harvey, 1990).

As Harvey (1993: 8) asked, "The question immediately arises as to why people accede to the construction of their places by such a process". In many cases they of course do not, communities may resist the change of the developers. For example, "political battles between residents and specially created redevelopment authorities have punctuated the urban renewal of Australian waterfronts" (Kelly and McConville, 1991: 91). However, while short-term opposition did save the physical fabric of many Australian inner-city communities, it is worthwhile noting that the social fabric has been changed through gentrification and touristification of many areas leaving only heritage facades (Hall and McArthur, 1996). Indeed, Harvey (1993) also noted that resistance has not checked the overall process of place competition. A mixture of coercion and co-optation centred around maintenance of real estate values, assumptions regarding employment and investment generation, and an assumption that growth is automatically good, has led to the creation of local growth coalitions. "Coercion arises either through interplace competition for capital investment and employment (accede to the capitalist's demands or go out of business; create a 'good business climate' or lose jobs) or more simply, through the direct political repression and oppression of dissident voices, from cutting off media access to the more violent tactics of the construction mafias in many of the world's cities" (Harvey 1993: 9).

The central concerns of politics and power are sometimes apparent in heritage conservation, management and interpretation, more often they are not. Ideology and power relations are inscribed not only in space through the uneven development of the qualities of places (Lefebvre, 1991), but also through the representation of heritage. As Norkunas (1993: 97) described with respect to heritage tourism in Monterey: "The ruling class carefully controls the form and content of historical re-creations and tourist landscapes, legitimizing itself by projecting its own contemporary sociocultural values upon the past. This struggle, the tension between groups with power and groups with varying but lesser degrees of power, is replayed in the many spheres in which the public enactment of identity is staged. The erection or non-erection of statuary is a physical manifestation of that tension; nostalgic reinterpretations of socially condemnatory fiction, which results in a humorous caricature of poverty is yet another manifestation of this struggle. Dominance is expressed not in terms of physical coercion but as rhetoric".

The representation and the creation of places, therefore, needs to be understood in a far wider context than has generally hitherto been the case. The application of models of community participation in tourism planning which assume the pluralistic allocation of power within a community may unwittingly serve to reinforce existing power structures and representations of history to the exclusion of oppositional and contrary local histories. In the case of many ethnic and working class communities who face the extinction of their past, "their systematic exclusion from official history fragments the community so that feelings of alienation and 'loss of soul' are experienced most deeply by minorities" (Norkunas, 1993: 99).

CONCLUSION

Research into heritage tourism, therefore, needs to consider the means by which power structures have potentially served to lead to a one-dimensional representation of heritage and place to visitors, which ignores the complex range of place histories that often exist. Host and guest exist in an ongoing dialectic. By revealing the richness of place and the power structures that often serve to restrict historical representation to visitors, students of heritage tourism may well reinforce the uniqueness that comes from place complexity rather than allow places to submit to the serial monotony of contemporary place competition.

ACKNOWLEDGEMENTS

The author would like to acknowledge provision of a grant from the Australian Research Council and the assistance of Nicolle Lavelle, Vanessa O'Sullivan, and Kirsten Short in the preparation of this chapter.

REFERENCES

Boniface, P., and Fowler, P.J. (1993). *Heritage and tourism in 'the global village'*. London and New York: Routledge.

Boyer, C. (1988). The return of aesthetics to city planning. *Society*, 25(4), 49-56.

Boyer, M.C. (1992). Cities for sale: Merchandising history at South Street Seaport. In M. Sorkin (Ed.), *Variations on a theme park: the new American city and the end of public space* (pp. 181-204). New York: Hill and Wang.

Britton, S.G. (1991). Tourism, capital and place: Towards a critical geography of tourism. *Environment and Planning D: Society and Space*, 9(4), 451-478.

Crenson, M.A. (1971). *The un politics of air pollution: A study of non-decisionmaking in the cities*. Baltimore and London: The John Hopkins Press.

Foucault, M. (1972). *The archeology of knowledge*, trans. A.M. Sheridan Smith. New York: Pantheon.

Gallie, W.B. (1955-56). Essentially contested concepts. *Proceedings of the Aristotelian Society*, 56, 167-198.

Hall, C.M. (1994).*Tourism and politics: power, policy and place*. London: John Wiley & Sons Ltd.

Hall, C.M., and Jenkins, J. (1995). *Tourism and public policy*. London and New York: Routledge.

Hall, C.M., and McArthur, S. (1992). Whose heritage, whose interpretation, and whose quality tourism?: Perspectives on the politics and sustainability of heritage tourism. In *Joining hands for quality tourism interpretation, preservation and the travel industry, Third global congress of Heritage Interpretation International* (pp. 157-159). Honolulu: Heritage Interpretation International.

Hall, C.M., and McArthur, S. (1993). Heritage management: An introductory framework. In C.M. Hall and S. McArthur (Eds.), *Heritage management in New Zealand and Australia: visitor management, interpretation and marketing* (pp. 1-17). Auckland: Oxford University Press.

Hall, C.M., and McArthur, S. (Eds.) (1996). *Heritage management in Australia and New Zealand: The human dimension*. Melbourne: Oxford University Press.

Hall, D.R. (1991). Albania. In D.R. Hall (Ed.), *Tourism and economic development in Eastern Europe and the Soviet Union* (pp. 259-277). London: Belhaven Press.

Hall, D.R. (1991). Contemporary challenges. In D.R. Hall (Ed.) *Tourism and economic development in Eastern Europe and the Soviet Union* (pp. 282-289). London: Belhaven Press.

Harvey, D. (1990). Between space and time: reflection on the geographic information. *Annals Association of American Geographers*, 80, 418-434.

Harvey, D. (1993). From space to place and back again: Reflections on the condition of postmodernity. In J. Bird, B. Curtis, T. Putnam, G. Robertson and L. Tickner (Eds.), *Mapping the futures: local cultures, global change* (pp. 3-29). London and New York: Routledge.

Haywood, K.M. (1988). Responsible and responsive tourism planning in the community. *Tourism Management*, 9(2), 105-118.

Hewison, R. (1987). *The heritage industry: Britain in a climate of decline*. London: Methuen.

Hollinshead, K. (1992). 'White' gaze, 'red' people - shadow visions: The disidentification of 'Indians' in cultural tourism. *Leisure Studies*, 11, 43-64.

Kelly, M., and McConville, C. (1991) Down by the docks. In G. Davidson and C. McConville (Eds.), *A heritage handbook* (pp. 91-114). North Sydney: Allen & Unwin.

Lasswell, H.D. (1936). *Politics: who gets, what, when, how?* New York: McGraw-Hill.

Lefebvre, H. (1991). *The production of space*. Oxford: Basil Blackwell.

Lindblom, C.E. (1959). The science of muddling through. *Public Administration Review*, 19, 79-88.

Lukes, S. (1974). *Power: A radical view*. London: MacMillan.

Lyden, F.J., Shipman, G.A., and Kroll, M. (Eds.) (1969). *Policies, decisions and organisations*. New York: Appleton-Century-Crofts.

Macintyre, B. (1994). Disney loses theme park battle. *Weekend Australian*, 1-2 October, 1994, 16.

Murphy, P.E. (1985). *Tourism: A community approach*. New York and London: Methuen.

Murphy, P.E. (1988). Community driven tourism planning. *Tourism Management*, 9(2), 96-104.

Norkunas, M.K. (1993). *The politics of memory: tourism, history, and ethnicity in Monterey, California*. Albany: State University of New York Press.

Papson, S. (1981). Spuriousness and tourism: Politics of two Canadian provincial government. *Annals of Tourism Research*, 8(2), 220-235.

Schattsneider, E. (1960). *Semi-sovereign people: A realists view of democracy in America*. New York: Holt, Rinehart and Wilson.

Simmons, R., Davis, B.W., Chapman, R.J.K., and Sager, D.D. (1974). Policy flow analysis: A conceptual model for comparative public policy research. *Western Political Quarterly*, 27(3), 457-468.

Sorkin, M. (1992). Introduction: Variations on a theme park. In M. Sorkin (Ed.), *Variations on a theme park: The new American city and the end of public space* (xi-xv). New York: Hill and Wang.

Thrift, N., and Forbes, D. (1983). A landscape with figures: Political geography with human conflict. *Political Geography Quarterly*, 2, 247-263.

Urry, J. (1990a). *The tourist gaze: Leisure and travel in contemporary societies*. London: Sage Publications.

Urry, J. (1990b). The 'consumption' of tourism. *Sociology*, 24(1), 23-35.

Wellington City Art Gallery. (1991). *Inheritance: art, heritage and the past*. Wellington: Wellington City Art Gallery.

Plate 8 Street scene, Barkerville
(photo courtesy of The Province of British Columbia) ➡

Urban Tourism and the Performing Arts

Howard L. Hughes

Manchester Metropolitan University, United Kingdom

The aim of this chapter is to determine the role and significance of the performing arts in urban tourism. Initially, concepts and definitions are examined in an attempt to clarify the terms of the analysis. The chapter considers the extent to which the performing arts act as a tourist resource in terms of visits by tourists to theatres and concert halls and in terms of how important those facilities are in the decision to visit a particular destination. Additionally, some of the wider implications of arts tourism are examined. The chapter includes a consideration of the way in which such tourism is evaluated.

It is argued that it is currently difficult to establish the role and significance of the performing arts because of a number of constraints identified in the chapter. A number of suggestions relating to further research in the tourism-performing arts relationship are considered.

URBAN ARTS AND TOURISM

Urban areas, as central service loci, are usually characterized by a high concentration of theatres and concert halls and of the arts performed in them such as drama, comedy plays, musicals, classical music, opera, and ballet. These, apart from any local function, are often regarded as part of the tourist product of many cities. In the tourism market, urban areas may have a comparative advantage with respect to the performing arts as they are resources that small towns, rural areas, and seaside resorts may not have. They may encourage tourist visits and lead to an injection of tourist expenditure that is usually considered beneficial to the wider urban economy.

For leisure tourists it is probable that the performing arts (and heritage) are a significant attraction of many cities. The exact significance will vary from one city to another and other attractions will include entertainment, shopping, and sport (Law, 1993). The performing arts do, nonetheless, appear to have the potential to be particularly strong tourist assets for many urban areas. In Glasgow, for instance, 'arts-related' tourism was estimated at 34 percent of all trips in 1986 (Myerscough, 1988). Such tourism was, however, widely defined as any which included arts in the trip and the arts were widely defined to include theatre, concerts, museums and art galleries. It was also estimated, in the same study, that in 1986 arts-related tourism constituted 41 percent of all expenditure by overseas visitors to UK and 13 percent of expenditure by domestic tourists.

The ability to discuss tourism relating to the performing arts is, however, constrained by a number of confusions of terminology, such as those cited above (Hughes and Benn, 1995). Much related work has been conducted under the umbrella of 'cultural tourism', 'arts tourism', or 'heritage tourism'. These terms are often used interchangeably to refer to tourism which includes visits to historic buildings and sites, museums and art galleries, and also visits to view contemporary paintings or sculpture, or to attend the performing arts. There has been a tendency to treat such tourism as a single entity, and studies do not usually address one particular aspect of 'culture' such as the performing arts or museums. These studies have not, either, normally included 'entertainment': activities such as variety shows, music hall, pantomime, band concerts, pop concerts, rock, reggae, jazz, folk music, dancing, circus, and magic. The significance of this 'popular' cultural activity may be considerable, especially in the tourism context (Hughes and Benn 1995).

Definitional issues, in themselves, need not be a particular problem, but they have contributed to an operational and research perspective which has clouded rather than clarified matters. It may be at the level of individual cultural forms or events that the tourism significance lies.

The focus of this chapter is the 'high' performing arts of theatre, music and dance. The term 'performing arts' refers to these activities and not, unless otherwise indicated, to the 'popular' arts of entertainment.

TOURISM POTENTIAL AND PARTICIPATION

The paths by which any one tourist arrives in the audience of the theatre or concert hall are many and varied. The concept of arts tourism is, however, applied loosely to cover a number of possibilities ranging from trips where the performing arts are the main activity and the prime motivation, through to trips where they are a secondary activity and an incidental motivation.

Some holiday choices will be made in order to experience the performing arts in preference to alternatives such as 'sun, sea and sand'. In addition, the presence of some tourists in audiences may arise primarily because of a decision to attend the performing arts. The availability of live performances is widespread but not universal, and some consumers may need to travel and become tourists in order to experience the product (Hughes, 1987).

Watching the performing arts seems to be the activity of relatively few tourists; UK national tourist board data indicates that the activity occurred on only 5 percent of domestic holiday trips (English Tourist Board et al., 1993). An earlier survey which focused on both the 'popular' and 'high' performing arts (confusingly) under the term 'entertainment', suggested higher participation (Research

Surveys of Great Britain, 1985). This showed that on 38 percent of holidays in England, British holiday-makers had gone to see some form of live entertainment. It was also more usual for holiday-makers to visit live entertainment while on holiday than when at home.

Most tourist surveys suggest that overseas visitors to Britain, and London in particular, are more likely to visit historic sites and houses than the performing arts. Theatre tends to be the most popular performing arts form with opera, ballet, or classical concerts significantly less popular (British Tourist Authority and English Tourist Board, 1986; British Tourist Authority, 1992).

A survey of European cultural tourism confirmed that heritage tourism was more important than performing arts tourism (Richards, 1994). Attendance at the performing arts when at home was more likely than when on holiday. This appears to contrast with the conclusions of the survey of entertainment in England and may reflect a difference between the (high) arts and entertainment.

DRAWING POWER

The participation rate in the performing arts on holiday may have little relation to the importance of these activities in the decision of tourists to visit a destination.

Research among British holiday-makers (Research Surveys of Great Britain, 1985) indicated that no respondents spontaneously mentioned the availability of live entertainment (which included the 'high' arts) as a factor when deciding where to go on holiday in England. It was only on a list of prompted factors that live entertainment assumed any significance in the holiday destination decision: a factor in 6 percent of inland town and city holidays. Other research shows that the vast majority of domestic holiday trips in the UK are undertaken without any particular activity specified as the main reason (English Tourist Board et al., 1993). 'Watching the performing arts' was the main reason for only 2 percent of all domestic holiday trips.

The Overseas Visitor Survey 1992 (British Tourist Authority and English Tourist Board, 1993) identified those factors which were considered as 'important' or 'very important' in the decision of foreign tourists to come to Britain on holiday. 'Heritage' was cited by over three quarters of respondents and 'arts and entertainment' by only half. If 'beautiful scenery or countryside' had been absent from Britain then most foreign visitors would not have come, whereas the relevant figure for theatre was only 42 percent (British Tourist Authority and English Tourist Board, 1985).

Some audience studies also give an indication of the importance of the event in the decision of the audience to visit the area. Only a small proportion (15 percent) of overseas tourists to London who had attended the arts gave 'visiting arts and cultural things' as the main reason for coming to London (Myerscough, 1988). Many of those attending the Edinburgh Festivals 1990-91, however, considered that the Festivals were the 'sole reason' for the visit to Scotland (Scotinform, 1991).

THE TOURISM-CULTURE COALITION

The development of both the performing arts and tourism in many cities has been, in part, a response to economic decline. Tourism strategies for urban areas have frequently been based on the regeneration potential of tourism. The English Tourist Board has been promoting the role of tourism in urban regeneration for some time, and the possible role of tourism is recognized by the UK government (English Tourist Board, 1980, 1981; Department of the Environment, 1990). The supposed benefits and disadvantages of tourism in urban areas are well rehearsed.

Concurrent with this has been the development of cultural policies (including the performing arts) for regeneration. Cultural policies may serve many purposes, but serving the objective of urban regeneration is a relatively recent development (Bianchini, 1993a). Urban regeneration through culture is assumed to be the consequence of several factors, including enhancing the image of the city ("place marketing"), thus enabling it to compete in the international market for inward investment and the employment and income effects of an injection of tourist expenditure (Booth and Boyle, 1993).

Cultural policies have, however, been the subject of some criticism largely because of these economic and tourism objectives (Bianchini 1993a, 1993b; Booth and Boyle, 1993; Griffiths, 1993; Boyle and Hughes, 1991). In particular, it is argued that local relevance and talent and the nurturing of long-term cultural development have been neglected and the emphasis has been on the high arts and prestige projects. Production and consumption may have been sacrificed to providing buildings; the cultural industries generally may have been disregarded in favour of activity in theatres and concert halls. (See, however, Myerscough, 1991, who was much more positive in many of these respects). The potential of tourism in cultural policy has been strong and has served to intensify these pressures.

A touristic perspective to the performing arts may have an effect similar to that observed in the case of heritage tourism. This has been criticized because of a possible contribution to the commodification, commercialization, and distortion of history (Ashworth, 1993; Hewison, 1987; Hughes, 1989). It is argued, too, that there has been an undue emphasis on the heritage of the white middle class at the expense of the culture and history of others in the UK (Stephenson, 1994).

Many tourist visits to cities will be motivated, in part at least, by the opportunity to attend musicals and plays. The commercial success of many of these is due, in part, to the numbers of tourists in the audience, especially in London (Gardiner, 1982, 1986, nd). The long term effect may be the demise of artistic activity that is not profit-making. Products may become commercialized and trivialized. Artistic aspirations and integrity may clash with the requirements of the market. In some cases the arts promoted for tourism are the 'high arts', especially in festivals, and these, in particular, may seem to lack local relevance and be open to charges of élitism. Tourism's espousement of the arts is contributing to the wider process that is making the arts more inaccessible and less stimulating, creative, and spontaneous. Manchester's City of Drama program (1994) has been criticized for not giving sufficient consideration to the development and promotion of indigenous talent and art forms (Thorber, 1994). This yearlong festival was, in part, justified by its presumed tourist effects (Manchester City Council, 1991).

Tourism strategies and cultural strategies have the joint and reinforcing effect of promoting a particular urban image and particular tourism and arts products. The new urban services class seeks to ensure that the city centre is created in a form suitable for its own recreation and identity-reinforcement and city centres have become gentrified and the preserve of a middle class élite (O'Connor and Wynne, nd). The middle service classes are in a strong position to bring about the development of urban areas and of those arts which are congruent with their tastes. The realities of the current economic climate are such that even the most left-wing of local governments are powerless to implement policies that do not recognize the necessity to operate in the market place and to cooperate with the capitalist system. The pursuit of urban regeneration and growth has served to unify otherwise disparate groups (Whitt, 1987) so that tourism authorities, development and promotional bodies, and industry all implicitly subscribe to a particular perspective of the arts and tourism. Frequently tourism policies have a pro-business bias reflecting the more powerful voices in the political process (Peck and Tickell, 1995). As a consequence, tourist policies may not be serving the public interest in anything other than a very narrow sense (Hughes, 1994a). The tourist industry's compliance in this white middle class coalition serves to augment the effects of cultural and regeneration policies in further marginalizing certain groups and sectors of society.

ECONOMIC PERSPECTIVE

Despite the emphasis on the contribution of tourism and culture to urban renewal, it is not, in practice, easy to determine the actual impact. Performing arts tourism may well be important, especially for urban areas, and is believed to be growing. It can generate many visitors, especially through special festivals and events (Zeppel and Hall, 1992; Bywater, 1993). In the case of Glasgow's year (1990) as European Community City of Culture, it is estimated that there were 81 percent more tourists at arts events and attractions than in 1986. It is not known, however, what the effect on the total number of tourists in Glasgow was (Myerscough, 1991). In the case of the Edinburgh Festivals in 1990-91, nearly half of the total audience of 1.3 million were from outside Scotland (Scotinform, 1991).

Inevitably, performing arts tourism is evaluated in economic terms: expenditure, income, and employment generated. In the case of the Edinburgh Festivals, the tourism impact is believed to be considerable: well over three-quarters of total direct expenditure of £43 million (Scotinform, 1991). Estimates of the direct effects of any form of tourism are, however, difficult to calculate given limited comprehensive data and the necessity to rely on survey material (Sheldon, 1990). Employment figures are frequently conversions of these unreliable expenditure figures. There are problems of attributing tourism (and its consequences) to the arts facilities and events and of making adjustment for any displacement of expenditure from other tourist attractions in the area (Hughes, 1993).

In addition to the direct effects, indirect and induced effects are estimated through multiplier analysis. This has many shortcomings, most of which are widely recognized, but it continues to be applied routinely and indiscriminately (Hughes, 1994b). Inadequate data and restrictive and unrealistic assumptions serve to limit the value of the multiplier technique. Calculated multiplier values are widely misunderstood and misused; the apparent precision of the technique leads to undiscriminating interpretation of values.

Additionally, the technique serves to distract from other fundamental issues. As a mathematical concept, it is relatively easy to estimate and it may overshadow issues that cannot be expressed so easily in figures.

Such considerations are not confined to arts tourism, but have been raised, for instance, in the case of major conference centres and concert halls and major sporting facilities and sports events (Loftman and Nevin, 1992; Baade and Dye, 1988a, 1988b, 1990; Critcher, 1992). The authors of a Birmingham study (Loftman and Nevin, 1992) concluded that prestige projects there (including those associated with the performing arts) may well have contributed to the physical regeneration of the city, but social inequalities were made worse by the uneven distribution of benefits and costs.

Many of these projects have not been conceived and implemented as the outcome of rational objective analysis and evaluation (Roche, 1994). Decisions have been the outcome of powerful leadership and power politics with justification and evaluation occurring subsequently (Peck and Tickell, 1995). Projects, including performing arts festivals and concert halls, may be activated without thorough evaluation. The effects may be overestimated and, in practice, are difficult to determine with any degree of precision. This is not to suggest that tourism and arts strategies generally have been poorly conceived and implemented, but rather that some elements within them may have been misjudged and inappropriate.

Given the nature of the urban problem the contribution of any form of tourism to regeneration is likely to be limited, anyway (Hughes, 1993).

CONCLUSIONS

Although urban centres have a tourism advantage with respect to the performing arts, for most it is probable that its drawing power in isolation is limited compared with heritage and other urban attractions. The performing arts in many cities, therefore, need to be viewed in context as a secondary tourist resource.

It would also appear that visits to the performing arts (though not entertainment) are less likely when on holiday than when at home. Visits to the theatre and to concerts are not, in most instances, generally perceived of as holiday activities.

However, there are a number of constraints on the ability to be more precise in assessing the role and significance of the performing arts. First, the dimensions of performing arts tourism are, in practice, difficult to determine. Terms such as cultural, heritage, or arts tourism are applied indiscriminately and in an all-embracing way so as to include any tourist trip that includes a visit to 'culture' or the performing arts. Little attempt has been made to separate out the individual components and identify whether distinct markets exist within the broad activity of cultural or arts tourism. Entertainment, which may well have a very important role to play in many forms of tourism, is rarely considered (Hughes and Benn, 1995).

The intent of tourists and the drawing power of the performing arts are also difficult to determine. Studies do not clarify whether the performing arts are important reasons for tourism in isolation or jointly. They do not indicate, either, whether the attractions are important to tourists only within a wider package of other attractions. Studies do not always give a clear indication of the relative importance of the performing arts, nor of their importance relative to other possible attractions.

Similar deficiencies are evident in many audience surveys, but in particular there has been a frequent failure to clearly identify those segments of audiences who are tourists. Audiences are inevitably categorized as visitors or by place of residence or distance travelled.

In both destination and audience studies, there has often been a failure to distinguish between those who visit a destination and only subsequently visit a theatre and those who visit a destination for a specific purpose such as seeing a particular play.

Notwithstanding these operational issues, it is arguable that tourist and arts policies have had a distorting effect by, for instance, being supportive of only the safe and the prestigious in the performing arts. This may have been at the expense of more indigenous and adventurous artistic activity. In effect tourism has contributed to the creation of city centres in the image of the white middle class. Tourism may have had a distorting effect on the performing arts encouraged in urban areas. It must, though, be acknowledged that in most cities there are relatively few tourists in performing arts audiences (with the exception of London and festivals). The influence of tourism on the urban performing arts product may be manifest but is limited. The nature of the performing arts in most urban areas is increasingly the outcome of commercial pressures regardless of the tourism dimension. Cultural policies may well though have intensified these influences by emphasizing the commercial and economic perspective through, in part, the tourism potential of the arts.

Finally, there is an obvious tendency to assess the worth of tourism in economic terms, often to justify public expenditure. Tourism is not often nor as easily evaluated in non-economic terms. It is evident that the determination of the economic effects of performing arts tourism is subject to considerable speculation and margins of error. The unreliability is especially acute in the case of indirect and induced effects which are estimated utilizing the multiplier technique.

The economic evaluation of effects is uni-dimensional in so far as it usually ignores wider issues such as opportunity costs. In the case of prestige arts events or projects, in particular, resources may be diverted from other uses which might be considered more 'productive' or 'useful' activities.

IMPLICATIONS

For the further development of the performing arts in an urban tourism context a number of issues need to be addressed. First it is necessary to identify the market more closely by focusing cultural tourism studies more: for instance, to individual art form levels such as drama, music, ballet, opera. Whether or not a trip should be defined as cultural tourism or arts tourism should be determined by the intent of the tourist and the tourist drawing power of the art form or event. There is a need, therefore, to assess drawing power at more focused levels and to determine the requirements of the tourist. At one extreme will be the tourist whose sole purpose is to attend a specific event and at the other will the tourist whose sole purpose initially is non-cultural and attends a concert subsequently because it is 'something to do'. A typology of performing arts tourism (or the wider concept of cultural tourism) may build on a matrix of degree of arts intent (primary, incidental or accidental) and of nature of arts interest (broad or narrow) on the part of the tourist. Additionally studies need to differentiate those whose main reason for travel was to see the performing arts and who subsequently became tourists and those who seek a holiday with varying degrees of performing arts input.

It may, in practice, be difficult to identify the relative pull of any one attraction since it may be a combination of factors that constitutes the attractiveness of a destination. It is, therefore, necessary to examine the joint influence of several factors including non-cultural attractions.

It is possible that the availability of the performing arts and entertainment has a significant *indirect* role to play in the choice of holiday destination, even if visitors do not actually visit the arts or entertainment. Entertainment may identify a tourist area as such. The presence of the performing arts of some standing may identify, increase awareness and enhance the 'attractiveness' of a destination even if tourists do not visit the event or facility. These issues remain to be explored.

The second issue that needs to be addressed is restoration of the credibility of the tourism industry and tourist boards by reconsidering the performing arts (and culture) that are promoted as the attractions of cities. Tourist boards may need to be more representative (Hughes 1994a). Policy, especially national, is handed to non-government organizations whose membership is narrow and is representative only of the interests of industry. Tourist boards need to draw on a wider constituency for their policy-making. The likely outcome is a perspective that recognizes the multifaceted nature of artistic activity in this country.

Those tourism policies need to relate to the cultural policy for any particular urban area since it is the local cultural resources that are being utilized for tourist purposes. It would be insensitive and inappropriate to pursue performing arts tourism policies that conflict with the interests of the local population. Urban cultural policies too should be interpreted more widely as an integral aspect of the quality of life of urban residents, in the determination of which the widest participation is to encouraged (Bianchini 1993b). Inevitably tourist boards and related organizations will have regard for those attractions that seem most likely to appeal to tourists but the policies adopted so far have not been unequivocally successful. It may be that a radical rethink could lead to the development of rather more successful and sustainable urban tourism.

Finally it is necessary to put the performing arts in context in the economic sense and be wary of over-exaggerating its significance. Currently, as performing arts tourism is not clearly defined it is difficult to be precise about its economic significance. Where it can be clearly defined and the pull identified it may be evident that the performing arts have less economic significance than previously thought. In addition there is still the danger of overestimation because of the widespread use of the multiplier technique. Its shortcomings need to be more widely recognized and the temptation to utilize this at all times and in all circumstances should be avoided.

The multiplier may also be a distraction from other issues and there is a need to extend the criteria by which tourism and cultural policies are judged so that opportunity costs and the distribution of income, for instance, are recognized. Strategies, projects and events should be subject to evaluation by the fullest criteria including social and environmental concerns. This is not to suggest that economic evaluation should not be undertaken nor that it is without merit but rather that it should be but one of many approaches to assessment.

The performing arts may well be a resource with which urban areas are particularly well endowed. The role and significance of the performing arts in urban tourism are, however, not yet clear and several fundamental issues remain to be addressed before they can be.

REFERENCES

Ashworth, G. (1993). Culture and tourism: Conflict or symbiosis in Europe? In W. Pompl and P. Lavery (Eds.), *Tourism in Europe: Structures and developments* (pp. 13-35). Oxford: CAB International.

Baade, R., and Dye, R. (1988a). An analysis of the economic rationale for public subsidisation of sports stadiums. *Annals of Regional Science*, 23, 37-47.

Baade, R., and Dye, R. (1988b). Sports stadiums and area development: A critical review. *Economic Development Quarterly*, 2(3), 265-275.

Baade, R., and Dye, R. (1990). The impact of stadiums and professional sports on metropolitan area development. *Growth and Change*, 21(2), 1-14.

Bianchini, F. (1993a). Remaking European cities: The role of cultural policies. In F. Bianchini and M. Parkinson (Eds.), *Cultural policy and urban regeneration: The West European experience* (pp. 1-20). Manchester: Manchester University Press.

Bianchini, F. (1993b). Culture, conflict and cities: issues and prospects for the 1990s. In F. Bianchini and M. Parkinson (Eds.), *Cultural policy and urban regeneration: The West European experience* (pp. 199-213). Manchester: Manchester University Press.

Booth, P., and Boyle, R. (1993). See Glasgow, see culture. In F. Bianchini and M. Parkinson (Eds.), *Cultural policy and urban regeneration: The West European experience* (pp. 21-47). Manchester: Manchester University Press.

Boyle, M., and Hughes, G. (1991). The politics of the representation of 'the real'. *Area*, 23(3), 217-228.

British Tourist Authority (1992). *Digest of tourist statistics. No 16.* London: British Tourist Authority and English Tourist Board.

British Tourist Authority and English Tourist Board (1985). *Overseas visitor survey 1984.* London: British Tourist Authority and English Tourist Board.

British Tourist Authority and English Tourist Board (1986). *Overseas visitor survey 1985.* London: British Tourist Authority and English Tourist Board.

British Tourist Authority and English Tourist Board (1993). *Overseas visitor survey 1992.* London: British Tourist Authority and English Tourist Board.

Bywater, M. (1993). The market for cultural tourism in Europe. *Travel and Tourism Analyst,* 6, 30-46.

Critcher, C. (1992). Sporting civic pride: Sheffield and the World Student Games of 1991. In J. Sugden and C. Knox (Eds.), *Leisure in the 1990s: Rolling back the Welfare State* (pp. 193-204). Eastbourne: Leisure Studies Association.

Department of the Environment (1990). *Tourism and the inner city.* London: Her Majesty's Stationery Office.

English Tourist Board (1980). *Tourism and the inner city: Planning advisory note.* London: English Tourist Board.

English Tourist Board (1981). *Tourism and urban regeneration: Some lessons from American cities.* London: English Tourist Board.

English Tourist Board, Northern Ireland Tourist Board, Scottish Tourist Board, Wales Tourist Board (1993). *The UK tourist: Statistics 1992.* London: ETB, NITB, STB, WTB.

Gardiner, C. (1982). *Audiences for London's West End theatres.* London: Society of West End Theatre (Unpublished).

Gardiner, C. (1986). *The West End theatre audience 1985-86.* London: Society of West End Theatre (Unpublished).

Gardiner, C. (nd). *The West End theatre audience 1990-91.* London: Department of Arts Policy and Management, City University (Unpublished).

Griffiths, R. (1993). The politics of cultural policy in urban regeneration strategies. *Policy and Politics,* 21(1), 39-46.

Hewison, R. (1987). *The Heritage Industry: Britain in a climate of decline.* London: Methuen

Hughes, H. (1987). Culture as a tourist resource: A theoretical consideration. *Tourism Management,* 8(3), 205-216.

Hughes, H. (1989). Tourism and the arts: A potentially destructive relationship. *Tourism Management,* 10(2), 97-99.

Hughes, H. (1993). Olympic tourism and urban regeneration. *Festival Management and Event Tourism: an International Journal,* 1(4), 157-162.

Hughes, H. (1994a). Government and tourism: A sub-set of leisure policy. In T. Seaton, R. Wood, P. Dieke and C. Jenkins (Eds.), Tourism: The state of the art (pp. 472-480). Chichester: John Wiley & Sons.

Hughes, H. (1994b). Tourism multiplier studies: A more judicious approach. *Tourism Management,* 15(6), 403-406.

Hughes, H., and Benn, D. (1995). Entertainment: Its role in the tourist experience. In D. Leslie (Ed.), *Leisure and tourism: Towards the Millennium. Vol II* (pp. 11-21) Eastbourne: Leisure Studies Association.

Law, C. (1993). *Urban tourism: Attracting visitors to large cities.* London: Mansell.

Loftman, P., and Nevin, B. (1992). *Urban regeneration and social equity: a case study of Birmingham 1986-92. Research Paper No 8.* Birmingham: Built Environment Development Centre, University of Central England in Birmingham.

Manchester City Council (1991). *Manchester City of Drama: Bid for 1994 Arts 2000 Initiative.* Manchester: Manchester City Council.

Myerscough, J. (1988). *The economic importance of the arts in Britain.* London: Policy Studies Institute.

Myerscough, J. (1991). *Monitoring Glasgow 1990.* Glasgow: Glasgow City Council (unpublished report).

O'Connor, J., and Wynne, D. (nd). *From the margins to the centre: Cultural production and consumption in the post-industrial city.* Manchester: Institute for Popular Culture, Manchester Metropolitan University.

Peck, J., and Tickell, A. (1995). Business goes local: Dissecting the 'business agenda' in Manchester. *Journal of Urban and Regional Research,* 19(1), 55-78.

Research Surveys of Great Britain (1985). *Holiday entertainment survey: A report on live entertainment in summer 1985.* London: RSGB for the English Tourist Board.

Richards, G. (1994). Developments in European cultural tourism. In T. Seaton, R. Wood, P. Dieke and C. Jenkins (Eds.), *Tourism: The state of the art* (pp. 366-376). Chichester: John Wiley & Sons.

Roche, M. (1994). Mega-events and urban policy. *Annals of Tourism Research,* 21(1), 1-19.

Scotinform (1991). *Edinburgh festivals study 1990-91. Visitor survey and economic impact assessment. Final report.* Edinburgh: Scottish Tourist Board.

Sheldon, P. (1990). A review of tourism expenditure research. In C. Cooper (Ed.), *Progress in tourism recreation and hospitality management. Vol. 2* (pp. 28-49). London: Belhaven Press.

Stephenson, M. (1994). The white of the eye: Perceiving Manchester's heritage. *Tourism in Focus,* 12, 14-15.

Thorber, R. (1994). Urban cosmetics. *Red Pepper,* July, 24-25.

Whitt, J. (1987). Mozart in the metropolis: The arts coalition and the urban growth machine. *Urban Affairs Quarterly,* 23(1), 15-36.

Zeppel, H., and Hall, C. (1992). Arts and heritage tourism. In B. Weiler and C. Hall (Eds.), *Special interest tourism* (pp. 47-68). London: Belhaven.

Plate 9 Totems in Stanley Park, Vancouver
(photo courtesy of The Province of British Columbia) ➡

Collusion, Collision or Challenge?: Indigenous Tourism and Cultural Experience in British Columbia, Canada

10

Heather Norris Nicholson
University College of Ripon & York St. John

INTRODUCTION

In recent years, political, economic, educational, and cultural goals have combined to make tourism important to many of Canada's indigenous communities.[1] These initiatives seek to stimulate economic activity and to strengthen collective identity and self-image. They may also attempt to inform about aboriginal culture and history (Norris Nicholson, 1992). This interweaving of ideology, cultural aspiration, and economic opportunism fosters community development where museum orthodoxy and established tourism are also challenged.

Indigenous tourism prompts the consideration of certain assumptions underlying cultural tourism (Parker, 1992; Stewart, 1992).[2] First, evidence suggests that culturally motivated tourism is stimulated by both supply and demand. Second, cultural products offered for tourism consumption are more heterogeneous than is sometimes acknowledged. Third, there may be implications for the future of such tourism where a mismatch arises between what tourists experience and what indigenous communities offer as their culture (Pearce and Butler, 1992).

This chapter discusses these issues in relation to the growth of indigenous tourism within British Columbia (Figure 10.1), particularly since 1980. It is suggested that indigenous-led tourism is usefully understood as part of a wider quest to achieve economic self-sufficiency as well as sociopolitical and cultural recognition. But *is* it possible to reconcile such potentially divergent goals within tourism activity without a clash of interests and unfulfilled expectations? Does the adoption of tourism as a panacea for economic needs prompt a level of expedient collusion between aboriginal and non-aboriginal groups? Is there a resultant collision between maintaining cultural integrity and satisfying tourism's appetite for cultural experience? This chapter considers some of these challenges faced by aboriginal communities as they adopt tourism strategies and tentatively offers some pointers as to where future attention and research may focus.

In less than two decades, aboriginal-led projects have assumed an important role in western Canada's tourism. They demonstrate the recognition both in and

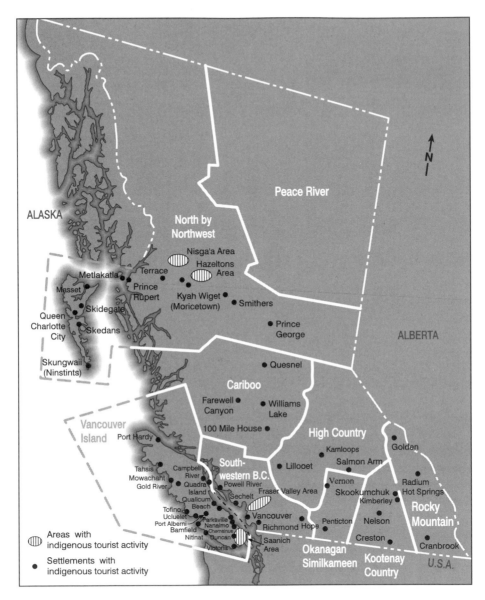

Figure 10.1   Indigenous tourism activity within British Columbia.

beyond First Nations' tourism marketing circles of an expanding interest in indigenous culture. These aboriginal initiatives may be seen as a means to utilize and more directly control tourism's voracious appetite for traditional encounter and cultural artefact (Weiller and Hall, 1992). Alternatively, they might be viewed as astute marketing strategies attuned to particular types of tourist interest and motivation (Figure 10.2) (Ashworth and Goodall, 1990).

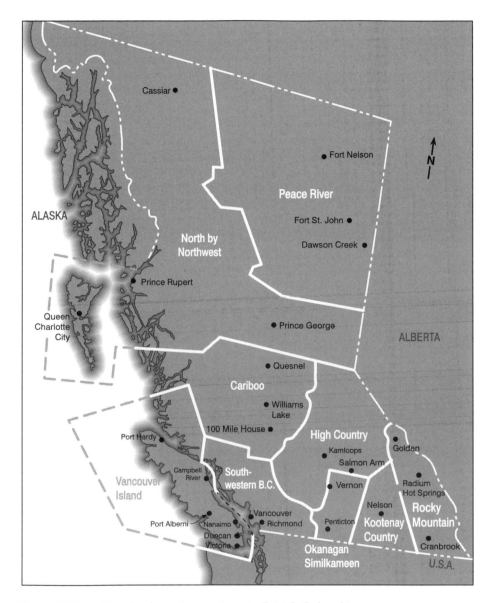

Figure 10.2   Standard tourism regions in British Columbia.

The analysis of culturally-orientated tourism prompts trying to identify the *cultural tourist*. One interpretation, as Hummon suggests, may be

> *the quintessential, if tragic modern person searching for authenticity in an increasingly modern world* (Hummon, 1988).

This fits with a view of contemporary existence in which inherited social, ideological, and moral certainties lack the reassurance of supposedly more consensual times.

But not all tourists who enjoy culture-related activity match this description. As with other types of tourism, variables such as ethnicity, language, age, gender, income level, education, and other personal attributes influence *who* goes *where*. The presence of aboriginal visitors at West Coast cultural attractions belie the idea of cultural tourists as primarily non-native professionals in a neo-colonial search of the Other.

On-site questionnaires and ticket sales, including concessions to local residents, point to a diverse group of visitors who are neither élitist nor exclusively culture-orientated. Visitor surveys indicate that other leisure pursuits include bingo, whale-watching, hockey, and theatre. More specialization occurs among long-haul than other visitors, but culture combined with varied outdoor activities is frequent.[3] Aboriginal developers of tourism activities tune their product accordingly and meet their customers' needs in different ways. As discussed later, the product on offer is no straightforward act of cultural collusion compelled by the quest for economic survival. Neither does tourism, on present evidence, suggest an inevitable collision of interests between host and guest.

If there are different kinds of cultural tourist, then is it possible to speak in general terms about cultural tourism? The abundance of alternative definitions (Figure 10.3) reflects the breadth of tourism studies, the industry's rapidly changing character and increasingly reflexive cultural discourse (Dann and Cohen, 1991; de Vries, 1978).

Figure 10.3   Definitions of cultural tourism.

- Cultural tourism is the consumption of cultural experiences (and objects) by individuals who are away from their normal place of habitation (John Kelly).

- Cultural tourism is a form of tourism based upon the enhancement and protection of cultural products for their fuller potential as resources for tourism. These resources include natural beauty, architecture, and urban forms, arts activity, and unique local and regional character (*Partners for Livable Spaces*).

- The World Tourism Oganization offer both a broadly and more narrowly based definition of cultural tourism. The latter "includes movements of persons for essentially cultural motivations such as study tours, performing arts, and cultural tours, travel to festivals, visits to sites and monuments, folklore and pilgrimages. In the broader sense, all movement of persons might be included in the definition because they satisfy the human need for diversity, tending to risk the cultural level of the individual and giving rise to new knowledge, experience and encounters (World Tourism Organization, 1985).

Source: *Planning for Cultural Tourism: A Symposium*, Calgary, 1989.

For the purpose of this chapter, however, one approach is to see indigenous tourism as an outcome of various strands of tourism activity which have emerged at different times (Figure 10.4). Changing political, socioeconomic, technological, educational, and cultural circumstances provide the context both for changing patterns of tourism and changing aboriginal involvement.

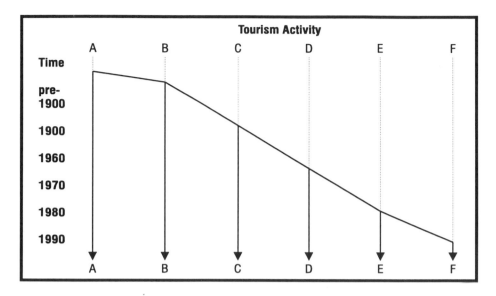

A: **Colonial tourism:** Travel (by individuals, government representatives and institutional agencies) is linked to wishes to explore and survey colonial territory, record and collect ethnographic detail and artefacts and encounter the western wilderness and cultural difference. Tourism in indigenous communities was predominantly determined by external processes.

B: **Outdoor tourism:** Rising levels of car ownership, leisure time, promotion of the "Great Canadian Outdoors" from the 1920s onwards encourage an increasingly urban population to join in with organized and independent travel to accessible and more remote wilderness destinations for outdoor activities (e.g., camping, hiking, canoeing and fishing). Indigenous involvement in tourism varied according to local circumstances, economic alternatives and is frequently externally determined

C: **Scenic sightseeing:** Independent and organized touring combine land and water travel to relatively undisturbed natural areas to enjoy the scenery and historical or cultural sights of different destinations. Urban localities acting as gateways to tourist hinterland promote their cultural and historical resources (e.g., museums, art galleries, heritage sites). Growing opportunities for indigenous involvement on own terms.

D: **Speciality tourism:** Improved access by land, water and air, changing tourist interests and widening range of tourist operators combine to provide a diverse range of tourism activities based in different locations and appealing to a wide range of domestic and long-haul tourists at varied prices. Unusual natural and cultural resources gain popularity in urban and remoter destinations. Increasing opportunities for participation on own terms.

E: **Adventure tourism:** Travel for speciality outdoor activities that tend to involve various degrees of (perceived) risk and exhilaration (e.g., wilderness backpacking, trekking or sea-kayaking). Indigenous controlled initiatives increased.

F: **Ecotourism:** A subset of Adventure and Speciality Tourism which seeks to respect the integrity of the ecosystem and traditional attachment to the natural environment or the Land. Ecotourism seeks to help further protection of natural and cultural resources while deriving economic benefit which produces conflicting goals (e.g., increased access to vulnerable sites might put natural or cultural resources at risk). Much current focus upon trying to develop sustainable forms of community-led tourism.

Figure 10.4 Strands of tourism activity underlying Indigenous Tourism.

Given that indigenous tourism functions as a subset within general tourism activity, some of its emerging diversity may be seen as a kind of continuum of tourist experiences and encounters (Figure 10.5). At one extreme are tourist activities specifically orientated towards lifestyle, tradition and custom, for instance dancing, storytelling, or visiting a carving shed: in contrast, are those activities which offer tourist experiences in a culturally distinctive locale or form, for example sea-kayaking in a native canoe or staying in a native-run lodge. Either may

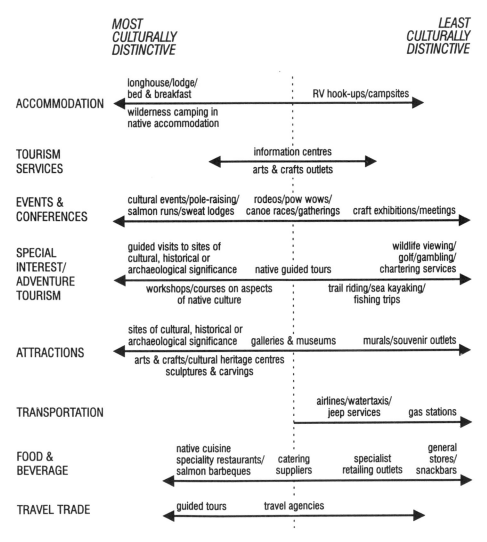

Figure 10.5 A classification of indigenous tourism and cultural distinctiveness.
(*Note: Positioning of listed activities is indicative only, as considerable variety exists within the emphasis and orientation of indigenous-led activities under any category.*)

offer some cultural contact, but their potential either to further cross-cultural understanding or, to prompt a clash of values, varies. Different facets of indigenous culture are clearly being used to create different tourist experiences for different consumer groups. An undifferentiated cultural tourism no more exists than the generic cultural tourist.

Acknowledging the diversity within consumer and market product leads on to consideration of those making the cultural experience available. Again, an undifferentiated notion of producer is inadequate. Those individuals, groups and communities so far involved in indigenous tourism activity are as diverse as the operators in any other sector of tourism (Figure 10.6) (Murphy, 1985).

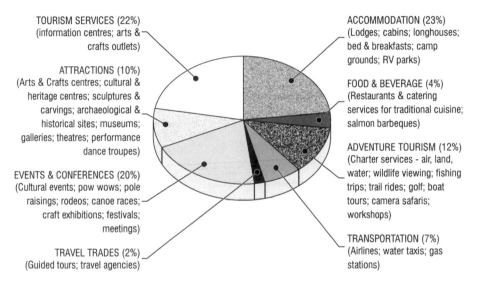

TOURISM SERVICES (22%)
(information centres; arts & crafts outlets)

ATTRACTIONS (10%)
(Arts & Crafts centres; cultural & heritage centres; sculptures & carvings; archaeological & historical sites; museums; galleries; theatres; performance dance troupes)

EVENTS & CONFERENCES (20%)
(Cultural events; pow wows; pole raisings; rodeos; canoe races; craft exhibitions; festivals; meetings)

TRAVEL TRADES (2%)
(Guided tours; travel agencies)

ACCOMMODATION (23%)
(Lodges; cabins; longhouses; bed & breakfasts; camp grounds; RV parks)

FOOD & BEVERAGE (4%)
(Restaurants & catering services for traditional cuisine; salmon barbeques)

ADVENTURE TOURISM (12%)
(Charter services - air, land, water; wildlife viewing; fishing trips; trail rides; golf; boat tours; camera safaris; workshops)

TRANSPORTATION (7%)
(Airlines; water taxis; gas stations)

Figure 10.6   Indigenous tourism: An indication of sectoral involvement within British Columbia

A discussion of culture within tourism—and tourism research—often starts from the asymmetrical relations between hosts and strangers (Pearce, 1988; Smith, 1989; Pearce and Butler, 1992). Prevailing sociocultural, economic and geopolitical conditions contextualize any decision to promote tourism. Indigenous involvement in tourism is no exception. Its development is indicative of the attempts by community leaders to tackle the enduring structural inequalities that beset many reserves. It is also a localized response to the flow of ideas, images, people, money, and resources which underlie trends in modern consumerism and global tourism (Appadurai, 1990).

The outcome of this interplay between past and present processes is more than cultural commoditization. It is too simplistic to condemn tourism's capacity to sell lifestyle and locality as another variant of neo-colonial domination. Tourism based upon marketing tangible cultural expression, does not automatically lead to cultural reification and trinketization. The West Coast fridge magnet, no more than the Anne Hathaway pencil sharpener, makes no claims to cultural enlightenment. Both are simply mementos within a similar price bracket. Any critique of culture-related tourism which dismisses this economic spin-off, while condoning the sale of art and quality reproductions, is itself élitist.

It is against this background that the development of aboriginal-led tourism in western Canada is set (see Figure 10.1). The extent to which these initiatives are on a collision course—whether through competition from over-provision or in reconciling producer aims with visitor expectations—is still unknown. Likewise, how present-day pragmatism and collusion with other economic and political processes will be viewed in the future is uncertain. Past experience elsewhere, however, shows that changes brought by involvement in tourism seem irreversible, so careful management and direction are essential.

ATTITUDES AND EARLY INDIGENOUS TOURISM

Aboriginal involvement in modern tourism represents a significant shift beyond earlier experiences (see Figure 10.4). Fascination with Canada's indigenous inhabitants as objects of spectacle, curiosity, and borrowed cultural resource predates even the country's emergence as a modern nation-state in the 1860s (Francis, 1992). Nineteenth century travellers searching for mystery and romance in the Canadian wilderness depended upon indigenous knowledge and guidance, just as European militia, explorers, and traders had relied on local expertise before them. Aboriginal guides viewed early tourism with ambivalence in their combined role as expert and servant (Jansen, 1993).

For much of the twentieth century, a fictive aboriginal identity, constructed from imposed economic, cultural, and sociopolitical inequalities, has featured in tourism and advertising. Stereotypes, both inherited and sometimes in self-conscious parody, still permeate popular culture and media. Neither domestic nor international visitors to indigenous tourist sites can be completely unaware of this legacy. Old prejudices lose credence slowly even if they do not match past movies, televised indigenous protests or romantic notions of aboriginal peoples as the Earth's original ecologists. The underlying racism of such imposed identities remains pervasive within much daily indigenous experience. Native tourism operators acknowledge a duty to inform the public about modern aboriginal life.

Much of the impetus for a culturally-based tourism run by aboriginal groups dates from the past 10 to 15 years (Murphy, 1985). The Native Brotherhood of British Columbia cautioned in 1980 against converting socially-orientated activities —integral to indigenous lifestyle—into tourism products. The discussion acknowledged that certain cultural activities had already lost their social role in succumbing to economic forces and tourist appeal (TISDA, 1980). A report by the provincial government, published in 1982, dealt with the "West Coast Indian Theme" in four brief paragraphs. After acknowledging "the exceptional nature of this Native Indian culture and its *relatively low profile*", the report continued:

> *The marketability of the West Coast Native Indian culture, its arts, crafts and ways of life is **quite high** . . . (and) **should be explored** (TREE, 1982) (author's emphasis).*

The goal of economic self-sufficiency eclipsed many doubts about tourism during the next decade (Cassidy and Seward, 1991). Different communities in British Columbia and elsewhere saw opportunities arising from widespread government promotion of tourism (Walker, 1987; Hirano, 1993). Added impetus came, in several instances, as at the U'Mista Cultural Centre in Alert Bay and the Kwagiulth Museum on Quadra Island, from the need to construct facilities adequate to re-house confiscated Potlatch ceremonial objects being returned from museums (Figure 10.1).[4]

Political changes during the early 1990s rekindled hopes of settling aboriginal land claims and gaining self-government rights (Richardson, 1989; Cassidy, 1991; Boldt, 1993). Greater optimism about the political future began to fuel indigenous communities' grasp of economic opportunities within provincial tourism.

Imaginative development plans and investment strategies for community businesses were indicative of new leadership styles on many reserves. In a modern outward-looking, entrepreneurial climate, interest in developing government-initiated Community Tourism Action Plans (CTAPs) has grown rapidly among aboriginal groups since the early 1990s. Although participation in the provincial program—open to *all* communities—brings no finance directly, it enables communities to tap into advisory support systems which may provide access to funding.[5]

Arguably, necessity rather than choice prompts aboriginal communities to respond to government encouragement of tourism. At one level, this is collusion borne of expedience. When wider societal trends start to place a monetary value on aspects of cultural identity and history which were once suppressed, the commercial implications are too significant to ignore. The internationally recognized and distinctive material heritage and art-forms of the West Coast represent an alternative product to the often vulnerable resource bases and short-term enterprises on which many community business interests initially focused. Yet, as tourism tends to perpetuate economic dependency, its ability to foster economic self-sufficiency is questionable.

Choosing to promote tourism based upon *culture, nature, history,* or *hospitality services* is largely a function of geographical location, resource availability and community inclination. Once the cultural and historical context are also taken into consideration, the present variety of activity reveals a growing need for greater precision and coordination between individual tourist operators (see Figure 10.6). Some recent initiatives are considered in the next section.

A NEED TO COORDINATE AND CLASSIFY?

The wide geographical distribution, socioeconomic disparities, and cultural diversity of the province's 196 aboriginal groups requires the careful planning of tourism initiatives (see Figures 10.7 and 10.8). The First Nations Tourism Association (FNTA) was set up in response to this need for coordination. Its short-lived existence and achievement reflected the financial impetus given by the UN 1993 International Year of Indigenous Peoples. By late 1994, the organization had reformed and relocated in Ottawa as the Canadian National Aboriginal Tourism Association (CNATA). This national coordinating body now has a council representing indigenous tourist operators and educators in different parts of Canada.[6]

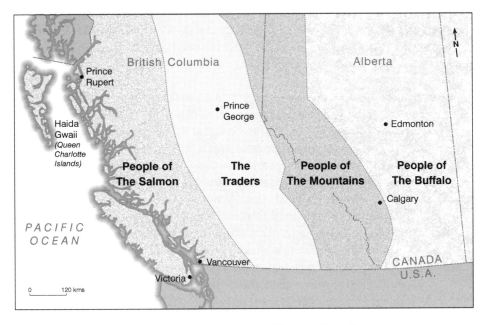

Figure 10.7   Cultural tourism groupings in Western Canada.
(This map shows the four historico-cultural groups which form the tourism regions of the provinces of British Columbia and Alberta, according to Kramer (1994). All entries in the guide are coded according to these regions.)

The FNTA's *First Nations Guide* (1993) was an impressive example of joint marketing for 10 contrasting cultural tourism operations in different parts of British Columbia. Its publication anticipated visitor interest during the Commonwealth Games held at Victoria in August 1994. The range of cultural products and tourist experiences being run by First Nations has widened further and another guide produced with the support of B.C. Tourism and *Beautiful British Columbia* magazine is currently in progress.[7] In September 1994, *The Sunday Times*, published in London, heralded indigenous tourism as "a driving force in the province's travel industry".

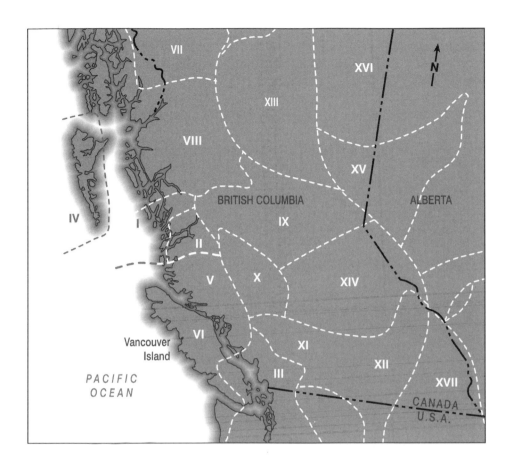

This map shows how the province's 196 aboriginal groups are members of the major Nations approximate to the cultural regions identified by Kramer (1994). Numbers refer to the names of each main Nation and indicate both familiar and alternative name:

Familiar name	Alternative name
People of the Salmon (within British Columbia)	
I Bella Bella	Heiltsuk
II Bella Coola	Nuxalk
III Coastal Salish	Coast Salish
IV Haida	Haida
V Kwakiult, Kwagiult	Kwakwaka'wakw'
VI Nootka	Nuu-chuc-nulth
VII Tlingit, Tlinkits, Chilkat	Tlingit
VIII Tsimshian	Nisga'a, Gitskan
The Traders (within British Columbia)	
IX Carrier	Carrier
X Chilcotin	Chilcotin
XI Interior Salish	Halkomelem

Familiar name	Alternative name
XII Okanagan	Okanagan
XIII Sekani	Sekani
XIV Shuswap	Secwepemc
People of the Mountains (within British Columbia)	
XV Beaver	Beaver
IX Carrier	Nuxälk-Carrier
XVI Slavey	Dene
XVII Kootnai, Kootenay, Kutenai	Ktunaxa, Kinbasket

Note: The Lillooet (Li'wat) are numerically small but a distinctive group of people. Traditionally, the Lillooet occupied a geographical position which reflected their origins as intermediaries between the Coast and Interior Salish.

Figure 10.8 Aboriginal Nations in British Columbia.

The evolution of aboriginal tourism is also evidenced by the provincial government's annual lists of cultural products and experiences. Although inevitably incomplete, these guides—produced more for tourism operators than visitors—indicate the geographical distribution of activity, range of operation and scale of different projects. There is an urgent need for more precise classification when producer, consumer, and product are so different: listing a school trail, the Museum of Anthropology in Vancouver, and a week's kayaking in the Gwaai Haanas (Queen Charlotte Islands) as similar activities illustrates the problem. Existing classification, developed for the Ontario context, does not quite match the mix of urban and remote tourism initiatives in western Canada (Robbins, 1992).

These ventures are clearly not all community initiatives. Enterprising individuals lead some projects, while others have institutional origins. Locations may be on, adjacent to, or far from, reserve land. Budgets vary from provincial government subsidy to those reliant on charity donations. Experience and expertise vary, as do levels of acceptance and integration into related areas of tourism promotion, research, and policy-making. Culture-related activities have different histories, status, and goals. A commitment to education, research, and cultural understanding underpins some activities; others are well-targeted responses to specific trends in niche marketing and speciality tourism.

An attempt to provide accessible tourist information on aboriginal sites was published in 1994 (Kramer, 1994). The pocket-sized handbook is a visitor's guide to sites in both Alberta and British Columbia. It was compiled in association with the FNTA and is now promoted by the CNATA, and its author works at the Native Education Centre in Vancouver, where an extensive program in Native Tourism for aboriginal students is now well-established. Its remit, in the words of its author, is "to discuss native-themed sites of interest to travellers" (Kramer, 1994: 6).

The publication concentrates on native-owned operations which are run by entire communities, individual native entrepreneurs, or as partnerships between aboriginal and non-native people. Visitor information is provided also on a selection of key non-native operations, including museums and sites with protected status. A range of practical details indicate where and how visitors may encounter aboriginal culture in positive ways.

This publication is striking evidence of the commitment to indigenous involvement in tourism and the professionalism of aboriginal operators who assisted with compiling the material. The combination of cultural background and community history with specific visitor information readily indicates the nature of tourism experience on offer. The entries are arranged according to broadly defined cultural labels which divide the two provinces into four geographical regions (see Figure 10.7). Each section is further divided thematically with entries on selected sites and types of activity. The publication is less comprehensive than the annual lists (mentioned earlier), but offers an important step towards providing a new kind of visitor literature. It also indicates an emerging awareness of the need for regional promotion even if native grouping does not readily equate with the standard subdivisions found in other tourist literature (see Figure 10.2).

DYNAMISM OF INDIGENOUS TOURISM

The vibrancy of aboriginal activity has affected British Columbia's tourism more widely. Other activities are being redefined as their promoters find ways to hint at North West Coast artistic and cultural tradition. Indeed, the recognition given to aboriginal culture and the participation of First Nations as co-hosts at the Commonwealth Games may represent this process in its most sophisticated form (Norris Nicholson, forthcoming).

There was recognizable media opportunism, political and commercial expedience, and cultural significance for those involved. An article in *Native Voice* expresses one perspective:

> *finally in this province and in this country, Aboriginal People are given a place that is more than token . . . the recognition from the Games Committee of the Aboriginal People here is some kind of medicine to our people as we march towards our collective wellness.*

Contemporary artwork depicting traditional myths and characters is currently utilized on covers and as illustrations for many tourist brochures throughout the province. Indigenous designs bring a distinctive artistic style to advertising for hotel facades, marinas, and outfitters, which until recently would have appealed to their customers in different ways. The message is clear: aboriginal culture is too important to ignore, even where tourist appeal has little to do with cultural activity.

TOURISM AND CULTURAL REGENERATION

The cultural revivalism associated with tourism is often dismissed as commoditization (Watson and Kopachevesky, 1994). Yet this ignores inherently complex processes. When traditions, languages, knowledge, and skills have been suppressed and sometimes virtually lost, cultural regeneration assumes symbolic significance. Attempts to revitalize tradition or to merge innovation with tradition become part of aboriginal adjustment to contemporary life (Elias, 1991: 137). Individuals, groups and whole communities now look to tourism, as a flexible tool for both cultural assertion and economic self-sufficiency, with much ingenuity. How far it is possible to reconcile such goals with visitor expectations has far-reaching implications for these attempts to combine education, entertainment, employment, and cultural recovery.

Indigenous tourism is an outcome of external dynamics and internal pressures. Marketing the material trappings of cultural identity, no less than putting traditional cultural practice and ceremonial regalia into museums and heritage centres, is fraught with ethical and interpretative problems (Clifford, 1991). Not all tourist operators wish, or have their community's approval, to put aspects of their culture on display. A few beaded bracelets on sale at a gas station, campsite, or concession store may be the only sign of local tradition.

Other tourist developers are prepared to tackle different issues. They may seek to present tradition as part of an evolving cultural identity through salmon barbecues or art events, or find ways to counter misunderstanding and ignorance through performance and exhibitions (Norris Nicholson, 1992). Tradition survives within contemporary aboriginal life in varied forms. The liberal tourist in search of ethnic encounters—and prepared to step beyond constructed images of *indianness*—must also accept diversity and dynamic cultural change. Were indigenous-led tourism merely to serve up anthropological animations, both visitors and employees would surely stop turning up.

At present, much culturally-based tourism, even where its overt focus is on maintaining past traditions, indirectly helps to fulfil the goals of cultural recovery and affirmation. Other interests merge with commercial concerns. Communities take pride in new facilities, employment, and training opportunities. Improved relationships with both neighbouring and more distant communities are widespread. Generational differences lessen where young volunteers work with elders who may be reasserting once denied traditions and skills.[8]

Since the early 1980s, aboriginal artistic output has expanded under the impetus of tourism. Encouraged by the proximity of ready buyers, artists experiment using new materials, motifs, and methods. Retailing outlets allied to tourist venues distinguish between popular appeal and specialist interest while acknowledging the economic importance of both. Gift-shop and gallery may sell different goods but both have a function in promoting community image, enhancing reputation and offering aboriginal youth an alternative to Skid Row. The professionalism of an indigenous carver, cashier, or on-site business manager gives cultural distinctiveness modern meaning. It may challenge some visitors' expectations. Where tourism meets culture, cultural encounter is about much more than resurrecting victims of history.

Participation as guide, carver, performer, and demonstrator affirms an identity: tourism need not prostitute cultural integrity nor become an act of servitude. Through tourism-related artistic activity, individuals may express new-found self-confidence, as well as a sense of belonging to wider cultural and occupational identities. The emergence of art forms distinctive from traditional practice reflects the potential vigour stimulated by a rediscovery process which is as much concerned with creating a future as with reclaiming a past.

Inviting tourists to share a tradition is a means to keep it alive as well as to reinvent it. Adaptability is not only the key to survival but the sign of cultural well-being. Where visitors are welcomed into cultural experiences as paying guests, participation is both an economic and a cultural transaction which acknowledges changing post-colonial relationships. The vanishing Indian of nineteenth century Euro-Canadian creation has gained a new visibility. An appropriated identity is being reclaimed and redefined: in the process, new forms of expression are tried, one being tourism.

CULTURAL CHALLENGES

Indigenous-run museums and cultural interpretation centres exemplify how tourism ventures challenge conventional museum practice (Ames, 1986; Clifford, 1993). They symbolize changing sociopolitical relations. They combine memory and vision with the role of mentor, communicator, entertainer, and host. While being showcases and treasure houses, they are also community centres and nursery business units (Norris Nicholson, 1992).

These community-run centres offer museum practitioners and others insights into the relationship between knowledge, marginalization, and under-representation.[9] Innovative display techniques, decisions about exhibition content, storage of cultural materials, and use of language all reflect the concerns of those who are well-placed to speak about themselves. Alternative approaches to interpretation and representation are spreading from community venues where education, entertainment, and economics closely interweave.

Decentralized archives, different notions of historical resources and the growth of cultural amenities in the communities they purport to concern, challenge museum orthodoxy. The development of cultural centres, accessible by boat and backpacking trails creates a rural version of cultural tourism compatible with outdoor recreation, nature, and adventure tourism. The eco-cultural tourist illustrates how pleasure peripheries constantly expand.

The historical aspect of culturally-related tourism seems likely to continue to be affected by changes introduced during 1994, in heritage legislation, archaeological site investigation, and interpretation. The politics of the present affect the politics of representing the past. Currently, heritage centres are celebratory; in time, they may also become commemorative of other painful experiences important for younger generations of native and non-native peoples to understand. Affirmation and assuagement must surely coexist if cultural healing is to take place.

Pro-active strategies should not slip unconsciously into reactive situations dictated by customer wishes if other objectives also underpin the tourism venture. At the Native Heritage Centre, Duncan, on Vancouver Island, a series of cedar long houses cater to tourists as they are invited to share in a celebration of Coastal Salish cultural distinctiveness. Traditional structures accommodate film studio, theatre, restaurant, gallery, and carving shed. Yet customer surveys reveal that some visitors regret the lack of teepees![10] Reconciling customer wishes with the needs of cultural integrity poses a dilemma in future planning: the long house is at the heart of a revitalized community spirit, yet West Coast visitors, steeped in filmic and artistic stereotypes, want Plains and Prairie culture (Ablers and James, 1983,1988).

However, visitor responses have prompted a debate about whether or not to put a teepee on site, which raises issues that go beyond consumer satisfaction. Although it might appear incongruous to the purist in search of Coastal Salish authenticity, the debate perhaps also acknowledges cultural exchange processes that have always been integral to aboriginal communities. Rodeos, powwows, and fancy dancing are as much a reflection of contemporary mobility and cultural dynamism amongst the aboriginal peoples of North America as a homogeneity imposed by tourist consumerism.

The multiple identities of indigenous culture may fit uneasily with anthropological schema, but better reflect the actuality of modern aboriginal living. At the Native Heritage Centre, the visitor with time and money may partake in a four-hour "Feast and Legends" program each summer evening. The salmon blessing and barbecue, storytelling and performance strengthen this distinctive encounter with Coastal Salish people, but the aboriginal participants, no less than their audience, do not function in cultural, geographical, or economic isolation.

If tourism is to be a means to sociopolitical ends, success depends on the careful development of priorities, policy, and practice. Community development and morale only suffer hardship from false starts, and dissatisfied visitors are hard to retrieve. The balance between education, entertainment, and economic gain needs to be identified from the outset. Cultural recovery may sometimes fit better with educational activity than marketing. Moreover, over-provision of similar products leads to competitive rather than complementary forms of tourism development.

Regional coordination and better recognition of how cultural activities combine with other visitor attractions seem critical for economic sustainability. Venues must not become over-congratulatory and complacent. Where presentation and promotional literature offer promises that outstrip visitor experience, both individual venues and indigenous tourism generally suffer. Over-pricing and unfulfilled expectations make return visits and recommendations less likely.

As tourism initiatives expand in number and in form, clearer identification will become increasingly important to promoters and visitors alike. Imprecise designation of visitor experience can exacerbate the problems of tourism management. There is a need to establish areas of complementarity so as to network between similar types of operators, avoid unfair bases of comparison while balancing ways to coordinate activity, and ensure adoption of appropriate standards. Cloning cultural products and tourist experiences meets neither economic nor sociocultural goals.

Tourism tends to transform private encounters into staged spectacles; this makes any community embracing tourism potentially vulnerable. Aboriginal tourism in British Columbia has so far avoided the intrusiveness which typifies much of tourism. Typically, tourist access blurs differences between public and private space. Communities might pre-empt such problems by ensuring that publicized codes of visitor conduct respect cultural integrity. Sensitivity in restricting access without racializing space protects cultural dignity and fosters social relations. Regulation and better coordination offer means to disseminate good practice among both suppliers and consumers of cultural experience. CNATA's role as coordinator seems essential to the future development of indigenous tourism.

Developing a tourism compatible with cultural resurgence requires raising public understanding of the ethnicity paradox. Cultural assertion may be an integral part of cross-cultural understanding, but it may appear contradictory (Richardson,

1992). Has a robust enough culturally-oriented tourism yet emerged to embrace such potentially turbulent currents? Any culturally-based activity requires integration within wider tourism management strategies. It must be based upon an understanding of visitor perception, interest, and participation in other leisure pursuits. Otherwise, the piecemeal consumption of cultural product and encounter will do little to contribute towards better inter-cultural understanding.

Tourism's capacity to ritualize and homogenize may appear at odds with tourist developers' wish to sustain or re-invent cultural distinctiveness. Without clear guidance, aboriginal tourism could become trapped between, on the one hand, a retreat into staged idiosyncrasy and cultural retrenchment, and on the other, creeping uniformity. Can the globalizing tendencies of modern consumerism really be reconciled with the promotion of cultural identity and dynamism? It will be necessary for those labelled as cultural tourists and those satiating their appetite for cultural experience to recognize the legitimate coexistence of multiple worlds. It has been suggested that the ultimate challenge of culture is to

> *find space for specific paths through modernity, paths where emerging traditions go on inventing themselves, where cultural dispersal does not necessarily spell disaster* (Clifford, 1988).

A self-regulated tourism is perhaps one temporary stage in the re-invention of tradition. If not, it is possible that culturally-led tourism carries the seeds of self-destruction.

DISCUSSION

Tourism's capacity for re-invention is well-known. Already aboriginal tourism is redefining its range of cultural products as it embraces traditional environmental knowledge in eco-tourism and develops other specialisms based on indigenous activity, management practice, and expertise. Attention is also shifting from culturally-specific activities to more generic leisure experiences within distinctive cultural contexts. Indigenous ventures into adventure/wilderness tourism, coastal cruising, and commercial vision quests are already emerging. Yet the multifaceted nature of cultural centres should secure their place in the foreseeable future: they may remain community facilities, rentable space, and training ground even if their function as a bridgehead for the curious visitor gradually shifts focus.

Contemporary indigenous tourism promoters may be trying to combine goals which, in the longer term, prove irreconcilable. But can aboriginal tourism developers offer a message about themselves and their modern identity that all their visitors will wish to hear? Fortunately, aboriginal Canadians have had enough experience of being framed by others (Cole, 1985): they are well aware that wherever tourism renders places, peoples, and cultural inheritance into spectacle, backcloth, and objects of ethnic voyeurism, its sociopolitical and cultural relevance is betrayed.

The accurate portrayal of indigenous history, as well as the representation of past and contemporary tradition, is vitally important to aboriginal peoples' own recovery of cultural identity and self-realization. Putting themselves in charge of the tourism impetus fuelled by wider governmental aims and societal trends implies foresight rather than collusion. Likewise, tour operators are not as yet on a collision course with their visitors as the balance between entertainment and education seems to be determined as much by cultural as by economic accountability.

On present evidence, it seems that indigenous tourism is not merely a damage-limitation exercise riddled with the scars of disillusion, compromise and unmet challenge. Within a relatively short time, expertise has grown rapidly and past mistakes have not been ignored. Schemes that fail, or come close to doing so, threaten communities which are beset by other forms of instability. Projects that lack the full support of community members, exceed their budgets, or become overambitious or over-reliant upon external agencies provide few but important reminders of what may go wrong. Wider exchanges of modern expertise and experience mean that the problems of isolation are beginning to lessen.

Tourism development is fostering new levels of community planning, land use management, and partnership in more equitable decision-making approaches. New ways to resolve struggles and rivalries based on age, gender, status, and family affiliation mean that community tensions are gradually becoming less of a threat as a shared realization about seeking stability continues to grow.

These developments have various implications which point to scope for further research both within and beyond aboriginal communities. First, as the economic, political, and cultural situation of Canada's First Nations continues to change, it seems likely that the nature of how they represent themselves in tourism will alter. Second, tourism's involvement of full-time, part-time, and voluntary female workers may provide much-needed opportunities for training, experience, and independence which will assist aboriginal women towards greater equity. This is likely to have significance in the emergence and retention of professional women within their communities and thus, in the longer term, may help to address other areas of socioeconomic provision, welfare need, and cultural instability.

Developments within indigenous-led tourism are also usefully understood within wider trends. Although marketing cultural experience has characterized much of indigenous-led tourism so far, this chapter indicates that it is only one of various strands of tourism activity. Equally, it must be acknowledged that this dimension has grown during a period when there has been much promotion of the arts and culture for tourism and leisure within mainstream Canadian society and, indeed, in most industrial nations (Knight and Gappert, 1989; Blanchini and Parkinson, 1993).

Cultural policies have become widely adopted within broader strategies to boost urban and regional development and to build new economic and employment opportunities, even though the economic returns from promoting *cultural capital* are hard to prove (Kearns and Philo, 1993). In such schemes, cultural activity and the arts are readily equated with efforts to *raise the image, counter stereotypes,* and *to improve quality of life* through *fostering a sense of identity.* Such terms, in current usage among policy-writers and arts fund-raisers, have a striking resemblance to many aims of indigenous tourism and indicate that there is an often under-acknowledged political agenda to much tourism promotion.

Perhaps the threat of cultural commoditization is more real in these contexts than within aboriginal communities, where the act of regeneration is the essence of cultural expression and recovery. Indeed, when that sense of affinity is part of the tissue of daily experience—the pain and the pleasure—the warnings about economic exploitation, social change, and cultural impoverishment are more appropriately directed towards tourism elsewhere.

In short, tourism has not put indigenous communities on a collision course which will compromise cultural integrity. Neither is the slur of collusion applicable when action which takes advantage of the government's tourism drive is clearly a means towards greater autonomy. Tourism challenges, and will continue to challenge, indigenous promoters as they contribute innovative new strategies to serve contemporary aboriginal life. As aboriginal tourism in British Columbia seeks to negotiate its ambitious future, it holds important messages for tourism research as well as those who find themselves the objects of tourist desire.

ACKNOWLEDGEMENTS

The author gratefully acknowledges funding from the UK Foundation for Canadian Studies, British Association for Canadian Studies, and from the University College of Ripon and York St John. She would like to thank staff, volunteers, artists, and Elders at the Native Heritage Centre (Duncan), U'Mista Cultural Centre (Cormorant Island), 'Ksan Historical Village Museum (Hazelton), Cape Mudge Museum (Quadra Island), Skidegate Cultural Centre, and Masset Museum (Haida Gwaii). Thanks are due to Sandra White (Canadian National Aboriginal Tourism Association/Native Tourism Development Program, Vancouver), Colin Campbell and Jennifer Nicol (Ministry of Small Business, Tourism and Culture, Victoria), to Professor Gregory Ashworth (University of Groningen) and Professor Peter Murphy (University of Victoria) for their invaluable comments at different stages and, lastly, to family members for their patience and help.

REFERENCES

Ablers, P.C., and James, W.R. (1983). Tourism and the changing photographic images of the Great Lakes Indians. *Annals of Tourism Research*, 10(1), 123-148.

Ablers, P.C., and James, W.R. (1988). Travel photography. A methodological approach. *Annals of Tourism Research*, 15(1), 134-158.

Ames, M. (1986). *Museums, the public and anthropology: A study of the anthropology of anthropology.* Vancouver: University of British Columbia Press.

Appadurai, A. (1990). Disjuncture & difference in the global cultural economy. In M. Featherstone (Ed.), *Global culture: nationalism, globalization and modernity* (pp. 295-310). London: Sage.

Ashworth, G., and Voogh, H. (1990). Can places be sold for tourism? In G.J. Ashworth and B. Goodall (Eds.), *Marketing tourism places* (pp. 1-22). London: Routledge.

Blanchini, F., and Parkinson, M. (Eds.) (1993). *Cultural policy and urban regeneration: the Western European experience.* Manchester: Manchester University Press

Boldt, M. (1993). *Surviving as Indians.* Toronto: University of Toronto Press.

Canada. British Columbia (1980). *TISDA. Travel industry development study agreement. The development of Native Tourism in British Columbia.* Government of Canada: Province of B.C.

Canada. Province of British Columbia (1991-1994). *First Nations products and events. Guide to Native sites etc.* Ministry of Small Business, Tourism and Culture, Ministry of Aboriginal Affairs & First Nations Tourism Association, Victoria.

Canada. Province of British Columbia (1992-94). *Community tourism action program reports.* Ministry of Small Business, Tourism and Culture, Victoria.

Canada. Province of British Columbia (1993). *British Columbia First Nations guide.* Ministry of Tourism and Ministry Responsible for Culture/First Nations Tourism Association, Victoria.

Canada. Province of British Columbia (1993). *Community tourism action program.* Ministry of Small Business, Tourism and Culture, Victoria.

Canadian Government Office of Tourism and Regional Economic Expansion (1982). *Province of British Columbia Tourism Development Strategy: The Vancouver Island Tourism Region,* Ottawa.

Canadian Government Office of Tourism and Regional Economic Expansion (1982). *Province of British Columbia tourism development strategy: The Vancouver Island tourism region,* Ottawa.

Cassidy, F. (Ed.) (1991). *Reaching just settlements.* Lantzville: Oolichan Books.

Cassidy, F., and Seward, S.B. (1991). *Alternatives to social assistance in Indian communities.* Lantzville/South Halifax: Oolichan Books & The Institute for Research in Public Policy.

Clifford, J. (1991). Four northwest coast museums: Travel reflections. In I. Karp and S. Lavine (Eds.), *Exhibiting cultures: The poetics and politics of museum display* (pp. 212-54). Washington, DC & London: Smithsonian Institution Press.

Clifford, J. (1993). On collecting art and culture. In S. During (Ed.), *The cultural studies reader* (pp. 49-73). London: Routledge.

Clifford, J.E. (1988). *The predicament of culture: Twentieth century ethnography, literature & art.* Cambridge, Mass.: Harvard University Press.

Cohen, E. (1993). The study of touristic images of native people: Mitigating the stereotype of a stereotype. In D.G. Pearce and R.W. Butler (Eds.), *Tourism research, critiques and challenges* (pp. 36-69). London: Routledge.

Cole, D. (1985). *Captured heritage. The scramble for Northwest Coast artifacts.* Seattle & London: University of Washington Press.

Cummings, M., and Katz, R. (Eds.) (1987). *The patron state, government and the arts in Europe, North America and Japan.* Oxford: Oxford University Press.

Dann, G., and Cohen, E. (1991). Sociology of tourism. *Annals of Tourism Research*, 18(1), 155-169.

De Vries, P. (1978). Towards an anthropology of tourism. *Canadian Review of Sociology and Anthropology*, 15, 478-484.

Elias, P.D. (1991). *Development of Aboriginal People's communities*. North York: Captus Press.

Francis, D. (1992). *The imaginary Indian. The image of the Indian in Canadian culture*. Vancouver: Arsenal Pulp Press.

Going Native on Canada's West Coast, *The Sunday Times* 18.9.94.

Harron, S., and Weiler, B. (1992). Ethnic tourism. In B. Weiler and C. Hall (Eds.), *Special interest tourism* (pp. 83-94). London: Bell Haven.

Heritage Conservation Statutes Amendment Act, 1994. Bill 21. Province of British Columbia. Ministry of Small Business, Tourism and Culture: Heritage Conservation Branch.

Hirano, R. (1993). *Keep our circle strong. A cultural renewal facility for the Peigan Nation. A consultative document*. Lethbridge: Robert Hirano Architect Limited.

Hummon, D.M. (1988). Tourist worlds: Tourist advertising, ritual and American experience. *Sociological Quarterly*, 10, 199-202.

Jansen, P. (1993). *Who's the boss? Native guides and white tourists in the Canadian Wilderness, 1850-1914*. Paper presented at the British Association for Canadian Studies Annual Conference, Cambridge, April 1993.

Kearns, G., and Philo, C. (Eds.) (1993). *Selling places: The city as cultural capital*. Oxford: Pergamon Press.

Knight, R.V., and Gappert, G. (Eds.) (1989). *Cities in a global society*. Beverley Hills: Sage.

Kramer, P. (1994). *Native sites in Western Canada*. Canmore: Altitude Publishing Canada Ltd.

Murphy, P. (1985). *Tourism: A community approach*. New York: Methuen.

Nash, D. (1978). Tourism as a form of imperialism. In V.L. Smith (Ed.), *Hosts and guests: The anthropology of tourism* (pp. 33-47). Oxford: Basil Blackwell.

Native Voice, 1994, May/June, 4-5.

Norris Nicholson, H. (1992). Cultural centres or trading posts. *Museums Journal*, 8(2), 31-34.

Norris Nicholson, H. (forthcoming). *The Commonwealth Games, tourism and cultural representation: The politics of being hosts in British Columbia*. Manuscript submitted for publication.

Parker, B. (1992). Aboriginal tourism in Canada. From perception to reality. In L.J. Reid (Ed.), *Community and cultural tourism. Conference proceedings* (pp. 14-20). Travel and Tourism Research Association/Statistics Canada.

Przeclawski, K. (1993). Tourism as the subject of interdisciplinary research. In D.G. Pearce and R.W. Butler (Eds.), *Tourism research, critiques and challenges* (pp. 9-19). London: Routledge.

Richardson, B. (Ed.) (1989). *Anger and renewal in Indian country*. Toronto: Summerhill Press/Assembly of First Nations.

Richardson, R. (1992). Introduction. In T. Modood (Ed.), *Not easy being British. Colour, culture and citizenship* (pp. 1-7). London & Stoke-on-Trent: Runnymede Trust & Trentham Books.

Robbins, M. (1992). Community-based tourism in remote native communities. In L.J. Reid (Ed.), *Community and cultural tourism. Conference proceedings* (pp. 133-136). Travel and Tourism Research Association/ Statistics Canada.

Stewart, K. (1992). Aboriginal tourism in Canada. Challenges in Community and Cultural Tourism. In L.J. Reid (Ed.), *Community and cultural tourism. Conference proceedings* (pp. 9-13). Travel and Tourism Research Association/Statistics Canada.

Walker, E.G. (1987). Native involvement in heritage resource development: A Sakatchewan example. *Native Studies Review*, 3(2), 123-131.

Watson, G.L., and Kopachevesky, J.P. (1994). Interpretations of tourism as commodity. *Annals of Tourism Research*, 21(3), 643-660.

ENDNOTES

[1]   The indigenous inhabitants of Canada sanction a variety of terms to define them-
      selves. These terms have been used interchangeably in this chapter for stylistic
      variation.

[2]   Indigenous tourism may be defined as a tourism business owned 51 percent or
      more by Aboriginal peoples.

[3]   Interview with Director of Sales, The Native Heritage Centre, July 1994.

[4]   Although the Potlatch or gift-giving ceremony was banned by Canadian law in
      1885, unofficial practice continued among the Kwakaka'waka' people of Alert
      Bay, off north east Vancouver Island. The ban was finally lifted in 1951 and the
      gradual process of returning Potlatch collections during the 1980s assumed
      considerable significance in the process of cultural and political revitalization.

[5]   Interview with Manager, Tourism Planning, Victoria, November 1994.

[6]   Interview with Board Member (British Columbia Region), Canadian National
      Aboriginal Tourism Association, November 1994.

[7]   Correspondence with Colin Coates, Centre of Canadian Studies, University of
      Edinburgh, April 1995.

[8]   Interviews at The Native Heritage Centre, Duncan, June-July 1994.

[9]   Interview with Deputy Editor, *Museums Journal*, November 1994.

[10]   Interview with Director of Sales, The Native Heritage Centre, Duncan, July 1994.

Linking Heritage and Tourism in an Asian City: The Case of Yogyakarta, Indonesia

Geoffrey Wall

Department of Geography, University of Waterloo

INTRODUCTION

In a frequently-cited paper on tourism and conservation, Budowski (1976) argued, in the context of natural areas, that three possible relationships exist: conflict, coexistence and symbiosis. These relationships are found with respect to all forms of heritage, built or living. In towns and cities throughout the world there is increasing interest in forging links between heritage and tourism as a means of attracting tourists, sustaining heritage, and stimulating economies (Ashworth and Tunbridge, 1990). Thus, means of achieving symbiosis between heritage and tourism are increasingly being sought.

At the same time, there are those, mostly academics, who fear the possibility of commoditization of culture and promote the maintenance of authentic experiences (Cohen, 1988). These are legitimate concern. Nevertheless, it is argued that commoditization and authenticity are relative rather than absolute terms, that there is tension between the two concepts, that neither concept alone is adequate as a basis for heritage management, and that compromise is required if a symbiotic relationship between heritage and tourism is to be fostered. Indeed, more than compromise is necessary if positive relationships and the mutual benefits of symbiosis are to be achieved: acceptable trade-offs should be actively sought. It follows that simplistic notions of carrying capacity are not very helpful in resolving complex planning and management issues and that concepts such as Limits of Acceptable Change (Stankey and McCool, 1984), which acknowledge that it is seldom possible to maximize benefits and minimize costs at the same time, have greater potential to empower local people and lead to more equitable decisions concerning the uses of resources.

Destination areas usually wish to be involved in tourism because of the perceived potential economic benefits. This requires that they have something to sell and, in many cases, this is likely to be rooted in aspects of their heritage, otherwise the experience is likely to be artificial. At the same time, in its purest form, authenticity would require the complete absence of tourists, so that an authentic touristic experience, as it relates to the heritage of others, is an impossibility, a juxtaposition of non sequiturs for, by definition, tourists are outsiders who arrive from another ·place. Thus, intermediate positions on the use-preservation continuum should be sought, maintained and enhanced through careful planning and management.

Heritage is often viewed as something that should be preserved. Other perspectives are that heritage can be conserved, enhanced and even used (Wall, 1989). Heritage may be viewed as a resource which can be managed and shared. This view is likely to receive considerable support in places where conventional resources are under pressure but heritage resources are plentiful. This is the case in many countries in the so-called developing world.

Many developing countries are blessed with rich heritage resources, including built structures such as monuments and archaeological sites, and cultural expressions such as music, dance, and drama. At the same time, such countries face substantial development challenges and, often, limited options in addressing those challenges. In such circumstances it is understandable that there is often a desire to employ heritage resources to meet development goals. However, it is not a simple task to sustain heritage and, at the same time, to stimulate economies. This chapter will examine and illustrate the opportunities and challenges in fostering symbiosis between heritage and tourism in cities of the South, through a discussion of the case of Yogyakarta, Indonesia.

YOGYAKARTA, INDONESIA

The City of Yogyakarta is located in Java, Indonesia, and is widely acknowledged as being the centre of Javanese culture (Figure 1,11). The city is the capital of Yogyakarta Special Province and the locus of the Yogyakarta Sultanate, which dates from 230 years ago. The city has a population of approximately 650,000, including the suburban area around Yogyakarta *Kotamadya* (Municipality).

The centre of Yogyakarta is dominated by the *kraton* (Sultan's palace) and Malioboro Street, which extends in a northerly direction towards Mount Merapi, an active volcano that erupted with considerable force and some loss of life late in 1994 (Figure 1,11). The *kraton* itself attracts tourists to its museums and cultural displays, and Malioboro Street, with its mix of souvenir vendors and department stores, is always crowded and vibrant. The city is well-served with commercial accommodation of many types: hotels are scattered throughout the city and two clusters of guest houses, restaurants, and souvenir outlets in Sosrowijayan and Prawirotaman cater especially to the needs of the budget traveller.

Yogyakarta has a wealth of both hard and soft heritage resources. Hard resources are archaeological sites, buildings and other structures, and Yogyakarta

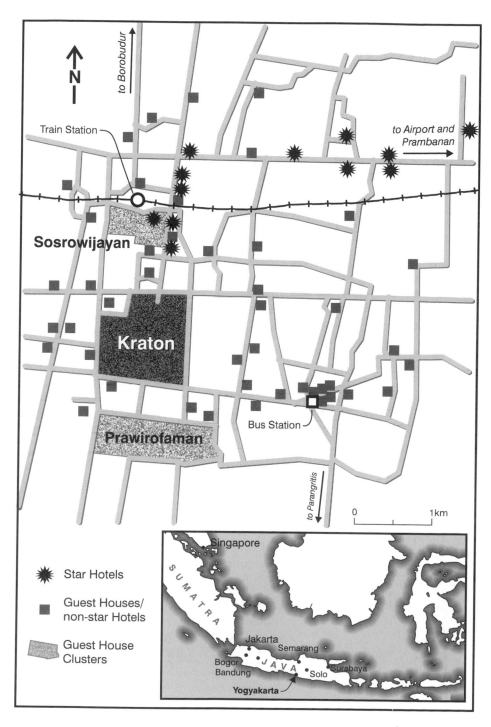

Figure 11.1   Map of Yogyakarta City.

and the surrounding area are particularly blessed with important historical places, including two UNESCO heritage sites, as well as a multiplicity of other important historic sites and monuments. Soft resources are other cultural expressions of a less tangible nature, such as music (e.g. *gamelan*), dance, drama, and *wayang kulit* (shadow puppets). Yogyakarta also possesses a wealth of arts and crafts, including batik, silver, leather, pottery, and wood products which are sold to tourists. In reality, these cultural expressions are not distinct, the one informing the other, and tourists may be interested in purchasing craft products for their own sake, or as mementoes of other heritage experiences. However, it is Borobudur and Prambanan, the two UNESCO heritage sites located a short distance to the north-west and east of the city respectively, which are of particular renown and which attract both international and domestic tourists.

SELECTED HERITAGE SITES IN YOGYAKARTA

In order to illustrate the wealth of heritage resources available in Yogyakarta, four of many built heritage sites will be described briefly (Oey, 1991).

1. Borobudur is located on the Kedu Plain amidst rice fields and coconut groves, approximately 42 kilometres west of Yogyakarta (Figure 11.2). To the north and west are volcanoes which reach 3,000 metres (10,000 feet) in height. Borobudur is the largest Buddhist monument in the world. There were five phases of construction, but it probably dates from 750-850 AD and includes 1,460 stone relief panels, on four levels, which portray the life of Buddha, as well as 432 Buddha statues, and 72 stuppa surrounding a massive central stuppa.

    The monument was first described for the west by Raffles in 1817 when it was still partially covered by volcanic debris. The first conservation measures were begun in 1870, and a major restoration took place from 1907 to 1911. However, deterioration continued and a major restoration effort was undertaken by the Indonesian Government and UNESCO from 1975 to 1984. One million stones were taken apart, treated and replaced on a concrete base, residents in the vicinity were relocated, and the surroundings were made into a park.

2. Prambanan is located approximately 10 kilometres northeast of the city (Figure 11.3). It consists of more than 50 structures, the most prominent of which is the Loro Jonggrang temple complex which was completed in 856 AD to mark the victory of Hindu King Rakai Pikatan over his Buddhist rival. The complex includes numerous Ramayana reliefs and both Buddhist and Hindu sites.

    Prambanan was "discovered" in 1871 by Mackenzie (Raffles's surveyor). Following some earlier efforts, restoration began on the main complex between 1930 and 1933 and was completed on the main Siva temple in 1953. Restoration of the Brahma temple was completed in 1987 and is continuing in other parts of the complex.

Figure 11.2   Borobudur.

Figure 11.3   Prambanan.

3. Taman Sari (Fragrant Gardens), or the Water Palace, was built by Sultan Hamengkubuwono I between 1758 and 1781 (Figure 11.4). It is located in the precincts of the *kraton* (the Sultan's palace) near the centre of the city and consists of 57 buildings, some of which are two stories in height, as well as sunken bathing pools, underground tunnels and secluded chambers for meditation. The hydraulic works proved difficult to maintain and they were damaged in the Java War, 1825-1830, and by an earthquake in 1867. Some restoration took place in the 1970s but only the central pools have been rebuilt, although they no longer contain water. Many buildings are in a poor state of repair and the area has been occupied by numerous settlers and their dwellings.

Figure 11.4   Taman Sari.

4. Ratu Boko Palace is located approximately 3 kilometres south of Prambanan and affords excellent views of the surrounding area (Figure 11.5). It was probably built in the eighth century and "discovered" by Van Boeckholtz in 1790. However, it is only in the last few years that it has attracted much attention. The site has five main groupings: the main gate, public audience hall, royal audience hall, princess' place and caves. The site is the shared responsibility of the Department of Archaeology (preservation), PT Taman (tourism) and a multisectoral coordinating group. Archaeological investigations are in progress and residents who have colonized the ruins are being displaced. However, the pressure to develop the site is such that tourism is being encouraged before the archaeological investigation has been completed.

Figure 11.5   Ratu Boko.

Space does not permit a more detailed description of the tourist attractions and opportunities of Yogyakarta. Indeed, books have been written on individual sites as well as on specific cultural expressions, such as Javanese dance and music. However, sufficient information has been presented to confirm the rich heritage and international significance of this Javanese City.

With two UNESCO World Heritage Sites on its periphery, a multitude of other monuments and archaeological sites, a rich heritage of music, dance, arts, crafts, and other cultural expressions, Yogyakarta would appear to possess ample heritage resources to attract tourists. However, a distinction should be made between tourism resources and tourism products which can be sold to potential visitors. The latter requires that resources be accessible and that supporting infrastructure be available to meet visitor needs.

TOURISM IN YOGYAKARTA

Yogyakarta is already a much-visited destination attracting large numbers of domestic and international tourists. In 1993, 910,251 visitors, of whom 610,251 were domestic and 299,433 foreign, stayed in Yogyakarta's hotels (Parpostel, 1994). Indeed, it is the second most-visited tourist destination in Indonesia after Bali. A substantial and varied supply of visitor accommodation exists and construction of additional accommodation for visitors is proceeding apace. However, occupancy rates are low. Average length of stay is only 1.7 days, slightly longer for domestic tourists and slightly shorter for international visitors. Average expenditure per visitor is also low when compared to other destinations in Indonesia such as Bali.

Some Challenges

Yogyakarta faces a great many challenges that will need to be addressed if the benefits from heritage tourism are to be increased. The opportunities have been recognized by UNESCO in its support of a cultural tourism plan for Yogyakarta and Central Java (Directorate General of Tourism, UNESCO/UNDP, 1992) and they have also been addressed from a marketing perspective by Wall (1992). Of the many challenges which could be identified, five have been selected for further discussion.

Site Maintenance

The large number and great size of the heritage sites mean that they cannot be sustained adequately with local resources. Some of these sites are of international significance and international money has been put into them, but the costs of restoration and maintenance, let alone interpretation, are enormous. Admission fees, even with differential fees for international and local users as currently exists, are unlikely to cover costs of preservation and restoration. Private investors, who gain from the existence of these sites, put their money into visitor accommodation, but do little to support the sites themselves or the broader infrastructure which tourists require. The costs fall primarily upon the public purse.

Involvement of Local People

In the case of three of the four sites described above, local people living in and around the sites have been displaced as the sites have been developed for tourism. In the case of Taman Sari, no official tourism development plan appears to exist. Many buildings are in a poor state of repair but many local residents are involved in activities, such as batik and painting, which have the potential to contribute to rather than detract from tourism experiences. If local people are to benefit economically from their built heritage, there is an urgent need to foster pride in and appreciation of local culture and to find ways for residents to participate in activities and decisions related to their monuments. Monument preservation, by itself, is insufficient.

Increasing Visitor Expenditures

It is self-evident but often overlooked that, in order to benefit economically from tourism, one must have something to sell. In Yogyakarta, the rich heritage of arts and crafts means that there is much to buy at reasonable prices. Unfortunately, the location of key sites on the periphery of the city takes visitors away from the core to places where there are fewer opportunities to spend money. Successful development of Ratu Boko could exacerbate this trend.

It is true that the daily average of more than 5,000 visitors to Borobudur provides direct daily employment in the informal sector for between 700 (in the low season) and 1,000 people (in the high season) who work as small-scale entrepreneurs selling souvenirs or food and beverages or acting as guides or working in guest houses in establishments which surround the site. More than 75 percent originate from the local community adjacent to the site (W. Nuryanti, personal communication, 1995). Nevertheless, there is a need to get people into the city centre and to retain them for longer periods so that they can spend money. Giving greater prominence to Taman Sari may assist in this direction.

Transportation

A distinction should be made between transportation to and within destination areas. Although it is easy to arrange tours and transportation to Borobudur and Prambanan from Yogyakarta, the city cannot be reached directly by international air transportation, and this has resulted in it being accorded the status of a secondary destination, particularly for international visitors. This situation is likely to remain unchanged and even become exacerbated by the construction of a new airport in Surakarta, approximately one-hour drive to the east. Increased frequency of domestic air services to and from Yogyakarta has had unexpected consequences: it has allowed visitors to fly from Jakarta and Bali, to see the main sites, and to move on or return on the same day, thus making it a day-trip destination, particularly for Japanese tour groups on short visits to Indonesia. Thus, while the number of visitors has increased, the length-of-stay problem has been magnified.

Many domestic visitors arrive by bus or by train, but although the services are cheap and reliable, they are also extremely time-consuming, increasing travel time by a factor of six or eight when compared to air travel. Thus, these forms of transportation are not popular among most international visitors.

Product Diversification and Market Positioning

Yogyakarta provides access to an extremely rich number and variety of high quality, hard and soft, heritage resources of interest to both domestic and international visitors. However, little information is available on domestic tourism in Indonesia although it is clearly of major significance to Yogyakarta.

In the international marketplace, the image of Yogyakarta is indistinct and dominated by the two UNESCO sites of Borobudur and Prambanan (Wall, 1992). Many travel agents in the west have never heard of Borobudur or Prambanan, cannot spell Yogyakarta, muddle it up with Jakarta, cannot find it on a map, and are ignorant of the cultural treasures to be found in this area. Lack of a clear image means that those international visitors who do visit Yogyakarta are not fully aware of the richness of the heritage, plan to stay only briefly, and move on with only a superficial exposure to Javanese history and culture.

For many potential international visitors, the area has no reputation at all: it is not on the list of possible vacation destinations. Alternatively, it is viewed as having a somewhat narrow set of offerings. Either way, the result is the same—the potential visitor does not come or, at best, stays only briefly.

It is true that opportunities for experiences other than world-class monuments, such as natural areas, fine dining, or night life, are limited in Yogyakarta, although it is a major university centre and has excellent shopping. However, evening cultural performances are widely available. Yogyakarta has more and greater diversity of offerings when placed in a broader regional context when the south coast of Java, the slopes of volcanic Mount Merapi and even the Dieng Plateau (an area of thermal springs and pools and ancient Hindu temples) fall within day-trip distance.

At present, however, Yogyakarta appears not to have a sophisticated marketing strategy nor the data on which one can be based.

CONCLUSION

It has been argued that, if heritage tourism is to be a reality and if a symbiotic relationship between heritage and tourism is to be forged, legitimate concerns about the provision of authentic experiences and commoditization of culture will need to be modified and softened. To date, in Yogyakarta, emphasis has been placed upon preserving the major archaeological sites and monuments, but securing the structures is only the first step in developing a tourist product. Although it is an important first step, other factors which require attention include interpretation to explain the significance of the monuments to visitors, transportation to convey international visitors to the city, the provision of supplementary services and activities to increase length of stay, improved marketing, the development of a stronger information base to inform decision makers, and improved coordination of those involved in different aspects of the tourist industry.

Heritage can be regarded as a resource; a resource with which many developing countries are well-endowed when other resources may be in short supply. However, the availability of a wealth of heritage resources does not automatically lead to the development of a successful tourism industry: the tourist product is made up of many components of which attractions, although important, are only one. Others include accommodation and restaurants, supporting infrastructure such as water and electricity supplies and sewerage systems, information, product packaging, and transportation to and within the destination area. This is a lesson which is relevant to all mid-sized and small urban places, both in developed and developing countries, especially those in rural areas or removed from the airports of hub cities or major highways.

ACKNOWLEDGEMENT

The comments of Ms. Wiendu Nuryanti, Lecturer in Architecture, Gadjah Mada University, Yogyakarta, and Director of STUPPA Indonesia, on a draft of this chapter, are very much appreciated.

REFERENCES

Ashworth, G., and Tunbridge, J. (1990). *The tourist-historic city.* London: Belhaven.

Budowski, G. (1976). Tourism and conservation: Conflict, coexistence or symbiosis. *Environmental Conservation,* 3, 27-31.

Cohen, E. (1988). Authenticity and commoditization in tourism. *Annals of Tourism Research,* 20(1), 371-386.

Directorate General of Tourism, UNESCO/UNDP (1992). *Cultural tourism development Central Java - Final report.* Yogyakarta.

Oey, E. (Ed.) (1991) *Java.* Berkeley and Singapore: Periplus Editions.

Parpostel (1994). *Statistik Pariwisata, Pos dan Telekomunikasi Daerah Istemewa Yogyakarta, Tahun 1993.* Yogyakarta: Departemen Pariwisata, Pos dan Telekomunikasi.

Stankey, G., and McCool, S.F. (1984). Carrying capacity in recreational settings: Evolution, appraisal and application. *Leisure Sciences,* 6, 453-474.

Wall, G. (1989). An international perspective on historic sites, recreation and tourism. *Recreation Resources Review,* 14(4), 10-14.

Wall, G. (1992). Cultural tourism: How do we market it? In W. Nuryanti (Ed.), *Universal tourism: Enriching or degrading culture? Proceedings of the International Conference on Cultural Tourism* (pp. 183-194). Yogyakarta: Gadjah Mada University Press.

An Institution in Transition: The Royal British Columbia Museum's Futures Project

Bill Barkley

Executive Director, Royal British Columbia Museum

INTRODUCTION

The last few years have seen some dramatic changes in our world. It is tempting to assume that what we are experiencing is not a permanent change but just part of a cycle—once the cycle is complete, everything will get back to normal. Political and economic events tend to indicate that the concept of what is normal is changing. Some observers have indicated that what we are experiencing will fundamentally change our societies. Institutions such as museums are part of the fabric of our society. They are being impacted, and they will have to adapt to this change if they are going to succeed and survive.

Poor economic conditions result in a priority being placed on what society believes is essential and, therefore, a diminishing funding of what is regarded as nonessential. Museums, art galleries, symphony orchestras, and theatre companies are currently suffering from the withdrawal of public and private funds. The inference is that these institutions have a low priority in the maintenance of a healthy society. This raises questions in the minds of people responsible for these types of institutions. Do the cultural institutions have an important role in a healthy community, or are they a frill to be funded only when surplus funds are available? Is there something these institutions are doing, or are not doing, that supports the public's decision to place these organizations low on the funding priority list?

In Canada, some institutions suffering from the decline in support have come to the attention of the news media. The Art Gallery of Ontario in Toronto, a large and successful institution, received a great deal of press for both extensive staff layoffs and a several-month closure of the gallery. The Vancouver Museum was closed for several months as the result of a dispute between management and staff over an operational restructuring designed to deal with a decline in available funding. The Glenbow Museum, in an effort to secure its economic future, reduced its staffing and offered part of its collection for sale. These are some notable Canadian examples. It is, however, a worldwide phenomena. In 1992, at the triennial meeting of the International Committee on Museums, the topic discussed both formally in the sessions, and informally amongst the delegates, was the funding crisis.

In the United States, the financial crisis was captured in a headline in *USA Today*: "Culture Shock: Museums Feel Cash Crunch" and in a quote by Robert Buck, Director, Brooklyn Museum: "It's a cultural Chernobyl."

THE ROYAL BRITISH COLUMBIA MUSEUM

The Royal British Columbia Museum (RBCM) is an established multi-disciplinary museum that was created in 1886 as the result of a public petition. The expressed public concern was that natural history objects and anthropological artefacts were being removed from the Province. It was deemed essential that the Province create an institution to collect and preserve the physical evidence of the human and natural history of the Province.

The RBCM is located in British Columbia's capital city of Victoria on Vancouver Island. Greater Victoria has a population just under 300,000. The mandate of the RBCM requires the institution to make its programming available throughout the Province.

Since its beginnings in 1886, the RBCM has amassed a vast collection numbering 10 million individual objects. Collections have been developed in natural history, recent history and aboriginal history. By mandate, the RBCM limits its collections to those of British Columbian origin.

The collections provide the basis for research at the RBCM. Research remains an active pursuit of the curatorial staff. Staff publish both in publications produced by the RBCM and in refereed professional journals.

The RBCM has had great success in its public programming over the last two and a half decades. Exhibits, publications, school programs and innovative community programming receive tremendous public response and are lauded by colleagues around the world. Attendance for the exhibitions has been between 800,000 and one million visitors per year since 1972.

The RBCM is housed in buildings constructed in 1967. The two main buildings are the 13-storey Fannin building, which houses most of the collections and the curatorial staff, and the three-storey display building, which provides space for exhibits and public programs.

The RBCM has 100 staff, 300 volunteers, and a membership of 10,000 via the Friends of the Royal British Columbia Museum organization. There is no board of directors, since the museum is run directly by the Province of British Columbia.

DIMENSIONS OF A PROBLEM

Throughout most of the eighties, the RBCM received cuts to its budget. The result was reduced programming and decreased staffing levels. In 1992, a 7 percent cut to the budget resulted in over 90 percent of the funds normally available for research, public programs, and acquisitions being reallocated to cover fixed costs. The situation had reached the point where the building's operating and maintenance costs, utility costs, and salaries were consuming the budget at an alarming rate. Clearly, we were reaching the point where no funds for program presentation or development would be available as fixed costs increased.

Adding to the impending financial problem were the 27 year old buildings. The Fannin building had recently been cleaned of asbestos at a cost of $8.5 million. That cost was amortized over 25 years and added to our growing building costs. The public display building, having had approximately 25 million pass through its portals, was in need of an upgrade. A number of issues related to building codes and completely worn-out and unreliable escalators needed urgent attention.

The lack of growth in budget allocation resulted in virtually no change to the exhibits. As a result, the annual attendance began to show a measurable decline. Declining attendance was reflected in decreasing revenues.

As a government agency, the museum's ability to raise funds through sponsorships and donations has always been limited. While the Friends of the RBCM have raised modest sums for special projects, they are hampered by a perception on the part of potential donors or sponsors that gifts are being given to the government.

Demands for product and information from many areas of the museum are increasing. The information contained in the biological collections is in demand by government agencies for studies related to environmental issues, such as biodiversity. Information from the aboriginal collection is in demand by both aboriginal groups and government, who are negotiating land claims. Furthermore, the public is demanding change in the galleries and in the program presentations.

The situation in which the RBCM found itself in 1992 is typical of that of many similar institutions. There are no quick or easy solutions.

THE FUTURES PROJECT

A gloomy future seemed projected by the situation just described. Increasing fixed costs and decreasing or static funding would result in reduced staff and decreased activity in public programming, research and collection acquisition. If this trend were to continue, within a decade, and without some kind of creative intervention, the RBCM would be non-functional or even non-existent.

Other boards and museum directors were faced with the same issue and the same tough decision. They could wait out the recession, in the hopes that when the economy strengthened, the museum would get increased funding and could be revived. The other option was to re-invent the museum to withstand and avoid the vagaries of the economy. After all, massive economic and social change was affecting every aspect of our society. It seemed reasonable, then, that our institutions must also change and adapt.

In the summer of 1992, we created the Futures Project. The purpose of the project was to create a positive future for the RBCM. The three staff assigned to the project were relieved of all other duties. The project was led by the senior manager of the institution (the author); his duties were reassigned to another manager. A Steering Committee was established that included staff from the RBCM and from two cooperating societies affiliated with the RBCM, the Friends of the RBCM, and the Fannin Foundation.

As the project proceeded, the Steering Committee developed an approach to its task that took shape in five phases.

THE PHASES OF THE FUTURES PROJECT

1.   Analysis and Recommendations

This stage began with a literature search. This included reviewing articles on changing directions in museums, reading other museums' annual reports, and examining their planning documents.

Having resolved to seek out a new model for the museum, the Steering Committee established a process whereby staff and museum volunteers undertook an examination of the past and made recommendations for the future.

In particular, four specific task groups were established, covering public programs, collections, research and support services, in order to review recommendations that came in from staff and volunteers. Their priorities were to look for ways to save money, earn money, and become more involved with the community. To ensure that the chairperson of each task group remained as objective as possible, no one was allowed to chair a task group assigned to their own field. For example, the chair of the public programs task group was a staff member from collections. Furthermore, each of the groups were represented by a cross-section of RBCM staff.

2.   Consultation

We determined early in the project that we would seek input from people outside the RBCM. Since the RBCM's mandate covered the entire province of British Columbia, we would obtain a sampling of opinion from communities across the Province.

We initiated a variety of methods to gather the input we sought. The entire museum staff worked together to produce an open house, where visitors were given the opportunity to comment on what they saw and what they would like to see. Formal focus groups, meetings with specific interest groups and meetings with invitees from a cross-section of each selected community were held across the Province. We hired a consultant to help us develop a process for community consultation, and a unique and successful technique was created. As an aid to the consultation sessions, a vision of the museum's future, as seen by the staff, was graphically represented on a nine-foot by three-foot mural. The focus group leader used this colourful, cartoon-like graphic very successfully to animate the discussions.

3.   Experimentation

Some promising ideas that emerged during the consultations were selected and immediately put into effect as experiments. These ideas were economic ventures of a risky nature. We knew that some might be successful, and would thus be continued, and that others would fail. The experiments that failed would be regarded as significant as the experiments that succeeded in terms of what each venture taught us about directing our new course.

4. Planning

A plan was necessary to organize the changing direction of the RBCM and to satisfy the governing body (the Province of British Columbia). A comprehensive five-year business plan and an annual plan for the first (and, thereafter, successive) year(s) were to be produced.

5. Implementation

The implementation strategy and approach were planned by the Steering Committee in consultation with the senior management of the museum.

THE RESULTS OF THE FUTURES PROJECT

The process outlined above did not occur in a linear fashion—some of the phases occurred simultaneously. The end product was a five-year business plan (1993-1998). The process took nine months to complete. The remainder of this chapter outlines the results of each of the phases.

1. Analysis and Recommendations

The analysis and recommendation phase produced over 300 recommendations from staff and volunteers. Many of the suggestions were both innovative and creative, and they guided the planning process.

2. Consultation

The consultation process emerged as a vital portion of the Futures Project. Altogether, several hundred people were met with, and information, suggestions and requests were tabled. Data gathered from the formal focus groups presented us with a range of conflicting expectations. The tourism focus group, for instance, wanted more money spent on the tourist product, while the scientific focus group wanted less attention paid to exhibitions and more attention paid to research. The public meetings held across the Province produced a great deal of useful information. While the input was often repetitive, new ideas and new perspectives emerged.

We compiled the results of the consultations into a report, the essence of which revealed that our public likes *what* we do, but wants us to change *how* we do it. The consultations affirmed that museums are considered important institutions in our society. It also became clear that there was a feeling that the relationship between the RBCM and its public needed attention. While we needed to continue to develop information through collecting and researching, and continue to provide the information in innovative forms of public programming, we needed to become more accessible, relevant and responsive to our public.

We were told that access to our collections, and the information they hold, needed to be made easier. In some cases, the barriers put in place for security reasons were perceived as obstructions to the serious user. As well, our public wanted more access to museum staff and affiliates. They regarded the people at the RBCM as a resource that they wanted to be able to access.

We were told that the RBCM needed to address its activities to issues that are relevant to the lives of individuals and to the society as a whole. This implies that the public should be more involved in planning and decision-making within the museum.

Finally, the consultation revealed a fair amount of consensus on how the RBCM should be funded. It was agreed that government needed to maintain its investment in the RBCM. It was also clear that government could not fund the RBCM in the future to the same degree as it had in the past. As well as carefully controlling costs, the RBCM had to earn more of its own revenue. As a result, the RBCM would need to examine areas of potential entrepreneurial activity.

3. Experimentation

As expected, some of the economic ventures were a success; others were not.

- Museums are storehouses of information, and it was felt that this information could be made more easily accessible by using computer technology. A large computer service organization donated the services of a media specialist. As the project unfolded, and a business case emerged, it became apparent that making information available in this format required a large, up front expenditure. At this point, the museum could not afford to fully exploit this opportunity, and the project was shut down. The only product that emerged from the project was a screen saver that displayed images from the collection.

- Not necessarily a new idea, but new to the RBCM, was a gallery rental program. After a pre-market survey was completed, groups were booked and the RBCM galleries were opened for receptions and dinners. This experiment was very successful financially, and it helped the museum establish new connections within the community.

- A series of eco-tours were designed that used our curatorial experts as guides and educational resources for each destination. These tours have been well received by the community and have been a modest financial success.

- Another series of tours were designed to show the public different parts of the large collection housed in the 13-storey Fannin building. While these group tours were a modest success, a three-day open house, where parts of the collection were temporarily displayed in the exhibits building, attracted 14,000 people.

- An idea that came to us from the Australian Museum in Sydney, Australia, addressed our desire to make the museum more relevant and accessible. We developed a "Quick Response Team". The idea was to identify current issues that the museum would be able to interpret to the community with useful information in a very timely and succinct manner. In the form of a small exhibit, objects from our collection, print material and newspaper articles would cover such topical issues as a dangerous, hallucinogenic plant discovered by teenagers, a women's issues celebration, a local woman's remarkable contribution to science, and an exhibit of World War II anniversary information related to British Columbians.

4. Planning

There were a number of planning documents produced at various stages in the project. The document, *Framework for the Museum's Future: Challenges and Changes*, January 1993, was published early in the project. This document was primarily intended to identify the problems faced by the museum and to outline possible solutions. A one-year annual business plan was produced for the 1993/1994 fiscal year. It established some of the directions that eventually emerged in the final document, *Five Year Business Plan: 1993-1998*.

As part of the process, another 17 strategy documents were produced. Some were specific to local issues, such as a downtown redevelopment plan. Others were directed to the functioning of the museum—a collections strategy, a computer systems strategy, a research strategy, for example.

5. Implementation

As with any change, implementation can be tumultuous. How does a "Futures Project" stop being a project and start becoming the future of the museum? While the Futures Project ended as a formal activity in July, 1994, the ventures it designed and promoted, and the new directions it charted are still being integrated into the existing operation. The implementation is gradual, and now in its third year at the point of writing this paper.

THE FUTURE OF THE RBCM

The Futures Project was essentially an appeal to the public to make some sense of, and help us find a solution for, the increasing budgetary cutbacks that threatened the museum's very existence. The public answered unequivocally the question about why institutions like the museum do not have priority in times of economic crises. They told us that what we do is extremely important, that it is of great value, BUT they don't like how we do it. Specifically, they feel that the information, the collections and the staff are inaccessible. If we are to get our share of the public purse, we must find a way to become more relevant to their lives.

We have begun the quest. It is exciting and, in specific areas, difficult. Some staff and stakeholders are embracing the changes enthusiastically, and a minority of others are reluctant to acknowledge the need for change. Even with the gradual approach to implementing the Futures Project, the museum has experienced its share of distress and disruption. There have been both disappointments and successes.

Some of the successes include 23 consecutive Sundays where we "trucked" out the collection in cooperation with interested community organizations for our public to see. We had audiences of 4,000 show up on rainy Sundays. We formalized the rental of our galleries for events, and not only are we making money, but we have an overwhelming expression of support from hoteliers and conference organizers. We offered a training program for aboriginal people to prepare them for the eventual return of their artefacts from museum collections. The results were exciting, and we learned as much from the aboriginal students as we taught them.

We are changing the way we work with our public. We are trying to find ways to include them in our planning and decision-making processes. As well, we are changing the way we work inside the institution. We are looking for ways to enable staff to work across the organization as well as in their own area of speciality. Decisions on which projects we undertake are now the responsibility of a rotating staff committee (inherited from the Futures Project's Steering Committee). Management's task is to ensure the projects are implemented. We continue to change and evolve in partnership with our community.

Our ultimate objective is to make the Royal British Columbia Museum an essential part of the lives of British Columbians. The early signs are that we are succeeding!

REFERENCES

Royal British Columbia Museum (1993). *Framework for the museum's future: Challenges and changes.* Internal Report.

Futures Project, Royal British Columbia Museum (1993). *1993 Public consultations final report.* Internal Report.

Royal British Columbia Museum (1993). *Five year business plan: 1993-1998.* Internal Report.

Biltmore Estate and the Business of Historic Preservation

W.A.V. Cecil
The Biltmore Company

INTRODUCTION TO BILTMORE ESTATE

The Legacy

Biltmore Estate, located in the mountains of western North Carolina, was established at the turn of the century by George Vanderbilt as a winter retreat and a home for his vast collection of art and antiques. It was then, and continues to be, a showplace for both architectural excellence and landscape design at its finest. It still maintains a working farm, oversees successful managed forestry operations, and is one of the biggest employers in the western portion of North Carolina. It is also self-sufficient, functioning as a private enterprise.

All of the above was true 100 years ago when my grandfather, George Vanderbilt, opened Biltmore to friends and family for the first time Christmas Eve 1895. But these similarities have not occurred simply by happenstance. Consistency with Mr. Vanderbilt's original vision is what we strive daily to achieve. It is challenging, of course, to balance maintaining the integrity of an 1890s property in a 1990s world. Still, we seem to be holding our own. What follows is an overview of what has happened to my grandfather's estate over the past century, how we manage it today, and a glimpse at some of the issues which will undoubtedly have an impact on us all in the future.

The Property And Its Growth

The centrepiece of Biltmore Estate is Biltmore House, the largest home in the United States with 250 rooms and approximately four acres of floor space (Figure 13.1). The house was designed by Richard Morris Hunt, one of the founders of the American Institute of Architecture and a longtime friend and resident architect of the Vanderbilt family. Within the house is George Vanderbilt's original collection of furnishings, art, artefacts, and books totalling somewhere around 70,000 objects. The collection is a true reflection of my grandfather's tastes: eclectic, worldly, intelligent, diverse.

Figure 13.1   Biltmore Estate (photo courtesy The Biltmore Company © James Valentine, photographer).

Surrounding Biltmore House is a property of 8,000 acres, substantially smaller than the original scope of the estate at 125,000 acres. The balance of the land was deeded to the government after my grandfather died, and is now the nucleus of Pisgah National Forest. The landscaping on Biltmore Estate and much of the overall conceptualization and design for the property was the genius of Frederick Law Olmsted. It was, in fact, Olmsted who first suggested to George Vanderbilt that he consider establishing a working estate on his land in North Carolina. Today the house grounds are comprised of approximately 75 acres of beautifully landscaped gardens. The rest of the property is forest and farmland.

In the late 1970s, it became apparent that the next generation would need to expand and grow with the property and its enterprises in order to meet the challenges of maintaining the estate. I researched and developed the concept of a state-of-the-art winery and productive vineyards. Today, the Biltmore Estate Winery is the most visited winery in the United States, welcoming half a million guests annually. We produce approximately 75,000 cases of varietal wines each year and harvest over 200 tons of Vitis Vinifera grapes each fall. While the majority of our wine sales take place on the estate, we also currently distribute our wines off-site in the southeastern United States and view this business as one with great potential for expansion.

The land has always been the core of Biltmore Estate's existence. During Mr. Vanderbilt's day, one of the first orders of business in creating the estate was the development of vast nurseries to supply the land with plantings. Before the destruction of Biltmore nurseries in the 1917 flood, it had, in fact, become not only highly successful in providing healthy plants for Olmsted's plans for Biltmore; it had also become a revenue producer for the property. Biltmore nurseries' mail-order business was one of the earliest and most lucrative in the Southeast and offered one of the first horticultural catalogues in the country. Beyond landscaping, however, the land was also managed as farm and home to Vanderbilt's famous herd of Jersey cattle. Biltmore milk and dairy products were synonymous with the highest quality, and the yellow delivery wagons (and later trucks) were a familiar sight throughout the region.

Still, it was Biltmore's role as the site of the first school of scientific forestry in America which, perhaps above all other accomplishments, rises as the most significant. It was Olmsted in the late 1880s, visiting the acres of overworked farmland a young George Vanderbilt had purchased, who first suggested emulating what Europe had already begun:

"Such land in Europe," Olmsted suggested, "would be made a forest; partly if it belonged to a gentleman of large means, as a hunting preserve for game, mainly with a view to crops of timber. That would be a suitable and dignified business for you to engage in; it would, in the long run, be probably a fair investment of capital and it would be of great value to the country to have a thoroughly well organized and systematically conducted attempt in forestry made on a large scale. My advice would be to make a small park into which to look from your house; make a small pleasure ground and garden, farm your river bottom chiefly to keep and fatten livestock with a view to manure, and make the rest a forest, improving the existing woods and planting the old fields."

Vanderbilt hired Gifford Pinchot (later governor of Pennsylvania), a recent graduate of Yale who had been studying forestry in Europe, to plan and direct the renovation of the woodlands into productive forests. Under Pinchot's leadership, the forestry operations at Biltmore soon became unique in the United States as a large scale demonstration of economical forest management. A few years later, Carl Schenck, a young German forester hired by Pinchot, began the first school of forestry. The school, which continued until 1909, trained some of America's first foresters. Today at Biltmore Estate, we continue modern forestry practices and research.

MAKING THE COURAGEOUS DECISION

> *"Whenever you see a successful business, someone once made a coura-geous decision."* (Peter Drucker)

In the early 1960s, Biltmore Estate was losing a quarter of a million dollars each year. The Depression, World War II, and the fact that the costs involved in operating the property were enormous and skyrocketing daily had all created financial hardships for the estate. It would have been much easier to stay at Chase Manhattan Bank, where I was working. And I might have, except that someone told me that saving my "white elephant" was an impossibility. That was the only gauntlet I needed.

MY DECISION FOR BILTMORE

At Biltmore, there was no book. We had to write it.

> *"It couldn't be done, but sometimes it don't work out that way."*
> (Casey Stengel)

For an historic house to open itself up to the public, spend money on advertising and promotion, and generally treat its operations as any business would was unheard of when I came back to Asheville. Historic properties were to be cared for by the government, run by volunteers, and positioned as an educational experience for school children until the property crumbled due to disrepair. For an historic property to be self-sufficient, private, and profitable was considered completely unrealistic and unattainable. And the concept of preservation and business working in tandem was absurd.

That was when we first started. By 1968, Biltmore Estate made its first profit of $16. By 1979, revenues were up to $3.5 million. By 1993, revenues were at $32 million, we had 750,000 guests visit us, and we employed over 600 people.

The Mission

As simple as it may sound, the first order of business was determining what questions had to be answered. In the early days, we had to re-examine the purpose of Biltmore Estate and the purpose of our efforts to keep it going. We determined a mission statement which has remained our guiding mandate:

> The mission of The Biltmore Company is the preservation of Biltmore Estate as a "privately owned, profitable, working estate."

This was and is a challenging goal. It is no easier in 1994 than it was in 1964, except that we have learned many valuable lessons along the way. And I think that we have successfully adhered to some basic tenets as well. We began with a review of basic principles of marketing and good sound business investment concepts. And each planning period, each decision is viewed with these same ideas in mind.

MARKETING

Our marketing plan examines the fundamentals of product, price, target markets, and promotion. We recognize the heart of our "product" as Biltmore Estate itself, the experience it offers guests, and the overall accomplishment of vision it represents. It is an isolated, single example of a short time period in American history and, as a shining example of the best of the Gilded Age, it is worthy of preservation. We are not alone in our thinking: In 1963, we were named a National Historic Landmark. We also acknowledge that the estate as a cultural attraction must keep up with the interests and needs of our potential guests, guests upon whom we rely to return again and again in order to pay the bills.

Product Development

One of the most significant lessons we've learned over the years is exactly how critical it is to listen to what our guests tell us; pay attention to what they like, what they need and what they want. It is because of guest feedback that we have developed new tours and attractions, special events, and valuable add-ons. The results have been rewarding and effective. Some examples of these results are as follows.

In 1980, we decided our guests might like to see the downstairs of Biltmore House, how the laundry and kitchens operated, how the gymnasium, bowling alley, and swimming pool functioned. The result was a 28 percent increase in visitation and a 55 percent increase in admission price in the first two years, and a substantial increase in our guests' satisfaction with their time at Biltmore.

In 1985, we opened a 90,000 square foot winery in an adapted structure once used as the main dairy barn. The results were a 12 percent increase in visitation and a 17 percent increase in admission price in the first two years. We also, of course, gained the additional benefit of making extraordinarily good wines and, as a consequence, created another source of revenue.

In 1989, we determined our guests really did want to see more of what was behind closed doors in Biltmore House, so we opened a portion of the third floor. A 22 percent increase in visitation and a 9 percent increase in admission price occurred.

Special Events

Perhaps our most glowing success story, however, is our use of special events designed to build traditionally slower seasons for travel in the Asheville area. The most impressive of these events is our re-creation of George Vanderbilt's turn-of-the-century Christmas with music, period decorations, and candlelit evenings. The results are evident. Admissions went from 24,476 in 1979 to 158,676 in 1993, or a 548 percent increase. In addition, the increase in admissions revenue totals more than 2,228 percent.

After Christmas became something our guests clearly enjoyed, we found that other seasons at Biltmore Estate merited special attention as well. Our grounds and gardens are beautiful in the spring, with 50,000 tulips, one of the most extensive collections of native azaleas in America, and a variety of rare and valuable plantings originating to Mr. Olmsted's plans. We have tried to maintain the integrity of his elaborate design for the three-mile approach road, a naturalistic garden in itself, designed as a suggestion of the subtropical for Vanderbilt and his guests weary of the cold of New York and Newport. Architect Hunt thought Olmsted would be remembered, if for no other work, for his creation of this approach.

We determined that Olmsted's legacy at Biltmore Estate, his last and largest project, was indeed most worthy of celebration. We also knew our guests revelled in the opportunity to see springtime at the estate every year. So, in 1986, we began our first Festival of Flowers, an event designed to acknowledge Olmsted's great contribution to the creation of Biltmore Estate and to draw attention to his work.

Not only did we pay special attention to the natural beauty on the estate; we also began our most serious attention to preservation and restoration of the landscape, an essential and integral part of Biltmore. We also understood the importance of promoting the landscape. During the festival, we added special events and music, interior decorations in Biltmore House, and an Easter egg hunt on the front lawn (last year it attracted 1,000 children).

Again, the response to our concept of a special event was rewarding. Admissions have increased from 95,751 in 1979 to 158,606 in 1994, or a 66 percent overall increase. Our admission revenues increased 204 percent during that time.

Pricing And Market Research

While product development is certainly a key element of marketing, our guests must feel that their time and money are well spent. As a result, we frequently examine pricing issues, determining the perceived value of a visit to Biltmore Estate versus the admission. We offer special pricing for groups, for special events and for optional add-ons, such as taped tours, guidebooks, and special behind-the-scenes tours.

We carefully analyse our audiences by geographic, demographic and psychographic determining factors. We dissect our target markets by those guests visiting us as individuals, couples, and families, or those who come as part of an organized group.

Promotions

Finally, we create and execute promotions, all of which have the same basic objectives:

- To create and maintain awareness of Biltmore Estate
- To provide information about Biltmore Estate
- To communicate a high-quality image of the Estate
- And to create the perception (and hopefully the reality) of high value

We have incorporated a far-reaching and diverse methodology in order to implement these promotions:

- Advertising
- Public Relations
- Direct Sales
- On-site cross-selling
- Opportunity Management
- Destination marketing organizations/ trade association

We feel that all this hard work has paid off so far. We continue to pay our bills, pay our taxes, and grow each year. We have seen visitation increase 96 percent from 361,000 in 1979 to over 750,000 in 1993. In 1979, we employed 129 people. Today, we employ 750. We have also evolved as a financially sound company.

THE BILTMORE COMPANIES

The Biltmore Company is actually divided into three legal entities, all owned by my family as Subchapter S corporations. Each company contributes to the overall financial strength of the Biltmore Company.

- The Biltmore Company was actually incorporated in 1932 and originally included the current estate operations as well as an operating dairy. In 1979, due to inheritance tax issues, my brother George and I split the company, and each of us took one segment of the business. George acquired the dairy and I took on the operation of the estate.
- Biltmore Estate Wine Company was incorporated in 1982 for the purpose of producing classic wines for sale both to estate visitors and through retail sales across the region. We opened the winery itself in 1985.
- Biltmore Estate Reproductions was incorporated in 1992 to sell reproduction furniture and decorative accessories, all based upon pieces in Mr. Vanderbilt's collection.

In order to make each of these businesses successful in contributing to the overall mission of the estate, we follow three basic financial policies.

- Businesses must be profitable. Since we do not receive subsidies from federal, state or local governments, it is essential that our businesses be profitable.
- We must finance internally. The reason that we finance everything internally is that our mission statement requires us to be privately owned. While taking some of our businesses public might generate additional cash to expand, we choose to maintain our private status at this time.
- The third guideline we live by is that the funds created by our businesses are reinvested into those businesses in order to expand and improve upon the products we deliver. We are firmly committed to the preservation of Biltmore and the ongoing growth of its companies.

REINVESTING IN PRESERVATION

Since 1979, we have invested over $35 million back into the property. These funds were either internally generated or borrowed from banks and repaid through earnings. Much of this reinvestment is for projects our guests don't even see:

- New plumbing. This may seem rather mundane, but it becomes more impressive when you tally the total cost of upgrading Biltmore House plumbing to accommodate 750,000 people annually. In 1993, for example, we spent an estimated $533,900 on plumbing repairs and upgrading.

- Better roads. Because we are a private property, we are responsible for our 12 miles of estate roads. In 1992, we spent $160,000 in an effort to improve and maintain our roadways.

- A cleaner Bass Pond. Mr. Olmsted went to great lengths to design an elaborate flume system beneath the Bass Pond at Biltmore Estate in order to avoid a build up of silt and to keep the water clean. After 100 years, some of the flumes had become clogged. Unclogging them cost us $423,000.

- All historic properties open to the public can attest to the continuous need for additional restrooms. Since 1982, we have spent $399,300 on the construction of new restroom facilities for our guests and employees.

While the aforementioned projects might not be as obvious to the average guest, other preservation efforts, on the other hand, are quite evident and impressive:

- The restoration of the Music Room. This was the first major restoration and preservation project I tackled when I came back to Biltmore Estate. Completed in 1976, the project included elaborate stencilling of the ceiling, installation of a carved stone mantel, and refurbishing the furnishings for this room.

- The re-creation of silk cut brocade for the Family Breakfast Room and my grandmother's bedroom. This project was an exciting one for me, enabling us to make contact with the weaving firm in Lyon, France, which had originally woven fabric to my grandfather's specifications for these rooms. Tassinari and Chatel still had the original jacquard cards matching the patterns precisely. They re-created the upholstery and draperies for these two rooms and completely renovated them at a total cost of nearly $600,000.

    In addition to the fabric, we restored the Breakfast Room to its original colour scheme. In the early 1980s we created a decorative arts, conservation, and restoration company called Biltmore Campbell Smith. Our company relied almost totally on European artisans because training for these skills in the United States was rare. We determined a need to begin a training model in America and in the late 1980s, Biltmore Company collaborated with Asheville's local technical college and the City Guilds of London to establish a decorative arts restoration and conservation program through the Asheville college. Today, the program is flourishing and students are being sent all over the United States to conserve, restore, preserve and repair structures and works of art. Some of the students came to Biltmore, conducted paint analysis on the Breakfast Room ceiling, and restored it to its original splendour.

- In 1987, we began the ambitious undertaking of conserving the eight priceless 16th century Flemish tapestries in the collection. We constructed our own wash bath, dye lab, and conservation studio inside Biltmore House and staffed with textile conservators from Hampton Court in England and St. John the Divine in New York. To date, five of the tapestries have been cleaned and conserved and our conservators have become sought-after consultants for other properties, including The Breakers Hotel in Palm Beach. Our total estimated expenditure for this project is $125,000 per year.

- We also have on staff at Biltmore House two of the finest furniture conservators in the United States. Werner Katzenberger and Tim Judson are constantly evaluating, repairing, and conserving the 16th, 17th, 18th, and 19th century pieces in Mr. Vanderbilt's collection.

THE FUTURE

In 1992, we adopted a long-range plan for the company, designed to improve the product our visitor experiences and to lead us into the next century with forethought and insight. Over the next 5 to 10 years, we will spend at least $15 million on enhancing that visitor experience.

We are, of course, pleased to be able to preserve, reinvest and expand. But these achievements do not come without a cost. As a for-profit business, the first reality is in knowing that the more successful you are, the more of your profits the government wants.

Since 1979, the Biltmore Companies have paid taxes at the federal and state levels of over $10.2 million. Certainly an additional $10 million would go a long way towards preservation of Biltmore. But we are for-profit and so we pay our fair share. The dilemma comes in dealing with the Catch-22 of inheritance taxes.

The government has, of course, standardized rules and regulations dealing with passing assets or property from one generation to the next. Current regulations require that the receiving party pay up to a maximum of 55 percent of the value of that asset as a tax. While we do not have an exact estimate of how the Internal Revenue Service would value Biltmore, there is no question that its value would be appraised at a substantial amount and that 55 percent of that value would translate into a great deal of money. There are no large coffers of cash hidden away within the Biltmore Company. On the contrary, all monies are reinvested into the property. And, ironically, that reinvestment in the property increases its value, which in turn increases the amount of tax due at death.

It is our hope that the government will consider Biltmore a model for other historic properties and allow it to remain in the for-profit sector. It is my belief that its future preservation and ongoing success relies on our ability to continue to operate as we currently do. As a footnote to this thought, consider the fact that in the 1970s our admissions revenues covered 100 percent of our operating costs. Today, admissions generates only 50 percent of the revenues needed for operation of the estate. The remaining funds are derived from retail sales and food and beverage profits. If Biltmore Estate were to become a non-profit organization, our ability to depend on retail to support us to this extent would disappear.

In closing, you'll remember I noted earlier that our approach to meeting the challenge of running Biltmore Estate began with an examination of questions which must be answered. As the owner of the estate, I have had to answer questions such as whether I was committed to the concept of long-range planning. I had to decide whether the estate should be private, public, or non-profit. I had to determine whether I was indeed the best person to manage the property.

I also had to surround myself with a team knowledgeable about the marketing and financial questions which have to be addressed: Is the project economically feasible? Is there a market for this enterprise? Who is our audience?

In retrospect, although it has appeared at times to be something of a Herculean task, I would do it again. It is time for the worlds of historic preservation and business to come together with a unified dedication to saving our historic properties and our cultural heritage. It can no longer be solely up to the government or to the benevolent few to protect our history. Legacies such as Biltmore Estate are worth the risks, the battles, and the pointed arrows. At Biltmore Estate, we don't preserve the property in order to make money. We make money in order to preserve Biltmore Estate. Of course, each historic property must determine how, when and in what manner it works towards its preservation. Certainly not all properties are like Biltmore, have the same issues as Biltmore or the same possibilities that Biltmore presents. Still, I am proud of what the marriage of good business and sound preservation has accomplished there, and I challenge others to find their own innovative approaches to saving these properties which tell us so much about who we are, where we have come from, and what our futures hold.

Plate 10 Granville Island Public Market, Vancouver
(photo courtesy of The Province of British Columbia) ➡

SECTION 3
MANAGEMENT
PARTNERSHIPS

Creating Value for Visitors to Urban Destinations

14

K. Michael Haywood

School of Hotel and Food Administration, University of Guelph

INTRODUCTION

Cities around the world are engaged in a relentless battle to revitalize their economies; and tourism, in combination with attraction, recreation, and entertainment complexes, has become a critical component in urban development strategies. Consequently, like market-driven businesses everywhere, cities have become fixated with communicating their special appeal to visitors. This expensive marketing approach, though relevant and advocated by well-known experts (Kotler, Haider and Rein, 1993; Ashworth and Vogel, 1990) has deficiencies. Most effort goes into building demand, but much less effort goes into urban design as it relates to tourism, improving hospitality, and generating interest in tourism from the perspective of the community at large. As a result, marketing, especially when stripped of its product design, development and value components, and ignorant of constituency requirements, is an inadequate vehicle for sustaining tourism and constantly improving its potential (Haywood, 1990).

Overemphasis on the economic rewards of tourism has been criticized roundly in the literature. What is often contemplated but rarely articulated is the loss of sense of place. Cities, particularly when pursuing tourism dollars, become arenas for conspicuous consumption—places removed from the lives of their residents and disconnected from their history, culture, and everyday experiences (Hiss, 1990). Tourism advertisements exacerbate this notion through the use of sanitized and commodified themes and images. By streaming people into specific areas of cities, by de-emphasizing ways in which visitors can experience the authenticity of cities, by failing to provide realistic orientations to city life, visitors become disenchanted. The economic result: shortened stays, failure to return, or unfavourable word of mouth.

The blandness of or difficulties associated with the urban tourism experience often result from the approach taken to develop tourism. Tourism proceeds on a project-by-project basis. It is rarely subjected to careful planning or viewed from the perspective of the city at large. Moreover, there is little consideration of the behaviour and requirements of visitors. As a community-embracing activity, tourism is ignored or misunderstood by urban planners. Ambivalent or angry with the hosting role or the dysfunctional aspects of tourism (e.g., congestion), residents ignore or are indifferent to the visitor. When this occurs, visitors remain strangers —unwelcome and unhappy.

Feeling disconnected from each other, both the resident and visitor can become disillusioned. In worst-case scenarios, tourism may become a morally bankrupt activity. Interactions are merely transactions. There is no caring, no understanding, no sharing. The quality of the visitor experience as well as the quality of urban life become negated (Haywood, 1989).

On the other hand, there are successes, and they are numerous, that can be attributed to urban tourism and marketing efforts. They have been built largely on the strengths of individual tourism enterprises. To remain profitable and competitive, these organizations—hotels, museums, parks, theatres—have dedicated themselves to pursuit of a broadened marketing approach. Explicitly or implicitly, they have adopted a total quality and customer approach to managing their enterprises. Through patience and fortitude some have achieved dramatic benefits by making sure that quality programs do not clash with other strategic initiatives, do result in financial improvement, and do create changes to operating procedures or practices—particularly those important to customers.

Whether visitors stay for a few hours or a few days, each encounters a wide range of people and organizations. Therefore, if cities want to enhance the visitor experience, it seems appropriate to suggest that marketers and planners view tourism from a perspective that takes into consideration the people who provide services as well as those who receive them—people living and working in communities and people visiting those communities. For marketing and quality improvement programs to be initiated and implemented successfully, the urban visitor's and community's tourism experiences need to be better understood (Haywood and Muller, 1988). Participating organizations in urban tourism must collaborate in more effective ways (Haywood, 1992).

In an attempt to help urban areas realize the benefits of community-wide initiatives to improve the tourism experience, an effort will be made to juxtapose existing with emerging strategic models associated with urban tourism. The emerging approach will then be anchored by a demonstration of management practices at Ritz Carlton Hotels. Finally, an example of an initiative in Rochester, New York, will be used to reveal how communities could apply total quality management on a community-wide basis.

EXISTING AND EMERGING STRATEGIC REALITIES

Current wisdom suggests that distinctive competitive advantage can only be achieved if cities exude "excellence" in hosting visitors. By itself, however, excellence is insufficient; today it only represents the price of entry. Excellence must be combined with innovation, that is, the ability to identify and capitalize on new chances to bring cities alive for visitors. Innovation is stalemated, though, unless it can be leveraged and carefully integrated with visitor and community expectations and desires. Being prepared to deliver on these expectations (excitement, learning, adventure, safety, quality of life) will require organizations and communities to cultivate new competencies, and to redesign the way work is done in a way that is valued by visitors and urban residents.

Anticipation of what is required to create and sustain value is the critical ingredient because tourism, and the way it is currently being managed, is undergoing dramatic change. The information contained in the following tables highlights three themes anchoring this paradigm shift: visitor and community value strategy; community/organization system; and continuous improvement.

Visitor and Community Value Strategy

Visitor and community value represent the net combination of benefits from tourism in consideration of the sacrifices that need to be made. The visitor value strategy represents both organizational and community plans and attempts to serve visitors. Included in this strategy are the numerous, disparate and interactive characteristics, attributes, and processes of the urban tourism product, and other necessary support services. It is important to emphasize that a visitor value strategy must be considered in conjunction with a community value strategy. As a community-based industry, tourism is legitimized when direct and indirect economic and social benefits of tourism can be earned in the community with full recognition given to any costs or negative impact (Haywood, 1989). Visitor value can only be achieved when people feel good about welcoming and serving visitors. So, visitor and community values resulting from tourism activity are intertwined.

As Table 14.1 indicates, the theme of visitor and community value strategy may be addressed under a number of topics. Of major consideration is "quality" which, in the new paradigm, represents only one component of visitor or community value. Quality, in contrast to what is currently happening, is not assured by weeding out the "bad" tourism products or services. To a large extent, it can be improved by reducing variations in processes and performances (the ways in which services are provided to visitors), or in closing gaps between expectations and actual experiences. However, quality must become broadly defined. In urban areas, there is a danger of destroying inherently attractive and regionally distinctive aspects of a community; homogeneity is not a desired state. As a consequence, measurement must shift from simplistic measures of conformation to broader measures associated with visitor and community value, particularly over a longer time frame. (Included should be all forms of economic, social and physical impact.)

The juxtaposition of visitor and community value strategies suggests that the positioning of cities as destinations should also shift from an overtly comparative, competitive stance to one in which appropriate urban attributes, highly regarded by residents and important to potential visitors, are emphasized. When this occurs, tourism's key stakeholders broaden from project owners to visitors and the people in the community who make them feel welcome. This revision of the urban area's tourism constituencies suggests that the needs of both residents and visitors be considered when designing or re-designing urban areas or when proposing new urban amenities. Of course, enlarged constituencies may create dilemmas that challenge the achievement of competitive advantages vis à vis competing destinations —hence the need to legitimize tourism as a valid economic sector.

Table 14.1 Existing and emerging paradigms on the theme of visitor and community value strategy.

Topic	Existing Paradigm	Emerging Paradigm
Quality	Meet specifications, conform. Inspect into product. Make trade-offs with costs.	Recognize as only one component of visitor value. Manage into process of providing value. Seek synergies with costs and impacts. Recognize impact of tourism on quality of life in community.
Measurement	Measure efficiency, productivity and profitability	Link all measures to visitor value and quality of life— benefits and costs.
Positioning Strategy	Position against competition	Position against visitor segments while maintaining integrity of community.
Key Stakeholders	Shareholders	Visitors, employees, tourism enterprises, community.
Product/Process/ Service/Design	Internal focus, sell what the organization can offer	External focus. Provide what visitors want. Design processes in such a way that value is enhanced.

Community/Organization System

The second overriding theme deals with the means associated with providing value to visitors and the community. These systems broadly include physical and human contributions, process technology, operating methods and work practices, streams of work activity, information flows, and decision-making. The approaches to managing these systems, as shown in Table 14.2, are: a functional/organizational approach, technology, employee/resident involvement, human resource management, role definition, culture, and structure. In the emerging paradigm it is important to note how managers and the community move from negotiating to gaining cooperation, and then to actually defining, owning, and optimizing cross-functional and cross-organizational systems that will result in valuable results for visitors and community. Technology becomes a vital tool in optimizing these systems for value; that is, by speeding up response times. Employees, similarly, concentrate more on contributing to visitor satisfaction and community wellbeing.

Table 14.2 Existing and emerging paradigms on the theme of community/organization system.

Topic	Existing Paradigm	Emerging Paradigm
Functional/ Organizational Approach	Negotiate across business functions to obtain cooperation	Define functional/organizational systems of importance to visitors and gain cooperation across the community to achieve visitor value
Technology	Use to eliminate people problems	Use to reduce complexity and add value for visitors and citizens
Employee/ Resident Involvement	Focus on issues that will lead to contentment and cost efficiency	Focus on strategic factors of primary importance in visitor value-added and community wellbeing
Human Resource Management	Staff responsibility with emphasis on labour costs	Regard as critical, strategic resource. Manage to allow people to excel.
Role Definition	Limits set by job descriptions	Shared vision of visitor value and role as host. Inspire flexibility.
Culture	Suppress emotion. Power and politics.	Connect with quality of life, individual sense of purpose
Structure	Specialize, functional emphasis	Integrate, team emphasis

From a managerial viewpoint, human resource departments relinquish their role as controllers of human behaviour. The idea is no longer to prescribe but to build shared visions and to inspire people to provide superior value to visitors. This will require changes to organizational cultures and structural arrangements within and among tourism organizations.

Continuous Improvement

As previously suggested, innovation and anticipation are of vital importance if organizations and community are to keep pace with the increasing rate of change in the external environment. The constant striving to make things better, as depicted in Table 14.3, should be aligned with occasions, approaches, responses to error, decision making perspectives, managerial roles, authority, focus and controls. Most urban areas have approached occasions for improvement by announcing new tourism-related projects. The emerging paradigm suggests a need to find more fundamental and down-to-earth occasions: all aspects of the visitor experience that

Table 14.3   Existing and emerging paradigms on the theme of continuous improvement.

Topic	Existing Paradigm	Emerging Paradigm
Occasion	Focus on new attractions, infrastructure, mega-projects. React to problems.	Focus of tourism on broader visitor and activity systems. Innovate and be proactive to opportunities, big breakthroughs and small improvements.
Approach	Hit or miss	Scientific, based on data as well as intuition
Response to Error	Employees/citizens responsible	Management/community responsible
Decision-Making Perspective	Political expediency. Short term focus.	Strategic, purposeful, long-term focus
Managerial Roles	Administer. Maintain status quo. Control others.	Prompt strategic improvement. Challenge status quo.
Authority	Top-down. Rules and policies.	Community generated. Customer-driven. Base on vision, empowerment.
Focus	Business results through quotas and targets	Business and community results through capable systems tied to results
Control	Score, report, evaluate	Study statistical variation. Understand causes.

take place in all settings with all sorts of people. By examining the systems designed to create value, there are opportunities for both big breakthroughs and small steps. Managers will need to approach these opportunities and problems more scientifically as well as intuitively. And whenever errors or breakdowns in delivering service occur, they should be viewed as opportunities for learning. Emphasis, therefore, is on improving the process or system, not on assigning blame.

Decision making in this context should be designed to serve long-term, strategic interests as related to the community, as well as individual businesses. Removed is the need simply to administer existing systems and maintain the status quo. Rather, the status quo must be challenged for strategic improvement to meet present and future demands. To be effective, the loci of authority will need to be altered to include top-down and bottom-up, particularly if community value is to be enhanced. Authority, therefore, needs to be imposed by communicating a vision, enabling people with systems, and empowering them to make the vision real. Results will be achieved by improving the capabilities of people and redesigning systems so that they result in higher levels of satisfaction.

RITZ CARLTON HOTELS

Superior value for visitors represents the strategic linchpin for competing in today's globally competitive environment. In the new paradigm, everyone needs to be involved in quality improvement for the purpose of enhancing visitor value. As leading firms operating in the tourism industry—Disney, Marriott, Four Seasons Hotels, SAS to name a few—can attest, results stem from a team effort, led by senior managers as part of strategic management in their firms.

Such dedicated effort paid off for the Ritz Carlton Hotel Company in 1992. They were awarded the prestigious and coveted Malcolm Baldridge National Quality Award, created by the U.S. government to promote and recognize quality achievement in U.S. businesses. Operating in what is one of the most logistically complex service businesses, the Ritz Carlton, which manages 25 luxury hotels in the United States and Australia, set out to identify the most important, yet least consistent quality concerns of its guests. The intent was to develop a way of understanding the individual expectations of hundreds of thousands of customers while also preventing difficulties from ever reaching them—an obvious concern because it is estimated that at the Ritz Carlton there are as many as one million employee-guest interactions each day. They then proceeded to build a reliable, customer-driven service delivery system, based largely on a commitment to a set of principles designed to provide premium service. The entire system was also designed to enable employees to instantly react to pacify a dissatisfied guest and correct their problem immediately. Employees also learned how to identify and resolve distinct patterns of recurring problems. Ritz Carlton Hotels set out to develop a competitive advantage by becoming defect free and to achieve 100 percent customer retention by 1996.

To put the Ritz Carlton's approach to total quality management into perspective, and provide benchmarks for similar tourism enterprises, the following discussion will be based on the seven Malcolm Baldridge award categories: leadership, information and analysis, strategic quality planning, human resources utilization, management of process quality, quality and operational results, and customer satisfaction (Hart and Bogan, 1992). It should be evident that each of these categories cuts across the three themes of the emerging paradigm shift.

Leadership

The senior management group doubles as the senior quality group. They devised the original quality strategies. The entire group monitors work areas, instills the Gold Standards (Table 14.4), models their relationship management approach, insists upon 100 percent compliance to customer's requirements and recognizes outstanding achievement.

Table 14.4   Ritz Carlton Hotels' Gold Standards

Component	Explanation of Standards
Credo	The Ritz Carlton Hotel is a place where the genuine care and comfort of our guests is our highest mission. We pledge to provide the finest personal service and facilities for our guests who will always enjoy a warm, relaxed, yet refined ambience. The Ritz Carlton experience enlivens the senses, instills wellbeing, and fulfils even the unexpressed wishes and needs of our guests.
The Three Steps Of Service	1. A warm and sincere greeting. Use the guest's name, if and when possible. 2. Anticipation and compliance with guest's needs. 3. Fond farewell. Give them a warm goodbye and use their names, if and when possible.
Ritz Carlton Basics	These describe the guest problem solving process as well as grooming, housekeeping, safety and efficiency standards. The lateral service principle makes known the value of internal customer satisfaction, It also serves to eliminate internal competition.
Motto	Ladies and Gentlemen Serving Ladies and Gentlemen.

Another primary responsibility of senior management is the protection of the environment and society at large with respect to Ritz Carlton's business activities. Accordingly life safety and security receive a high priority and are considered part of everyone's job.

The lessons to be learned from Ritz Carlton's approach to leadership: when senior management personally instill a strong vision and a set of principles in their employees and then give them the confidence, freedom, and authority to act, people take responsibility for their jobs and do whatever is necessary to satisfy their customers.

Information and Analysis

The Ritz Carlton's approach allows every employee to collect and use quality-related data on a daily basis. The information is critical and responsive and includes on-line, guest preference information, quantity of error-free products and services, and opportunities for quality improvement. Their automated property management systems enable this information to be collected and inspected by all employees.

A quality production reporting system is used to aggregate hotel-level data from two dozen sources into a summary format. It serves as an early-warning system and facilitates analysis. The reporting system allows team improvement mechanisms that are functional (within a work area) and cross-functional (within a hotel or across hotels) to function effectively.

Ritz Carlton uses a benchmarking approach which focuses entirely on hotel industry best practices and performances. They also study the best practices in any industry through the use of industry-watchers and consultants.

Lessons learned: Ritz Carlton needs immediate responses from listening posts, combined with system accessibility to all, just to keep pace with ever-changing individual customer demands.

Strategic Quality Planning

Ritz Carlton's quality plan is their business plan. The primary objectives are to improve the quality of its products and services, reduce cycle time, and improve price-value and customer retention. At each level of the company—from corporate leaders to managers and employees in the 720 individual work areas—teams are charged with setting goals and devising action plans which are reviewed by the corporate steering committee. These teams enhance quality and productivity by:

- aligning all departments around a common vision and objectives;
- encouraging all people to think beyond the demands of day-to-day activities;
- increasing communication among the diverse functions that make up the hotel chain;
- simultaneous, integrated problem-solving.

Lessons learned from quality planning: action plans developed by each level of the organization must be screened to ensure they have been adequately researched, and contain no complexity before they are undertaken.

Use of Human Resources

All hotels have a director of human resources and a training manager. They are assisted with their planning efforts by the hotel's quality leader. Each work area has a departmental trainer on staff who is charged with the training and certification of new employees of that unit.

Ritz Carlton's commitment to planning and realizing the full potential of its people begins with the selection process. They use a highly productive "character trait" instrument to determine the capability of each candidate to meet the requirements of each of their 120 job positions. The orientation period to a hotel is two days with a follow-up session three weeks later to monitor the effectiveness of the instruction and to make necessary changes. All employees undergo a comprehensive training period to master the procedures of their respective positions and must pass written and skill demonstration tests to become certified. During daily meetings, each employee is trained to become a certified quality engineer: they must become capable of identifying the wasteful complexity within their work, that is, mistakes, rework, breakdowns, delays, inconsistencies, and variations.

Effective involvement and empowerment of employees is encouraged. Each individual can:

- contact appropriate employees to help resolve a problem swiftly;
- spend up to $2000 to satisfy a guest;
- decide the acceptability of products and services;
- become involved in setting plans for their work area.

There are many opportunities for employee recognition; and employees are surveyed annually to ascertain their levels of satisfaction and understanding of the quality standards.

Lessons learned: a collective quality commitment must be gained by the entire workforce. There is no substitute for selecting employees who believe in the organization's values.

Management of Process Quality

Ritz Carlton's product management process has three integral parts: an interactive team pyramid (with the guest at the pinnacle, followed in order by the customer interaction employee, the training certification, problem solving and strategic planning teams, the hotel executive committee, and the corporate steering committee/developers); a basic product management process; and, regional product management process. Several critical aspects, to name a few, contribute to the effectiveness of the product management process: forced interface of all design, marketing, operations, and legal functions; a concentrated focus on basic, regional, and individual customer requirements; and continuous emphasis on their principles and prevention of problems.

In delivering quality in their hotels there are a few systematic control systems: self control of the individual employee based on spontaneous and learned behaviour; a basic control mechanism that allows any employee to take decisive, corrective action; and a critical success factor control to measure quality, speed, and cost performance against benchmarks and customer satisfaction data. Ritz Carlton employs eight mechanisms to improve the quality of its processes, products, and services and conducts periodic self audits and outside audits.

Lessons learned: new products and services that get off to a good start are the most reliable and efficient. The major thrust of this quality effort is to prevent difficulties from ever reaching a customer.

Quality and Operational Results Over the Past Eight Years

Independent testing and consumer measurement organizations have determined that the Ritz Carlton has become the consistent benchmark for quality hotel products in the United States. They maintain a 10 percent performance gap over their best competitor and 95 percent over the industry average. Their quality conscious culture has led to significant improvements in process measurement: they have achieved 100 percent completion and delivery of new ready-to-rent guest rooms on time since 1989; their employee turnover rates have been reduced 47 percent or 16 percent better than the industry average; the number of hours worked per guest room has been reduced 8 percent over a three year period; and cooperation ratings between departments improved from 78 percent in 1989 to 86 percent in 1991; and the chain has been recognized as "industry best" at generating revenue per available room.

Lessons learned from quality and operational results: The Ritz Carlton never underestimates the value of even one idea or quality improvement effort.

Customer Satisfaction

Customer satisfaction data is separated into major customer segments and product lines, then given comprehensive analysis. Individual hotels are responsible for their units' performance, while the senior leaders concentrate on the problems of the entire system. Direction for change is set at both the local and national levels. Annually, the data passes through the strategic planning process to establish objectives and action plans. At the Ritz Carlton, the objective of their quality effort is: "never lose a single customer".

Lessons learned: Ritz Carlton has avoided the failures often attributed to total quality management (TQM). The word "total" conveys the idea that employees, throughout every function and level of the company, pursue quality. "Quality" suggests excellence in every aspect of the organization. "Management" refers to the pursuit of quality results through a quality management process. It begins with leadership and strategic management processes and extends through design, operations, marketing and finance in a never ending process of improvement.

The Ritz Carlton model of TQM will not work for every organization. As firms in the tourism industry move from traditional approaches to managing towards new and emergent approaches there will need to be considerable experimentation. Organizations will continue to shift and managers will invest and test new approaches to management that fit their unique circumstances.

The emergence of a new paradigm, as noted in tables 14.1, 14.2, and 14.3, however, implies a need to define and improve quality. The concepts of visitor value and quality of community life will necessitate the integration of each function or activity which defines and improves quality with all other activities of all other managerial functions. From an urban destination perspective it identifies how the interrelated dimensions of visitors' experiences could be managed to achieve satisfaction during the entire visit.

QUALITY URBAN TOURISM

To what extent can total quality management, developed as an organization-specific tool, be implemented throughout an urban region? Interest in community-based quality efforts is growing rapidly, though little effort has yet to be channelled toward tourism (Getz, 1993). While awards for excellence do exist, a lot more could be done. For example, many communities in both the United States and Canada have started networks of "excellence councils" to enhance quality improvement efforts and education.

It sounds like a dream: citizens pulling together to create a community where quality is a way of life not a buzz-word; where workers, managers, educators and government officials cooperate to gather data, solve problems and serve visitors. This vision can become a reality. Indeed, in places like Rochester, New York, it is a reality, though in regard to another industry (Gaber, 1991). For much of the past century, Rochester, a city of 230,000, had vested its wellbeing almost entirely in the performance of a few large companies—Kodak, Xerox and Bausch and Lomb. Each was involved in optics, the science of light and vision. But the industry was evolving quickly, and with it a fundamental shift was occurring in how firms were managed. Rochester was about to lose an entire industry and with it, thousands of jobs. Where the old approach relied on proprietary inventions such as xerography, film and photo-processing patents and on individual scientific breakthroughs, the new model stressed the constant improvement of non-proprietary technologies and cooperation within and between companies. Rochester's leading firms, their local suppliers and the city were facing potential disaster, so they began to coalesce around a new strategy: working together to achieve and maintain global competitiveness.

The upshot, resulting from a desire to maintain leadership in the optics industry, has been astounding: collaboration in projects; education reform; a local drive for quality improvement; quality training and establishment of venture capital fund.

Rochester's experience provides a reminder that the key elements of economic performance and economic strategy are intensely local—that the core competencies for creating the future are ultimately at the command of the local community.

Lessons learned: tourism enterprises must learn how to collaborate more effectively. The effort begins with a few individuals committed to enhancing the visitor and community value to be derived from tourism. The essential factors in creating a widespread community endeavour are as follows:

Energetic Champions

Numerous barriers stand in the way of quality improvements: complaisance about competitiveness, resistance to change, and suspicions about motives. It takes enormous energy to overcome these barriers, so the need for strong, energetic champions is critical.

The Right Mix of People

It is important to get involvement early on from key decision-makers (such as the Mayor) and well-renowned experts. The group should have the following characteristics: power or access to power; education in total quality management; risk taking and an action orientation; a mind-set for collaboration, not competition; perseverance and commitment; and a belief in breaking down the barriers of parochialism.

A Need, a Frustration, an Opportunity

No one jumps on the quality or value bandwagon if they think everything will continue to function well. It is necessary to work with the people involved in tourism to identify the following: what is or is not performing correctly in tourism enterprises and the community; where there are gaps in services, or even just a feeling things could be better; what resources and skills are available, and how can they can be capitalized upon.

A Vision

People need to develop a common vision as a guidepost for quality in community tourism. Such a vision will create constancy of purpose and help them to determine their own and their community's priorities.

A strategy for involving others

For total quality management to take root, thought should be given to questions such as:

* In five years, what kind of participation in quality efforts will be required? Who are the people that can make the vision come true?
* Who are the influence wielders in the community?
* Who are the "willing workers," the people likely to have the time and ability to carry out the tasks?
* What people or organizations will benefit most from the efforts? Are they already interested in quality management? What will grab their interest? What's the best way to bring them into the group and develop their ownership in the efforts?

Something Visible and Concrete

Some people never believe in anything new until they see concrete results, so one element of a strategy should be an early demonstration project—something that says "This is the way it's done. This is what you can accomplish."

An Event

Another way to generate enthusiasm around quality efforts—not to mention revenues to support them—is to create an event that brings tourism decision makers together.

Publicity

Publicity helps because press coverage is one of the best ways to get a message out to the broader public, and it adds prestige and credibility to the efforts. Attaching press clippings or other articles to funding proposals, business plans, annual reviews, and so on, makes them more impressive.

Money

Company leaders, department heads, and high level officials may support total quality management verbally, but the rank and file are not going to believe a word of it until two things happen: (1) they see top management using the principles themselves; and (2) the money and resources are allocated to help support projects and other quality-focused activities.

CONCLUSION

Managers of tourism enterprises, particularly those operating in an urban setting, are starting to recognize that the prevailing ways of managing are undergoing radical change. As a result, the management practices of leading firms such as Ritz Carlton Hotels are evolving significantly. Senior management can lead a superlative quality management effort. The Ritz Carlton approach is based on a customer-focused vision, personal commitment to continuous improvement, and a cultural transformation to integrate the efforts of the entire organization toward this vision.

To enhance the urban visitor experience, however, a broad scale application of a total quality management approach is necessary. It could revitalize urban destinations. The success of Rochester, New York in turning around its optics industry represents a benchmark for the tourism industry. Success will require, however, a major transformation of how tourism enterprises are currently managed and relate to each other. A strategy of enhancing visitor value and community wellbeing needs energetic, and skilled champions who believe in collaboratively implementing quality programs on a community-wide basis.

REFERENCES

Ashworth, G.J., and Voegel, H. (1990). *Selling the city*. London: Belhaven Press.

Gaber, A. (1991). Rochester focuses: A community's core competence. *Harvard Business Review*, July-August, 116-126.

Getz, D. (1993). Planning for tourism business district. *Annals of Tourism Research*, 20, 583-600.

Hart, C., and Bogan, C. (1992). *The Baldridge*. New York: McGraw-Hill.

Haywood, K.M. (1990). Revising and implementing the marketing concept as it applies to tourism. *Tourism Management*, 11(3), 195-205.

Haywood, K.M. (1989). Tourism, Toronto and quality of life: Visitor opinions as revealed through their photographs. Presentation made at the Third Quality-of-Life/Marketing Conference, Virginia Polytechnic University and State University, Blacksburg, Virginia.

Haywood, K.M. (1992). Identifying and responding to the challenges posed by urban tourism. *Tourism Recreation Research*, 17(2), 9-23.

Haywood, K.M. (1989). Responsible and responsive approaches to tourism planning in the community. *Tourism Management*, 9(2), 105-118.

Haywood, K.M., and Muller, T.E. (1988). The urban tourism experience: Evaluating satisfaction. *Hospitality Education and Research Journal*, 12(2), 453-459.

Hiss, T. (1990). *The experience of place*. New York: Alfred A. Knopf.

Kotler, P., Haider, D., and Rein, I. (1993). *Marketing places*. New York: The Free Press.

15

Improving The Tourist's Experience: Quality Management Applied To Tourist Destinations

Albert Postma

Leisure Management School Leeuwarden
Faculty of Economics and Management, CHN North Netherlands

Andrew K. Jenkins

Hotel Management School Leeuwarden
Faculty of Economics and Management, CHN North Netherlands

INTRODUCTION: QUALITY CONTROL AS A COMPETITIVE TOOL

If we look at current developments in the tourist industry, quality improvement must be seriously considered as a useful instrument in achieving competitive advantage, as a strategy to reduce uncertainty and improve the results of tourist organizations. Since the end of the Second World War the tourist sector has experienced considerable growth facilitated by technological advancement, the rise in popularity of the package tour, the development of mass tourism, mass production, and mass marketing. However, there are a number of developments that may lead to a turning point in tourism development, such as the negative images of mass tourism. These include a tourist industry which cannot keep abreast of the latest technological developments in information, reservations, transport, and new types of recreation. The tourist industry is losing control of a growing number of factors, such as mass production, over-building of hotels (affected by property speculation), mega-carriers, charter flights, oil prices, and the decline of cities. The tourist industry is becoming increasingly dependent on developments such as peace, wellbeing, or economic recession, paid holidays or reduction of holiday budgets, regulation or deregulation of air traffic, as well as the individualization of increasingly unpredictable tourist behaviour (Jansen-Verbeke, 1994).

One way of dealing with this vulnerability and reducing the uncertainty is to develop and implement strategic quality control programs. The combination of service and quality might be of great importance in the competitive struggle, as has been proved in the manufacturing sector. Yet, quality control is not widely used as a source of competitive advantage in the service sector (Grönroos, 1990). Because tourism belongs to the service sector, many ideas from service marketing and quality management have been put into practice in tourism organizations and companies, especially the larger ones. However, when we talk about a tourist destination, such as a city, only a few articles on the subject exist and there is little empirical experience to draw upon. When looking at the current problems facing the tourism industry, it is high time that the various organizations tried to improve tourists' experiences in close cooperation.

The central question in this chapter is to examine recent developments in the field of service management and service marketing, and the possibilities of applying it to the management and marketing of tourist destinations.

COOPERATION

Although it is claimed that many large organizations strive for certain quality improvements in their provision and delivery of services, this appears not to be enough for a destination to be competitive. Today, there is a real danger that tourist organizations are focusing on quality improvement simply because every other organization is doing so, and see quality improvement as a goal in itself. Then, to some degree, organizations or companies that are affected by tourism don't always consider themselves part of tourism and there is little notion of the role regarding the service in, or the contribution to, the total experience of a tourist. These companies possess a "myopic" view of their business interests (Mill and Morrison, 1993).

It is preferable that organizations take the destination as a starting point for their quality improvement program, instead of their own firm. When we talk about a tourist destination such as a city, the tourist "product" is an amalgam of various attractions, facilities, and services. The tourist interacts with service providers and, as such, creates an individual and unique "product" (Ashworth and Voogd, 1990; Jansen-Verbeke, 1994). The tourist destination (the city) is actually the core product of the tourists' experiences, but it is the tourist who puts together several secondary and additional sub-products. The individual character of such an aggregated product must be stressed (Dietvorst, 1993; Jansen-Verbeke, 1988). Only through cooperation will it be possible to give a proper answer to these individual interests.

From the viewpoint of quality control it is important that forms of cooperation focusing on the consumer be developed (Jansen-Verbeke, 1994). A first appropriate form of strategic alliance would be a geographically restricted aggregation of sub-products. This means that the various sub-products must be adjusted to each other by strategic alliances between local/regional organizations. This aggregation must be based on the Tourist Opportunity Spectrum, the offer of opportunities a tourist expects at the destination. This requires a good knowledge and insight into the different organizations involved and the relative importance of its product(s)/ service(s) in the behaviour and experience of the tourist at the destination. The tourist needs to be informed about the possibilities at the destination and this gives an added value to his/her experience. A relevant argument for cooperation in such a strategic alliance could be the development of a cultural identity and image for the destination, and a shared interest in the quality of the physical environment.

Another appropriate type of strategic alliance, sequential aggregation of sub-products, is based on the sequential chain of these sub-products from the moment the tourist prepares his vacation at home until the moment he returns home and evaluates his experiences. Cooperation in this form could result in a service-packet being offered (for example, information, travel, lodgings, relaxation, travel insurance, payments) based on a total quality concept (adjusted to each other, complete and accurate information about the total course). The adjustment between the various sub-products, the guarantees, the quality label of the total service, and the savings (because the customer only has to deal with one organization), offer a certain added value to the vacation experience. A relevant argument to participate in such alliances is more flexible opportunities for product differentiation and synergy between sub-products, so that it is possible to develop innovative product aggregations. By offering a certain quality standard during the vacation a relationship can be established between the service-chain and the customer. This relationship may be disconnected from the destination or the type of vacation.

In all probability, a combination of the two strategies is the most difficult to achieve, but the best solution from the tourist's viewpoint. The combination of various attractions is the reason a tourist visits a specific destination, at least in terms of the first visit. The tourist's decision to visit the destination area for a vacation is influenced by the degree to which the opportunity set of the resources and attributes matches the aspiration level (Ashworth and Voogd, 1990). The tourist is persuaded to visit the destination because he thinks this set will satisfy his needs during the vacation. The second type of alliance is important for the tourist to enjoy the product and for it to satisfy him/her. The combination of opportunity set and service-chain will persuade the tourist to visit the destination again, or to recommend it to relatives and friends.

However, a destination can only be successful if the tourist organizations realize that it is part of a system. According to Mill and Morrison, this system consists of four elements: destination, market, travel and marketing (Mill and Morrison, 1993). In accordance with this viewpoint, change in one part of the system will be felt throughout the whole system. Understanding the links in the system and the factors that affect the decision to become a tourist can make every organization in the system anticipate changes in the number and characteristics of tourists.

QUALITY MANAGEMENT

Quality has become a "cult-status" topic of today's management, education and practice. The concept of quality has aided the impact of Japanese management philosophy on the management philosophies of Western societies. However, it is not always clear what is meant by quality and quality control. Normann states that the concept of quality seems to refer to several different areas: the quality of the product or output, the quality of the process, the quality of production or delivery system and quality as a general philosophy pervading the whole organization. As Normann quite rightly points out, good service companies should have quality as a general philosophy (Normann, 1991). This can be applied to an (urban) tourist destination as well. In this section two models will be discussed which are useful for understanding the management function in quality control.

First of all, Grönroos' *Perceived Service Quality Model* (see Figure 15.1), is a helpful instrument to understand factors that effect customer perceived quality. It has proven a help for managers in understanding how different internal factors[1] affect the customer's perceptions of quality in a company's service.

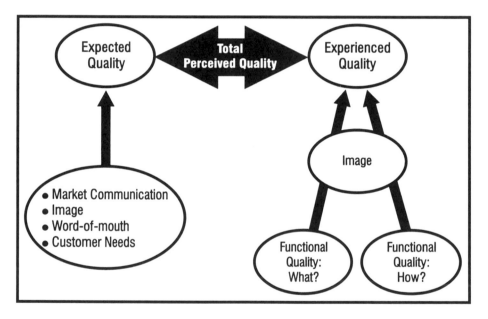

Figure 15.1   Model of the total perceived quality (Source: Grönroos, 1990).

Secondly, in defining the objectives of quality management, it is very helpful to take the (conceptual) *Service Quality Model* (see Figure 15.2) of Parasuraman, Zeithaml, and Berry as a starting point. As with Grönroos' model, it is basically customer-oriented. It helps to explain processes in the creation of service, the so-called co-service process.

The model is based on empirical research undertaken in different sectors of the service industry. It has been developed for quality improvement programs and the starting point is the conditions that give form to the co-service process between the service provider and the customer. According to the model consumers' quality assessment will be influenced by a series of four distinct "gaps" in this co-service process (Edvardsson et al., 1994).

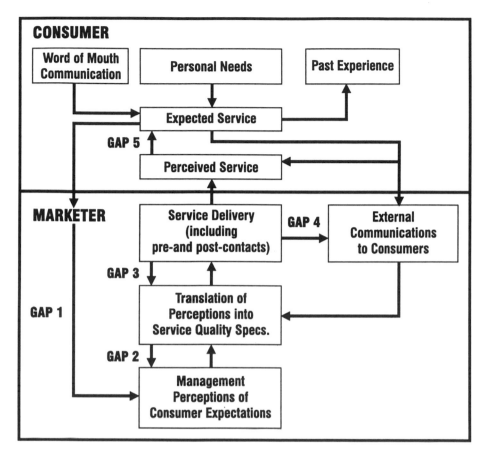

Figure 15.2   Model of service quality—the gap analysis model
(Source: Edvardsson, 1994).

The "gaps" are as follows:

Gap 1:   The difference between what the customer expects and what the management perceives the customer expects.

Gap 2:   The difference between what the management perceptions of consumer expectations of the service and its quality are, and specifications regarding service quality.

Gap 3:   The difference between the specifications regarding service quality and the service which is actually delivered.

Gap 4:   The difference between the service delivery and what is communicated in marketing to the customer regarding the service.

Gap 5:   The difference between what the consumer expects and what the consumer perceives.   The gap is influenced by the size and direction of the other four gaps.

For managers, the gap analysis model has proven to be a useful tool in examining their own perceptions of quality, and to recognize how much they actually understand customers' perceptions. Quality management programs must attempt to close the five gaps in the model and to improve the quality of service as experienced by the customer by means of a comparison between expected and perceived quality after the customer has received the service.

In further developing the gap model, Zeithaml et al. mention some interorganizational factors which affect the different gaps, and should receive, therefore, attention in the management of destinations (Edvardsson et al., 1994).

Gap 1:   - marketing research orientation
- upward communication
- levels of management

Destination management should understand how the service should be designed, what support or secondary services the customer requires, and what the right quality for the customer would be.

Gap 2:   - management commitment to service quality
- goal setting
- task standardization
- perception of feasibility

This means destination management should not reduce costs by placing internal restrictions on how a service is to be performed, so that the staff can't meet customer expectations.

Gap 3:   - teamwork
- employee-job fit
- technology-job fit
- perceived control
- supervisory control systems
- role conflict
- role ambiguity

Destination management should not only specify the quality of the service properly, but should pay attention to the personal contacts between customer and tourism staff as well.

Gap 4:   - horizontal communication
- propensity to over promise

This means that the management should not promise the customer more than the destination can deliver, but, at the same time, should inform customers about the efforts being made to increase quality.

Gap 5:   - reduce difference between expected and actual experience

All items will indirectly influence gap 5 as well, where the emphasis is on delivering the promised and expected level of service experience.

RELATIONSHIP MARKETING

In the previous section, the factors and processes have been described that will facilitate customer-oriented quality management improvement programs. According to the tourism system, dependence on an internal company management focus is not sufficient for destination quality improvement programs. The market and marketing are parts of the system as well. In this section, the Grönroos concept of relationship marketing will be discussed as a useful strategy to deal with this external part of the system.[2]

In the service industry, it is the client who determines the quality of the service. Because services are unrepeatable, a certain quality can only be achieved if services are not offered anonymously. Service organizations, therefore, need to develop and maintain a good relationship with the client, which can be seen as a life cycle (see Figure 15.3).

Figure 15.3   The customer relationship life cycle (Source: Grönroos, 1990).

To develop and maintain this relationship between service provider and customer, an optimal communication is required. According to Grönroos, this can be achieved by Relationship Marketing, which he defines as "to establish, maintain, and enhance [usually, but not necessarily always, long-term] relationships with customers and other partners, at a profit, so that the objectives of the parties involved are met. This is achieved by a mutual exchange and fulfilment of promises".

Looking at the various phases in the Customer Relationship Life Cycle, this implies that relationship marketing takes place before (giving promises to establish the relationship), during (fulfilling the promises to maintain the relationship), and after the transaction (offer a new set of promises, with the fulfilment of earlier promises as a prerequisite) to enhance the relationship. If the satisfied customer recommends the service organization to his/her friends and relatives, they might be persuaded to become acquainted with the service. Thus, the initial customer is functioning as a marketer him/herself and relationship marketing can be seen as an instrument to communicate with the customer's network as well (Grönroos, 1990).

The total perceived quality will be partly affected by the core product of the destination (for example, an historic building which is closed to the public), but also by secondary and additional products; these are the services that make it possible for the customer to experience the core product (gap 1). The total perceived quality to provide customer satisfaction requires quality in the separate service organizations and the way they are interconnected to reinforce the total perceived quality (Jansen-Verbeke, 1994). However, we need to realize that the different services do not have the same weight in the tourist's experience (Braithwaite, 1992). At the same time this is one of the greatest challenges in developing good quality management programs.

To improve the quality of separate service organizations and the total perceived quality of the aggregated product presupposes cooperation. The customer relationship life cycle focuses on the relationship between the service provider and the customer, as well as between the different companies and organizations at the destination and, as such, supports the sequential form of strategic alliance discussed in the previous section. This is the reason a destination service organization needs to see marketing as its central management function, responsible for the whole communications policy, both internally (management) and externally (marketing) (Grönroos, 1990).

Referring to the sequential type of alliance and the life cycle concept, it is important that services communicate in a coordinated way with the customer before, during and after the vacation. To offer the destination to potential customers, the services must be made known and the promises that are made must be understood and delivered. In order for the communication to be successful, the service organizations should (Vogelezang and Hageman, 1993):

- get the potential visitor to select the service (destination) from all information that he receives. Marketing needs to attract the visitor's attention; if the potential visitor is interested and feels that the service (destination) might be able to satisfy his needs, it results in interest in the service (destination).

- in weighing up the pros and cons of using the service, give the potential visitor the benefit of the doubt. Marketing needs to inspire confidence, to present the service (destination) attractively, to create the right expectations and to translate the offer to the situation and needs of the potential visitor. If the service promises to offer what the customer wants, a positive decision of first purchase may be made.

   For a tourist destination, the central goal must no longer be to attract a large number of visitors, but to take the tourist seriously and be honest with him/her. This means, for example, more finely tuned promotion. The so-called demarketing might be important in avoiding the development of a negative image when the region/city is unable to deliver the required products or when tourism has become harmful for the local environment (Dietvorst, 1993).

- use marketing in order to verify the promises about the service (destination) by adjusting the experience of the tourist with his expectations and needs.

- get the visitor to return to the same service (destination) or recommend it to others. As with confidence at the interpersonal level, image is the impression something or someone leaves behind. The gained experience (positive, ambivalent, or negative) results in an image, established by means of word-of-mouth, publicity, rumours, or watching the performance/form of the communication, such as the promises concerning a service. Thus, the image influences the attitude of potential customers. In this way, image can be seen as a powerful means of communication and has become an important management instrument in quality control programs. During the after-use evaluation, a satisfied customer might opt for a new or prolonged usage of the service. In addition, if the evaluation of the stay is positive, there is a reasonable chance that the experience will be conveyed by word of mouth to others. This is the best way for a service to become known, since quality services can't be offered anonymously.

MONITORING

Because there are a number of business participants in the destination's co-service process (staff, customer, providers), each with their own subjective interpretations of quality, destination programs involving quality control can only be successful if the management bases its policy on a permanent feedback concerning the perceived quality and the experienced quality. Only then can the destination organization hold a mirror to itself in relation to quality (Gummesson, 1993; Vogelezang and Hageman, 1993). The perceived quality needs to be measured, both internally and externally. The experienced quality must be evaluated by communicating between organization and customer about the quality criteria the service organization tries to meet. In this way, the service organization shows its own intentions, and respectively what the customers might expect from the service, but also what the organization might expect from the customer. This type of self-reference gives the service organization a steering mechanism by which to navigate. Quality programs must give the means and instruments to improve the service.

To manage the quality of the tourism system properly, the achievement of, or progress toward, the desired outcomes must be monitored, by continuous measurement of the perceived quality (Grönroos' Perceived Service Quality Model) both internally and externally.

Internal measurement refers to the measurement of objective quality criteria developed and/or posed by the destination organization. The related concepts are technical quality, process quality, functional quality, and relational quality. All four are integrated under the heading of total quality, and Total Quality Management

(TQM) is perhaps the most well-known term. It is the responsibility of management to measure the gaps in the model of Zeithamml, Parasuraman and Berry, and suggest relevant response strategies.

The research methods that can be applied must also be objective. Phenomena must be reduced to their simplest elements, and this requires methods where concepts are operationalized so they can be measured. Attribute-based methods, therefore, offer the best possibilities. A popular technique is SERVQUAL, developed by Zeithaml Parasuraman and Berry, which attempts to measure the five main characteristics of service quality: tangibles, reliability, responsiveness, assurance, and empathy. These characteristics correspond with the gaps 1 to 5 in the gap-model. With SERVQUAL, organizations are able to permanently monitor the internal routine service quality (Easterby-Smith et al., 1993; Fick and Brent Ritchie, 1991; Staus and Hentschel, 1992).

The external measurement refers to the subjective expectations, needs, wants, and experiences of the customer. The related quality concepts are expected quality, experienced quality, and perceived quality. Management strategies aim at improving the relationship between service provider and customer, and the respective co-production. Research methods which apply to this viewpoint need to focus on the totality of each situation and, therefore, need to establish different views of phenomena.

Useful methods are the incident-based methods, of which the Critical Incident Technique (CRIT) is often used. The results are collected from small samples investigated in depth over time and used to try to understand what is happening in the various "moments of truth". With CRIT the organizations are able to understand customer problems and resolve them in a flexible way (Easterby-Smith et al., 1993; Scheuing and Christopher, 1993). The CRIT deserves special attention, given the discussion above in relation to the development and interpretation of the product, the widening of the domain of marketing, and the quest for quality improvement.

Research has demonstrated that the customer wants to have at least the feeling that he/she has a certain influence on the service process. When this feeling is absent, it will lead to a lower appreciation of the service. If the service in reality differs from the image the customer has, the result is a critical situation (loss of control) that can be harmful for the service organization. If the organization is able to solve the incident (recovery), the service can be saved. But if the organization fails, a negative evaluation will follow. Such situations have a strong influence on the image and reputation of the organization. Therefore, it is very important for management to recognize these situations and to solve them. "One single failure in an unexpected situation can turn a good quality assessment which was built up carefully over years into the opposite. In this way, even long-lasting relationships between customers and service providers may come to a sudden end. But the message for managers responsible for service quality is also: do not only be prepared for when things go wrong, also plan and create positive surprises for your customer!" (Staus and Hentschel, 1992). The critical incident technique can be an important aid in this process.

A MONITORING SYSTEM FOR TOP OF HOLLAND

In 1993, the Institute for Service Management[3] started building a marketing monitoring system for a destination organization called "Top of Holland" (Institute for Service Management, 1994). The goal of this organization is to stimulate foreign tourism to the three northern provinces of the Netherlands (Friesland, Groningen and Drenthe), in such a way that the growth, in percentage terms, is the same as the growth of foreign tourism in the Netherlands as a whole. Actually, Top of Holland is an organization which comprises attractions and service providers in the three provinces and the foreign tourist market. It can be seen as being responsible for relationship marketing, although in fact all attractions and service organizations are participants in the marketing process.

To be able to manage the marketing, Top of Holland needs a continuous systematic evaluation, which informs it about the results of the marketing efforts and areas in which improvement is required. The monitoring system the Institute for Service Management (ISM) has developed has been built around the viewpoints discussed in the previous sections: the concepts of a tourism system, quality management, and relationship marketing.

To stimulate the growth of incoming foreign tourism by improving marketing, four questions are important.

1. *Communication:* through which channels does Top of Holland provide generic information (about the whole region, for the whole market) respectively and contingent information (specific information for a specific market segment about a specific product profile) about the destination?

2. *Empowerment:* does the information lead to a 'purchase'?

   It is necessary that a potential tourist is informed about the product, but that doesn't necessarily mean that he/she is going to visit the destination. Possibly the product profile and consumer profile do not match each other, for example because of the destination's image, or the income, or cultural background of the customer. But in the decision making process, all other factors are important. Some factors can be influenced by Top of Holland, but other environmental factors cannot be influenced by this organization. If a potential tourist fails to visit the destination, this doesn't necessarily mean the customer is not interested in the product profile: it might be that the information to persuade him/her is inadequate.

   Empowerment is relevant to both general information and contingent information, but especially the latter. To the customer it is relevant in that he/she can express complaints about the product profile. These can be used as an indicator to match the product profile and consumer profile.

3. *Legitimation:* does the information reflect the product, in that it is understandable and honest?

   The information about the product (profile) needs to be correct, understandable and honest. It may mean a positive contribution in the decision making process of the potential tourist to visit the destination. Moreover, it gives the tourist a normative structure to his/her destination decision-making.

In relation to the Top of Holland, legitimation has to do with a certain responsibility to the tourist: the experiences of the vacation should match the expectations of the tourist. On the other hand, the tourist must be able to express complaints about the product profile.

4. *Co-production:* how can the growth of foreign tourism be stimulated by the co-production (co-service) between Top of Holland and the potential tourist?

Top of Holland is able to support the decision making process of the tourist, but cannot influence it. This support can be achieved by adequate relationship marketing.

But in its marketing, Top of Holland is confronted with a dilemma. On the one hand, it needs to offer product profiles for which interest exists in the foreign market. On the other hand, it needs to identify market segments to which the North of the Netherlands has something to offer. In short, Top of Holland cannot define product profiles as long as it does not know the market profile and cannot define a market profile as long as the product profile is unknown. Actually, we need to define them at the same time.

From the product side, we need to investigate to which consumer profiles something can be offered. From the consumer's side, we need to investigate for which product profiles there is interest. Top of Holland needs to communicate between product and market, and needs to mediate between their respective interests.

For optimal effect, this process needs to be continuous. Therefore, it is necessary that information be collected about the co-product. This gives Top of Holland the possibility of evaluating and adjusting its objectives, tactics, and targets as often as is necessary. In this way, Top of Holland is able to steer the development of the co-product. There are a number of important conditions:

a) Because Top of Holland mediates between both the interests of the product and the tourists, it is unable to offer certain product profiles, as well as preventing certain consumer profiles.

b) There are conditions that are relevant to all product or consumer profiles, and conditions that are only relevant to one product or consumer profile. The lack of conditions of the second type cannot be compensated by conditions of the first type. This hinders the development of the co-product and the growth of incoming tourism.

c) To be able to mediate between the interests of both customer and service provider, Top of Holland requires a lot of knowledge and expertise about the service providers and the consumer.

To build a monitoring system that continuously gives insight into these questions, the ISM has developed a research strategy that contains the following steps. Every step is finished by giving summarized information to Top of Holland, providing them with the possibility of reacting to it in their marketing campaign.

1. An overview of the marketing program (Faulkner and Shaw, 1991), undertaken once a year:

   - An overview of the objectives in a hierarchy. The objectives at the lowest level are the most easy to reach. The higher the level, the more external factors influence the results. The objective at the highest level is: "growth of incoming tourism from abroad".

- An overview of the strategies (tactics/methods) that are used to reach every objective in the hierarchy.

- An overview of the target(s) for every objective in the hierarchy Top of Holland would consider as a success. The target for the highest objective is: "a growth of at least the same as the national growth".

- An overview of the performance indicators that can be used for measuring the targets of the marketing campaign.

2.   An overview of the developments in the performance indicators undertaken throughout the year.

3.   Suitability analysis:

- *product profile analysis, undertaken once a year*
The destination mix (attractions and services) of North Netherlands will be developed. In the first cycle of this continuous process, this will result in one list of product elements. But every subsequent cycle results in a classification that is based on conditions the interested consumer profiles require. These profiles are not static. In following cycles, product profiles might be added, eliminated, or adjusted. Furthermore, the analysis implies a first evaluation of the promotion material.

- *consumer profile analysis, undertaken once a year*
The foreign market that is relevant to Top of Holland will be developed. In the first cycle, key informers are confronted with the destination mix. Open interviews must lead to a segmentation of the market into consumer profiles on the basis of shared product conditions. In following cycles, the key informers are confronted with the product profiles and it will be discussed whether the consumer profiles need to be adjusted, added, or eliminated.

- *mismatch analysis, undertaken once a year*
The recursive process from product and consumer profile analysis implies a mismatch analysis in every cycle. This will be done with the help of Top of Holland and key informers in the market place.
The mismatch analysis will give insight as to whether it will be necessary to develop new product profiles, finish or adjust existing product profiles. At the same time, this means the start of a product profile analysis of a new recursive cycle.

- *breakdown analysis, undertaken every season (three times a year)*
If the experiences of the tourist match the expectations, every service is seen as self-evident. Mostly, it is only during critical situations that existing expectation patterns breakdown and consumers suddenly don't behave according to their conditions. Such positive or negative critical experiences are important for the image of the destination in relation to holiday-making. To establish such critical situations, the Critical Incident Technique is used. It gives qualitative information about satisfaction and appreciation.

Because the Top of Holland needs to mediate between the interests of the service providers and the tourists, the CRIT will be used to understand the experiences from the viewpoint of the service provider.

CONCLUSIONS

In this chapter, the central issue was to discuss recent developments in the field of quality management and service marketing and the possibilities of applying these developments to the management of a tourist destination. Attention has been paid to important elements in the strategy of quality management to improve the quality of offered services and the way in which they are interconnected; relationship marketing as a strategy to keep the tourist coming back; the value of an information system to monitor the progress in management and marketing; and cooperation in management, marketing and monitoring are seen as the necessary conditions to deliver quality management for a destination. Finally, Top of Holland is discussed as an example in which these ideas have been applied to a monitoring system.

ACKNOWLEDGEMENTS

The authors appreciate Klaes Eringa's constructive comments on the paragraphs about service management; Jim Slevin for writing the research proposal for Top of Holland; and Cameron Scouler for improving the style and grammar.

REFERENCES

Ashworth, G.J., and Voogd, H. (1990). *Selling the city; marketing approaches in public sector urban planning*. London: Belhaven Press.

Brathwaite, R. (1992). Value chain assessment of the travel experience. *Cornell Quarterly*, 33(5), October, 41-49.

Dietvorst, A. (1993). *Tourist recreation development and spatial transformations*. Wageningen, Netherlands: Agricultural University.

Easterby-Smith, M., Thorpe, R., and Lowe, A. (1993). *Management research: An introduction*. London: Sage Publications.

Edvardsson, B., Thomasson, B., and Ovretveit, J. (1994). *Quality of service—Making it really work*. London: McGraw-Hill.

Faulkner, B., and Shaw, R. (Eds.) (1991). *Evaluation of tourism marketing* (BTR Occasional paper No. 13). Canberra, Australia: Bureau of Tourism Research.

Fick, G.R., and Brent Ritchie, J.R. (1991). Measuring service quality in the travel and tourism industry. *Journal of Travel Research*, Fall.

Grönroos, C. (1990). *Service management and marketing: Managing the moment of truth in service competition*. Lexington, Massachusetts: Lexington Books.

Gummesson, E. (1993). *Quality management in service organisations: An interpretation of the service quality phenomenon and a synthesis of international research* (ISQA Research Report No. 1). USA: International Service Quality Association.

Institute for Service Management (1994). *Effectrapportage Top of Holland*. Leeuwarden, Netherlands: ISM.

Jansen-Verbeke, M. (1988). *Leisure, recreation and tourism in inner cities* (Netherlands Geographical Studies, Vol. 58). Nijmegen, Netherlands: Katholieke Universiteit.

Jansen-Verbeke, M. (1994). *Toerisme Quo Vadis? Agenda voor een krisismanagement*. Rotterdam, Netherlands: Stichting Bewetour.

Mill, R.C., and Morrison, A.M. (1993). *The tourism system*. Englewood Cliffs, NJ: Prentice Hall.

Normann, R. (1991). *Service management: Strategy and leadership in service business*. Chichester: John Wiley and Sons, Ltd.

Scheuing, E.E., and Christopher, W.F. (Eds.) (1993). *The service quality handbook*. New York: AMACOM.

Staus, B., and Hentschel, B., (1992). Attribute-based versus incident-based measurement of service quality: Results of an empirical study in the German Car Service Industry. In P. Kunst and J. Lemmink (Eds.), *Quality management in services* (pp. 59-78). Assen, The Netherlands: Van Gorcum.

Vogelezang H., and Hageman, T. (1993). *Servicemanagement—de sociale contructie van diensten*. Baarn, Netherlands: Nelissen.

ENDNOTES

[1] Internal factors are those that can be influenced by the organizations themselves.

[2] Thus, relationship-marketing is different from the traditional marketing-mix approach (product, place, price, promotion, and sometimes even people, public relations, and politics). This approach primarily aims at the sale or transaction of the product, service or idea, and as such communication primarily takes place before this transaction. Furthermore, the market is seen as an abstract mass which is always present somewhere, and customers are seen as numbers who replace each other. As such, relationship marketing can be seen as an alternative approach for the marketing of destinations.

[3] The Institute for Service Management is the service centre which belongs to the Faculty of Economics and Management of the CHN North Netherlands, Leeuwarden, the Netherlands. The institute develops international, national, and regional projects in cooperation with students of the Hotel Management School, the Leisure Management School, and the Retail Management School of the faculty.

Plate 11 The Royal British Columbia Museum, Victoria
(photo courtesy of The Province of British Columbia) ➡

'Visioning' for Sustainable Tourism Development: Community-based Collaborations

16

Tazim B. Jamal and Donald Getz

Tourism and Hospitality Management,
Faculty of Management, University of Calgary

INTRODUCTION

One of the principles of sustainable development outlined by the Brundtland Commission's report of 1987 (*Our Common Future*) is that of holistic planning and strategy making. As described by Bramwell and Lane (1993: 3), sustainable tourism is a "positive approach intended to reduce the tensions and friction created by the complex interactions between the tourism industry, visitors, the environment and the communities . . . ." In trying to develop measures of local sustainability, however, the Sustainable Community Roundtable in Washington's Thurston County realized that it needed to have a vision of what sustainability meant for them locally. It thereafter compiled a comprehensive picture of a sustainable community, by drawing on the existing visions of various local organizations.[1] While the term 'sustainable tourism' is being debated, many tourism destinations and other communities are grappling with issues related to its philosophy, such as managing growth and development for the long-term wellbeing of the community, its visitors and the environment. Various organizational and inter-organizational initiatives are evolving in these communities in light of these challenges. This chapter describes collaborative, vision-based exercises for strategic destination planning and management in four communities: Jackson Hole (Wyoming) and Aspen (Colorado) as resort destinations, Calgary (Alberta) as an urban tourist destination, and Revelstoke (British Columbia) as an emerging tourist destination.

The main aim of this exploratory research is to examine these strategic visioning exercises from a content, process, outcome perspective, and evaluate their potential for assisting local planners and other stakeholders with sustainable destination management. The merits and weaknesses of the various processes utilized in the visioning exercises are discussed in the context of participatory planning and effective destination management. Propositions for directing further research into vision-based exercises for strategic destination planning are presented.

THEORETICAL PERSPECTIVES

Collaboration in community tourism planning

Tourism literature abounds with studies pointing to the dynamic character of tourism destination communities, where resident views vary considerably depending on the perceived impacts of tourism, the type and level of tourism development, as well as socioeconomic factors such as education and employment in the tourism industry (Allen et al., 1988; Milman and Pizam, 1988; Keogh, 1990; Long et al., 1990; Johnson et al., 1994). Growing awareness of the fragmented nature of the tourism industry and the adverse impacts of tourism development on environmental and sociocultural sustainability, has led to a call for integrating tourism within the overall planning framework of the destination, developing growth management strategies and involving the local community in the planning process (see Murphy 1985; Getz, 1987; Haywood, 1988; Dredge and Moore, 1992; Gill and Williams, 1994). However, Ryan and Montgomery (1994: 369) warn against assuming the existence of a common community consensus view, and hence the danger of community-responsive tourism becoming "tourism promotion aimed at those who wish to become responsive, thereby making more explicit the community differences that exist." The challenge in tourism destination management then becomes being able to incorporate the often diverse views of the community's multiple stakeholders and the fragmented control over community goods and resources (both public and private), into the local planning process.

Discussing the pluralist nature of American society, which enables power diffusion and the formation of interest groups, Buchholz (1993: 104) points out that a pluralist system is a system of conflict because interest groups compete for attention and influence in the public policy process. Such competing interests "do not necessarily result in the best public policy decisions" and, furthermore, some interests (e.g., minorities or poorer elements of society) are not well represented. The special features of tourism development at the community level suggest that participation techniques applicable to tourism planning need to be developed and evaluated; required is an ongoing participation process that is educational for all parties involved (Simmons, 1994). Applying a three-stage participation program (interviews, focus groups, and surveys) to residents in Huron County (Ontario, Canada), Simmons notes that surveys can reach a broad spectrum of residents and efficiently provide quantifiable data on known issues, but offer only one-way communication, tend to require high user sophistication, and rate poorly as an educational device.

Jamal and Getz (1995) argue for the need of a community-based tourism planning process, based on collaboration between autonomous and key stakeholders in the community tourism domain. Collaboration theory provides an effective framework for designing multi-stakeholder, consensus-based processes to advance shared visions or resolve complex problems. The *domain* is inter-organizational, requiring multi-stakeholder response to issues which are beyond the capability of any single individual or group to resolve single-handedly (Gray, 1989). According to Trist (1983: 270), inter-organizational domains are "functional social systems that occupy a position in social space between the society as a whole and the single organization." As defined by Gray (1989), *stakeholders* are the actors with an interest in a common problem or issue and include all individuals, groups, or organizations directly influenced by the actions taken by others to resolve the problem or issue. A *consensus* approach involves joint decision making by the stakeholders involved in the collaboration process, who are also *autonomous*, since they retain independent decision-making powers while abiding by the collaboration's shared rules. Examples of local area initiatives involving community cooperation and collaboration include the *Local Area Tourism Initiatives* in the UK (Bramwell and Broom, 1989), the *Community Tourism Action Plan* initiated in the mid-1980s in Alberta (Canada), and *Vision 2020*, a provincial initiative to enable Alberta communities to develop a vision which could guide their future direction and development.

A case study by Getz and Jamal (1994) in the growing mountain community of Canmore, Alberta (Canada), demonstrated that collaborative processes related to tourism planning and development were occurring at various levels of the destination development domain, for example, between local municipalities, as well as between environmental groups and the local resident organization (BowCORD). The *Vision 2020* initiative enabled a community vision statement to be formed in Canmore in the late 1980s, through the participation of a diverse group of community members. This community vision has subsequently been invoked by concerned stakeholders during various development and planning initiatives, including the revision of the town's General Municipal Plan. In light of the multiple stakeholders of a community tourism destination, the diversity of community views and the complexities of the tourism 'product,' it can also be argued that a community vision statement should be formed with the active input of the stakeholders in the community domain.

Strategic Visioning

Unlike those of a firm, the processes of strategic planning and management of a destination are not well defined theoretically. The transposition of corporate strategic planning techniques to the public sector has been perceived both positively and negatively (see Bower, 1977; Bryson et al., 1986; McGill, 1988; Skok, 1989). Nevertheless, some valuable lessons on the strategic process can be learned and applied from the corporate literature to a community domain. For example, Mintzberg (1994: 328) has criticized the traditional planning schools for having relegated the creative process of strategy-making to corporate planners. Formal, systematic analysis does not encourage creativity; it is "a convergent process, in search of a solution, and a deductive one, oriented more to decomposition than to design." Strategy-making conversely, he states, is an intuitive and creative process of *synthesis* requiring both soft and hard data, where strategies can be formed deliberately or may *emerge* over time. Generally, it is the managers (and not the planning analysts) who have access to soft information, and who therefore should (i) take active charge of the strategy making process, (ii) make use of tacit knowledge and intuitive processes, and (iii) have intimate contact with their organization's operations and external environment (Mintzberg, 1994: 269). From a study of three Ohio state agencies, Wechsler and Backoff (1987) also concluded that if planners are to play a significant role, it will usually be in support of general managers rather than as strategists themselves.

Enclosed within the strategy-making process is the concept of a strategic vision (or mission), which embodies the desired direction and values of the organization and its stakeholders. As summarized by Westley and Mintzberg (1989), strategic vision or 'visioning', as the process has been referred to, contains three distinct stages: (1) envisioning 'an image of a desired future organizational stage', (2) effectively communicating the vision to followers, which then serves to (3) empower those followers to be able to enact the vision. Mintzberg suggests that the visionary approach is more flexible in dealing with an uncertain world; vision sets out the broad outlines of a strategy, but specific details can be worked out or may emerge. A sufficiently robust vision enables the organization to adapt, learn, and thereby more easily accommodate change (Mintzberg, 1994: 209-210). At a destination level, competition for scarce resources (e.g., government funds, tourist dollars, investment, and taxable revenues) and an increasingly competitive global environment, increase the challenge of creating sustainable communities. For instance, the reallocation of destination resources to hosting mega-tourist events can serve to decrease the wellbeing of certain groups in society, especially the powerless and disadvantaged (Hall, 1994a). The management, representation, and preservation of heritage is also closely linked to broader political issues of values, interests, and control (Hall, 1994b). Who, then, are the 'managers' of a tourism destination, and how can public-private sector interests be balanced for the overall benefit of the community's stakeholders (internal and external)?

Haywood (1988) has suggested a diversified approach to planning for tourism, where planning is a process for designing the future, for innovation, for learning, for influencing, and for managing. Haywood (1994) discusses the need for destinations to engage in continuous innovation and strategic improvements, in order to keep pace with the increasing rate of change in the external environment. This entails that decision-making become more bottom-up than top-down, where authority can be imposed by communicating a vision, enabling people with systems, and empowering them to make the vision real. Tourism enterprises, he suggests, must learn how to collaborate more effectively if they are to survive. A vision is one essential factor for creating a widespread community endeavour towards quality destination management, since it "will create constancy of purpose and will provide a guidepost for people to determine their own priorities and those of the community effort" (Haywood, 1994: 433). As pointed out by Ritchie (1993: 381), while the choice of the vision is critical for any entity or firm, it is absolutely critical for a tourism destination "as it will set in motion the development of facilities, events and programmes which will do much to define the very essence of that destination for years to come." Discussing key challenges that face place marketing (such as growing competition and increasing self-reliance), Kotler (1993) also suggests that one response to organizing for change is for places to establish a *strategic vision* to face these challenges.

It follows that strategic visions for specific destination objectives, such as marketing and tourism development, need to be consistent with the community's overall vision of its future, which provides guidance for the development of specific initiatives. The concept of an overall vision has also been advocated by the Successful Communities program (initiated by the U.S. based Conservation Foundation in 1988) as one of the success factors identified for managing growth and change within communities. According to this guideline, a community should *"build land-use policies around a vision of what the community should be. A positive, shared vision is critical . . ."* (Abberger and Propst, 1991-2). Luther Propst also stated in Muller (1990: 11) that "the principle shortcoming of many communities is local land use policy that is reactive rather than proactive. The vision, the goal, needs to stay out front." Vision statements help to describe the community's shared beliefs and values, its cultural image, its desires for its future direction (i.e., what it wants to see for the community's future). Ideally, they are uplifting and enduring, the foundations upon which goals and plans are based (Schechter, 1990).

Methodology

The complexity of community tourism domains leads to the tentative proposition that a collaborative, community-based, 'visioning' approach is required for effective strategic planning and management of local destinations. Four communities were picked for exploratory study: Jackson Hole (Wyoming), Aspen (Colorado), Revelstoke (British Columbia), and Calgary (Alberta). These were selected in order to examine specific 'visioning' exercises that have been conducted within each one. Data was gathered using (a) existing published literature sources, and (b) new data through telephone interviews and document reviews. In order to obtain a richer insight into these processes, interviews followed a qualitative method, using an iterative approach with open-ended questions. Data analysis involved using a set of criteria for inputs and outputs of the collaborative process. Inputs included: (i) types of stakeholders present; (ii) reasons for the initiative; (iii) decision making (consensus-based?); (iv) initiator of the exercise; (v) strategic process. Outputs involved: (i) content of vision statement, strategies; (ii) focus on tourism; (iii) implementation plan; (iv) implementing organization (structure, continuity).

Community Planning Collaborations

Jackson Hole, Wyoming

Jackson Hole's image has been changing from a traditionally ranching community to a more commercial tourism one, aided by the establishment of national parks followed by a ski resort in the mid-1960s. This has brought with it the typical problems of rising real estate values, lack of affordable housing, and a conflict over community identity and values. While most of the county is federally-owned, the ranching owners exert a strong influence over the community due to their large land holdings. In 1979, the Jackson Hole Alliance for Responsible Planning (referred to as 'the Alliance' henceforth) was formed as a non-profit advocacy group, with the purpose of enforcing Jackson Hole's first land-use plan (passed in 1977), as well as to monitor and guide growth management and planning issues in the community. Its 1,164 members come from diverse backgrounds, with about half coming from outside of Teton County. With a professional staff augmented by volunteers and an annual budget of around $260,000, this is one of the largest memberships in the country. Despite the conflicting values of the various stakeholders in the area and in the Alliance membership, this advocacy group has been able to exert a strong influence over decision-making in Jackson Hole, and demonstrates "that consensus-building can give an organization real teeth."[2] While surveys play a role in choosing positions on issues, its 18-member board, which attempts to contain ideological diversity, often makes the final decision, using a joint decision-making approach.

Recognizing the need for organizing the divergent community interests, protecting the community's distinct character and the ecological integrity of its environment, a Successful Communities program was initiated in March 1990, under the guidance of the Conservation Foundation. Of the 5,500 town residents (and over 11,000 people who reside permanently in Teton County, inclusive of the town), over 300 people attended one or more of the workshop sessions. Ten random groups were formed, each of which developed a vision statement. Common themes in the statements reflected shared community values and desires for the community's future. Additionally, the participants developed action steps by which the community could bring about the future represented by the vision statements (see Schechter, 1990). The 10 statements were synthesized into one overall vision by a workshop organizer, as follows:

> *Jackson Hole is a diversified yet cooperative community. It acts through a unified representative government that is responsible to a concerned and involved constituency, and dedicated to managed growth—acknowledging that as in all communities there is a limit to the development which any area can support—using a variety of new as well as "tried and true" planning techniques to promote:*
>
> *The enhancement and protection of all our natural resources, including the maintenance of open spaces between diverse housing development;*
>
> *The maintenance and enhancement of our unique and small-town Western heritage, which not only welcomes others but has a very special interest in caring for its own;*
>
> *The preservation of our historical heritage; and*
>
> *The growth/development of a diverse economy not dependent on any one segment of economic life.*

A steering committee (*Successful Communities Dialogue*), formed to convene, organize, and lead the workshops, continued after this visioning exercise, and held subsequent workshops. It also initiated a Roundtable of diverse interest groups (August 1992 to February 1993) to discuss issues related to the Comprehensive Plan being developed then by local policy makers. The Roundtable discussions aided in improving cooperation among some of the diverse interests in the community, while the vision statements developed by the Successful Communities workshop have had a strong positive impact on the new Comprehensive Plan (a joint Town and County plan). The community character-based nature of this plan was developed based on the vision statements.

The Comprehensive Plan replaced the old 1978 Plan which had generated strong controversy from dissatisfied stakeholders. The new Plan has been formed under intense scrutiny from the public, whose participation ranged from attending public hearings, informal public meetings, and public information sessions, to forming ad hoc committees to address various issues. One major stakeholder group formed in opposition to some of the proposed regulations. The Alliance played an active role throughout the process, but though public interest was strong, the complexity of the Plan and the lengthy formation time caused some attrition in public participation. As put succinctly by a Jackson Hole planner, the planner's job should be to help the community determine what it needs, not to tell it what it needs. Hence, the existence of an ongoing citizen's roundtable group, it was felt, would be very helpful.

Aspen, Colorado

State-wide legislation requiring a growth management strategy has been in effect for over a decade in Colorado, where growth management is a "systematic impact management strategy" which attempts to "capture the benefits of growth while mitigating the consequences" (Gill and Williams, 1994: 213). Subsequent to the establishment of Aspen as a skiing destination in 1950, the population of the surrounding Pitkin County grew rapidly, reaching 12,661 in 1990 and swelling to a peak of 35,000 at the height of the tourism season. Aspen's current metro population is 7,800 and swells to about 23,400 during the peak season. The 1976 Aspen/ Pitkin County Growth Management Policy Plan (GMPP), intended to replace the more traditional multicoloured comprehensive planning map, recognized the interdependence of population, housing, new business formations, skiing, community services and the environment. Additionally, it acknowledged that Aspen has historically valued its small town uniqueness and its natural environment. Subsequently, the Valley has experienced several planning problems, including (i) runaway growth in other communities down the Roaring Forks Valley (partly attributable to growth limitations in Aspen), (ii) lack of affordable housing for local employees, due to rising real estate prices and a large increase in the number of second homes, (iii) displacement of workers and business owners to further down the valley due to housing problems, leading to a concern about eroding community values and a diminishing permanent resident population. Between 1987 and 1991, the proportion of employees working within the community who also lived in the community dropped from 60 percent to 45 percent (AACP, 1993: 8).

These difficulties indicated that the 1976 GMPP had not anticipated or planned for social consequences, nor similarly for qualitative issues. For example, while the 3.7 percent growth limit was not exceeded, the design and character of the residential housing being developed were not in keeping with Aspen's perceived character. Hence, an innovative exercise was funded by City and County elected officials in 1990 (Fall) to create a community-based, comprehensive land use plan, the Aspen Area Community Plan (AACP). The main purpose of this process was to develop a character-based and action-oriented plan, built upon a citizen-based vision for the future of City of Aspen and its immediate 'metro area' in Pitkin County (Figure 16.1).

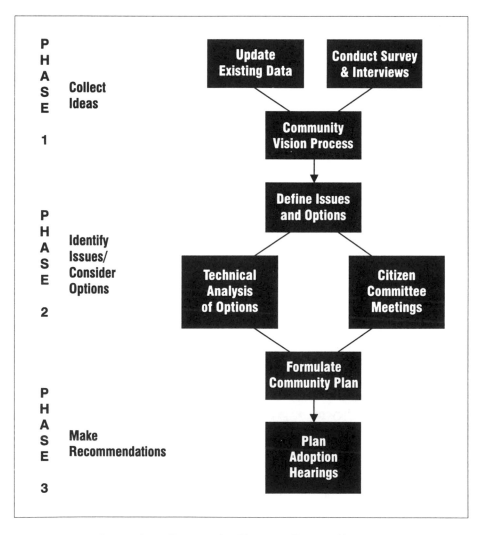

Figure 16.1   Aspen Area Community Planning Process (Source: AACP, 1993).

The process of creating the AACP can be characterized by the following:

1. Maximal citizen involvement. Major issues facing the community were identified via personal interviews and community-wide meetings, using a consensus approach. Five Issue Committees of citizens from diverse backgrounds were formed (participation open to all residents), which interacted closely with an Oversight committee comprised of County and City officials. This enabled eventual "buy in" of the AACP by the elected officials responsible for plan implementation.

2. A multi-stakeholder and consensus-based approach was used to formulate the plan, which helped ensure approval by the overall community and the elected officials. Involvement in the planning process was open to all citizens; over 400 participated.

3. A vision statement was developed by the citizen committees, based on four themes identified by participating citizens: (i) revitalizing the permanent community, (ii) providing transportation alternatives, (iii) promoting environmentally sustainable development, and (iv) maintaining design quality/historic compatibility. In addition, five main Community Development Features were identified to help direct future planning, which formed the focus of the five committees. Six *action plans* were created by the citizen committees, in order to help implement the vision. Each plan was organized under three subheadings: intent, philosophy and policies. The plan avoided traditional limits to growth such as infrastructure and water, focusing instead on the 'quality' of the built environment and the character of the social fabric of the community.

After two and a half years in formulation, the AACP was adopted formally in January, 1993. It has enabled community-wide support for several planning programs being developed by local planners in sensitive areas such as traffic mitigation, street design/enhancement efforts and affordable housing. The GMPP was being revised, with the assistance of the AACP and the citizen committees formed during the AACP process, who continued to operate and provide advice. Hence, not only did the citizens write the plan, they also continued to stay involved, ensuring continuity and commitment to the plan over the long run. In this sense, the plan retained a dynamic character.

Revelstoke, British Columbia (B.C.)

Located strategically along the major Trans Canada Highway and the Canadian Pacific railway route in the interior of B.C., Revelstoke has experienced a boom and bust industry based on the cycles of the forestry, mining, and transportation sectors. Situated adjacent to two national parks, and encircled by the North Columbia Mountains, its potential for skiing and summer park visitation makes it an attractive area for tourism development. Tourism currently comprises roughly a quarter of the local economy. In Fall/Winter 1995/1996, the City of Revelstoke has been evaluating proposals from developers to assist in developing the city's Mount Mackenzie ski hill into a first class destination resort.

Wishing to shape their own future and create an integrated expression of community values, the community leaders of this town of 8,000 inhabitants initiated a visioning exercise in November 1991. An interdisciplinary team was formed, called the Revelstoke Community Vision Committee, whose members consisted of 37 citizens from various sectors. Visionary speakers were hosted, and a facilitator appointed. By May 1992, a draft vision was formed, which sought for the historic alpine town to be a leader in achieving sustainable development by balancing environmental, social and economic values. Feedback from the resident public on the draft vision statement was sought via a community-wide survey and the results of a research team comprised primarily of Earthwatch volunteers (*Mountain Town with a Vision* Research Project) which interviewed over 300 individuals (including residents and visitors) to obtain their comments on the visioning process (Feick, 1994, 1995). Based on the information received, the draft vision statement was revised and submitted to City Council, which ratified it in February 1994. The statement reads as follows:

> *Revelstoke will be a leader in achieving a sustainable community by balancing environmental, social and economic values within a local, regional and global context.*
>
> *Building on its rich heritage, this historic mountain community will pursue quality and excellence. Revelstoke will be seen as vibrant, healthy, clean, hospitable, resilient, and forward-thinking. It will be committed to exercising its rights with respect to decisions affecting the North Columbia Mountains.**
>
> *Community priorities include: opportunities for youth; economic growth and stability; environmental citizenship; personal safety and security; a responsible and caring social support system; a first-class education system; local access to lifelong learning, spiritual and cultural values; and diverse forms of recreation.*
>
> *All residents and visitors shall have access to the opportunities afforded by this community.*
>
> * An area roughly bounded by Eagle Pass(W), Donald (E), Mica (N), and Trout Lake (S).

In 1993, the town became the first community in B.C. to purchase its own timber license in order to exercise local control of timber harvesting operations. This step reflected the environmental philosophy espoused in the draft vision document in process at that time. Additionally, the official Community Plan is expected to reflect portions of this vision statement. Several stakeholders have also suggested that steps should be taken to ensure that the vision document is carried beyond formulation into action (e.g., by forming an implementation committee).

The change in local officials during the Fall 1993 elections has been providing a test of the ability of the vision statement to guide future tourism development in Revelstoke. While it is too early to judge the overall impact of the visioning process on the community, the vision-setting exercise appears to have helped some individual participants to become more aware of different issues and points of view, as well as of the value of collaboration.

Calgary, Alberta

Following the successful hosting of the 1988 Winter Olympics in Calgary, community leaders initiated a process which involved getting together the thoughts and views of over 100 of its approximately 660,000 residents, to determine how best to direct the city's future economic direction and continue diversifying away from the traditional oil and gas sector. Subsequent to this, a 'Core Group' of 12 volunteer citizens was formed (aided by four staff from the City Administration), which developed a report in April 1989, entitled "Calgary . . . Into the 21st Century: A Strategy for Economic Development." It incorporated the views of the initial 100 residents, as well as additional research and experts' opinions. This report contained a vision statement "as a measure of what success would look like." Additionally, three primary goals and ten strategic challenges were arrived at, plus a number of facilitating actions to assist in achieving the outlined goals were outlined. Based on this, ten task forces were set up to expand upon and create implementation steps for the key strategies and major challenges. Over 150 volunteers took part in this stage. The Calgary . . . Into the 21st Century report obtained broad circulation worldwide and locally. It was hoped that this document would receive community ownership, encourage economic development, and be a catalyst for an ongoing implementation plan.[3]

Task Force No. 6 undertook the responsibility of trying to establish Calgary as 'Host, Consultant and Educator to the World'. The 18 members of the task force, representing various industry sectors, met monthly between March 1990 and February 1991. As its prime mandate, a vision statement was created of the kind of tourist destination Calgary should become as it moves into the 21st century. The nine vision statements reflected two general categories: first, some general values upheld by the city, and second, the key aspects of the city's character upon which tourism should be built (Ritchie, 1993). Based on this statement, nine key strategies and a series of action steps to implement the strategies were developed by the task force. One of the action steps recommended was to consider applying to host an international world exposition (Expo 2005) on the Province's 100th birthday. The city is currently putting together a proposal to host the Expo world fair in 2005, which is a direct outcome of this task force's recommendations. The task force followed a consensus-based decision making approach.

In order to ensure that the Calgary vision is communicated and the action steps implemented, a coordinating body was launched (The Strategic Alliance for "Calgary . . . Into the 21st Century") and an implementation report generated.[4]

Founding members consisted of prominent citizens with links to local community and business leaders. Nine new task forces were set up by the Strategic Alliance to implement the plan, working together with sponsoring organizations from the business and academic community. The Strategic Alliance group was replaced by a new body (Cal 21 Executive Group), which provides coordination between implementation groups and ensures the continuity of the exercise. This economic visioning project is currently facing some funding and organization challenges, related to the restructuring of the project's original sponsor, CEDA (Calgary Economic Development Authority, a joint venture between the local Chamber of Commerce and the City of Calgary).

The applications of this economic visioning exercise range well beyond that of the immediate project. The political action plan created by Calgary's City Council in 1990 ("Charting Calgary's Future") relied on several local strategic planning exercises including "Calgary . . . Into the 21st Century" and "Calgary 2020." While the former provided an economic vision and strategy, the latter "Calgary 2020" exercise was conducted in response to a provincial initiative to get local governments to prepare "preferred vision" statements to help shape their future.[5] City Council responded and created a task force which invoked citizen participation. Over 300 members participated, in the form of 33 diverse groups representing community associations, native Indian and ethnic members, heritage, natural environment, economic development, religious denominations, seniors, and other community segments. Members of "Calgary . . . Into the 21st Century" inputted into the "Calgary 2020" vision via the economic development subgroup. The hopes and issues within the 2020 vision reflect common consensus among the community groups involved.

ANALYSIS

The usefulness of a community vision statement as a destination planning and management tool may vary considerably, and could depend on factors such as (i) the specificity of community values, desires and aspirations, (ii) the process and type of community involvement in the visioning exercise (degree of formalization of the process, who participated and why, resources available to conduct the process, active and broad community participation versus passive survey feedback, etc.), and (iii) the utilization of the vision statement in strategic planning and development initiatives related to the community. Tables 16.1 and 16.2 compare the visioning exercises that were undertaken in these four communities, from a content and process perspective. The vision statements vary in specificity with respect to stating community characteristics, values, and desired future direction. Detailed descriptions of existing community characteristics and values to be preserved, as well as those to be developed, are seen in Aspen's vision statement. Jackson Hole's vision contains some specific guidelines for directing future growth (e.g., maintenance of open spaces between diverse housing developments; managed growth; diverse economy). Aspen's vision, more detailed than Jackson Hole's or Revelstoke's, identifies four themes as a framework of action, as well as some overall strategies. It recognizes that tourism is the economic force of community, and also recognizes the interdependence between the community and the tourism industry. Revelstoke's statement is 'succinct' and attempts to portray how it wishes to be perceived and what its community priorities are. Neither Revelstoke's nor Jackson Hole's overall vision make direct reference to the role of tourism in their community's future, though Revelstoke's statement refers to offering visitors access to the opportunities afforded by its community (Table 16.1). Calgary's economic vision is also quite specific and oriented towards future development. Of the five themes outlined as to its future character, the 'host, consultant and educator to the world' focuses on developing Calgary as a major tourism, conference, and business destination.

Active, community-wide involvement was encouraged in forming Jackson Hole's vision statement, which has since been utilized in the formulation of the new joint town and country Comprehensive Plan. Aspen's vision statement was developed as part of a process of formulating an action-oriented Community Plan (Figure 16.1). As the Plan states, its purpose is "to determine the future character and vision for the City of Aspen and surrounding area" and is therefore a character-based plan "reflecting the energy, creativity and commitment of Aspen Area citizens" (AACP, 1993: 9,10). Imparting the community vision to the Plan was facilitated by the full involvement of the area residents. It can then be argued that, transferring the somewhat intangible qualities of shared values and beliefs, plus desires for the community's future, into a community plan can be facilitated by involving the residents and citizens to whom they belong. Furthermore, since the Aspen Area Community Plan contains distinct action steps developed jointly by the citizens and the local authorities, both sides can take ownership for directing future development and growth issues.

Conversely, Revelstoke's visioning exercise was more restricted in the degree of community-wide participation. Like Jackson Hole's process, Revelstoke's exercise was primarily to form a vision statement, which also stated broad community priorities. In Revelstoke's case, community leaders participated in formulating the vision, while community-wide participation was primarily in the form of surveys and over 300 interviews (of locals and visitors). Calgary's economic visioning exercise, ongoing with respect to implementation, relied primarily on task forces interacting with a 'core' group. One consideration in the outcome of the Calgary exercise is the separation of formulation and implementation task forces. The first set of task forces was responsible for the formulation of the strategies plus action steps for implementation, while the subsequent new task forces were mandated for implementation. Though there was overlap in some members between the old and new task forces, this may account for some of the delay between the formation and the implementation of the strategies and actions devised.

Table 16.1   Content summary of the visioning exercises in the four communities

Content of the visioning exercise	Aspen	Jackson Hole	Revelstoke	Calgary (economic vision)
Environmental considerations	One of four major vision themes (environmentally sustainable development and lifestyles)	Wildlife protection; environmental stewardship	Environmental citizenship; balancing environmental, social and economic values within local, regional and global context	"values and preserves . . . minimize impact on the environment"
Economic considerations	Bring back local serving businesses into Aspen area; tourism is economic force	Diversified economy	Economic growth plus stability	Strong emphasis: expanding and diversifying; innovation and entrepreneurship
Social considerations	People should take precedence; vitality eroded by inability of working people to live in town	Maintain social diversity, recreation opportunities	Youth opportunity; access to education, responsible social support, personal safety and security, diverse recreation	Quality of life, education and training, encourage arts and entertainment, parks and recreational opportunities
Community "culture and values"	Diverse mix of people is its key resource; must recreate "messy vitality"	Historic, unique small-town Western heritage (ranching)	Build on rich historic heritage; spiritual and cultural values	Value rich heritage, integrated community of many cultures and ethnic origins
Tourism	Interdependence between tourism industry and community recognized	No direct emphasis	Indirect reference (visitors shall have access to afforded opportunities)	Well specified as a priority ("host, consultant and educator to the world")

DISCUSSION

A preliminary investigation of visioning exercises in the communities of Jackson Hole, Aspen, Revelstoke, and Calgary shows that collaborative visioning exercises are occurring, often initiated by the need to manage growth (e.g., Aspen, Jackson Hole), establish future direction (e.g., Calgary, Revelstoke), and/or integrate the views of multiple stakeholders in the community domain (e.g., Jackson Hole). While North American firms have typically had short planning horizons, destinations by their very nature require long-term planning frameworks, within which short- and

Table 16.2   Visioning processes in the four communities

	Aspen	Jackson Hole	Revelstoke	Calgary
Name of project	Aspen Area Community Plan (AACP)	Successful Communities Workshop	Revelstoke Community Vision Committee	"Calgary . . . Into the 21st Century"
Strategic Plan in same process? (Community plan; strategy/ action steps)	Yes. AACP formed as one continuous process	No. Some action steps developed at workshop	No. Community priorities identified in vision statement	City vision, action steps and implementation in sequence of different processes
Public involvement via **1a** full participation **1b** stakeholder representation via committees &/or task forces **2** surveys, interviews, focus groups, opinion polls **3** public meetings, information sessions **4** limited resident representation	**1a** >400 participated via interviews, surveys, community meetings, focus groups plus 5 'open' citizen committees (formed to work with "oversight committee" and form action plan). Committees focus: growth, transportation, community character, open space/recreation and environment. Oversight committee: 2 members each from City Council, Board of County Commissioners, City P&Z, County P&Z	**1a** Full participation. >300 attended 1 or more of 3 workshops. Sponsored by >50 local organizations (public, private, non-profit)	**1b + 2** Vision created by Revelstoke Community Vision Committee (comprised of community leaders). Feedback from community residents via community surveys, interviews and focus groups. Draft statement revised by Vision Committee to reflect feedback.	**1b + 4** Over 100 residents participated initially in brainstorming sessions which led to formation of a Core Group to develop a Strategy report on "Calgary . . . Into the 21st Century". This report was circulated locally and internationally. Task forces formed for creating action steps plus new ones formed for implementation
Decision-making: consensus-based approach?	Yes: consensus = general agreement (can live with a recommendation even if not first choice)	Yes: consensus = all parties are seen and heard; does not mean everyone agrees	Yes: approach attempted to incorporate community views	Yes: joint decision-making approach
Ongoing organizational body/bodies to help monitor &/or implement vision/plan?	Yes: Citizen committees formed during AACP process still ongoing and provide feedback	No? Alliance continues watchdog role. Successful Communities Dialogue still present	No.	Yes: New task forces formed to try to implement vision plus action strategy
Comments about process &/or plan	Plan is character-based and action-oriented	Some workshop participants felt not all resident voices present e.g. worker	Vision statement ratified by Council in February 1994	Economic vision and strategic plan; ongoing process

medium-term strategies can be developed. Vision statements provide a continuity through changing electorates and demonstrate to government authorities, incoming developers, and new residents, the sense of place (both present and future) desired by the local people. The vision statement can be invoked in community meetings on planning issues and during election campaigns. A well-formulated statement can provide a benchmark for assessing the value of proposed development projects to long-term community wellbeing. Additionally, the articulation of a shared community philosophy can act as a *proactive* guide to stakeholders involved in planning and developing a destination's resources. It could be argued, then, that the vision statement needs to be formally ratified into the community's official plan if it is to carry adequate weight. It would be reviewed by newly elected officials to ensure compatibility with public policy goals. Due to the dynamic nature of destination communities, such statements need to be 'revisited' periodically by the community to ensure its continued representation of their culture and aspirations.

The vision-based processes examined in this chapter indicate that visioning exercises may be a useful mechanism for raising citizen awareness of their community's identity, values, and aspirations. Stokowski (1992) mentioned that the introduction of specific tourism development strategies in mountain communities requires a re-definition and re-organization of social relationships and communal meanings, which are embedded in institutionalized social structures and are fundamental elements of community cohesiveness, stability and quality of life. Hence, "the more intimate, internal issues of community vision and meaning are difficult to identify and express, and even more difficult to incorporate into the planning process" (Stokowski, 1992: 37). Active citizen participation in a community visioning exercise (where the vision statement is an outcome of the joint process), could be one way to incorporate intangible community aspects into overall destination planning and could help to ensure a 'sense of place'.

Other benefits can also accrue from a collaborative visioning exercise, such as the fostering of better understandings between stakeholders, developing a sense of shared values, and increased recognition of interdependence among the destination's stakeholders. As noted by Trist (1983), collaboration is the value base appropriate for the adaptive cultivation of interdependence. Through processes that enable shared appreciation to evolve, stakeholders can attempt to develop a common value base, thereby leading the domain closer towards a negotiated order (Trist, 1983). While some of these collaboration benefits were noted in the case studies (e.g., among participants in the Revelstoke Vision Committee), the exploratory nature of the study did not permit a detailed examination of these factors. However, theoretical considerations and preliminary results from this study indicate that a multi-stakeholder visioning exercise may be one process for attaining a 'shared appreciation' plus better ordering within a tourism planning domain. Johnson and Bauen (1994: 1,4) note that "developing a community vision can help unite people with different viewpoints and create a positive goal towards which to work". A similar view is stated by the Sustainable Community Roundtable in its State of the Community Report for Thurston County, Washington.

Involving local citizens in the visioning process also provides an opportunity for planners to share their knowledge (as planners cum educators) with the community, and serves to empower local participation and action in destination planning and development. Alexander and Calliou (1991) compare community education with the visionary tradition in planning, and call for a new planning practitioner to tackle the challenges of a sustainable future. This new practitioner, they suggest, is one who combines the holism of visionary planning with the empowerment of community education, to be a social teacher and a learning practitioner. The community's citizens would be an integral part of the cyclical social learning process, where new experiences are learned from, and modification of future action can occur through active dialogue, experimentation, reflection, and evaluation (Alexander and Calliou, 1991). Jackson Hole's community vision statement assisted in establishing the character-based nature of the town and county's new comprehensive plan. The Aspen Area Community Plan, developed as a collaborative effort between the planners and the citizens, provided an opportunity for both groups to learn and exchange knowledge related to community needs and planning issues.

Several propositions emerge from this study of community visioning to guide future research in the content, process, and outcomes of community-based vision statements:

Proposition 1

> *A well-articulated, community-based vision statement offers effective direction to the public and private sector for managing a community's tourism-related resources over the long term.*

The term well-articulated as used in this context refers to the creation of a vision statement that reflects, as clearly as possible, those aspects of a community's character and values which are to be nurtured, and also the community's hopes and aspirations for their future direction. While the statement should reflect a clear community philosophy, it should avoid less than broad strategies or detailed action steps which may be considered unacceptable to incoming stakeholders, who were not involved in their formulation. A vision statement may be able to specify that small-scale developments are desired, but the policies and strategies enabling this can be outlined in the official comprehensive or community plan. One question to be addressed in this context is whether the local Council should be required to ratify the community vision statement, or whether an unendorsed community vision statement is adequate or even preferable. A resulting corollary from the above proposition is that a collaborative, visioning process is more likely to obtain community consensus than traditional land-use planning methods (which typically involve planners as 'experts') for directing destination development.

Proposition 2

> *The success of a community-based vision statement in achieving community consensus on destination planning and development is directly related to the level of community involvement in the vision formulation process.*

The ability of the visioning exercise to achieve consensus (rather than dissent) within the community, both on the outcome of the exercise plus on future planning and development efforts, may be directly related to the level of broad and active community involvement in the visioning process. Involvement here consists of (a) all key stakeholders to be selected by the community to represent various public/private community interests, and/or (b) community surveys to obtain input on the vision statement formulated by key stakeholders (e.g., Revelstoke), and/or (c) full participation requested of all residents and community stakeholders (e.g., Aspen; Jackson Hole). In keeping with collaboration theory, the decision making process should follow a consensus-based approach and involve key stakeholders in the community-based process. Careful identification and inclusion of the various stakeholder groups in the domain should help to address the contentious issue of how to balance out the voices of more powerful community and advocacy groups. Additionally, it might provide an answer to the oft-voiced complaint of how to include the 'silent majority' within a community.

Proposition 3

> *The effectiveness of a community visioning exercise to aid public and private planners will be enhanced by the existence of an ongoing representative body or bodies, to ensure implementation, monitoring and revision of the vision and/or of the strategic outcomes of the visioning exercise.*

An example of such an organizational form would be the citizen committees formed in the AACP process in Aspen, which continue to provide valuable feedback and assistance to the ongoing planning efforts in the town and area. Trist (1983), while acknowledging the role of vision-led individuals in forming networks during the early phases of domain development, also argues that purposeful domain transformation will not occur without the assistance of a structured and ongoing 'referent' organization to enable purposeful action. A research question of interest in the community planning domain is the role of local citizen advocacy groups: do such groups provide broad representation of the local community and, if so, how well can they fulfil the role of an ongoing monitoring and change ('referent') organization? It must be noted, however, that a case study by Westley and Vredenburg (1992) suggests that the movement from network to referent organization may be circular and interactive, rather than linear. Their study also questions the desirability of evolution from network to referent organization under certain circumstances.

CONCLUSIONS

The need to manage growth and changing community identities, combined with global concerns of sustainability, indicate that in order to be sustainable, communities need to become "learning communities". This means to be engaged in an interactive learning relationship with the internal and external environments, aided by flexible communication and public participation structures which could enable information flow, and flow of educational learning among stakeholders. Such a community would be one of empowered stakeholders, whose planning and development is guided by visionary planners cum educators. As noted by Alexander and Calliou (1991), the new planner may require educational as well as planning theory. A community-based visioning exercise could provide a flexible mechanism for enabling the community members to develop a better awareness of interdependence and an appreciation of jointly held values, needs, and aspirations. By providing a sense of future direction for a destination, a community vision statement may assist with achieving the philosophy of sustainable development, which "seeks to meet the needs and aspirations of the present without compromising the ability to meet those of the future (WCED, 1987: 40).

While the community-based visioning exercises examined in this study demonstrate strong potential for assisting both private and public authorities in determining (and regulating) the type, scale, and pace of tourism development desired by the local community, detailed longitudinal studies are required in order to address the following issues:

- What are the most effective mechanisms for representing broad community views in the visioning process?

- What should be the extent of community involvement: vision formulation only, leaving strategy development and implementation to the public officials, or should the community be fully involved in plan formulation (as in the Aspen community plan)? How does the presence of a visionary community leader influence the visioning process?

- What is the effect of community size on the visioning and planning process? For example, can Aspen's community plan process (AACP) be effectively used in larger communities?

- How helpful is a shared community vision to enabling sustainable tourism development for the community and region? As a tool for directing a community's future, the usefulness of a vision-based community exercise may vary depending on its content and process.

It is hoped that this chapter will assist planners, destination managers, and researchers to undertake examination of the merits of community-based visioning exercises, and to develop effective community participation mechanisms for the visioning and planning process. It should be recognized that the vision is only the first step in a strategic planning process, leading to the development of objectives, strategies, and action plans. However, the vision statement can also be used by itself to inform developers and other newcomers to the community of its values and future aspirations, as well as be a guiding statement for other local initiatives within the community. King Solomon is believed to have said: "Without a vision, people will perish."

ACKNOWLEDGEMENTS

The authors thank all those who participated in providing data and information for this exploratory study. In particular, we wish to acknowledge the valuable time and assistance of the following individuals: Mike Facey, Jenny Feick, Cynthia Houben, Barbara Gray (of Jackson Hole), and Bill Collins.

REFERENCES

AACP (1993). *Aspen Area Community Plan*, January 1993. Developed by citizens of Aspen, Colorado, with technical assistance provided by Aspen/Pitkin Planning Office.

Abberger, W., and Propst, L. (1991-2). *Successful Communities: Managing growth to protect distinctive local resources*. Final report of the Successful Communities program. World Wildlife Fund (incorporating the Conservation Foundation), WA.

Alexander, D., and Calliou, S. (1991). Planner as educator: A vision of a new practitioner. *Plan Canada*, 31(6), 38-45.

Allen, R.L., Long, P.T., Purdue, T.T., and Kieselbach, S. (1988). The impact of tourism development on residents' perceptions of community life. *Journal of Travel Research*, 27(1), 16-21.

Bower, J.L. (1977). Effective public management. *Harvard Business Review*, March-April, 131-140.

Bramwell, B., and Lane, B. (1993). Sustainable tourism: An evolving global approach. *Journal of Sustainable Tourism*, 1(1), 1-5. Quote on p. 3.

Bramwell, W., and Broom, G. (1989). Tourism Development Action Programmes—An approach to local tourism initiatives. *Insights*, A6-11-A6-17. Discussed in Long, P. (1994). Perspectives on partner organizations as an approach to local tourism development. In A.V. Seaton et al. (Eds.), *Tourism: The state of the art* (pp. 481-488). West Sussex, UK: John Wiley & Sons Ltd.

Bryson, J.M., Freeman, R.E., Roering, W.D. (1986). Strategic planning in the public sector: Approaches and directions. In B. Checkaway (Ed.), *Strategic Perspectives on Planning Practice* (Chapter 5). Lexington, MA: Lexington Books.

Buchholz, R.A. (1993). Public policy and the environment, Chapter 3, in *Principles of Environmental Management*. Prentice-Hall, Inc. New Jersey.

Calgary Economic Development Authority (1992). *Calgary into the 21st Century: A Plan for Implementation*. Published for The Strategic Alliance by the Calgary Economic Development Authority, May 1992.

Calgary Economic Development Authority (1989). *Calgary into the 21st Century: A Strategy for Economic Development*. Calgary, Alberta: Calgary Economic Development Authority.

City of Calgary (1989). *Calgary 2020*. Calgary: Public Information Dept., p. 1.

Dredge, D., and Moore, S. (1992). A methodology for the integration of tourism in town planning. *The Journal of Tourism Studies*, 3(1), 8-21.

Feick, J. (1994). Studying sustainable development in action. *Research Links*, 2(1), 11-12.

Feick, J. (1995). *Mountain town with a vision: A case study in sustainable community development in Revelstoke, British Columbia*. Master's thesis, Faculty of Environmental Design, University of Calgary, Calgary, Alberta, Canada, July, 1995.

Getz, D. (1987). *Tourism planning and research: Traditions, models and futures*. Proceedings of The Australian Travel Research Workshop, Banbury, W. Australia, Nov. 5-7, 1987.

Getz, D., and Jamal, T. (1994). The environment-community symbiosis: A case for collaborative tourism planning. *Journal of Sustainable Tourism*, 2(3), 152-173.

Gill, A., and Williams, P. (1994). Managing growth in mountain tourism communities. *Tourism Management*, 15(3), 212-220.

Gray, B. (1989). *Collaboration: Finding common ground for multiparty problems*. San Francisco: Jossey-Bass.

Hall, M.C. (1994a). Mega-events and their legacies. In P.E. Murphy (Ed.), *Quality management in urban tourism: Balancing business and the environment* (pp. 109-122). Conference Proceedings, Nov. 10-12, Victoria, B.C.: University of Victoria.

Hall, M.C. (1994b). The politics of heritage tourism: Place, power and the representation of values in the urban tourism conflict. In P.E. Murphy (Ed.), *Quality management in urban tourism: Balancing business and the environment* (pp. 203-214). Conference Proceedings, Nov. 10-12, Victoria, B.C.: University of Victoria.

Haywood, M.K. (1988). Responsible and responsive planning in the community. *Tourism Management*, June, 105-118.

Haywood, M.K. (1994). Quality imperatives and beyond: Creating value for visitors to urban destinations. In P.E. Murphy (Ed.), *Quality management in urban tourism: Balancing business and the environment* (pp. 424-435). Conference Proceedings, Nov. 10-12, Victoria, B.C.: University of Victoria.

Jamal, T., and Getz, D. (1995). Collaboration theory and community tourism planning. *Annals of Tourism Research*, 22(1), 186-204.

Johnson, J.D., Snepenger, D.J., and Akis, S. (1994). Residents' perceptions of tourism development. *Annals of Tourism Research*, 21(3), 629-643.

Johnson, K., and Bauen, R. (1994). Sustainability: Guiding community action. *Community and the environment*. A supplement to the Northwest Policy Center's *The Changing Northwest*, June, pp. 1, 4.

Keogh, B. (1990). Public participation in community tourism planning. *Annals of Tourism Research*, 17, 449-465.

Kotler, P. (1993). *Marketing places*. New York: The Free Press.

Long, P.T., Perdue, R.R., and Allen, L. (1990). Rural resident tourism perceptions and attitudes by community level of tourism. *Journal of Travel Research*, 28(3), 3-9.

McGill, R. (1988). Planning for strategic performance in local government. *Long Range Planning*, 21, (October), 77-83.

Milman, A., and Pizam, A. (1988). Social impacts of tourism on Central Florida. *Annals of Tourism Research*, 15(2), 191-204.

Mintzberg, H. (1994).*The rise and fall of strategic planning: Reconceiving roles for planning, plans, planners*. New York: The Free Press.

Muller, C. (1990). More than 350 show for workshop. *Jackson Hole News*, Wed. March 07, 1990, p. 11.

Murphy, P.E. (1985). *Tourism: A community approach*. New York: Methuen.

Ritchie, J.R.B. (1993). Crafting a destination vision: Putting the concept of resident responsive tourism into practice. *Tourism Management*, 14(5), 379-389.

Ryan, C., and Montgomery, D. (1994). The attitudes of Bakewell residents to tourism and issues in community responsive tourism. *Tourism Management*, 15(5), 358-369.

Schechter, J. (1990). *Planning for a successful community*. Jackson, Wyoming: Pioneer of Jackson Hole.

Simmons, D.G. (1994). Community participation in tourism. *Tourism Management*, 15(2), 98-108.

Skok, J.E. (1989). Towards a definition of strategic management for the public sector. *American Review of Public Administration*, 19(2), 133-147.

Stokowski, P.A. (1992). Place, meaning and structure in community tourism development: A case study from Central City, Colorado. In A. Gill and R. Hartmann (Eds.), *Mountain Resort Development* (pp. 32-40). Proceedings of the Vail Conference, April 1991, Vail, Colorado. Burnaby: The Centre for Tourism Policy and Research, Simon Fraser University. Quote on p. 37.

Trist, E. (1983). Referent organizations and the development of interorganizational domains. *Human Relations*, 36, 269-284.

Wechsler, B., and Backoff, R.W. (1987). The dynamics of strategy in public organizations. *APA Journal*, Winter, 34-43.

Westley, F., and Mintzberg, H. (1989). Visionary leadership and strategic management. *Strategic Management Journal*, (Special Issue) 10 (Summer), 17-32.

Westley, F., and Vredenburg, H. (1992). Managing the Ark: Interorganizational collaboration and the preservation of biodiversity. *Working Paper #92-11-16*, Faculty of Management, University of Calgary, Canada.

World Commission on Environment and Development (1987). *Our common future*. (Brundtland Commission report). Oxford: Oxford University Press.

ENDNOTES

1 Commentary on the Sustainable Community Roundtable in *Community and the Environment*. A Supplement to the Northwest Policy Center's *The Changing Northwest*. June 1994, p. 3.

2 *Jackson Hole Guide*, May 04/94; p. A8

3 *Calgary into the 21st Century: A Strategy for Economic Development*. Published by the Calgary Economic Development Authority, Calgary, Alberta, 1989, p. 8.

4 *Calgary into the 21st Century: A Plan for Implementation*. Published for The Strategic Alliance by the Calgary Economic Development Authority, May 1992.

5 *Calgary 2020*. Published by the City of Calgary, Public Information Department, Calgary, 1989, p. 1.

Attraction Land Use Management in Disney Theme Parks: Balancing Business and Environment

17

Peter E. Murphy

Tourism Programs,
Faculty of Business, University of Victoria

INTRODUCTION

When one thinks of the wide range of tourism attractions available in today's market it is amazing how frequently the Disney theme parks are cited by both the media and the consumer. These parks have caught the imagination of the world through their bold innovation and meticulous planning. Their success is reflected in their attendance figures, which, even in tight economic times, still dominate the industry. In 1993, Tokyo Disneyland attendance was 15.8 million, Walt Disney World 12 million, Disneyland 11.4 million, and Euro Disneyland 10 million (Sterngold, 1994). They have become benchmark operations in the true sense of the word, setting the standards not only for successive theme park copies, but for the attractions sector and industry as a whole. Many museums and interpretation centres have embraced the imagineering concepts of Disney, and many more tourism and service businesses have adopted the Disney approach to training.

There are many lessons that can be learned from the Disney approach to attraction development, including its relations with internal and external environments. Given the conference emphasis, this chapter will focus on but two—how this company has striven to develop a balance between its business goals and its responsibilities to the internal and external environment. Internally, it will examine how the theme parks have developed their physical site, in order to create a "safe adventure" environment (Caproni, 1992). Externally, it will examine the relations with host communities, to gauge the impact of such major attractions on surrounding socioeconomic and environmental conditions. The question of developing a tourism attraction in harmony with the natural and local environment is certainly a relevant one for tourism, and Walt Disney was one of those very concerned about the harmony between his business objectives and surrounding land uses.

The theme parks to be examined will be the three Disney controlled developments, where the Disney company has specific control over the locational and development strategies. Therefore, the Tokyo Disneyland will not be discussed because it is owned and operated under a franchise agreement by the Oriental Land Company. The balance between each Disney park and its internal/external environment will be explored, focusing on the impacts on the surrounding natural environment and upon the socioeconomic fortunes of the host community. The data base for the chapter is primarily secondary sources supplemented by personal observation of the three operations. The three theme parks will be examined in chronological order to illustrate the Disney learning curve regarding the management of what was an original attractions concept, followed by a discussion of the general lessons that can be learned from this business-environment interaction.

DISNEYLAND, CALIFORNIA (1955)

Although Walt Disney was a successful movie producer, his vision for a new type of attraction led him into a business area where he had no track record. Like all new business ventures, he had to work hard to convince backers of this new concept's viability. He went about this in a professional manner, conducting research on the existing fairground competition, developing an alternative based on his successful movie studio characters, and creating a business plan that demonstrated its feasibility. Even so, he needed the financial backing and exposure opportunity presented by a partnership with the fledgling American Broadcasting Company to bring these plans to fruition (Mosley, 1985); a partnership that has gone full circle recently with Disney's purchase of the television company in its bid to become a fully integrated communications-entertainment company.

The initial business plan included an independent locational analysis by the Stanford Research Institute, something considered essential for a business concept that would require a great deal of land and good access to the new automobile generation. The analysis pinpointed an agricultural area on the outskirts of Los Angeles in Anaheim County. This site was chosen because it lay between the two principal and expanding cities of southern California, Los Angeles and San Diego, was adjacent to a planned freeway exit, had a good climate, and lay in a pro-development jurisdiction (Walsh, 1992); a confluence of ideal locational characteristics.

Despite this ideal site and the substantial financial backing from ABC, Disney could not afford to buy as much land as he would have liked. He purchased only 75 hectares of orange groves, later to be expanded to 93 hectares with the purchase of some adjacent property. This meant that the whole initial site had to be committed to the theme park concept, leaving no room for the lucrative support function of accommodation. Traditionally in the USA, the largest tourist spending occurs in the transportation sector (41 percent), followed by meals (25 percent) and lodging (16 percent), with the attractions sector a relatively low 10 percent (Gee, Makens and Choy, 1989: 325). True, the Disneyland theme park also served meals and souvenirs which would increase its revenue share, but nothing to compare with the room and meal revenues of surrounding hotels which developed largely because of the Disney presence. It was not until years later that Disney was able to purchase the current Disneyland Hotel, across the street from the theme park. This meant that, while Disneyland was becoming the major tourism magnet for southern California, Disney felt he was not receiving his appropriate share of tourist expenditures.

Learning Curve

Disneyland proved to be a pioneer business in many ways, including its relationship with the environment. Internally, the theme park set a new and higher standard for cleanliness and trouble free operation, based in part on the considerable planning and investment that went into its infrastructure. Externally, its impact was just as dramatic. Walsh's (1992) study of its evolution, using the Butler resort life cycle framework, shows the local agricultural area was transformed into a tourist service area over a relatively short period. However, he notes that the City of Anaheim, with its own major convention centre investment, along with regional dynamics and changing consumer tastes, helped to fuel broader changes in the local economy. Therefore, Disneyland alone could not be held accountable for the reported 25 percent a year increases in Anaheim land values over the next 25 years (Flower, 1991); but it was certainly a factor and probably the catalyst. Indeed, the very locational characteristics that attracted Disney to the Anaheim site were harbingers of more extensive suburbanization trends, as the rural-urban fringe accommodated Los Angeles' growth needs.

Within this growth certain lessons regarding external environment relationships did arise for Disney. The most obvious was the contrast between the Disney standard of development and that of surrounding land uses. "If Walt could have turned back the clock to the early 1950s and started all over again, he obviously would have acquired more land" (Elder, 1980). A larger site would have facilitated expansion and development, rather than forcing the company into expensive land purchases. A larger site would have enabled Disney to develop a buffer between his "fantasy" creation and the real world, and to build revenue generating hotels on site. Another lesson was that, although the park benefited from a large year round regional demand, it was well removed from the major population concentration and tourist market area in the country—the northeast urban-industrial belt. A positive lesson was the return from the locational analysis. The selected site confirmed the significance of "location, location, location" to an open air attraction dependent on good weather and the highway traveller.

WALT DISNEY WORLD, FLORIDA (1971)

Walt Disney World was also a personal Walt Disney creation, although he had passed away by the time it opened in October, 1971. As such, it is easy to see the learning curve resulting from his experiences in Anaheim. Once again, a careful locational analysis was conducted. Florida was chosen as a good potential location due to its closer proximity to the northeast market and because it was a traditional holiday destination for many in that part of the United States. Within the state locational analysis revealed the area around Orlando had many of the same characteristics that had worked so well in California. It was a service centre for an agricultural area, some of which was in orange production, but other areas were little more than scrub ranchland. Its central location and freeway connections, existing and future, would provide it with both north-south and east-west links within the state, enabling it to intercept a portion of the traffic travelling to the established beach resort destinations.

The next step was to assemble an area of land that would provide sufficient space not only for the Disney attractions, but support facilities such as hotels, restaurants and shops, plus room for future on-site expansion, plus a buffer zone between the Disney creation and the outside commercial world which was sure to congregate around the site once it was operational. A big difference between this and the Anaheim development was that Disney now had a track record in the tourism business and there were people and banks willing to invest in such a venture. On the down side, such a high profile meant that an open purchase of the necessary land would come at a premium. Consequently, the 11,088 hectares, or 20.7 square kilometres, was assembled in secret, at a cost that truly reflected the value of the swamp and scrub rangeland—namely, less than $81 per hectare or $200 per acre (Zehnder, 1975: 14).

Land assembly was only the first and minor financial step in the creation of a second and superior Disney theme park. To create the type of attraction that Walt Disney envisaged would require an investment of $600 million for the first phase alone, compared to the land investment of $5.5 million. Before Disney was willing to invest such an amount he wanted assurances that the freeway system would be extended by his site and that he could develop to a higher standard than was then required in central Florida. To do this Disney wanted complete autonomy over the land he had purchased, which meant the existing county jurisdictions would have to give up their control and rights pertaining to his land area.

This desire for complete development control and government infrastructure assistance meant political negotiation, and thanks to the track record and reputation of the first Disney theme park the Disney company could negotiate from strength. They were offering to transform poor agricultural land into a more productive land use, plus provide a 3,035 hectare conservation area that would bring back the disappearing central Florida wetlands. In the process it was anticipated that during the construction phase and first 10 years of operation the theme park would generate $6.6 billion in economic benefits to the state, including 50,000 jobs, of which half would be in Walt Disney World (Zehnder, 1975: 92-93). After two years of negotiation it was agreed that a new jurisdiction called the Reedy Creek Improvement District would be carved out of Orange and Osceola counties. This district was primarily created to facilitate the extensive water management operations which would be the keystone to the whole project, but it also allowed the Disney company to establish local building codes and to levy taxes. One other tangible benefit was that, as a government agency, the District could now enter the tax free bond market.

Disney's plans and dreams for Walt Disney World were intended to set a new standard for theme parks and tourism in general. To highlight but a few of its features that relate directly to the business-environment interface, one needs to start with the phenomenal investment in site preparation and infrastructure that has led to all succeeding developments and triumphs. The basis of this theme park is water management. A must in an area that experiences distinct wet and dry seasons, with a natural landscape of swamps in the low lying areas and grassland in the higher elevations. To regulate the flow of water across the Reedy Creek Improvement District, 17 self-adjusting barrages control the amount and quality of water entering the district, and a system of rivers, runoff channels, and lakes (natural and artificial) accommodate the water once it is on-site. Because of the susceptibility to flooding, all major capital investments, including the individual attractions of the Magic Kingdom and EPCOT, have been placed either on high ground or upon artificially created islands. This is the practical reason behind the imagineers fantasy water entrance to the Magic Kingdom. Where an investment has been placed in a floodplain, such as in the case of some housing clusters next to a golf course, units are built upon pedestals to minimize any flood losses.

Nature's water is not the only water distribution that a theme park attracting millions of visitors needs to consider, so equal attention was paid to the problem of waste water. A state of the art tertiary sewage treatment plant was erected, with its waste water recycled back into the land through the irrigation of golf courses and the ornamental tree plantations. In this way waste water management contributes to the landscape's green appearance, and more importantly replenishes the local subterranean water table. So the district's water table level and environmental stability have been maintained, while nearby Orlando's water table dropped 3.7 to 7.3 metres between 1960 and 1985 (Newsweek, 1985), and parts of central Florida are experiencing the plunging experience of sink holes.

In addition to carefully developing the site for long-term commercial purposes, the original Disney plan for a non-commercial conservation area has been fulfilled. Separated from the developed and developing area by a freeway is the Reedy Creek Swamp. This is the drainage pool for the creek and other district water that has been allowed to regenerate back to the original central Florida wetland habitat and wildlife state. What such stringent planning and management have achieved is a nature sanctuary adjacent to a world class tourism destination that attracts millions of visitors each year, and demonstrated that such diametrically opposed functions can coexist!

The Walt Disney World impact on the external socioeconomic environment of central Florida has been equally dramatic, but less controlled. Just as the Disney experience and state studies predicted, there has been a major transformation in the economy and life style of local communities. The lure of the Disney development attracted an immediate in-migration of people looking for work and excitement, so that the character of Orlando began to change almost immediately.

Zehnder (1975) reports that there was an overbuilding of hotels and motels, shortages of water and low cost housing, and some dramatic increases in land prices. Since those early days, the success of Walt Disney World along with the locational advantages and growing accommodation base of central Florida has attracted an increasing number of additional theme parks and tourism businesses to the region. Such a transition has provided a wider range of employment prospects for local communities and a larger tax base, but it has also eliminated their more tranquil rural lifestyles.

Learning Curve

The success of Walt Disney World was immediate and justified the time and trouble setting up this premier attraction, which has evolved into a multiple theme park resort destination. The central place location proved to be viable even though this was the first major Florida attraction not to be sited on the shoreline, because it enabled Disney to intercept established tourist flows to the south and provided him with development opportunities at lower land prices. The purchase of such a large parcel of land ensured that this theme park did not suffer from the cramped conditions and unwelcome neighbours of the first park. This large land base proved also to be the jewel in the Disney crown during the unwelcome takeover bid of the eighties. It was seen as an undervalued asset by Steinberg and was used by the company as a principal attraction for its eventual partnership with the property developers Bass Brothers Enterprises of Texas (Flower, 1991: 99-115). The political autonomy and financial assistance that Disney received from the State of Florida set the foundation for the building of a world class resort destination and mixed economy that generally satisfied the expectations of both parties; although there are some prominent Floridians like Carl Hiaasen (1986 and 1991) who regret the increasing tourism and urban development of Florida.

However, everything has not run according to plan since opening day. With the death of Walt Disney and changing financial conditions within the company, some of the early plans have been changed. Walt Disney's concept of an Experimental Prototype Community of Tomorrow (EPCOT) was changed from an urban planning experiment into a permanent world's fair, with most attractions consisting of company or national pavilions. The large land mass assembled for future development within a greenbelt setting has witnessed continued development over the past 25 years, with the pace picking up over the last decade as the value of this asset accelerated and the destination responded to new consumer demands with new and different attractions (Hasek, 1994). In an attempt to provide all the recreation needs of its visitors and to keep them on-site, the Disney company has provided not just accommodation, but night clubs, golf courses, water slide parks, shopping complexes and artificial beaches in Walt Disney World. Some questions concerning the carrying capacity of this land area have started to arise along with concerns about Disney's commitment to the environment. Recently, Walt Disney World has been charged with polluting local waterways, and it received widespread negative press on its handling of a protected bird species (Champion, 1989; Painton, 1991). But not all the environmental news is bad. Lueck (1990) reports that the Disney Company has been working quietly and successfully with the University of Florida to demonstrate that aquatic plant waste water treatment could be a cost effective alternative to conventional treatments, especially if the methane by-product was marketed to offset operating expenses.

What was good for Disney was generally good for the surrounding communities and the state, especially in the early years. They received the anticipated economic boost, not only from the Disney development but also from the spate of hotel and other support development in Orlando and Kissimmee. Both communities grew at a phenomenal rate after the construction started in 1968, with Orlando becoming the fastest growing metropolitan area in the country and its land values increasing by 30 percent every year over the next 20 years (Flower, 1991: 207). The resulting economic transfusion brought both socioeconomic benefits and costs. Benefits like employment and investment provided additional taxes that could be used to increase amenities and services; but growth also brought burdens, such as increased land prices and social problems, to say nothing of a lost innocence and tranquil lifestyle (Zehnder, 1975: 275-278).

Painton (1991) reports that the relationships with Disney are now mixed. She confirms the early growth rates continued, with the Orlando area possessing the largest concentration of hotel rooms in the U.S., with the highest occupancy rates, and more than 18 million passengers arriving at Orlando International Airport, three times the number that arrived 10 years prior. The vacation spirit has spread throughout the region, with "restaurants, hotels, shops, and golf courses all want(ing) to be theme parks . . . it's not clear where Disney World begins and ends" (Painton, 1991: 49). However, the area "has begun to chafe at Disney's power" and has threatened to challenge the company's self-governing status. One factor which upset local politicians and residents was Disney beating them to the gate and taking all of the state's $57.7 million regional tax exempt bond allocation for one year, to upgrade its sewer system. This was particularly galling given that Disney announced "25 years earlier that the use of such money for private projects is repugnant to us" (Painton, 1991: 55). Not surprisingly, some residents, including a past mayor, have found the new pace and style overwhelming, and have moved away for their retirement.

EURO DISNEYLAND (1992)

Given the outstanding success of Walt Disney World in Florida and the fact that this location attracted a surprisingly large proportion of visitors from Europe, it is no surprise that the Disney organization should consider using the same strategy in its first overseas venture.

Consequently, we find Disney looking for an identical rural location, close to a major urban market and within easy reach of a significant regional market, that could accommodate a large scale multi-theme park resort destination. In addition, it was looking for a government that would be willing to assist in its development in return for the employment and taxes that would be generated.

After deliberating over two short-listed sites, one in France, the other in Spain, Disney selected the Marne-la-Vallee site, 32 kilometres east of Paris. The company committed to spending $4.4 billion to develop an all-weather theme park, adjacent to "a high-tech retro-cute amusement park, six ambitious new hotels (containing 5,200 rooms), 50 restaurants, a convention center, a campground, an 18-hole golf course and a cluster of nightclubs" (Corliss, 1992: 66). The amount of land needed to construct the above facilities is less than one-tenth of the 2,000 hectares Disney either owns or upon which it has future development rights. "The park would come first, but piece by piece it would become surrounded by nearly eight square miles (20 square kilometres) of development—all designed and controlled by Disney" (Flower, 1991: 207). When Disney takes up its full options on the land it will control an area a fifth the size of Paris. It will be a real estate development, much along the lines of Walt Disney World over the past 10 years, based on "two theme parks, various hotels offering 18,000 rooms, a camping ground, entertainment centre, office blocks and warehousing, distribution centres, stores, golf courses, 2,500 family homes, 3,000 apartments and 2,400 time-share units" (Sandford, 1989: A4).

The Disney company was able to assemble such a large amount of land thanks to the assistance of the French government, which owned the land and had been leasing it to local farmers but was eager to see economic development in this part of rural France. "The land was artificially valued at $5,000 per acre ($2023 per hectare), its value as agricultural land in 1971, and that value was guaranteed for 20 years . . . . The French would improve the highways to the site and extend the TGV express train at their own expense . . . . The French government would loan Disney as much as $770 million for the project at an artificially low interest rate of 7.85 percent, with no repayments for the first five years" (Flower, 1991: 208). The complex financial structure which was needed to build the initial $4.2 billion park and support facilities involved the establishment of interlocking companies that gave Disney effective control while owning less than half of the European company. "The entire $4.2 billion project cost the company only $160 million in equity. In return for that investment, Disney would receive 10 percent of all admissions, 5 percent of all concessions, and 49 percent of all profits" (Flower, 1991: 216). It received this favourable treatment because the national government expected a repeat of the economic development and employment generation that occurred in Florida. An expectation that has been fulfilled according to *The Economist* (1994), which reported an investment of over $4.2 billion plus the creation of 40,000 jobs, up to that point in time.

Since the Euro Disneyland theme park was announced in March 1987, there have been some notable changes to the physical and socioeconomic environment of the Marne-la-Vallee area. The most notable physical change to the landscape is increased accessibility afforded by the new freeway system and improvements to the rail system. The site and local area are now better connected to Paris via the

A4/E50 Expressway and the Metro subway system, which offers a 30 minute ride to central Paris and a brand new station right opposite the gates to Euro Disney. In the fall of 1994 this metro system was augmented by an adjacent new station linked to the TGV system, which, with the opening of the Channel Tunnel, places Euro Disney within 3½ hours of London. The developed Euro Disney site is compact and built to the usual high Disney standards. Along with the normal pre-development infrastructure, an infirmary for both visitor and resident needs has been built. The park site is surrounded by active farming, centred on three local villages. At present, the physical impact on these villages is minimal as Disney has provided abundant visitor accommodation on site (5,200 rooms), and for those who wish to stay elsewhere, Paris is a natural lure. But in the future all this will change as the rural landscape evolves into a satellite residential community, not based on industrial parks as was the case with London's new towns, but on service sector parks including the leisure industry of theme parks.

Learning Curve

The move to Europe was Disney's first independent expansion outside of the United States and its sunbelt. As such it proved to be a cross-cultural and climatic test of their successful U.S. strategies. The socioeconomic impacts and lessons have been well reported because these represent the most visible results to date (Sasseen, 1993). Unlike the U.S. experience, Disney found their agricultural host community actively hostile to its presence. The initial local shock came when the long-term farming community discovered its paternal landlord was prepared to seek another client and land use for this area of France. The farmer demonstrations against the construction of the Disney project, therefore, were as much a protest against changed French government policy as they were against the Disney company. Likewise, the cultural concern over a dual language facility in France, along with the imposed dress and behaviour codes of the Disney organization, have a nationalist context to them over and above concerns relating to this specific project (Bagwell, 1992; Drozdiak, 1992). The more northerly location has meant that this theme park has experienced more severe seasonal peaks and valleys in attendance than the U.S. parks (Hartley, 1995: 119). After some initial reluctance, the company has been forced to accept this reality and to offer seasonal discounts to attract the out-of-summer visitor, and tour bus discounts to tap into that major form of European travel.

Its locational and transport analysis was one of the factors which drew Disney to the French site over the Spanish option, outside of Barcelona. The Marne-la-Vallee site placed the theme park within a two hour drive of 17 million people and a four hour drive of 41 million (Hartley, 1995: 115), which meant it had a substantially larger regional market than either of the two U.S. parks. However, such short distances to the park have meant it has received far more daytrippers than expected, especially as Europeans seem to be more content to let someone else do the driving as they relax on a bus. Consequently, the one area overwhelmed during the first year of operation was the initial bus parking facility.

Hartley (1995: 119) maintains "the problems of Euro Disney were not public acceptance, despite the earlier critics. Europeans loved the place. Since the opening it attracted just under one million visitors a month, thus easily achieving the original projections". The problems were primarily the external conditions of a recession, which made patrons more frugal than expected, and "the crash of the Paris real estate market as Euro Disneyland opened its doors to the public" (The Banker, 1994: 21). This meant that Disney was unable to either fill or sell its on-site hotels as planned, resulting in the much publicized loss of $921 million in the first year of operation and the need for refinancing.

The fact that a refinancing package has been approved, and that a "financial angel" has been found in the form of Prince Al-Walid bin Talal of Saudi Arabia, indicates there is still long-term confidence in this project. The Prince has invested up to $500 million for a 24 percent stake in Euro Disneyland, which will be used in part to start work on the delayed twin MGM studios theme park (Corporate Growth Report, 1994). It is hoped that the presence of two theme parks will encourage more visitors to come and to stay overnight.

However, the real hope for Euro Disney lies not so much in its tourism potential as it does with its real estate potential. The development rights on a huge piece of land within Europe's "Golden Triangle of London, Paris and Brussels", along with high speed rail connections to these three capitals, and local subway and freeway connections to Paris suggest a healthy investment return once the real estate market recovers. Thus, the Disney project should be viewed not simply as a theme park development, but as a new town development within one of the fastest growing areas of western Europe.

GENERAL LESSONS

The Disney experience offers important general lessons regarding a tourism attraction's relations to its external environment, from both a company and host community perspective. From a company's perspective, if it is hoping to create a magical experience it must place the time and effort into careful locational analysis, infrastructure development, and creating a sustainable competitive advantage. From a host community's viewpoint it must be prepared to accept the socioeconomic and physical changes that a successful theme park will bring, and hopefully be able to integrate them into the type of future it wishes to see for itself.

The strategic importance of location, finding rural areas close to major urban markets that have good highway and airline access to the wider national market, has been a key feature in the Disney success and should be a prominent consideration for all major attractions. The importance of locational selection to the success of the U.S. Disney theme parks is clearly evident, although as Solomon (1994) observed, a company hubris may have developed from its run of success in this area. In the short term, the Euro Disney site selection, using the same locational criteria as in the U.S., has proven to be a big gamble. By locating in the more northerly latitudes Disney has created its first winter theme park destination, and despite its largely enclosed attractions it is having difficulty drawing sufficient numbers in the winter months. By locating within Europe's golden triangle Disney has placed the parks within easy reach by car and bus. This made the latest theme park a short-haul destination for daytrips rather than the standard long-haul and over-night destination of the past (Bennett, 1992).

The importance of a fully prepared and serviced site to fulfil the fantasy has been a cornerstone of the Disney theme park philosophy, but as the projects have become grander the need for partners has increased. One obvious partner is gov-ernment, and the Disney Company has built on its past economic success to be-come a tough negotiator with various levels of government. In Florida and Europe it took substantial government concessions and subsidies before Disney would convert project proposals into actual entities. But Disney has also needed corpo-rate partners to help build its parks. Even in the first theme park one section was set aside for corporate investment, with several major companies transferring their New York World's Fair pavilions to Disneyland's "Tomorrow Land". This partner-ship continued at Disney World with the corporate involvement in EPCOT and the joint development of several hotel properties; and in Euro Disney with franchise agreements.

In the competitive world of tourism Disney has set a new standard in theme park attractions which has been emulated by others, necessitating Disney to con-tinually re-invent itself with new rides and attractions to maintain its pre-eminence. This process has been accompanied by a steady shift of business emphasis; from a simple theme park attraction status in California to that of a self-contained resort in Florida, and a new town in France. As a result, the Disney company is diversify-ing its product and ensuring it captures more of the local tourism market. Such a strategy reflects the limited financial returns associated with remaining in only one sector of tourism, and the advantages of capturing the synergistic natural linkages of this industry through vertical linkage. The lesson to other attractions is to buy as much extra land as possible and, failing that, to look for synergistic business partners.

In every theme park, Disney has built to the highest standard and been sensi-tive to the natural ecosystem, because it is in the company's self-interest. This is particularly noticeable in Walt Disney World. However, one wonders how much of that original theme park-environment harmony (Murphy, 1986) can be main-tained as the company moves from a park orientation to a real estate orientation. Disney has come under increasing scrutiny for its environmental problems in Florida, and it has responded to such scrutiny with new investment and policies. It is to be hoped that Disney's early strategic commitment to environmental carry-ing capacities will be continued with each successive phase so that an optimum development level can be recognized and adhered to, and other companies can use its environmental-business interactions as role models.

The issue of carrying capacity is certainly a key one for host communities. It is clear from past park experiences and from the eventual plans in Europe that a

Disney theme park will result in substantial socioeconomic and cultural change. However, such change should be viewed in perspective. In the case of Disneyland and Euro Disney, these parks are on the outskirts of growing metropolitan centres which were bound to change over time due to the urban growth process. In the case of Orlando, the Walt Disney World park had a more direct bearing on the urban growth rate, but with the rising popularity of Florida and its expanding retirement-leisure industries, some change would have occurred without the Disney intervention. Consequently, potential host communities of major attractions must recognize them as agents of change which, in conjunction with other forces of change, will help to create a different community and lifestyle. The key is to influence and direct such change in terms of the "public good", if it can be defined and agreed upon within the community.

The socioeconomic bases of the host communities and their lifestyle will be changed forever. They will receive the benefits of land development, increased employment, and an increased tax base; but with these benefits will come the problems of an increasingly transient community, with rising social costs and a 24-hour operational day. In addition, they can expect the attraction developer to ask for some form of public assistance in bringing about this change.

Perhaps the most significant change, yet hardest to quantify, will be with regard to lifestyle. Some individuals will benefit enormously from the attraction development through investment and employment, others will be indirect beneficiaries. But, because this is an industry that brings its customers to the point of production, many others will be impacted by the congestion, by the new demands, and by the rising prices. It is only natural for rural area inhabitants to bemoan the loss of old ways of life, but are they still viable in a world of limited resources and growing population? One can only hope that potential host communities learn from past experiences, such as the Disney record, and include as comprehensive a cost-benefit analysis as possible in the deliberations about their own future.

SUMMARY

It is apparent that a benchmark company can provide examples of both good and bad judgement, which may guide other attraction developers and host communities. Up to now, Disney's theme park operations have struck a fairly acceptable balance between business and environmental considerations, but a danger lies in their complacency. It is evident that the same development model does not necessarily work as well in different cultures or at different times. Furthermore, in a business where the consumer is always demanding something new, the pressure to build and become bigger places an increasing strain on the local environment, possibly endangering established carrying capacities. If the attraction and its host community are to become long-term sustainable partners they both need to consider the delicate and changing balance between the individual business and its surrounding environment.

REFERENCES

Bagwell, S. (1992). Taking le Mickey in Paris. *Sydney Morning Herald Magazine*, April 11,55-57.

Banker (1994). Euro Disney's property poser. *The Banker*, 144(815), 20-21.

Bennett, R. (1992). How will EuroDisney affect the European Market? *Tourism Management*, 13(2), 155-156.

Caproni, J.S. (1992). Travel as theatre: A new challenge to the credibility of tourism. *Journal of Travel Research*, XXX, 54-55.

Champion, M. (1989). Disney World charged with beating wild vultures to death. *Vancouver Sun*, October 7, A11.

Corliss, R. (1992). Voila: Disney invades Europe. Will the French resist? *Time*, April 20, 66.

Corporate Growth (1994). A Saudi prince comes to Euro Disney's aid. *The Corporate Growth Report*, No. 798, June 13, 7291 and 7302.

Drozdiak, W. (1992). Disneyland meets Europe and two cultures collide. *Vancouver Sun*, March 7, B6.

Elder, N. (1980). Attraction development. *Resort of the Eighties: Keynote Addresses*. Ottawa and Victoria: Travel Industry Subsidiary Agreement, Ministry of Tourism.

Economist (1994). Meltdown at the cultural Chernoble. *The Economist*, February 5, 34-39.

Flower, J. (1991). *Prince of the Magic Kingdom*. New York: John Wiley & Sons Ltd.

Gee, C., Makens, J., and Choy, D. (1989). *The travel industry* (Second Edition). New York: Van Nostrand Reinhold.

Hartley, R.F. (1995). Euro Disney: A successful format does not transfer well to Europe. *Marketing mistakes* (Sixth Edition). New York: John Wiley & Sons Ltd., 113-128.

Hasek, G. (1994). Disney development soars. *Hotel and Motel Management*, 209(8), 3 and 25.

Hiaasen, C. (1986). *Tourist season*. New York: Warner Books

Hiaasen, C. (1991). *Native tongue*. New York: Ballantine Books.

Lueck, G.W. (1990). A growing interest in wastewater Plants. *Waste Age*, 21(6), 87-92.

Mosley, L. (1985). *Disney's World*. New York: Stein and Day.

Murphy, P.E. (1986). Conservation and tourism: A business partnership. *Tourism and the environment: Conflict or harmony?* Edmonton: Canadian Society of Environmental Biologists, 117-127.

Newsweek (1985). Orlando's Magic Kingdom. *Newsweek*, September 2, 43.

Painton, P. (1991). Fantasy's reality. *Time*, May 27,46-55.

Sandford, G. (1989). Sacreblue! Mickey Mouse vient a Paris. *Globe and Mail*, November 6, A4.

Sasseen, J. (1993). Disney's bungle book. *International Management*, 48(6), 26-27.

Sterngold, J. (1994). A tale of two Mickeys. *Globe and Mail*, March 8, A9.

Solomon, J. (1994). Mickey's trip to trouble. *Newsweek*, February 14, 34-39.

Walsh, D.J. (1992). The evolution of the Disneyland environs. *Tourism Recreation Research*, 17(1), 33-47.

Zehnder, L. (1975). *Florida's Disney World: Promises and problems*. Tallahassee, Florida: Peninsular Publishing.

Plate 11 The Empress Hotel, Victoria
(photo courtesy of The Province of British Columbia) ➡

Researching Tourism Partnership Organizations: From Practice to Theory to Methodology

18

Philip E. Long

School of Leisure and Food Management, Sheffield Hallam University

INTRODUCTION

'Partnership', 'cooperation', and 'collaboration' are ubiquitous terms in the policy and strategy documents of agencies concerned with the development of tourism at national, regional and local levels in rural, coastal, and urban areas. The fragmented nature of the tourism industry comprised, in most areas, of large numbers of small- to medium-scale enterprises, together with a wide range of interest groups from public sector agencies to community groups in destinations, is increasingly recognized, and arrangements to bring these interests together are now widespread in the United Kingdom and elsewhere.

The Scottish Tourism Coordinating Group (1994), for example, notes the need for, or existence, of partnership or collaborative arrangements in 17 different contexts in Scottish tourism development. The Wales Tourist Board (1994) has identified 13 other statutory agencies with whom it collaborates in the development of tourism in the Principality. Throughout the 1980s and 1990s, the English Tourist Board has been instrumental in establishing formal locally-based partnership organizations in the Tourism Development Action Programs and more recent Local Area Tourism Initiatives.

The pilot local tourism development partnership program in England was centred on the city of Bristol in 1984. A number of subsequent programs were developed in urban locations in England, for example, in London, Manchester, Birmingham, Leeds and Leicester. These programs have been concerned with, for example, the tourism dimension of inner-city regeneration, the development of arts and cultural districts and events, and the promotion of business and convention tourism.

The programs in England have been discussed elsewhere by the author in terms of their locations, characteristics, membership, program content, and rationales for involvement from public and private sector perspectives. Potential contributions to the study of partnership arrangements from the fields of Policy Studies, Political Geography, and Organization Theory were also outlined (Long, 1994).

This chapter takes the analysis further by elaborating on the potential contribution of theories of inter-organizational collaboration (IOC) to the study of partnerships in tourism development. The chapter goes on to discuss some methodological considerations which might inform the development of research programs in this, to date, neglected line of enquiry into urban tourism.

TOURISM AND INTER-ORGANIZATIONAL COLLABORATION

Studies of inter-organizational collaboration appear to be particularly relevant at a time when public, private and, to an extent, voluntary sectors are increasingly forging partnership arrangements to plan, implement, and evaluate tourism development strategies and programs. These partnerships have in places adopted distinct organizational structures, as in the case of the local area tourism initiatives in England.

This phenomenon would bear scrutiny in respect of, for example, establishing the preconditions that would favour or hinder collaboration, presenting alternative organizational structures, defining organizational boundaries, recognizing and reconciling conflicts of interest, evaluating outcomes, and maintaining partnership arrangements in the long-term. Such research that has taken place has usually either been commissioned or conducted internally by partner organizations and pragmatically focused on the operating program (Long, 1994).

Additionally, Organization Studies has been a neglected subject area in the field of tourism (Pearce, 1992). Much work has been done in relation to planning for tourism development (for example, Gunn, 1988; Inskeep, 1993; W.T.O., 1994) and (following Murphy, 1985) in involving host communities in planning and management processes. However, these studies have generally not addressed organizational dimensions as being of central concern.

The potential contribution of Organization Studies is implicit in a recent Delphic process which sought to establish key issues and a research agenda for tourism (Pearce and Butler, 1993). Proposed research issues included:

- establishing public and private partnerships in the context of defining carrying capacities issues in destinations;
- achieving a balance among economic, social, and environmental objectives in community tourism planning and development efforts;
- the tourism industry adopting a more proactive stance in the political process in the promotion and practice of sustainable development;
- encouraging all sectors of the tourism industry to actively cooperate in the development of training and education programs;
- expanding the concept of tourism policy in which tourism development may be more thoroughly integrated with the overall economic and social policy of a country, region or locality.

The broad policy context for tourism in the United Kingdom also encourages a research agenda that makes organizational aspects more central. Relevant policy issues include:

- central government policy to extend private sector involvement in local and regional planning and development activity and the emergence of new institutions with extensive powers and interests in tourism. Examples in urban areas include development corporations and enterprise boards, along with an array of policy instruments *requiring* a partnership approach to urban development;
- the associated erosion of local government powers and resources and an increased recognition from local government of the value of partnerships;
- the increasing significance of European Union funded programs and projects which commonly require a partnership approach, particularly in terms of matching resources and cross-border initiatives;
- the catalytic role of the national tourist boards during the 1980s and 1990s in the formulation of partnership arrangements in local areas and the more recent reduction in their resources for this purpose;
- the emergence of the concept of sustainable tourism including the notion of involving 'stakeholders' in the development process, and a tourism 'policy community' seeking to put such ideas into practice.

All of these issues support the contention that Organization Studies and, in particular, perspectives on IOC might make a significant contribution in terms of the development of theory and practical guidance in the design of collaborative partnerships for tourism development.

From Cooperation, to Coordination, to Collaboration, to Partnership

Levels and degrees of interactions between interest groups involved in tourism development range from ad hoc, informal arrangements for specific purposes to highly structured formal and long-term relationships. The identification and definition of generalizable categories of interaction will be necessary if research is to move beyond the analysis of case studies towards distinct *forms* of cooperation, collaboration and partnership. Dictionary definitions highlight that the distinction between these terms is principally one of degree, with organizational definitions also moving from the loose notion of cooperation to the tighter concept of partnership. Thus, cooperation 'involves working together to some common end'. In organizational terms, this definition lacks the detailed preconditions and process characteristics described by the other terms. 'Coordination' may be defined more formally as 'the process whereby two or more organizations create and/or use existing decision rules that have been established to deal collectively with their shared task environment'. The dictionary definition of 'collaboration', 'to work in association', is similar to that offered for 'coordination', though sometimes given an invidious usage in English as compared with the more harmonious implications of coordination. However, in the context of inter-organizational relations, 'collaboration' has received considerable acceptance in recent years. Wood and Gray (1991: 146) present a definition which, they argue, encompasses the elements of a number of authors' approaches to the subject:

> *Collaboration occurs when a group of autonomous stakeholders of a problem domain engage in an interactive process using shared rules, norms and structures to act or decide on issues related to that domain.*

The elements of this definition, and examples of issues arising from it that may be operationalized, are as follows:

- the extent to which *'stakeholders'* exhibit common or contrasting definitions of the issues and how for these perceptions may change over time; whether the collaboration involves full or partial stakeholder representation.

- how far individual organization's *'autonomy'* is relinquished to the collaborative arrangement.

- whether the *'interactive process'* results in changes to actors' perceptions as a consequence of their involvement with other collaborators.

- the extent and direction of changes in the collaboration's *'shared norms, rules and structures'*.

- whether *'actions or decisions'* are intended rather than achieved; anticipated and/or unanticipated.

- the consequences of changes in the *'problem domain'* for the collaborative arrangement.

'Partnership' in the tourism development context implies similar characteristics to those defining collaboration with the added dimensions of cross-sectoral representation and the definition of geographical boundaries.

Waddock (1991) has identified three forms of partnership arrangement which may be advanced according to the nature of the issues to be addressed and the organizational level involved in the partnership. These three forms, with tourism examples are:

(i) **Programmatic** — The partnership tends to be technical or operational and commonly involves a contractual relationship between a few partners. The emphasis tends to be on products or outputs and is usually a short-term arrangement. The Scottish Tourist Board, Highlands and Islands Enterprise, Scottish Enterprise and the Association of Scottish Visitor Attractions jointly employing a Visitor Attractions Development Officer illustrates this approach.

(ii) **Federational** — The partnership comprises industry groupings and/or a regional coalition. 'The sweep is broader than that of the programmatic partnership but still limited by the bounded context in which the problem is defined.' The partnership tends to adopt a proactive stance towards coalition building, issue identification and purpose formulation and in consequence is a more complex arrangement than in programmatic partnerships. Examples of this approach include the English local area tourism initiatives.

(iii) **Systemic** — The partnership is concerned with broad, system wide societal issues and is dominated by process rather than products. The emphasis is upon system benefits rather than gains for individual participants, and representation tends to come from senior managers and officials across participating sectors. The Scottish Tourism Coordinating Group is an example of this form of arrangement.

An empirical question arising from these distinctions of partnership forms is whether, in this case tourism development, issues are misdefined by bringing in either too wide or too limited a range of actors to deal with them.

In the context of tourism development, a working definition of partnership may be derived from incorporating elements of the collaboration concept as follows:

> *Tourism development partnerships may be defined as the collaborative efforts of autonomous stakeholders from organizations in two or more sectors with interests in tourism development who engage in an interactive process using shared rules, norms and structures at an agreed organizational level and over a defined geographical area to act or decide on issues related to tourism development.*

This definition offers conceptual and empirical validity and allows for the application of theoretical perspectives from the IOC and partnership field which, in turn, give rise to the specification of research methodologies.

Tourism and Theories of Inter-Organizational Collaboration

Organization Studies has generally been concerned with studies of individual, focal organizations. However, research upon inter-organizational collaboration began to appear in the 1960s, initially in the form of case studies written by participants (Levine and White, 1961; Litwak and Hylton, 1962). Empirical research on coordination emerged in the late 1960s (Emery and Trist, 1965; Warren, 1967), with advances in conceptualization and modelling taking place from the 1970s (Hall et al., 1977; Rogers and Whetten, 1982; Waddock, 1991). The development of the field has, therefore, coincided with a period of increasing environmental turbulence and complexity for organizations of all kinds. The need to manage uncertainty has been recognized by organizational theorists and practitioners alike, and has contributed to the increasing attention to issues of cooperation, collaboration, and partnership.

This section briefly reviews six theoretical perspectives which have developed within the IOC field, and highlights research questions emerging from these perspectives which may be applied to tourism partnerships.

According to Gray and Wood (1991), each perspective shares a common interest in three overriding concerns:

- the preconditions that give rise to collaborative alliances;
- the form of the collaboration; and,
- the expected outcomes of the collaboration.

The roles of individual coordinators in inter-organizational collaboration provides a further dimension that may be addressed from each perspective.

The primary focus and associated research questions that emerge from theoretical perspectives on IOC are as follows.

Resource Dependence

This approach examines how focal organizations might reduce environmental uncertainty and work towards achieving stability in their domain by seeking necessary resources externally. The focus is on minimizing inter-organizational dependencies and preserving the organization's autonomy while recognizing that inter-organizational relationships are necessary in order to acquire resources.

This perspective, therefore, addresses the overall allocation of resources among all players in, in this case, the urban tourism development domain.

Research issues that might emerge from this problematic include:

- ways of achieving stability and reducing uncertainty with respect to the environment while minimizing dependencies on other organizations;
- the circumstances in which stakeholders adopt collaborative alliances;
- the patterns of inter-dependencies that result from resource exchanges.

In the case of urban tourism development, contracting budgets in the public sector and small scale operators in the private sector highlight resource dependencies in, for example, marketing campaigns.

Corporate Social Performance

This perspective focuses on stakeholders defining and achieving social and institutional legitimacy for their collaborative actions. The Corporate Social Performance approach therefore moves beyond narrow organizational concerns to examine wider, societal consequences of partnerships. Research issues would include:

- the roles that businesses might play as social institutions;
- the allocation of responsibilities for social issues among partnership actors; and,
- the ways in which collaborative alliances mediate between the interests of their participant organizations and those of the wider environment.

Achieving urban tourism development which is sustainable in economic, environmental, and community terms is high on the agenda of local area tourism initiatives in England, particularly in securing the participation of the private sector in sustainable tourism policies and programs. The Corporate Social Performance approach is, therefore, highly relevant in the context of private sector involvement in partnerships for tourism development in urban areas.

Strategic Management

This perspective is primarily concerned with strategy within independent, focal organizations. However, in terms of partnerships, the ways in which participants in an alliance might regulate their self-serving behaviours so that collective gains can be achieved would be a legitimate area of enquiry from a strategic management viewpoint.

The extent to which local area tourism development partnerships can mediate between their members in reconciling potentially conflicting strategic objectives would be a relevant approach in the context of urban tourism development.

Microeconomics

Achieving transaction efficiencies in markets is the main concern of this approach in an inter-organizational context. The emphasis would, therefore, be on ways in which inter-organizational partners might overcome impediments to efficiency in their bilateral transactions. A wider question would involve an examination of the overall efficiency of resource use within an entire inter-organizational network, for example in overcoming 'free-rider' effects and other impediments.

Improving transaction efficiencies within urban tourism development domains in, for example, training and technology initiatives would be a legitimate line of enquiry in this context.

Institutional/Negotiated Order

This perspective focuses on the institutional environment within which partnerships operate. The emphasis is, therefore, upon the norms and ideologies present in the institutional environment, and ways in which alliances might adjust to or seek to influence these dominant ideologies and norms.

Negotiated Order Theory focuses on the symbolic and perceptual aspects of inter-organizational relationships, particularly on the evolution of shared (and conflicting) understanding among stakeholders of the collaboration's structures and processes, limits and possibilities.

Identifying the norms and ideologies which are dominant within the tourism 'policy community' and how they may change as a consequence of involvement in inter-organizational collaboration would be a valid line of enquiry in the context of urban tourism development

Political Theory/Political Geography

Access to and distribution of power and resources is a central concern of this approach. A geographical component would also take into account the definition of boundaries and spatial impacts of a partnership's operation. Issues of accountability, legitimacy in the community, and winners and losers from collaborative alliances represent major research interests in this context.

Achieving an equitable distribution of power and resources, both within partnerships and spatially, is also pertinent in the case of urban tourism development. An interesting locational characteristic of a number of urban tourism development partnerships in England has been their local focus within defined boundaries. Examples include: Islington and Docklands within London, Leeds Waterfront, and the Castlefield district in Manchester.

All of these positions can, therefore, contribute to the development of a theoretical basis for the analysis of inter-organizational collaboration and partnership in tourism development.

However, in order to develop theory and associated appropriate methodologies, it will first be necessary to consider the basic assumptions that might underlie the analysis of inter-organizational collaboration and tourism development.

FROM PRACTICE TO THEORY TO METHODOLOGY

The specification of the assumptions underlying the selection of research methodologies is often lacking in tourism studies (Dann, Nash and Pearce, 1988; Dann and Cohen, 1991). For Pearce and Butler (1993: 6), there is a '. . . need for tourism researchers to be more explicit in what they do. We should not take for granted the methods, concepts or data that we use, but rather examine these critically, exploring, appraising, setting out and justifying underlying assumptions, theoretical considerations, technical factors and limitations in use'.

The previous section identified perspectives which might be applied from theories of inter-organizational collaboration to the study of tourism partnerships. Such an application would move the analysis beyond a descriptive, ideographic, case study approach towards the development of generalizable theory. However, it will also be necessary for researchers to identify and specify their ontologies, epistemologies, and socio-organizational models if the development of theory is to be rigorous and transparent. This section briefly considers these philosophical issues in relation to the study of inter-organizational collaboration, and identifies the methodological choices which arise from the adoption of a particular set of assumptions. Burrell and Morgan's (1979) seminal 'Sociological Paradigms and Organizational Analysis' has been highly influential in questioning the basis of organization studies and highlighting the choices that are available within the field. Their starting point is the identification of the subjective-objective dimension of research (Figure 18.1).

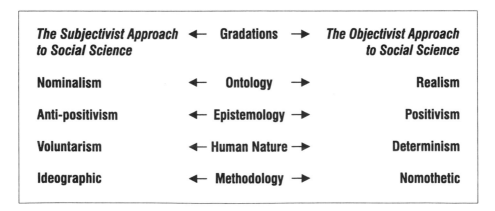

Figure 18.1 The subjective/objective dimension of research
(Source: Burrell and Morgan, 1979, p. 3).

An extreme Subjectivist position would, therefore, be based on assumptions that the social world external to individual cognition is made up of nothing more than names, concepts, and labels. The social world is essentially relativistic and can only be understood from the viewpoint of the individuals who are directly involved in the activities which are to be studied. Researchers can only understand phenomena by 'getting inside' the subject under investigation. In contrast, an Objectivist approach postulates that the social world external to individuals comprises distinct, tangible structures. The research task is to explain and predict phenomena by searching for regularities and causal relationships between constituent elements. Emphasis is placed upon systematic standardized research protocols and techniques (Burrell and Morgan, 1979: 3-7).

A further set of assumptions arises from the researcher's position on the essential characteristics of social, in this case inter-organizational, systems. Thus, a set of assumptions which views inter-organizational systems as being concerned with, for example, consensus, cohesion, cooperation, and order will contrast with a position which emphasizes, for example, dissension, division, and conflict. Burrell and Morgan combine the subjectivist/objectivist and order/conflict dimensions into a 2 x 2 matrix resulting in four paradigmatic positions within which inter-organizational analysis can be located. Burrell and Morgan's position that 'a synthesis (of the 4 paradigms) is not possible since in their pure forms they are contradictory, being based on at least one set of opposing meta-theoretical assumptions' is contentious (Willmott, 1993). However, a recognition of these 'ideal-types' does assist in the critique of existing studies of inter-organizational collaboration and in the specification of research methodologies for the future. A brief discussion of the principal characteristics of each paradigm in relation to inter-organizational analysis follows (Figure 18.2).

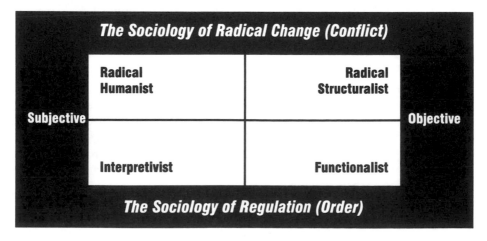

Figure 18.2   Sociological paradigms and organizational analysis
(Source: Burrell and Morgan, 1979, p. 22).

Functionalism

The functionalist position generally assumes that organizations are rational, purposive and goal seeking. The purpose of research is to seek practical solutions to practical problems and is primarily concerned with management and administrative priorities.

Methodology is commonly based on the assumption that the social world is composed of comparatively concrete empirical artefacts and relationships that can be identified, studied, and measured through approaches derived from the natural sciences (Burrell and Morgan, 1979: 26-30). Functionalist perspectives have dominated the field of organization studies from Classical Management Theory (Taylorism) through varieties of Systems Theories to more recent analyses of organizational pluralism. In tourism studies, the only text that explicitly adopts an organization theory framework is also clear about its focus, 'the concern is with what tourist organizations actually do, a concern expressed by focusing on their goals and functions' (Pearce, 1992: 19). However, while functionalism, whether explicit or implicit, remains dominant in the organization studies literature, alternative approaches have challenged the orthodoxy.

Interpretivism

In contrast to functionalism, an interpretivist position is concerned with understanding the world as it is at the level of subjective experience. The emphasis, therefore, is upon individual consciousness with research adopting the participants' rather than the observer's frames of reference. The implication for the study of inter-organizational collaboration is that the pre-eminence of structures should be rejected. Organizational partnerships are, therefore, 'no more that the subjective construction of individual human beings who, through the development and use of common language and the interactions of everyday life, create and sustain a world of inter-subjectively shared meanings' (Burrell and Morgan, 1979: 260).

Radical Humanism

This paradigmatic position may in this context, be best described as 'anti-organization' theory. From this perspective organizations are viewed as an alienating force, concerned with the wrong issues and the wrong problems. Organization studies is, therefore, 'an essentially conservative enterprise which underpins the present system of ideological domination within contemporary society' (Burrell and Morgan, 1979: 312). Inter-organizational collaborations may, therefore, be judged on the extent to which they represent a radical departure from 'conservative' organizational structures and involve local communities in the planning and implementation of their programs.

Radical Structuralism

A radical structuralist position shares with functionalism a set of assumptions about the reality of social structures and systems, but is concerned with developing a critique of the functionalist position. Approaches within this paradigm have developed into two principal frameworks derived from the later works of Karl Marx and from radical interpretations of Max Weber. They both, however, share the core concepts of:

- 'totality'—the need to study total social formations as a means of understanding the elements of a social system;
- 'contradiction'—organizations are viewed as the stage upon which deep seated divisions within society as a whole are most visible;
- 'crises'—contradictions and changes in the totality will, of necessity, result in changes of organizational form (Burrell and Morgan, 1979: 369).

The principal differences in emphasis between a Marxian and Radical Weberian approach can be represented in the primacy accorded to economic and political theory respectively and may be summarized as follows:

Marxian Structuralists Stress:		Radical Weberians Stress:
(i) Political economy	—	Political science
(ii) Economic structures	—	Political administrative structures
(iii) Monopoly capitalism	—	Corporatism
(iv) The Catastrophe analogy	—	The factional analogy.

This presentation has greatly simplified the core features of the four paradigms representing contrasting assumptions about the nature and purpose of organizations. The intention has been to highlight alternative assumptions that might be adopted in analyses of inter-organizational collaborations in urban tourism development. Examples of research issues which follow the identification of underlying assumptions are illustrated in Figure 18.3 below.

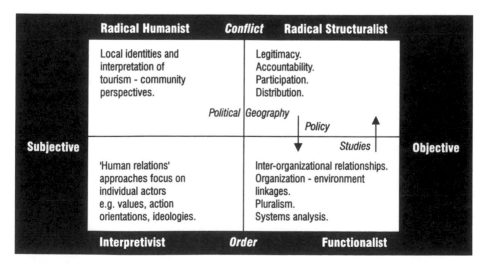

Figure 18.3 Sociological paradigms and the analysis of tourism partnership organizations (adapted from: Burrell and Morgan, 1979, p. 29).

Burrell and Morgan have been criticized for presenting an 'arbitrary' division of subjectivist and objectivist forms of analysis and for unjustifiably labelling the four paradigms as being mutually exclusive (Willmott, 1993). In the context of inter-organizational collaboration in urban tourism development, there would appear to be no reason why future research should not adopt a combination of positions within individual studies of tourism partnerships. It would indeed be desirable given the validity and saliency of the issues highlighted in Figure 18.3. Urban tourism development partnerships might, for example, be researched in terms of:

- the extent to which the partnership offers genuine opportunities for community participation;
- degrees of legitimacy and accountability within the political system, and equity within geographical boundaries;
- relationships, values and ideologies of participants; and
- the partnerships' place within the overall tourism and urban systems and the design of optimal organizational systems.

Given the nascency of the subject area within tourism studies, and the legitimacy of each paradigmatic position in the context of inter-organizational analysis, approaches which adopt a variety of methods and which are explicit about their working assumptions offer the best way forward.

CONCLUSION

Partnership and collaborative arrangements of various kinds between the actors and interest groups that make up the mixed economy of urban tourism are already widespread and are likely to develop further. Inner city regeneration programs, arts and cultural festivals and special events and place promotion campaigns now typically involve a partnership approach. Inter-organizational collaboration has thus become a *modus operandi* for public, private and voluntary sectors alike in policy and program formulation and implementation.

Tourism as a social and economic system is ideally suited to the development of forms of partnership given the range and diversity of organizational and community interests and involvement. It is therefore surprising that theories of inter-organizational collaboration and partnership have received scant attention in the tourism and organization studies literature. This chapter has sought to indicate some applicable perspectives from the IOC literature and to highlight the importance of specifying working assumptions in designing research that will develop this approach to the study of tourism development.

A paradigmatic perspective, as advocated by Burrell and Morgan (1979) is useful in making explicit assumptions about the nature of inter-organizational phenomena and the relationship between structures and individual agency (Giddens, 1984).

Other considerations which might inform future research in this field include the level adopted in a study, as summarized below (Figure 4.18).

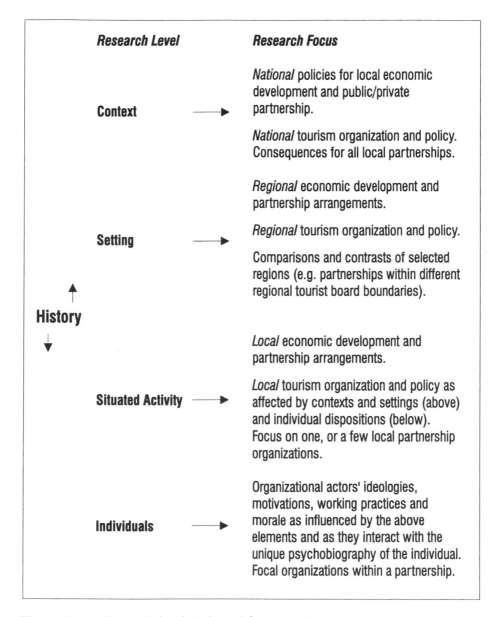

Figure 18.4   Research levels (adapted from Layder, 1993: 72).

The selection of levels of analysis will then give rise to choices about appropriate research strategies as summarized below (Table 18.1):

Table 18.1 Research strategies (adapted from Sayer, 1992: 243).

	Intensive Strategy	*Extensive Strategy*
Research Questions	How does a partnership work in a particular case or small number of cases? What causes local changes? What are the roles of local actors?	What are the regularities, common features, differences of a population of partnerships? Distribution of processes and characteristics.
Relations	Substantial local partnership relations of connection.	Formal relations of similarity and dissimilarity.
Type of Groups Studied	Causal partnership groupings.	Taxonomic groups.
Type of Account Produced	Causal explanation of partnership structures and processes though not necessarily representative.	Descriptive 'representative' generalizations, lacking in explanation.
Typical Methods	Qualitative studies of individual actors in causal contexts.	Surveys and representative samples: formal, standardized, quantitative.
Limitations	Patterns and relations unlikely to be 'representative' or generalizable.	Limited explanatory power. Problem of 'ecological fallacy' in making inferences about individual partnerships.
Appropriate Tests	Corroboration	Replication

This chapter has sought to justify the validity and relevance of adopting an inter-organizational approach to the analysis of urban tourism development and has outlined some fundamental methodological issues which may inform the design of future research. The theories of IOC and methodological considerations discussed here may be applied in any locational context, it is hoped that empirical studies will follow.

REFERENCES

Aiken, M., and Hage, J. (1968). Organizational interdependence and intra-organizational structure. *American Sociological Review, 33*, 912-930.

Aldrich, H. (1979). *Organizations and environments.* New York: Prentice Hall.

Alter C., and Hage, J. (1993). *Organizations working together.* Beverly Hills, CA: Sage.

Astley, W.G, and Brahn, A. (1989). Organizational designs for post-industrial strategies: The role of inter-organizational collaboration. In C.C. Snow (Ed.), *Strategy, organizational design and human resource management* (pp. 102-129). Chicago: JAI.

Bramwell, W., and Broom, G. (1989). *Tourism development action programs—An approach to local tourism initiatives.* Insights A6-11/A6-17, English Tourist Board.

Britton, S. (1991). Tourism, capital and place. Towards a critical geography of tourism. *Environment And Planning: Society And Space*, 9, 451-478.

Burrell, G., and Morgan, G. (1979). *Sociological paradigms and organizational analysis.* London: Heinemann.

Carroll, A.B. (1979). A three-dimensional conceptual model of corporate social performance. *Academy of Management Review*, 4, 497-505

Dann, G., and Cohen, E. (1991). Sociology and tourism *Annals of Tourism Research*, 18(1), 155-169.

Dann, G., Nash, D., and Pearce, P. (1988). Methodology in tourism research. *Annals of Tourism Research*, 15(1), 1-28.

DiMaggio, P.J., and Powell, W.W. (1983). The iron cage revisited: Institutional isomorphism and collective rationality in organizational fields. *American Sociological Review*, 48, 147-160.

Edwards, J., and Deakin, N. (1992). Privatism and partnership in urban regeneration. *Public Administration*, 70, 359-368.

Emery, F., and Trist, E. (1965). The causal texture of organizational environments. *Human Relations*, 18, 21-32

Employment Department, Northern Ireland Office, Welsh Office, Scottish Office (1992). *Tourism in the United Kingdom—Realizing the potential.* HMSO.

English Tourist Board (1991). *Planning for success—A tourism strategy for England 1991-1995.* English Tourist Board.

Fitzgerald, J. (1990). Partners in urban regeneration. *The Planner*, 76, 79-81.

Fleisher, C.S. (1991). Using an agency-based approach to analyze collaborative federated interorganizational relationships. *Journal of Applied Behavioural Science*, 27, 116-130.

Freeman, R.E. (1984). *Strategic management: A stakeholder approach.* Boston, Massachusetts: Pitman.

Giddens, A. (1984). *The constitution of society: Outline of the theory of structuration.* Cambridge: Polity Press.

Golich, V.L. (1991). A multilateral negotiations challenge: International management of the communications commons. *Journal of Applied Behavioural Science*, 27, 87-109.

Gray, B., and Wood, D.J. (1991). Collaborative alliances: Moving from practice to theory. *The Journal of Behavioural Science*, 27(1), 7.

Gunn, C. (1988). *Tourism planning.* London: Taylor and Francis.

Hall, C.M. (1994). *Tourism and politics—Policy, place and power.* Chichester: John Wiley & Sons Ltd.

Hall, R.H., Clark, J.P., Giordano, P.C., Johnson, P.V., and Van Rockel, M. (1977). Patterns of interorganizational relationships. *Administrative Science Quarterly*, 22, 457-474.

Hassard, J., and Pym, D. (1990). *The theory and philosophy of organizations: Critical issues and new perspectives.* London: Routledge.

Hicks, H.G., and Gullett, C.R. (1975). *Organizations: Theory and behaviour.* New York: McGraw Hill.

Hunter, C., and Green, H. (1995). *Tourism and the environment—A sustainable relationship?* London: Routledge.

Inskeep, E. (1991). *Tourism planning—An integrated and sustainable development approach.* New York: Van Nostrand Reinhold.

Inskeep, E. (1994). *National and regional tourism planning.* London: Routledge.

Karpik, L. (Ed.) (1978). *Organization and environment: Theory, issues and reality.* London: Sage.

Layder, D. (1993). *New strategies in social research.* Cambridge: Polity Press.

Levine, S., and White, P.E. (1961). Exchange as a conceptual framework for the study of interorganizational relationships. *Administrative Science Quarterly*, 4, 583-601.

Lincoln, Y.S. (Ed.) (1985). *Organizational theory and inquiry—The paradigm revolution*. Beverly Hills, CA: Sage.

Litterer, J.A. (1973). *The analysis of organizations*. Chichester: John Wiley & Sons Ltd.

Litwak, E., and Hylton, L.F. (1962). Inter-organizational analysis—A hypotheses on co-ordinating agencies. *Administrative Science Quarterly*, 5, 395-420.

Logsdon, J.M. (1991). Interests and interdependence in the formation of social problem-solving collaborations. *Journal of Applied Behavioural Science*, 27, 204-231.

Long, P.E. (1994). Perspectives on partnership organizations as an aproach to local tourism development. In Seaton, A.V. et al (Eds.), *Tourism—The state of the art* (pp. 239-257). Chichester: John Wiley & Sons Ltd.

Murphy, P.E. (1985). *Tourism: A community approach*. New York: Methuen.

Nathan, M.L., and Mitroff, I. (1991). The use of Negotiated Order Theory as a tool for the analysis and development of an interorganizational field. *Journal of Applied Behavioural Science*, 27(2), 163-180.

Northern Ireland Tourist Board (1992). *Annual Report Volume 44 1991-1992*.

O'Toole, L.J. (1983). Inter-organizational cooperation and the implementation of local market training policies: Sweden and the Federal Republic of Germany. *Organization Studies*, 4(2), 129-150.

Organization for Economic Co-operation and Development (annual). *Tourism Policy and International Tourism in OECD member countries*. Paris.

Pasquero, J. (1991). Supraorganizational collaboration: The Canadian environmental experiment. *Journal of Applied Behavioural Science*, 27, 38-64.

Pearce, D. (1992). *Tourist organizations*. London: Longman.

Pearce, D., and Butler, R. (Eds) (1993). *Tourism research—Critiques and challenges*. London: Routledge

Preston, L., and Post, J. (1975). *Private management and public policy: The principle of public responsibility*. New York: Prentice Hall.

Raelin, J.A. (1982). A policy output model of inter-organizational relations. *Organization Studies*, 3(3), 243-267.

Reed, M. (1991). Scripting scenarios for A New Organization Theory And Practice. *Work Employment And Society*, 5(1), 119-132.

Roberts, N.C., and Bradley, R.I. (June 1991). Stakeholder collaboration and innovation: A study of public policy initiation at the state level. *Journal of Applied Behavioural Science*, 27(2), 210-225.

Rogers, D.L., and Whetten, D.A. (1982). *Inter-organizational co-ordination: Theory, research and implementation*. Des Moines: Iowa State University Press.

Sayer, A. (1992). *Method in social science—A realist approach*. London: Routledge.

Scottish Tourist Board (1992). *Twenty Third Annual Report 1991-1992*.

Scottish Tourism Co-ordinating Group (June 1994). *Scottish tourism—Strategic plan*.

Sharfman, M.P., Gray, B., and Yan, A. (1991). The context of interorganizational collaboration in the garment industry: An institutional perspective. *Journal of Applied Behavioural Science*, 27(2).

Shaw, K. (1992). The development of New Urban Corporatism: The politics of urban regeneration in the North East of England. *Regional Studies*, 27(3), 251-286.

Silverman, D. (1979). *The theory of organization*. London: Heinemann

Smallbone, D. (1990). Enterprise agencies in London—A public-private sector partnership. *Local Government Studies*. September/October 17-32.

Smallbone, D. (1991). Partnership in economic development: The case of UK Local Enterprise Agencies. *Policy Studies Review*, 10(2/3), 87-98.

Taylor, P., and House, J. (Eds.) (1984). *Political geography: Recent advances and future directions*. New York: Croom Helm.

Turner, G. (1992). Public/private sector partnership—Panacea or passing phase? *Insights*, March A-85/A91, English Tourist Board.

Valler, D. (1991). Strategy and partnership in local economic development—A case study in local economic strategy making. *Policy Studies Review*, 10(2/3), 109-116.

Waddock, S.A. (1991). A typology of social partnership organizations. *Administration and Society*, 22(4), 480-515.

Wales Tourist Board (1993). *Annual Report 1992-1993*.

Wales Tourist Board (1994). *Tourism 2000—A Strategy for Wales* .

Warren, R.L. (1967). The inter-organizational field as a focus for investigation. *Administrative Science Quarterly*, 12(3), 396-419.

Warriner, C.K. (1984). *Organizations and their environments: Essays in the sociology of organizations*. Chicago: JA1 Press.

Westley, F., and Vredenburg, H. (1991). Strategic bridging: The collaboration between environmentalists and business in the marketing of green products. *Journal of Applied Behavioural Science*, 27, 65-90.

Williamson, O.E. (1985). *The economic institutions of capitalism*. New York: Free Press.

Williamson, O.E. (1991). Comparative economic organizations: The analysis of discrete structural alternatives. *Administrative Science Quarterly*, 36, 269-296.

Willmott, H. (1993). Breaking the paradigm mentality. *Organization Studies*, 18, 681-719.

Wood, D.J., and Gray, B. (1991). Toward a comprehensive theory of collaboration. *Journal of Applied Behavioural Science*, 27(2), 146.

Plate 12 Butchart Gardens—the Sunken Garden in Summer (photo courtesy of The Butchart Gardens Ltd.) ➡

Botanical Garden and Satisfaction of the Tourist: An Exploratory Measurement of the Experience

19

Laurent Bourdeau
Université de Moncton

Sylvie Paradis
Université du Québec à Montreal

Simon Nyeck
Université Laval

INTRODUCTION

In most cities, numerous urban attractions are discovered that attract tourists. Among those we can think of are museums, historical sites, parks, and gardens. In Montreal, the Botanical Garden is one of the urban attractions attracting touristic clientele.

The kind of visit made in a botanical garden would appear to be a hedonic experience due to the elements surrounding the consumption experience: "... that relate to the multi-sensory, fantasy and emotive aspects of one's experience with products" (Hirschman and Holbrook, 1982: 92). In others words, according to Hirschman and Holbrook (1982) and to Holbrook and Hirschman (1982), the visits made in a botanical garden are seen as hedonic consumption activities.

Moreover, the intangible characteristics associated with the visit to a botanical garden permits us to classify this type of consumption experience among those in the services industry. In a general sense, we can suggest that a visit to the Montreal Botanical Garden is a hedonic service, whereby the visitor lives the service experience across some aspects that relate to the senses (i.e., the view of the flowers) and to fantasy (i.e., the visit is often a leisure activity). It is only following the visit, or the hedonic experience across the botanical garden, that the consumer will experience a feeling of satisfaction or dissatisfaction.

Because of the nature of the hedonic experience, it is not obvious for the manager of a botanical garden to know the satisfaction of the visitor and the reasons that influence it. The task is to measure an abstract feeling which the negative outcome can damage the attitude of the tourist through enterprise.

This chapter briefly discusses the nature of satisfaction with respect to the consumer's literature. More precisely, this study focuses on the feeling of satisfaction and on the variables that compose it. The objective of this study is twofold: 1) to develop an exploratory measure of the satisfaction of the visitor of a botanical garden; and 2) to discover which variables influence the satisfaction of the tourist who visits a botanical garden. The data collection and the methodology used in the framework of this research will also be presented. The chapter discusses the research results and concludes with a discussion on the possible implications.

THE STUDY OF SATISFACTION

The study of consumer satisfaction, without a doubt, began in 1965 with an article by Cardozo. Since that time, numerous articles have been published with expectancy theory becoming the most widely used to explain the satisfaction phenomenon of the individual consuming the product.

In expectancy theory, the satisfaction of the buyer is determined by the narrow relationship between the expectations and the perceived performance of the product. On an empirical basis, Swan and Combs (1976) demonstrate that when the performance of a product fails to respond to the expectations of the consumer, dissatisfaction occurs, and when the performance of the product does respond to the consumers expectations, satisfaction occurs. Generally, we can assert that the greater the distance between the expectations and the performance, the greater the feeling of satisfaction/dissatisfaction that may arise. From an expectancy theory perspective, Howard (1977: 57) defines satisfaction: ". . . as the consumer's mental state of being adequately or inadequately rewarded for the sacrifice he or she has undergone. The degree of adequacy results from comparing actual past experience with the reward that was expected from the brand in terms of its potential to satisfy motives served by its product class."

In expectancy theory, satisfaction results, therefore, from a comparison between the actual performance and the anticipated performance. It is interesting to note that the affect of the individual (here, the feeling of satisfaction) is the result of a cognitive process. In other words, the satisfaction of a product is based on a process where the consumer compares his expectations with the product's performance, then, subsequently derives a feeling of satisfaction or dissatisfaction. The consumer is thus traditionally perceived as a rational human being, where the affect is dependent on the cognition.

Satisfaction with Respect to the Consumption of a Service

In the 1980s, we see the appearance of some studies centred on satisfaction with respect to the consumption of a service. In many of these studies, satisfaction is defined as an affective response resulting from the comparison of expectations and a purchase experience (Pizam, Neumann and Reichel, 1978). In certain studies, satisfaction depends on the expectations and the intangible elements of performance (i.e., a travel experience). For example, Pizam et al. (1978) indicate to us that, on the one hand, a tourist is satisfied when the experience of travelling compared to the expectations produces a feeling of gratification. On the other hand, dissatisfaction occurs when the experience of travelling compared to expectations produces displeasure. From another perspective, Whipple and Thach (1988) demonstrate that the satisfaction of a tourist towards a trip organized by bus depends on the response to expectations with regards to the performance of the tourist services support, of the convenience of departure points, and of sightseeing. We can therefore see that the intangible elements of a hedonic service influences the satisfaction of a consumer. Whipple and Thach (1988) empirically support that the realization of expectations influence the satisfaction and suggest that the performance of services and attractions is an indicator of future purchase intentions.

We notice that despite the development within the literature focusing on satisfaction in the services industry, and more precisely, in the tourism industry, many of these studies have supported the hypothesis of expectancy in the case of the consumption of a service, consequently adhering to the perspective of the rational human being.

The Role of Expectations

In the expectancy theory, the expectations of the consumer plays a major role. However, in the application of the expectancy model in the services sector, Jayanti and Jackson (1991) suggest that expectations play a minor role due to the subjective nature of services (e.g., due to the intangibility). Similarly, Hill (1986) adds that the more a service becomes intangible, the more difficult it becomes for the consumer to evaluate the service. For example, we may think that prior to visiting the Montreal Botanical Garden, a tourist should have no idea of what to expect during this consumption experience. In this case, the tourist would develop a feeling of satisfaction/dissatisfaction resulting from the confirmation of blurry or vague expectations, or resulting from a more global attitude upon the completion of the visit.

In this study, it appears important for us to adopt a perspective where the feeling of satisfaction/dissatisfaction towards a hedonic experience, develops from a global post-consumption attitude, so this study is similar to others conducted by some other authors (Cooper-Martin, 1991; 1992; Hirschman, 1984; Price and Ridgeway, 1983; Venkatraman and MacInnis, 1985). This perspective is inspired by the blurry and vague characteristics of certain expectations as well as by the certain intangible elements encompassing the visit. In addition, this perspective appears to consider service characteristics that involve evaluation processes different from those used by the consumer of tangible products (Berry, 1980; Eiglier and Langeard, 1979; Shostack, 1977).

The Measure of Satisfaction

In the literature, the majority of researchers measured the satisfaction of consumers in either one or two stages. In the studies where satisfaction was measured in only one stage, subjects were asked to evaluate the product or service after the consumption experience or purchase (e.g., Dubé-Rioux, 1990; Oliver and Desarbo, 1988). In the studies where satisfaction was measured in two stages, subjects were asked to evaluate the product or service before and after the consumption experience or purchase (e.g., Tse and Wilton, 1988; Whipple and Thach, 1988).

In a general sense, the measure of satisfaction in two stages is associated to the expectancy theory, whereby the researcher measures the expectations (before the consumption experience), and the performance of the product or service (after the consumption experience). Conversely, the goal of measuring satisfaction in only one stage is to define a global measure of satisfaction (after the consumption experience). By adopting the perspective of a visitor who doesn't know exactly what to expect during the consumption experience of a tourist site, notably due to the intangibility characteristics surrounding the service, it seems important to us to investigate and measure the feeling of visitor satisfaction immediately after leaving the botanical garden. We are therefore searching to measure the feeling of satisfaction without directly taking into account the tourists' expectations.

METHODOLOGY

To become familiar with the variables that influence visitors to the Montreal Botanical Garden, we have constructed a measurement instrument containing 18 variables. Preliminary exploratory research conducted with a reduced sample (n=37), permitted us to derive this grouping of variables that explained the satisfaction towards a visit to the Botanical Garden.

From an exploratory perspective, we have regrouped in four categories the variables defined in the measurement instrument. The first category regroups variables that encompass the various attraction points discovered on the grounds of the Montreal Botanical Gardens; that is to say, the evaluation of the visit to the Chinese Garden (V39), the Japanese Garden (V53), the Insectarium (V48), and the visit to the greenhouses (V43). The second category regroups variables that feature the functioning of the site, more precisely, the evaluation of the accessibility of the site (V37), the quality of equipment found on the site (V38), the cleanliness of the site (V42), the opening hours of the site (V50), the availability of parking (V51), the admission price (V41), and the signposting on the site (V52). The third category concentrates on the content of the visit, such as the evaluation of the collection of plants, flowers, and trees presented on the grounds (V45), the information obtained on the site (V46), the brochures and pamphlets offered (V47), the exterior arrangements (V54), and the competency of personnel (V49). Finally, a last category of variables will permit us to measure the evaluation of the visitors towards relational aspects, for example, the welcoming by the personnel of the botanical garden (V40) and the general ambience (V44).

It is also important to mention that we have added a variable allowing us to know the general satisfaction of the visitors (V36) with respect to the Botanical Garden visit. This last variable is appropriately defined as the dependent variable of this study. The scale used to measure this variable is a five point interval scale (1 indicating very dissatisfied to 5 indicating very satisfied). All the other scales used to measure evaluation of cues are five point interval scales (1 indicating very bad (worst) evaluation to 5 indicating very good (best) evaluation).

The data gathering procedures took place at the Montreal Botanical Garden during the summer season of July 31, 1993 to August 16, 1993. All respondents participating in this study were tourists and visitors to the Botanical Garden. In this research, we defined a tourist as a person who travels more than 100 kilometres from his home. In the questionnaire, we controlled this by questions on the profile of the tourist. The respondents of this study were tourists who visit Montreal. Respondents were approached by interviewers at one of the exits on the site and responded themselves to the questionnaire. The questionnaire was therefore completed immediately after their visit to the Botanical Garden. The sample was probabilistic with the collection being completed on a random basis of only one person or part of a group or family, every five minutes (n=228). All respondents were over 18 years of age (66.1 percent of respondents were between the ages of 18 and 44).

ANALYSIS OF RESULTS

We have divided the analysis of results in two large stages. In the first stage we have measured the reliability (internal consistency) of the measurement instrument. Subsequently, in stage two, we searched for the variables or groups of variables that influence the general satisfaction of visitors to the Botanical Garden.

The reliability (internal consistency) of the measurement instrument consists of identifying possible interrelations between the variables of the measurement instrument. The results of the first factorial analysis, containing the entire set of variables in the measurement instrument, permits the elimination of the variables that are weakly correlated with the overall variables of the measurement instrument. Variables V37, evaluation of the accessibility of the site; V41, evaluation of the admission price; and V54, evaluation of the exterior arrangements, are eliminated due to their weak communalities that are less than .45 (refer to Table 19.1). After having eliminated these three variables from the measurement instrument, we conducted a second factorial analysis.

Before studying the results of this factorial analysis, the appropriateness of the factorial model was investigated by calculating two tests. The analyses focusing on the sphericity of the distribution (Bartlett's sphericity test) allowed us to reject the hypothesis according to which the matrix would be unitary (test statistic = 608.96841, = .00000). This result implies that the variables contained in the factorial

Table 19.1   Factorial analysis results.

Variable	Communality	Factor	Eigenvalue	Percent of Variance	Cumulative Percent
V37	.41842	1	7.64264	42.5	42.5
V38	.54725	2	2.00055	11.1	53.6
V39	.54594	3	1.24943	6.9	60.5
V40	.71087				
V41	.44150				
V42	.56812				
V43	.76001				
V44	.67117				
V45	.74729				
V46	.80631				
V47	.72281				
V48	.50626				
V49	.54319				
V50	.64048				
V51	.69876				
V52	.74531				
V53	.48845				
V54	.33048				

model are not independent. There should, therefore, exist some interrelations between the variables of the model. The Kaiser-Meyer-Olkin permits the measurement of the appropriateness of the sample. In fact, it concerns: "... an index which compares the magnitudes of the observed correlation coefficients to the magnitudes of the partial correlation coefficients ... Small values of this index imply that a factor analysis may not be appropriate because correlations between pairs of variables cannot be accounted for by other variables" (Büyükkurt and Everett, 1993: 221). In our case, we observe the results of the sampling adequacy measure to be .76553, which can be subsequently qualified as "middling". The results from Bartlett's sphericity test as well from the Kaiser-Meyer-Olkin test permit us to confirm the appropriateness of employing a factorial model in this study.

In the next stage, the data were analysed favouring the utilization of the factorial extraction method of principal components. The adjustment criteria of the factorial structure used is the varimax rotation. We can explain the utilization of this criteria because: "It is a precisely defined method that approximates simple structure" (Büyükkurt and Everett, 1993: 221). We can observe in Table 19.2 that the factor loadings are all higher than .50. Highlighting the fact that the majority of the communalities are higher than .60 indicates the strong correlations between the indicators and the associated factors.

Table 19.2 Varimax rotated factor matrix.

Variable	Factor 1	Factor 2	Factor 3	Final Communality
V38	**.72425**	.17999	.12406	.57233
V39	**.70875**	.01590	.21721	.54975
V40	**.60665**	**.55690**	.05836	.68157
V42	**.71678**	.34418	.00244	.63225
V43	.07082	.39620	**.79249**	.79003
V44	.47012	.19864	**.62452**	.65049
V45	.49279	.05944	**.72756**	.77571
V46	.24556	**.85985**	.15060	.82233
V47	.08632	**.78473**	.35035	.74600
V48	.32266	.24327	**.54103**	.45601
V49	**.53862**	.49711	.25180	.60063
V50	**.73093**	.05328	.34032	.65291
V51	**.76006**	.07498	.35517	.70945
V52	.03134	**.86506**	.19291	.78653
V53	**.54230**	.12662	.43592	.50015

The results of the factor analysis indicate that three factors explain 66.2 percent of the total variance of the phenomenon studied (refer to Table 19.3). The first factor is associated with the facilities found on the site and explains 45.1 percent of the variance. The variables directly associated with the facilities having the highest factor loadings are the availability of parking, the opening hours, the quality of equipment and the cleanliness of the grounds. The second factor regroups variables that feature the orientation of the visitor on the site and explains 13.0% of the variance. The third factor would appear to be strictly revolving around the attractions and content of the visit, and subsequently explains only 8.1% of the variance. These factors are presented in a decreasing order with respect to their eigenvalues, and permits us to discover the different interrelations from the initial proposal. Contrary to our belief, we discovered three groups of variables amongst the measurement instrument, and not four. In addition, the nature of the factor groupings are slightly different than what we had elaborated at the outset. The factors fail to revolve around the attraction points, the functioning of the site, the content of the visit, and the relational aspects, but more so with elements that seem to be directly related to the attraction of the site.

To know the internal consistency of each of the factors of the measurement instrument, we used a Cronbach's alpha test as summarized in Table 19.3. The results obtained from this test allows us to confirm the attainment of a relatively high level of internal consistency associated with each of the factors. We can thus confirm that at the interior of the factors, the variables are correlated between each other and subsequently measure the same construct.

Table 19.3   Ranking of factors by eigenvalue and reliability measures.

	Factor Loadings	Eigenvalue	Percent of Variance	Cronbach's Alpha
Facilities Found on the Site				
V51 Parking spaces	.76006	6.75866	45.1	.8710
V50 Opening hours	.73093			
V38 Quality of equipment	.72425			
V39 Chinese Garden	.70875			
V42 Cleanliness of the site	.71678			
V40 Welcoming by the personnel	.60665			
V53 Japanese Garden	.54230			
V49 Competency of the personnel	.53862			
Orientation of the Visitors on the Site				
V52 Signposting on the site	.86506	1.95684	13.0	.8409
V46 Information available	.85985			
V47 Brochures and pamphlets	.78473			
Attractions and Content of the Visit				
V43 Visit to the greenhouses	.79249	1.2106	8.1	.7597
V45 Plants and flowers collection	.72756			
V44 General ambience	.62452			
V48 Visit of the Insectarium	.54103			

DISCUSSION

To explain the behaviour of tourists, we utilized a multiple regression model to uncover the variables that influence the general satisfaction of the tourist with respect to the visit to the Botanical Garden. The independent variables of the regression model are the three orthogonal factors—obtained through the factor analysis—as well as variable V41 associated with the evaluation of admission price. Table 19.4 presents a description of all variables in the linear regression model. We observe that the relations between the independent variables and the general satisfaction is statistically significant ($F = 13.81482$, df = 4,55; $p = .000$) with $R^2 = .50576$ and the adjusted $R^2 = .46915$. We can observe that only the independent variables FACTOR 1 and FACTOR 3 have beta coefficients (second column of Table 19.4) that are statistically significant at the alpha level = 0.05 (last column of Table 19.4).

The final regression model is therefore the following:

(V36: General satisfaction) = 4.81955 + 0.27471 (FACTOR 1) + 0.15166 (FACTOR 3).

This model signifies that the management staff of the Montreal Botanical Garden must increase the level of efficiency of their facilities and attractions that one finds on the site, with the ultimate goal of increasing the general satisfaction of the tourists. In the analysis of this model, we must also note that the evaluation of admission price is not a variable influencing the general satisfaction of the tourists.

Table 19.4 Multiple regression analysis results.

Variable	B	SE B	Beta	T	Sig T
V41	-.01769	.06075	-.03359	.291	.7719
FACTOR3	.151627	.04319	.345259	3.510	.0009
FACTOR1	.274713	.04574	.625529	6.005	.0001
FACTOR2	.057431	.04622	.130771	1.243	.2194
Constant	4.81955	.25668		18.77	.001

Multiple R = .71117 R^2 = .50576Adjusted R^2 = .46915
F = 13.81482   Sig. F = .0000

We can then argue that in this situation, where the price is 7 dollars (CDN), it seems that for a tourist, when the price is not too expensive it doesn't explain the overall satisfaction of the visit.

CONCLUSION

With the goal of better understanding these results, it would appear useful to underline the limitations of this research. Firstly, we must emphasize that the research conducted was exploratory in nature, with the results permitting us to clarify the problem associated with the comprehension and the measurement of tourist satisfaction to a botanical garden. It would be interesting to conduct an additional study testing the validity and reliability of the measurement instrument developed by using another sample. Secondly, the data originates solely from the Montreal Botanical Garden, thus the generalization of these results towards other botanical gardens is somewhat limited.

In this study, we adopted a perspective whereby the tourist who visited the Botanical Garden developed his/her feeling of satisfaction/dissatisfaction resulting from a post-consumption attitude. In this perspective, the tourist would develop a feeling of satisfaction/dissatisfaction resulting from the confirmation of blurry or vague expectations, or resulting from a more global attitude upon the completion of the visit. Upon leaving the site, we find three variable groupings (cues) that explain the general satisfaction with: a) the facilities on the site; b) the orientation on the site; and c) the attractions and contents on the site.

In this study, we highlighted the absence of regroupments among the variables directly associated to relational aspects. Nevertheless, careful attention is warranted. Firstly, we had a relatively small amount of variables on that topic. Secondly, the ambience and the welcoming by the personnel of the Botanical Garden could affect the post-consumption attitude of the visitors, albeit these variables do not seem to be major determinants of satisfaction.

The results from the multiple regression analysis indicate that the regroupment of variables related to the facilities on the site, and the regroupment of variables related to the attractions and contents discovered on the site, are significant predictors of the general satisfaction of the tourists who visit the Botanical Garden. These results imply that managers wishing to increase the level of tourist satisfaction with their botanical garden should increase the satisfaction towards the facilities and the ambience of the site. In other words, we can suggest increasing the performance of the variables contained in the factors of the regression model. The managers may work either: a) directly on the variables (e.g., by increasing or maintaining a certain number of assigned employees to the cleanliness of the site); or b) indirectly on the variables (e.g., by improving the cleanliness perception of the site with the help of a publicity campaign).

Tourism and a visit at a botanical garden are considered as hedonic consumption activities. The predominance of hedonic implication facets assumes that experiential activities are more commonly associated with leisure. Moreover, in the case of a visit to a botanical garden, a tourist has to deal with the intangible characteristics associated with services. We can suggest that the feeling of satisfaction towards a visit to the botanical garden is developed from a global post-consumption attitude that takes into account the evaluation of tangible cues. Tangibles cues should be what the tourist can measure concretely in accordance with hedonic experience. These principal tangible cues are the variables of the first factor; the facilities found on the site. For instance, the consumer probably prefers, among other things, to use as tangible cues the evaluation of the parking spaces and opening hours, than to use the information available on the site about the flowers, trees, and the collection of plants. At first glance, the cognitive informations seem to be a tangible cue, but for the hedonic consumers, tangibles cues seem to be related to what they experienced (i.e., the visit) and/or what they can measure (e.g., opening hours). We can explain this by the fact that the tourist visits a botanical garden for fantasy and the emotive aspects of one's experience.

The principal contribution of this research was to develop an instrument for the measure of satisfaction of the tourists who visit a botanical garden and to identify the groups of variables that influence the satisfaction. After having used the services offered by a botanical garden, the tourists develop consumption experiences that may influence the recommendation of this type of urban site. Hence, the results of this study can become a rich tool for the manager who wants to positively influence the satisfaction of the tourist and the recommendation of the urban site.

ACKNOWLEDGEMENTS

The authors gratefully acknowledge a grant from the Chaire du Tourisme of the University of Québec at Montréal and from the Montréal Botanical Garden which supported part of this study. Also, Lynda Hénault's assistance (from the Centre de Recherche en Gestion of the University of Québec at Montréal) in typing and editing is very much appreciated.

REFERENCES

Berry, L.L. (1980). Service marketing is different. *Harvard Business Review*. May-June, 24-29.

Büyükkurt, M.D., and Vass, E.C. (1993). An investigation of factors contributing to satisfaction with end-user computing process. *Canadian Journal of Administrative Sciences*, 10(3), 212-228.

Cardozo, R.N. (1965). An experimental study of customer effort, expectation, and satisfaction. *Journal of Marketing Research*, 2, 244-249.

Cooper-Martin, E. (1991). Consumers and movies: Some findings on experiential products. In R. Holman and M.R. Solomon (Eds.), *Advances in consumer research Vol. 18* (pp. 372-378). Provo, UT: Association for Consumer Research.

Cooper-Martin, E. (1992). Consumers and movies: Information sources for experiential products. In J.F. Sherry and B. Sternthal (Eds.), *Advances in consumer research Vol. 19* (pp. 756-761). Provo, UT: Association for Consumer Research.

Dubé-Rioux, L. (1990). The power of affective reports in predicting satisfaction judgments. In M.E. Golberg, G. Gorn and R.W. Pollay (Eds.), *Advances in consumer research Vol. 17* (pp. 571-576). Provo, UT: Association for Consumer Research.

Eiglier, P., and Langeard, E. (1979). A note on the commonality of problems in service management: A field study. In P. Eglier et al. (Eds.), *Marketing consumer services: New insights* (pp. 31-58). Cambridge, MA: Marketing Science Institute.

Hill, D.J. (1986). Satisfaction and consumer services. In R.L. Lutz (Ed.), *Advances in consumer research Vol. 13* (pp. 311-315). Ann Arbor, MI: Association for Consumer Research.

Hirschman, Elisabeth C. (1984). Experience Seeking: A Subjectivist Perspective of Consumption, *Journal of Business Research*, 12, 115-136.

Hirschman, E.C., and Holbrook, M.B. (1982). Hedonic consumption: Emerging concepts, methods and propositions. *Journal of Marketing*, 46, 92-101.

Holbrook, M.B., and Hirschman, E.C. (1982). The experiential aspects of consumption: Consumer fantasies, feelings, and fun. *Journal of Consumer Research*, 9, 132-140.

Howard, J.A. (1977). *Consumer behaviour: Application of theory*. Montréal: McGraw-Hill.

Jayanti, R., and Jackson, A. (1991). Service satisfaction: An exploratory investigation of three models. In R. Holman and M.R. Solomon (Eds.), *Advances in consumer research Vol. 18* (pp. 603-610). Provo, UT: Association for Consumer Research.

Oliver, R.L., and Desarbo, W.S. (1988). Response determinants in satisfaction judgements. *Journal of Consumer Research*, 14, 495-507.

Pizam, A., Neumann, Y., and Reichel, A. (1978). Dimensions of tourist satisfaction. *Annals of Tourism Research*, 5, 314-321.

Price, L.L., and Ridgeway, N.M. (1983). Development of a scale to measure use innovativeness. In R.P. Bagozzi and A.M. Tybout (Eds.), *Advances in consumer research Vol. 10* (pp. 679-684). Ann Arbor, MI: Association for Consumer Research.

Shostack, L.G. (1977). Breaking free from product marketing. *Journal of Marketing*, 41, 73-80.

Swan, J.E., and Combs, L.J. (1976). Product performance and consumer satisfaction: A new concept. *Journal of Marketing*, 40, 25-33.

Tse, D.K., and Wilton, P.C. (1988). Models of consumer satisfaction formation: An extension. *Journal of Marketing Research*, 25, 204-212.

Venkatraman, M.P., and MacInnis, D.J. (1985). Epistemic and sensory exploratory behaviours of hedonic and cognitive consumers, *Advances in Consumer Research*, E.C.

Whipple, T.W., and Thach, S.V. (1988). Group tour management: Does good service produce satisfied customers? *Journal of Travel Research*, 22, 16-21.

Author Index

A

AACP (Aspen Area Community Plan) 206, 211, **218**

Abberger, W. 203, **218**

Ablers, P.C. 129, **134**

Aiken, M. **248**

Akis, S. 200, **219**

Alberta Tourism, Parks and Recreation 28, **36**

Aldrich, H. **248**

Alexander, D. 215, 217, **218**

Allen, L. 57, **65**, 200, **219**

Allen, R.L. 200, **218**

Alter, C. **248**

Altman, I. 59-60, **65**

Ames, M. 129, **134**

Appadurai, A. 121, **134**

Ashworth, G. 75, **85**, 106, **111**, 137, **148**

Ashworth, G.J. 1-2, **8**, 25, 29, **36**, 116, **134**, 169, **182**, 184, 185, **196**

Asian Coalition for Housing Rights 81, **85**

Astley, W.G. **248**

B

Baade, R.A. 33, **36**, 108, **111**

Backoff, R.W. 202, **220**

Bagozzi, R.P. **263**

Bagwell, S. 229, **233**

The Banker 230, **233**

Barkley, B. 6, 149

BarOn, R.V. 9, 10, 20, **22**

Bauen, R. 214, **219**

Beason, K. 3, **8**

Belisle, F. 10, **22**

Beliveau, D. 76, **87**

Bell, D. 48, **53**

Benn, D. 104, 109, **112**

Bennett, R. 231, **233**

Berry, L.L. 3, **8**, 255, **263**

Bianchini, F. 30, **36**, 52, **53**, 106, 110, **111**

Birmingham City Council (UK) 44, 46, 48, 49, **53**

Birmingham Economic Information Centre (UK) 50, **53**

Blanchini, F. 132, **134**

Bogan, C. 175, **182**

Boldt, M. 123, **134**

Boniface, P. 94, **100**

Bonn, M.A. 9, **22**

Bonnemaison, S. 82, **85**

Booth, P. 106, **111**

Bordeau, L. 7, 253

Bower, J.L. 201, **218**

Boyer, C. 98, **100**

Boyer, M.C. 97, 98, **100**

Boyle, M. 106, **111**

Boyle, R. 106, **111**

Bradley, R.I. **250**

Brahn, A. **248**

Braithwaite, R. 190, **196**

Bramham, P. 75, 79, 81, 84, **85**, **86**

Bramwell, B. 199, **218**

Bramwell, W. 201, **218**, **249**

Brent Ritchie, J.R. **196**

Brewer, J. 74, **74**

British Tourist Authority 105, **112**

British Tourist Authority and English Tourist Board 105, **112**

Britton, S.   249

Britton, S.G.   94, **100**

Broadway, M.J.   25, **36**

Brooke, M.Z.   9, 20, **23**

Broom, G.   201, **218, 249**

Bryson, J.M.   201, **218**

Buchholz, R.A.   200, **218**

Buckley, P.J.   9, 20, **23**

Budowski, G.   137, **148**

Burns, J.P.A.   76, **85**

Burrell, G.   242, 243, 244, 245, 246, **249**

Butler, R.   5, 9, 236, 242, **250**

Butler, R.W.   13, 15, 16, 20, 21, **22,** 115, 121, **134, 135**

Büyükkurt, M.D.   258, **263**

Bywater, M.   107, **112**

C

Calantone, R.J.   9, **22**

Calgary Economic Development Authority   **218**

Calliou, S.   215, 217, **218**

Canada. Province of British Columbia.   **134**

Canadian Government Office of Tourism and Regional Economic Expansion   **134**

Caproni, J.S.   221, **233**

Cardozo, R.N.   254, **263**

Carlzon, J.   4, **7**

Carroll, A.B.   **249**

Cassidy, F.   123, **134**

Castells, M.   84, **86**

Caulfield, J.   **22**

Cecil, W.   6, 157

Chacko, H.   68, 70, **74**

Champion, M.   227, **233**

Chapman, R.J.K.   92, **101**

Chavis, D.M.   56, **65**

Checkaway, B.   **218**

Chianello, J.   32, **37**

Chivers, B.   33, **37**

Choy, D.   222, **233**

Christopher, W.F.   192, **197**

City of Calgary   **218**

Clark, J.P.   239, **249**

Clarke, A.   10, **22**

Clifford, J.   127, 129, **134**

Clifford, J.E.   131, **134**

Cohen, B.   48, **53**

Cohen, E.   118, **135,** 137, **148,** 242, **249**

Cole, D.   131, **134**

Collins, M.   26, **37**

Collins, J.R.   3, **8**

Combs, L.J.   254, **264**

Construction News   50, **53**

Cooper, C.   9, **22, 36,** 113

Cooper-Martin, E.   255, **263**

Coopers & Lybrand   32, **37**

Corliss, R.   228, **233**

Corporate Growth   230, **233**

Cosenza, R.   57, **65**

Crenson, M.A.   94, **100**

Critcher, C.   108, **112**

Crompton, J.L.   82, **86**

Cummings, M.   **134**

D

Dann, G.   118, **135,** 242, **249**

Davies, D.   57, **65**

Davis, B.W.   92, **101**

Day, P.   81, **86**

Deakin, N.   **249**

Debord, G.   83, **86**

Department of the Environment (UK)   106, **112**

Desarbo, W.S.   256, **263**

Desfor, G.   29, **37**

de Vries, P.   118, **135**

Dieke, P.   10, **22, 113**

Dietvorst, A.   184, 191, **196**

Dimanche, F.   5, 67

Directorate General of Tourism, UNESCO/UNDP   145, **148**

DiMaggio, P.J.   **249**

Donatos, G.   10, **22**

Donelly, J.H.   3, **8**

Drakatos, C.G.   10, **22**

Dredge, D.   200, **218**

Drozdiak, W.   229, **233**

Dubé-Rioux, L.   256, **263**

Dudycha, D.   25, **39**

Dye, R.   33, **36,** 108, **111**

E

Eadington, W.R.   **23**

Easterby-Smith, M.   192, **196**

The Economist   228, **233**

Edvardsson, B.   186, 187, 188, **196**

Edwards, J.   **249**

Eiglier, P.   255, **263**

Elder, N.   223, **233**

Elias, P.D.   127, **135**

Emery, F.   239, **249**

Employment Department, Northern Ireland Office, Welsh Office, Scottish Office   **249**

English Tourist Board   26, **37,** 106, **112, 249**

English Tourist Board, Northern Ireland Tourist Board, Scottish Tourist Board, Wales Tourist Board   104, **112**

Esolen, G.   70, **74**

Euchner, C.G.   32, **37**

F

Faulkner, B.   194, **196**

Featherstone, M.   **134**

Feick, J.   208, **218**

Fesenmaier, D.R.   9, **23**

Fick, G.R.   **196**

Fine, S.H.   **38**

Fitzgerald, J.   **249**

Fleisher, C.S.   **249**

Fletcher, J.   9, **22**

Flower, J.   223, 226, 227, 228, **233**

Forbes, D.   92, **101**

Foreshaw, J.   80, **86**

Foucault, M.   93, **100**

Fowler, P.J.   94, **100**

Francis, D.   122, **135**

Freeman, R.E.   201, **218, 249**

Furr, H.L.   9, **22**

G

Gaber, A.   180, **182**

Gallie, W.B.   92, **100**

Gappert, G.   **37,** 132, **135**

Gardiner, C.   106, **112**

Gazillo, S.   25, **37**

Gee, C.   222, **233**

Getz, D.   6, 13, **23,** 25, 32, **37,** 67, 68, **74,** 76, **86,** 180, **182,** 199, 200, 201, **219**

Gibson, J.L.   3, **8**

Giddens, A.   246, **249**

Gill, A.   **65,** 200, 205, **219, 220**

Gill, A.M.   55, 58, 60, 61, **65**

Giordano, P.C.   239, **249**

Golberg, M.E.   **263**

Goldrick, M.   29, **37**

Golich, V.L.   **249**

Goodall, B.   75, **85,** 116, **134**

Goodwin, D.   9, **23**

Gordon, D.   **53**

Gordon, J.R.   4, **7**

Gorn, G.   **263**

Gray, B.   200, 201, **219,** 238, 239, **250, 251**

Green, H.   **249**

Greenpeace Australia   80, **86**

Greenwood, J.   58, **65**

Greiner, N.   80, 82, **86**

Griffiths, R.   30, **37,** 106, **112**

Grönroos, C.   184, 186, 189, 190, 191, **196**

Gullett, C.R.   **249**

Gummesson, E.   191, **197**

Gunn, C.   236, **249**

H

Hage, J.   **248**

Hageman, T.   190, 191, **197**

Haider, D.H.   2, **8,** 36, **37,** 169, **182**

Hall, C.   107, **113, 135**

Hall, C.M.   5, 70, **74,** 75, 78, 79, 81, **86,** 91, 92, 94, 95, 98, **100, 249**

Hall, J.   **37**

Hall, M.   67, **74**

Hall, M.C.   202, **219**

Hall, P.   26, **37**

Hall, R.H.   239, **249**

Hannigan, J.A.   9, **22**

Harron, S.   **135**

Hart, C.   175, **182**

Hartley, R.F.   229, 230, **233**

Hartmann, R.   9, 10, 11, **22, 65, 220**

Harvey, D.   79, 80, 82, 83, **86,** 98, 99, **100**

Hasek, G.   226, **233**

Hassard, J.   **249**

Haywood, K.M.   3, 6, **7,** 72, **74,** 93, **100,** 169, 170, 171, **182**

Haywood, M.K.   200, 202, **219**

Heath, E.   2, **8**

Henry, I.   75, 79, 81, 84, **85, 86**

Henry, S.   83, **86**

Hentschel, B.   192, **197**

Hewison, R.   92, 94, **100,** 106, **112**

Hiaasen, C.   226, **233**

Hicks, H.G.   **249**

Hill, D.J.   255, **263**

Hiller, H.H.   82, **86**

Hillery, G.A., Jr.   56, **65**

Hillman, S.   77, **86**

Hirano, R.   123, **135**

Hirschman, E.C.   253, 255, **263**

Hiss, T.   169, **182**

Holbrook, M.B.   253, **263**

Hollinshead, K.   92, **100**

Holman, R.   **263**

Hopkins, J.S.P.   16, **22**

Hough, M.   52, **53**

House, J.   **250**

Houser, B.   15, **23**

Houston, W.   33, **37**

Howard, J.A.   254, **263**

Hoy, D.   10, **22**

Hoyle, B.S.   **37, 38**

Hu, Y.   77, **87**

Hughes, G.   106, **111**

Hughes, H.L.   5, 77, 85, **86,** 103, 104, 106, 107, 108, 109, 110, **112**

Hummon, D.M.   117, **135**

Hunter, A.   74, **74**

Hunter, C.   **249**

Hunter, M.   **37**

Husain, M.S.   **37, 38**

Hutchinson, J.   25, **39**

Hylton, L.F.   239, **250**

I

Innes, J.E.   61-62, **65**

Inskeep, E.   236, **249**

Institute for Service Management
    (Netherlands)   193, **197**

Interim Steering Committee Inc.   33, **37**

Ircha, M.   29, **38**

Ivancevich, J.M.   3, **8**

J

Jackson, A.   255, **263**

Jackson, E.E.   16, **22**

Jamal, T.B.   6, 199, 200, 201, **219**

James, W.R.   129, **134**

Jansen, P.   122, **135**

Jansen-Verbeke, M.   81, **86,** 183, 184,
    190, **197**

Jayanti, R.   255, **263**

Jenkins, A.K.   6, 183

Jenkins, C.   **113**

Jenkins, J.   92, 94, **100**

Johnson, A.T.   32, 33, **37**

Johnson, J.D.   200, **219**

Johnson, K.   214, **219**

Johnson, P.V.   239, **249**

Jotindar, J.S.S.   9, **22**

Judd, D.   50, **53**

Judd, D.R.   26, **37**

K

Kang, Y.-S.   68, 69, 74, **74**

Karpik, L.   **249**

Katz, R.   **134**

Kearns, G.   132, **135**

Kelly, J.   118

Kelly, M.   98, **101**

Kemper, R.   9, **23**

Keogh, B.   200, **219**

Kidd, B.   33, **37**

Kieselbach, S.   200, **218**

Klenke, M.   29, **37**

Knapper, C.   25, **39**

Knight, R.V.   **37**, 132, **135**

Knox, C.   **112**

Kopachevesky, J.P.   127, **135**

Kotler, P.   2, **8**, 36, **37**, 169, **182,**
    202-203, **219**

KPMG Peat Marwick   46, 47-48, **53**

Kramer, P.   126, **135**

Kroll, M.   92, **101**

Kunst, P.   **197**

L

Landry, C.   52, **53**

Lane, B.   199, **218**

Langeard, E.   255, **263**

Lanken, D.   26, **37**

Lasswell, H.D.   92, **101**

Lavery, P.   **111**

Law, C.   25, 26, **37**, 49, 50, **53,** 103, **112**

Law, C.M.   2, **8**, 68, **74,** 75, **86**

Layder, D.   247, **249**

Leahy, G.W.   29, 30, **37**

Lee, J.   27, **37**

Lefebvre, H.   99, **101**

Lemmink, J.   **197**

Leroux, C.   79, 85, **87**

Levine, M.V.   26, **37**

Levine, S.   239, **249**

Lewis, N.   42, **53**

Lincoln, Y.S.   **250**

Lindblom, C.E.   92, **101**

Litterer, J.A.   **250**

Litwak, E.   239, **250**

Loftman, P.   41, 47, 48, **53,** 108, **112**

Logsdon, J.M.   **250**

Long, P.E.   7, 235, 236, **250**

Long, P.T.   57, **65**, 200, **218**

LORD Cultural Resources Planning and Management   30, 31, **38**

Lorimer, J.   **37**

Lowe, A.   192, **196**

Lueck, G.W.   227, **233**

Lui, J.   57, **65**

Lukes, S.   92, 93, **101**

Lutz, J.   5, 41

Lutz, R.L.   **263**

Lyden, F.J.   92, **101**

M

MacGregor, S.   **36**

MacInnis, D.J.   255, **264**

Macintyre, B.   95, **101**

MacIsaac, M.   27, **38**

Mahoney, E.M.   9, **23**

Makens, J.   222, **233**

Manchester City Council   107, **112**

Mao, B.   5, 9

Market Facts of Canada   1, **8**

Marris, T.   77, **86**

Marshall Macklin Monaghan Limited in association with Christopher Lang and Associates Ltd.   32, **38**

Mathieson, A.   10, **23**

McArthur, S.   91, 94, 95, 98, **100**

McCaw, F.   75, **87**

McConville, C.   98, **101**

McCool, S.F.   137, **148**

McGill, R.   201, **219**

Mckay, S.L.   82, **86**

McMillan, D.W.   56, **65**

Merrens, R.   29, **37**

Mieczkowski, Z.   12, 13, **23**

Mill, R.C.   184, 185, **197**

Milman, A.   200, **219**

Ministry of Tourism and Recreation (Ontario)   18, **23**

Mintzberg, H.   201, 202, **219**

Mitchell, L.S.   10, **23**

Mitroff, I.   **250**

Mommaas, H.   75, 80, 81, 83-84, **85, 87**

Mondy, R.W.   4, **7**

Montgomery, D.   200, **219**

Montgomery, R.   78, **87**

Moore, S.   200, **218**

Morgan, G.   242, 243, 244, 245, 246, **249**

Morrison, A.M.   184, 185, **197**

Mosley, L.   222, **233**

Mount, J.   79, 85, **87**

Mules, T.J.   76, 78, **85**

Muller, C.   203, **219**

Muller, T.E.   3, **7**, 170, **182**

Murphy, P.   10, **23**, 47, **53**

Murphy, P.E.   3, 4, 6, **8**, 9, 10, 15, 21, **23**, 25, **38**, 93, **101**, 103, 105, 106, 107, **113**, 121, 122, **135**

N

Nash, D.   11, **23, 135**, 242, **249**

Nathan, M.L.   **250**

Netherlands: Ministerie van Economische Zak   10, 11, 20, **23**

Neumann, Y.   255, **263**

Nevin, B.   41, 47, 48, **53**, 108, **112**

Newsweek   225, **233**

Nielsen, N.A.   3, **8**

Norkunas, M.K.   95, 96, 97, 99, **101**

Normann, R.   4, **8**, 185-186, **197**

Norris Nicholson, H.   5, 115, 127, 128, 129, **135**

Northern Ireland Tourist Board   **250**

Nuryanti, W.   **148**

Nyeck, S.   7, 253

O

O'Connor, J.   107, **113**

Oey, E.   140, **148**

L'Office des Congrès et du Tourisme du Grand Montréal   26, **38**

Olds, K.   78, 81, 82, **87**

O'Leary, J.T.   9, **23**

Oliver, R.L.   256, **263**

O'Reilly, A.M.   55, **65**

Organization for Economic Co-operation and Development (OECD)   **250**

O'Toole, L.J.   **250**

Ovretveit, J.   186, 187, 188, **196**

Owen, C.   26, **38**

P

Page, S.   2-3, 4, **8**, 25, **38**

Painton, P.   227, **233**

Pannell, Kerr Forster, Campbell Goodell Consultants Limited   34, **38**

Papson, S.   95-96, **101**

Paradis, S.   7, 253

Parasuraman, A.   3, **8**

Parker, B.   115, **135**

Parkinson, M.   **111**, 132, **134**

Parpostel   144, **148**

Pasquero, J.   **250**

Peake, L.   **22**

Pearce, D.   1, **8**, 236, 242, 244, **250**

Pearce, D.G.   9, **23**, 115, 121, **134, 135**

Pearce, P.   242, **249**

Peat Marwick Stevenson and Kellogg   26, 28, 34, **38**

Peck, J.   107, 108, **113**

Perdue, R.   68, 70, 74, **74**

Perdue, R.R.   57, **65**, 200, **219**

Peters, J.   77, 78, **87**

Philo, C.   132, **135**

Pimlotts, B.   **36**

Pinder, D.   **37, 38**

Pizam, A.   200, **219**, 255, **263**

Pollay, R.W.   **263**

Pompl, W.   **111**

Pope, J.   72, **74**

Porter, M.E.   4, **8**

Post, J.   **250**

Postma, A.   6, 183

Powell, W.W.   **249**

Premeaux, S.R.   4, **7**

Preston, L.   **250**

Price, L.L.   255, **263**

Propst, L.   203, **218**

Prosser, G.   78, **87**

Przeclawski, K.   **135**

Purdon, M.   31, **39**

Purdue, T.T.   200, **218**

Pym, D.   **249**

R

Raelin, J.A.   **250**

Reed, M.   **250**

Regional Planning Services, Calgary Regional Planning Commission   28, **38**

Reichel, A.   255, **263**

Reid, L.J.   **135**

Rein, I.   2, **8**, 36, **37**, 169, **182**

Research and Development Department of the Greater Montréal Convention and Tourism Bureau   27, 28, 34, **38**

Research Surveys of Great Britain   104-105, **113**

Resort Municipality of Whistler (BC)   58, 62, **65**

Richards, G.   105, **113**

Richardson, B.   123, **135**

Richardson, R.   130-131, **135**

Ridgeway, N.M.   255, **263**

Ritchie, J.R.B.   27, 32, **38**, 68, **74**, 76, 77, 85, **87**, 202, 209, **219**

Robbins, M.   126, **135**

Roberts, D.   33, **38**

Roberts, J.   9, **23**

Roberts, N.C.   **250**

Roche, M.   68, 71, **74**, 79, **87**, 108, **113**

Roering, W.D.   201, **218**

Rogers, D.L.   239, **250**

Ronkainen, I.   9, **23**

Ross, E.   **37**

Royal British Columbia Museum   **156**

Ryan, C.   5, 41, 47, 51, **53**, 200, **219**

S

Sager, D.D.   92, **101**

Sandford, G.   228, **233**

Sasseen, J.   229, **233**

Saxby Payne and Cook Inc.   32, **38**

Sayer, A.   248, **250**

Schattsneider, E.   92, **101**

Schechter, J.   203, 204, **220**

Scheuing, E.E.   192, **197**

Schuyler, G.   29, **38**

Scotinform   105, 107, **113**

Scottish Tourist Board   **250**

Scottish Tourism Co-ordinating Group   **250**

Seaton, A.V.   **218**

Seaton, T.   **113**

Selin, S.   3, **8**

Seward, S.B.   123, **134**

Sharfman, M.P.   **250**

Sharplin, A.   4, **7**

Shaw, G.   9, 16, **23**, 58, **65**

Shaw, K.   **250**

Shaw, R.   194, **196**

Sheldon, P.   107, **113**

Sherry, J.F.   **263**

Shipman, G.A.   92, **101**

Shoalts, D.   33, **37**

Shostack, L.G.   255, **264**

Silverman, D.   **250**

Simmons, D.G.   57, **65**, 200, **220**

Simmons, R.   92, **101**

Sinclair, M.T.   20, **23**

Sinnott, J.   25, **38**

Skok, J.E.   201, **220**

Smale, B.J.A.   13, 20, **22**

Smallbone, D.   **250**

Smith, B.H.   32, **38**, 85, **87**

Smith, S.L.J.   25, **38**

Smith, V.L.   **23**, 57, **65**, 121, **135**

Snepenger, D.   15, **23**, 200, **219**

Snepenger, M.   15, **23**

Snow, C.C.   **248**

Solomon, J.   230, **233**

Solomon, M.R.   **263**

Sorkin, M.   96, **101**

Spotts, D.M.   9, **23**

Stankey, G.   137, **148**

Staus, B.   192, **197**

Stein, J.M.   **65**

Stephenson, M.   106, **113**

Sterngold, J.   221, **233**

Sternthal, B.   **263**

Stokowski, P.A.   214, **220**

Sugden, J.   **112**

Sutcliffe, C.M.S.   20, **23**

Swan, J.E.   254, **264**

Sydney Morning Herald   83, **87**

Sydney Olympics 2000 Bid Ltd.   79-80, **87**

T

Taylor, P.   **250**
Taylor, S.   32, **38**
Thach, S.V.   255, 256, **264**
Thomasson, B.   186, 187, 188, **196**
Thorber, R.   107, **113**
Thorpe, R.   192, **196**
Thrift, N.   92, **101**
Tickell, A.   107, 108, **113**
TISDA   123
Tobin, G.   **37**
Tourism Canada   26, 28, **38**
Tourism Vancouver   32, **38**
TREE   123
Triste, E.   201, 214, 216, **220**, 239, **249**
Tse, D.K.   256, **263**
Tunbridge, J.E.   2, **8**, 29, 30, **36**, **38**, 137, **148**
Turner, G.   **251**
Tybout, A.M.   **263**

U

Upton, C.   44, 46, **53**
Urry, J.   2, **8**, 80, **87**, 94, **101**
Uysal, M.   9, **22**, **23**

V

Valler, D.   **251**
van der Poel, H.   75, 80, 81, 83-84, **85**, **87**
Van der Werff, P.   10, **23**
Van Rockel, M.   239, **249**
Var, T.   57, **65**
Vass, E.C.   258, **263**
Venkatraman, M.P.   255, **264**
Vogel, H.   169, **182**
Vogelezang, H.   190, 191, **197**
Voogd, H.   2, **8**, 184, 185, **196**
Vredenburg, H.   216, **220**, **251**

W

Waddock, S.A.   238, 239, **251**
Wales Tourist Board   236, **251**
Walker, E.G.   123, **135**
Walker, J.R.   68, 70, **74**
Wall, G.   2, 5, **8**, 10, 12, **23**, 25, 31, **38**, **39**, 137, 138, 145, 146, **148**
Walsh, D.J.   222, 223, **233**
Wanhill, S.   9, **22**
Warren, R.L.   55, 56, 58, 62, 65, **65**, 239, **251**
Warriner, C.K.   **251**
Watson, G.L.   127, **135**
Wechsler, B.   202, **220**
Weiler, B.   **113**, 116, **135**
Wellington City Art Gallery (NZ)   91, **101**
Wenban-Smith, A.   48, **53**
Westley, F.   216, **220**, **251**
Whelan, R.K.   26, **39**
Whetten, D.A.   239, **250**
Whipple, T.W.   255, 256, **264**
White, P.E.   239, **249**
Whitt, J.   107, **113**
Wicks, B.   76, **86**
Williams, A.M.   9, 16, **23**, 58, **65**
Williams, P.   **37**
Williams, P.W.   61, **65**, 200, 205, **219**
Williamson, D.   58, **65**
Williamson, O.E.   **251**
Willmott, H.   243, 246, **251**
Wilton, P.C.   256, **264**
Witt, S.   9, 20, **23**
Wood, D.J.   238, 239, **251**
Wood, R.   **113**
World Commission on Environment and Development (WCED)   217, **220**
World Tourism Organization   15, **23**, 118

Wright, G.   44, 45, 50, **53**
Wynne, D.   107, **113**

Y
Yacoumis, J.   15, **23**
Yake, G.A.   78, **87**
Yan, A.   **250**

Z
Zairis, P.   10, **22**
Zehnder, L.   224, 226, 227, **233**
Zeithmal, V.A.   3, **8**
Zeppel, H.   107, **113**

Subject Index

A

aboriginal culture   115, 126, 127

aboriginal tourism   124, 126, 130, 131, 133, 135, 136

absentee property owners   58

accommodation   10, 13, 16, 18, 19, 21, 28, 39, 46, 47, 58, 59, 64, 76, 138, 144, 145, 147, 222, 226, 229

accountability   132, 241, 246

action plan(s)   49, 123, 177, 179, 207, 201, 210, 213, 217

adventure tourism   119, 129

advertising   73, 122, 127, 135, 160, 163

aggregated product   184, 190

allocation   60, 99, 227, 240

analysis   2, 6, 7, 8, 13, 38, 39, 53, 85, 91, 92, 93, 94, 101, 103, 108, 111, 152, 153, 164, 175, 176, 177, 179, 187, 188, 195, 201, 203, 210, 222, 223, 224, 229, 230, 232, 236, 237, 241, 242, 243, 245, 246, 247, 248, 249, 250, 251, 257, 258, 259, 260, 261, 262

arts   5, 31, 36, 39, 103-113, 118, 123, 132, 133, 134, 164, 212, 235, 246

arts tourism   103-111

Aspen, Colorado   61, 205, 218

attendance   31, 32, 34, 67, 105, 150, 151, 229

attraction development   221, 232, 233

attraction(s)   3, 6, 10, 12, 13, 14, 15, 16, 17, 20, 21, 22, 25, 26, 27, 28, 29, 30, 31, 35, 36, 38, 69, 71, 72, 74, 76, 77, 78, 79, 84, 86, 87, 95, 103, 107, 108, 109, 110, 118, 130, 144, 147, 161, 169, 174, 184, 185, 193, 195, 221-233, 238, 253, 255, 256, 259, 260, 261, 262

attractions sector   221, 222

audience   27, 32, 104, 105, 106, 107, 109, 112, 130, 143, 166

audience studies   105, 109

authenticity   117, 129, 137, 138, 148, 169

authority   93, 105, 112, 173, 174, 176, 202, 210, 218, 220

B

Biltmore Estate   6, 157-166

Birmingham   5, 41-53, 108, 112, 235

British Columbia   3, 4, 5, 20, 34, 55, 56, 57, 97, 115-136, 149-153, 156, 199, 203, 207 business environment   4

business interests   77, 123, 184

business management   3

business marketplace   75

business tourism   16, 46

business tourists   16

business travel   16

C

Calgary   27, 28, 31, 32, 33, 37, 38, 79, 82, 86, 87, 199, 203, 209-213

Canadian National Aboriginal Tourism Association   124, 133, 136

capital   9, 47, 49, 77, 79, 82, 94, 98, 99, 100, 132, 135, 138, 150, 159, 180, 225, 249

carrying capacity   55, 65, 137, 148, 226, 231

casino   72, 74

central place location   226

citizen advocacy   216

citizen awareness   214

citizen committees   207, 216

citizen involvement   207

citizen participation   210, 214

city planners   30

city renewal programs   77

climate   10, 11, 12, 21, 82, 100, 107, 112, 123, 222

climatic conditions   13, 16, 17

CNATA   126

co-option   82

co-producer   4

co-product   192, 194

co-service   186, 191, 194

coalition   95, 106, 107, 113, 238

coercion   82, 93, 98, 99

collaboration   7, 48, 79, 180, 199-220, 235-251

collaborative alliances   239, 240, 241, 249

collaborative arrangements   235, 246

collaborative process   201, 203

Colonial tourism   119

commodification   35, 106

commoditization   121, 127, 133, 137, 147, 148

community aspirations   4, 7

community characteristics   210

community consensus   200, 215, 216

community development   62, 115, 130, 207, 219

community expectations   170

community groups   33, 35, 81, 210, 235

community initiatives   126

community interests   83, 204, 216, 246

community involvement   210, 216, 217

community leaders   121, 208, 209, 211

community life   179, 218

community needs   5, 61, 62, 215

community of interest   82, 83

community participation   99, 210, 217, 220

community philosophy   214, 215

community plan(s)   61, 171, 206, 208, 211, 213, 215, 217, 218

community planning   132, 203, 206, 216

community resources   56

community structure   81

community subgroups   58

community tourism   55, 56, 123, 134, 181, 200, 201, 203, 219,
    220, 236

community values   171, 204, 205, 208, 210

community vision   6, 201, 208, 210, 211, 213, 214, 215, 217

community wellbeing   172, 182, 214

community-responsive tourism   200

competition   4, 13, 28, 50, 55-65, 79, 82, 98, 99, 122, 172, 176, 180,
    196, 202, 222

competitive advantage   3, 4, 170, 175, 183, 184, 230

concert halls   103, 106, 108

consensus   62, 154, 200, 201, 203, 204, 207, 209, 210, 213, 215,
    216, 243

consensus-building   62, 204

conservation   91, 92, 98, 99, 135, 137, 140, 148, 164, 165, 203, 204, 218,
    224, 225, 233

constituencies   171, 172

consumer   3, 4, 6, 7, 20, 28, 51, 104, 121, 126, 129, 130, 131, 178, 184, 186, 187, 193, 194, 195, 221, 223, 226, 232, 253, 254, 255, 262, 263, 264

consumer demands   226

consumer expectation   187

consumer measurement   178

consumer profiles   194, 195

consumer satisfaction   7, 129, 254, 264

consumerism   121, 130, 131

consumption   35, 65, 83, 84, 94, 96, 98, 106, 115, 118, 131, 169, 253, 254, 255, 256, 261, 262, 263

control   55, 58, 91, 92, 93, 97, 116, 119, 154, 173, 174, 178, 183, 184, 185, 186, 188, 191, 192, 200, 202, 208, 221, 224, 225, 228

controlling   3, 154

convention(s)   19, 25-30, 33-36, 41-52, 57, 71, 73, 74, 80, 223, 228, 235

convention centre(s)   25, 26, 27, 29, 34, 35, 36, 42-51, 71, 73, 74, 223

cooperation   62, 156, 172, 173, 179, 180, 184, 185, 190, 196, 197, 201, 205, 237, 239, 243, 250

cooperative marketing   3

coordination   62, 65, 123, 124, 130, 147, 210, 237, 239

core product   184, 190

corporate investment   231

corporate involvement   231

corporate partners   231

corporate social performance   240, 249

corporate strategic planning   201

creativity   52, 201, 211

crisis of the local state   79, 84

critical incident technique (CRIT)   192, 195, 196

cross-cultural understanding   121, 130

cultural activities   12, 122, 130

cultural attractions   110, 118, 123, 126, 133

cultural capital   132, 135

cultural change   86, 128, 232

cultural concerns   95

cultural development   106

cultural diversity   21, 124

cultural experiences   118, 128

cultural expressions   138, 140, 144

cultural heritage   91, 166

cultural identity   123, 127, 128, 131, 132, 185

cultural institutions   31, 149

cultural integrity   115, 128, 129, 130, 133

cultural policies   106, 109, 110, 111, 132

cultural product   131

cultural resources   110, 119

cultural resurgence   130

cultural strategies   107

cultural tourism   5, 25, 28, 30, 31, 100, 105, 110, 112, 113, 115, 118, 121, 124, 129, 134, 135, 145, 148

cultural tourists   30, 118, 131

cultural values   91, 208, 212

culture   1, 5, 23, 75, 83, 84, 91, 94, 95, 97, 106, 107, 110, 111, 112, 113, 115, 116, 118, 121, 122, 123, 126, 127, 128, 129, 130, 131, 132, 133, 134, 135, 137, 138, 145, 147, 148, 150, 169, 172, 173, 179, 212, 214

customer   4, 7, 129, 170, 174, 175, 176, 177, 178, 179, 182, 185, 186, 187, 188, 189, 190, 191, 192, 193, 194, 263

customer approach   170

customer relationship life cycle   189, 190

customer retention   175, 177

customer satisfaction   175, 176, 178, 179, 190

D

decision-making   6, 61, 63, 93, 94, 132, 154, 156, 172, 174, 193, 201, 202, 204

decision-making approaches   132

decision-making process   6, 93, 94

delivery system   175, 186

Delphic process   236

demand   2, 9, 15, 16, 20, 21, 23, 25, 27, 28, 33, 56, 59, 61, 63, 71, 76, 82, 84, 93, 99, 115, 151, 169, 223

demarketing   191

design   38, 79, 80, 157, 158, 162, 164, 169, 172, 178, 179, 201, 206, 207, 219, 237, 246, 248

destination areas   12, 13, 20, 21, 173, 146

destination association   3

destination awareness   35

destination development   201, 215
destination management   188, 199, 200, 202
destination managers   217
destination marketing   6, 163
destination planning   199, 210, 214, 215, 216
destination region(s)   10, 13, 14, 16, 21, 85
destination resources   202
destination service organization   190
destination setting   3
developing countries   138, 147
development control   224
development goals   138
development model   232
development plans   123
development strategy   32, 35, 36, 37, 38, 49, 55, 134, 169, 214, 236
differential pricing   20
differentiation strategies   4
Disneyland   221, 222, 223, 227, 228, 230, 232, 233
distribution of income   111
diversified (multiple) attractions   13
diversity   21, 52, 63, 68, 79, 94, 97, 118, 120, 121, 124, 128, 147, 201, 204, 212, 246
domestic tourists   104, 140, 145
drawing power 105, 108, 109, 110

E
eco-cultural tourist   129
eco-tours   154
economic benefits   26, 32, 35, 48, 67, 74, 81, 137, 224
economic change   26, 27, 48, 50
economic climate   107
economic development   5, 25, 26, 30, 32, 35, 37, 47, 49, 77, 79, 84, 100, 111, 209, 210, 218, 220, 228, 250, 251
economic effects   9, 33, 71, 109
economic evaluation   109, 111
economic growth 42, 48, 51, 208, 212
economic impact   33, 35, 37, 38, 39, 46, 47, 53, 67, 68, 71, 82, 86, 113

economic needs   115

economic opportunities   123

economic performance   180

economic restructuring   35, 56, 97

economic returns 9, 132

economic rewards   42, 169

economic self-sufficiency   115, 123, 127

economic strategy   42, 180, 251

economic survival   118

economic sustainability   130

economic visioning   210, 211

ecosystem   119, 231

ecotourism   119

education   3, 7, 28, 37, 47, 51, 118, 126, 127, 129, 130, 132, 180, 182, 185, 200, 208, 212, 215, 236

emerging tourist destination   199

employment   9, 10, 26, 27, 35, 38, 42, 46-51, 64, 79, 81, 82, 84, 85, 98, 99, 106, 107, 127, 128, 132, 146, 200, 226, 227, 228, 232, 249, 250

employment generation   49, 228

entertainment   44, 72, 76, 97, 103, 104, 105, 108, 109, 110, 112, 113, 127, 129, 130, 132, 169, 222, 228

environmental concerns   79, 111

environmental effects   10, 82

environmental impacts   44

environmental objectives   236

environmental philosophy   208

environmental quality   63

environmental stability   225

ethnic   11, 12, 31, 81, 96, 97, 99, 101, 128, 131, 135, 203, 207, 210, 212

Euro Disneyland   221, 227, 228, 230

evaluation processes   255

event tourism   37, 76, 78, 86, 87, 112

events   12, 13, 14, 17, 21, 22, 28, 31, 32, 33, 35, 36, 57, 67-74, 75-87, 95, 97, 104, 107, 108, 109, 111, 113, 128, 134, 149, 156, 161, 162, 202, 219, 235, 246

excellence   157, 170, 179, 180, 208

expectancy theory   7, 254, 255, 256

expected quality   192

experienced quality   191, 192

exterior environment   17

external environment   3, 4, 173, 202, 221, 222, 223, 230

external environments 3, 217, 221

F

facilities   2, 4, 7, 11, 13, 16, 21, 25, 26, 29, 30, 33, 38, 41, 42, 43, 44, 51,
    56, 57, 61, 62, 72, 75, 77, 79, 80, 103, 107, 108, 123, 128, 131, 164, 176,
    184, 202, 224, 228, 259, 260, 261, 262

factorial analysis   257, 258

festival marketplace   29, 30, 43, 50, 71, 98

festivals   13, 17, 20, 22, 25, 31, 32, 38, 74, 75, 76, 78, 86, 105, 106, 107,
    108, 109, 113, 118, 246

finance   53, 75, 83, 123, 163, 179

First Nations   124, 127, 132, 134, 135

flagship projects   49

franchise agreements   231

functional quality   191

functionalism   244

future purchase intentions   255

Futures Project   149, 151, 152, 153, 155, 156

G

gap analysis model   187, 188

geographical boundaries   238, 246

geographical location   123

global economy   37, 97

global tourism   5, 121

government   3, 25, 26, 29, 31, 32, 33, 34, 41, 42, 47, 50, 57, 59, 61, 74,
    77, 82, 83, 84, 96, 106, 110, 123, 126, 151, 154, 158, 160, 165, 166, 175,
    180, 202, 210, 214, 224, 225, 228, 229, 231, 237

government involvement   92

green spaces   52

greenbelt   226

growth   6, 42, 56, 58, 68, 69, 71, 81, 107, 115, 129, 151, 157, 163, 183,
    193, 194, 195, 206, 207, 208, 210, 211, 213, 223, 227

growth management   55, 61, 62, 63, 65, 199, 200, 203, 204, 205, 212, 217

growth management strategy(ies)   200, 205

H

Halifax   29, 38

hallmark event(s)   13, 68, 70, 74, 76, 77, 79, 81, 82, 86, 87

hedonic experience   253, 255, 262

hedonic service   253, 255

heritage   2, 5, 6, 15, 16, 21, 28, 20, 30, 31, 37, 63, 89, 91-101, 103, 104,
     105, 106, 108, 109, 112, 113, 119, 123, 127, 129, 130, 133, 134, 135, 137,
     138, 140, 144, 145, 146, 147, 166, 202, 204, 208, 210, 212, 219

heritage centres   127, 129

heritage conservation   91, 92, 98, 99, 135

heritage legislation   129

heritage management   91, 92, 100, 137

heritage policy   92

heritage product   97

heritage representation   92, 94, 97

heritage resources   138, 140, 144, 146, 147

heritage sites   29, 119, 140, 144, 145

heritage studies   91

heritage tourism   6, 91-100, 105, 106, 113, 145, 147, 219

high season   12, 13, 14, 21, 146

historic district   29, 72

historic property   160, 166

history   29, 70, 83, 95, 96, 97, 99, 106, 115, 123, 126, 128, 132, 147, 150,
     161, 166, 169

holistic planning   199

homogeneity   30, 36, 98, 130, 171

hospitality   6, 7, 34, 36, 71, 74, 113, 123, 169, 182, 199

host community(ies)   4, 7, 8, 75, 81, 94, 221, 222, 229, 230, 231,
     232, 236

host location   76

hosts   3, 65, 69, 121, 127, 135

hotel(s)   3, 16, 18, 19, 25, 26, 28, 29, 43, 46, 47, 48, 57, 64, 67, 71, 72, 73,
     74, 80, 81, 82, 127, 165, 169, 170, 175, 176, 177, 178, 179, 180, 182,
     183, 197, 222, 223, 224, 226, 227, 228, 230, 231, 233

housing   32, 47, 51, 58, 59, 61, 63, 65, 77, 78, 81, 84, 85, 87, 203, 204,
     205, 206, 207, 211, 225, 226

human resource management   172, 248

human resources   175, 177

I

identity   5, 51, 91, 94, 95, 99, 107, 115, 122, 123, 127, 128, 131-133, 185, 203, 214

ideology   94, 95, 96, 97, 99, 115

image(s)   5, 6, 27, 30, 32, 35, 36, 42, 49, 51, 60, 68, 73, 75, 76, 78, 79, 80, 82, 85, 86, 96, 97, 106, 107, 109, 115, 121, 128, 132, 134, 135, 146, 162, 169, 183, 185, 191, 192, 193, 195, 202, 203

imagineering concepts   221

imaging   36, 42, 76, 77, 79, 80, 81, 83, 84, 96

impact data   68, 74

impact measurement   68

implementation   21, 63, 153, 155, 203, 207-211, 216-218, 220, 244, 246, 250

index of seasonality   17

indigenous communities   115, 119, 133

indigenous tourism   115-136

industrial heritage   96, 97

information   3, 16, 50, 53, 126, 147, 151, 162, 172, 175, 176, 183, 185, 190, 193, 194, 195, 196, 201, 205, 208, 217, 218, 220, 256, 260, 262, 263

information system   196

Infrastructure   64, 71

infrastructure   2, 3, 10, 21, 27, 32, 35, 48, 49, 61, 62, 63, 64, 68, 69, 71, 73, 75, 77, 78, 82, 83, 85, 144, 145, 147, 174, 207, 223-225, 229, 230

inner-city   30, 77, 78, 81, 83, 84, 96, 97, 98, 235

innovation   52, 127, 170, 173, 202, 212, 221, 250

Institute for Service Management   193, 197

institutional   10, 11, 13, 15, 31, 95, 119, 126, 240, 241, 249, 250

institutional environment   241

inter-organizational relationships   3, 240, 241, 249

inter-urban competition   50, 79

interest groups   92, 152, 200, 205, 237, 246

International Convention Centre   41, 42, 43, 44, 45, 46, 47, 48, 49, 50, 52

international tourism   18, 23, 68, 74, 250

international visitors   46, 122, 145, 146, 147

interplace competition   82, 98, 99

interpretation   95, 97, 99, 100, 108, 117, 129, 145, 147, 192, 197, 221

interpretivism   244

investment   8, 9, 27, 29, 31, 35, 36, 37, 42, 43, 46, 48, 49, 51, 52, 57, 62, 68, 70, 71, 74, 77, 78, 82, 84, 85, 98, 99, 106, 123, 154, 159-160, 202, 223-232

IOC   237, 239, 240, 246, 248

J

Jackson Hole (Wyoming)   199, 203, 204, 205, 212, 213, 216, 218, 219

job creation   25, 48

jobs   26, 27, 30, 33, 35, 42, 47, 48, 49, 50, 82, 84, 99, 176, 180, 224, 228

L

land development   232

land prices   226, 227

land use(s)   38, 63, 64, 132, 203, 206, 221, 223, 224, 229

leadership   48, 95, 108, 123, 159, 175, 176, 179, 180, 197, 220

leading   3, 4, 26, 33, 68, 71

legacy(ies)   27, 67, 68, 73, 75, 76, 79, 122, 166, 219

legislation   6, 11, 129, 205

legitimacy   84, 95, 236, 239, 240, 241, 242, 243, 244, 246, 248

leisure   11, 16, 22, 50, 51, 60, 78, 79, 83, 84, 85, 86, 87, 97, 100, 101, 103, 112, 118, 119, 131, 132, 148, 183, 197, 229, 232, 235, 236, 253, 262

leisure experiences   131

leisure tourists   103

length of stay   145, 147

lifestyle   30, 31, 58, 83, 87, 120, 122, 227, 232

limits of acceptable change   137

local area tourism   201, 235, 236, 238, 240, 241

local community   55, 69, 146, 180, 200, 210, 216, 217

local control   55, 208

local culture   86, 100

local environment   191, 221, 232

local government   37, 41, 50, 53, 61, 84, 107, 219, 237, 250

local growth coalitions   81, 82, 83, 99

local histories   99

local participation   215

local residents   3, 16, 17, 19, 65, 145

local sustainability   199

locality   63, 122, 236

locational advantages   226

locational analysis   222, 223, 224, 230

locational characteristics   222, 223

locational features   50

locational selection   230

Louisiana World's Fair (LWF)   5, 67-74

low season(s)   17, 21, 146

M

management philosophy   185

management process   3, 62, 178, 179

management systems   176

managerial roles   173, 174

managerial viewpoint   173

market awareness   1

market demand   63

market profile   194

market regions   17

market research   57, 162

marketplace(s)   28, 29, 30, 35, 43, 50, 51, 71, 75, 98, 146

mass marketing   183

mass production   183

mass tourism   25, 183

measure of satisfaction   256, 262

media   33, 47, 67, 69, 72, 73, 82, 99, 122, 127, 149, 154, 221

mega-event(s)   5, 27, 28, 32, 35, 38, 67-74, 75-87, 113, 219

mega-event research   71

microeconomics   241

modifying process   13

monitoring system   6, 63, 64, 193, 194, 196

Monterey, California   65, 96, 97, 99, 101

Montréal   7, 16, 25-39, 53, 253, 257, 263

Montréal Botanical Garden   253, 255, 256, 257, 261

multiplier technique   108, 109, 111

multipliers   47, 50

municipal post-modernism   51

municipalities   26, 62, 77, 201

museum(s)   2, 4, 16, 25, 35, 49, 80, 95, 98, 103, 104, 119, 123, 126, 127, 129, 134, 135, 136, 138, 149-154, 170, 221, 253

N

natural environment   119, 205, 210, 222

nature   123, 129, 225

Negotiated Order Theory   241, 250

New Orleans   13, 67, 68, 69, 70, 71, 72, 73, 74

niche marketing   126

non-urban tourist destinations   15

non-urban tourist origin regions   15

O

occupancy levels   19

off-peak seasons   20

off-season   12, 13, 14, 18, 19, 20, 21

Olympic Movement   79

operations   2, 11, 97, 124, 126, 157, 159, 160, 163, 178, 179, 202, 208

opportunity costs   41, 47, 109, 111

organization studies   236, 237, 239, 242, 244, 246, 250, 251

organization system   171, 172, 173

organizational approach   172, 248

organizational performance   3

Ottawa   18, 19, 30, 31

outdoor tourism   119

outside visitors   30, 31, 32

overnight visitors   28, 46

overseas market   28

P

package tour   183

parks   2, 4, 6, 28, 36, 170, 221, 222, 225, 226, 229, 231, 232, 253

partnership   5, 6, 7, 49, 80, 132, 156, 222, 226, 231, 233, 235-251

partnership arrangements   235-238

partnership organizations   235, 245, 250, 251

pattern of seasonality   17, 19

peak demands   61

peak season   14, 15, 20, 22, 205

peaking   17, 20, 76, 77

perceived performance   254

perceived quality   186, 188, 190, 191, 192

Perceived Service Quality Model   186, 191

performance indicators   48, 195

performing arts   5, 31, 103, 104, 105, 106, 107, 108, 109, 110, 111, 118

performing arts tourism   105, 107, 108, 109, 110, 111

permanent resident population   58, 205

place   1, 2, 4, 5, 8, 17, 18, 36, 37, 45, 52, 56, 58, 60, 63, 74, 75, 76, 77, 81, 82, 83, 86, 91, 92, 94, 96, 97, 98, 99, 100, 106, 107, 118, 127, 159, 169, 182, 197, 202, 214, 219, 220, 226, 246, 249

place competition   98, 99

place histories   99

place marketing   106, 202

place promotion   76, 77, 246

planners   30, 34, 71, 169, 170, 199, 201, 202, 207, 215, 216, 217, 219

planning   2, 3, 4, 6, 7, 25, 28, 30, 31, 37, 38, 43, 49, 52, 53, 55-65, 70, 74, 76, 82, 83, 86, 87, 93, 99, 100, 101, 112, 118, 124, 129, 132, 136, 137, 138, 152, 153, 154, 155, 156, 160, 166, 169, 175, 177, 178, 179, 182, 196, 199-220, 221, 223, 225, 226, 236, 237, 244, 249

planning decisions   61, 62

planning issues   204, 214, 215

planning process   57, 62, 82, 83, 86, 153, 179, 200, 206, 207, 214, 217

pleasure tourism   16

pleasure tourists   16, 19

policy-making   84, 93, 110, 126

political agenda   93, 133

political analysis   91, 92

political framework   94

political geography   101, 235, 241, 250

political perspective   93

political process(es)   92, 107, 122, 236

political realities   96

political structure   56, 94, 95

political theory   241, 245

politics   37, 39, 70, 74, 75, 86, 87, 91, 92, 94, 98, 99, 100, 101, 108, 111, 112, 129, 134, 135, 173, 197, 219, 249, 250

positive imaging   96

post-industrial urban environment   81

power   6, 47, 50, 51, 58, 74, 78, 84, 86, 91, 92, 93, 94, 95, 96, 97, 98, 99, 100, 101, 105, 108, 109, 110, 173, 180, 200, 219, 227, 241, 248, 249, 263

power arrangements   92

power politics   108

power structures   99

premium service   175

preservation   6, 26, 37, 72, 91, 94, 96, 97, 98, 100, 138, 143, 145, 157, 160, 161, 162, 163, 164, 165, 166, 202, 204, 220

pricing   13, 20, 130, 162

private developers   30

private enterprise   96, 157

private investment(s)   29, 36, 46, 49, 71

private sector   27, 35, 43, 46, 49, 50, 83, 202, 215, 235, 237, 240, 250, 251

process quality   175, 178, 191

product aggregations   185

product delivery   3

product design   169

product development   5, 161, 162

product differentiation   185

product management   178

product matrix   3

product profile   6, 193, 194, 195

production   6, 51, 65, 71, 94, 96, 101, 106, 113, 177, 183, 186, 192, 194, 232

program formulation   246

promotion strategies   75

promotions   53, 162, 163

property development   42, 48, 49, 50

property management   176

public consultation   43

public expenditure   61, 75, 109

public funds   35, 46

public good   232

public interest   107, 205

public investment   31, 57, 77

public involvement   57, 63

public meetings   62, 63, 153, 205

public monies   76, 82

public participation   51, 62, 205, 217, 219
public relations   53, 70, 73, 163, 197
public sector   2, 7, 33, 49, 50, 51, 83, 196, 201, 218, 220, 235, 240
publicity   67, 70, 72, 73, 181, 191, 262

Q

quality assessment   186, 192
quality control   183, 184, 185, 186, 191
quality criteria   191
quality destination management   202
quality improvement   69, 170, 175, 176, 179, 180, 183, 184, 186, 189, 192
quality management   1, 3, 4, 6, 170, 175, 179, 180, 181, 182, 183-197, 219
quality of life   52, 72, 86, 110, 133, 171, 172, 173, 182, 212, 214
quality planning   175, 177
Quebec City   13, 29, 31, 33, 37, 38, 39

R

radical humanism   244
radical structuralism   244
re-imaging   36, 42, 76, 79, 83
real estate   59, 75, 82, 98, 203, 205, 228, 230, 231
reallocation   84, 202
recreation   1, 16, 18, 19, 22, 23, 28, 30, 36, 37, 38, 51, 53, 57, 58, 61, 63, 64, 72, 81, 107, 113, 129, 148, 169, 182, 183, 196, 197, 208, 212, 213, 226, 233
redevelopment   5, 36-39, 43, 44, 53, 75, 76, 77, 78, 81, 83, 84, 97, 98, 155
regeneration   25, 26, 30, 35, 36, 37, 38, 41, 42, 45, 47, 50, 53, 68, 76, 85, 86, 106, 107, 108, 111, 112, 127, 133, 134, 235, 246, 249, 250
regional development   22, 132
regional economy   28, 47
regional planning   28, 38, 87, 237
regional promotion   126
regional tourism   75, 87, 249
reinvestment   52
relational quality   191
relationship marketing   189, 190, 193, 194, 196, 197
remote areas   18
research methodologies   239, 242, 243

research strategy   74, 155, 194

reservations   22, 73, 183

resident dislocation   81

resident populations   55

resident satisfaction   68

resort   1, 22, 55-65, 199, 203, 208, 220, 223, 224, 226, 228, 231, 233

resort community   55, 57

resort management   55, 61

resort product   61

resorts   1, 12, 13, 15, 18, 19, 20, 21, 55, 60, 61, 103

resource allocation   60

resource dependence   240

resource use   58, 241

restoration   21, 29, 30, 110, 140, 143, 145, 162, 164

Revelstoke, B.C.   199, 203, 207, 208, 209, 212, 213, 214, 216, 219

revitalization   30, 35, 37, 38, 42, 73, 75, 76, 77, 78, 79, 80, 136

revival policies   51

Ritz Carlton Hotels   170, 175, 182

Rochester, New York   6, 170, 180, 182

Royal British Columbia Museum   6, 149-156, 197

rural areas   18, 103, 147, 230

rural destinations   15, 16

S

Saint John   29

scenic sightseeing   119

seasonal demand   16

seasonal factors   11, 12, 15

seasonal fluctuations   16, 20, 21

seasonal generating process   13

seasonal pattern(s)   11, 14, 12, 13, 15, 16, 20, 21, 22

seasonal peaking   17

seasonal receiving process   13

seasonal variations   9, 11, 12, 16, 76

seasonal workers   58, 59

seasonality   5, 9-23, 87

seasonalized pricing   13

secondary benefits   73
secondary destination   146
secondary tourist resource   108
service characteristics   255
service delivery   175, 187
service industry   4, 186, 189, 197
service management   8, 184, 193, 196, 197, 263
service marketing   184, 196, 263
service organizations   189, 190, 193
service provider   186, 189, 190, 192, 194, 196
service quality   3, 4, 8, 69, 186, 187, 188, 191, 192, 196, 197
service sector   42, 58, 59, 184, 229
services industry   253, 255
SERVQUAL   192
shopping   15, 16, 22, 45, 71, 80, 97, 103, 147, 226
short-term economic gains   74
social benefits   77, 171
social equity   47, 53, 112
social factors   11
social impact(s)   23, 57, 82, 219
social issues   240
social welfare   84
socioeconomic environment   225, 228
socioeconomic impacts   229
sociological paradigms and organizational analysis   243, 249
source areas   12
space   34, 43, 45, 50, 51, 53, 56, 59, 60, 63, 78, 79, 83, 86, 95, 97, 99, 100, 101, 130, 131, 144, 150, 157, 201, 213, 249
special events   17, 22, 31, 67-74, 75, 76, 77, 85, 86, 161, 162, 246
speciality tourism   119, 126
spending patterns   30, 33
sports   11, 12, 21, 27, 29, 30, 32, 33, 35, 36, 37, 77, 103, 108, 111
sports tourism   30, 32, 33
staff   3, 133, 149-156, 165, 173, 177, 188, 191, 204, 209, 261
staffing   9, 149, 150
stakeholder(s)   6, 56, 63, 155, 171, 172, 199-217, 238, 239, 240, 241, 249, 250
standardized tourism space   51

standards   3, 29, 59, 80, 130, 175, 176, 178, 221, 229

staying visitors   46

strategic alliances   184

strategic destination planning   199

strategic improvements   202

strategic initiatives   170

strategic interests   174

strategic management   175, 179, 220, 240, 249

strategic models   170

strategic objectives   241

strategic planning   62, 178, 179, 201, 203, 210, 217, 218, 219

strategic quality control   183

strategic vision   202, 203

strategy   6, 13, 25-38, 41, 42, 49, 53, 55, 61, 73, 74, 76, 77, 78, 79, 85, 87, 134, 147, 153, 155, 171, 172, 180, 181, 182, 183, 189, 194, 196, 197, 199, 201, 202, 205, 209, 210, 213, 217, 218, 220, 227, 231, 235, 240, 248, 249, 251

structural economic change   27

sub-products   184, 185

supplementary services   147

support organizations   3

sustainability   55, 100, 130, 199, 200, 217, 219

sustainable community   199, 208, 215, 219, 220

sustainable competitive advantage   230

sustainable development   61, 80, 199, 207, 208, 217, 218, 236, 249

sustainable partners   232

sustainable tourism   6, 199, 217, 218, 219, 237, 240

sustainable urban tourism   6, 111

Sydney   79, 80, 82, 83, 87, 97, 101, 154

Sydney Olympics 2000 Bid   79, 80, 87

T

tax base   84, 226, 232

tax revenues   26

technical quality   191

technology   4, 29, 38, 80, 85, 154, 172, 173, 188, 241

territorial behaviour   59

the Netherlands   6, 86, 193, 194, 197

theatres   16, 103, 106, 112, 170

theme parks   6, 221, 222, 225, 226, 227, 228, 229, 230

themes   169, 171, 175, 204, 207, 211, 212

time-sharing developments   20

Top of Holland   193, 194, 195, 196, 197

Toronto   16, 18, 19, 22, 26, 27, 28, 29, 31, 33, 34, 37, 39, 149

total quality concept   185

total quality management (TQM)   6, 170, 175, 179, 180, 181, 182, 191

tourism communities   55, 56, 59, 65, 219

tourism consumption   115

tourism development   6, 22, 25, 34, 35, 38, 41, 49, 55, 61, 67, 70, 72, 74, 85, 86, 92, 95, 96, 130, 132, 133, 134, 145, 148, 183, 199, 200, 203, 207, 209, 214, 217, 218, 219, 220, 235-250

tourism facilities   21, 42

tourism industry   13, 22, 23, 58, 61, 68, 69, 73, 74, 85, 96, 110, 147, 175, 179, 182, 184, 196, 199, 200, 211, 235, 236, 255

tourism initiatives   124, 126, 130, 201, 218, 235, 236, 238, 240, 249

tourism interests   60

tourism literature   70, 200

tourism market   5, 28, 38, 46, 57, 75, 76, 103, 231

tourism organizations   173, 184

tourism partnerships   239, 242, 246

tourism policies   107, 110, 240

tourism policy   48, 65, 93, 220, 236, 250

tourism potential   49, 104, 109, 230

tourism product(s)   6, 27, 38, 71, 122, 144, 171

tourism promotion   69, 126, 133, 200

tourism research   2, 8, 22, 23, 25, 30, 37, 38, 39, 65, 74, 87, 92, 98, 101, 113, 121, 133, 134, 135, 148, 182, 196, 219, 249, 250, 263

tourism researchers   70, 242

tourism seasons   15

tourism strategy(ies)   26, 49, 79, 106, 107, 115, 249

tourism studies   76, 92, 110, 118, 218, 242, 244, 246

tourism system   55, 56, 189, 191, 193, 197

tourism-related development   61

tourist activities   13, 60, 120

tourist behaviour   183

tourist boards   110, 237

tourist consumerism   130

tourist destination(s)   2, 15, 16, 25, 26, 27, 144, 183, 184, 186, 190, 196, 199, 209

tourist environment   96

tourist expenditure(s)   32, 103, 106, 223

tourist experience(s)   2, 3, 4, 7, 36, 112, 120, 121, 124, 130

tourist facilities   16, 62

tourist gaze   2, 8, 87, 96, 101

tourist histories   97

tourist landscape(s)   35, 36, 95, 96, 99

Tourist Opportunity Spectrum   184

tourist origin areas   15, 20

tourist product(s)   2, 7, 27, 28, 31, 81, 103, 147, 153

tourist resource   103, 108, 112

tourist revenue   32

tourist satisfaction   12, 261, 262, 263

tourist season   21, 31, 233,

tourist seasonality   11

tourist sector   183

tourist service area   223

tourist visitation   15, 16, 35, 36

tourist-historic city   29, 148

training   48, 128, 131, 132, 156, 164, 177, 178, 180, 212, 221, 236, 241, 250

transport   50, 76, 77, 80, 183, 229

transportation   13, 15, 16, 17, 26, 29, 32, 63, 64, 146, 147, 207, 222

trickle down economic theory   47

U

urban attractions   108, 253

urban design   169

urban destination(s)   5, 17, 22, 169, 179, 182, 219

urban development   15, 16, 37, 77, 169, 226, 237

urban entrepreneurialism   79

urban growth   79, 113, 232

urban growth coalitions   79

urban heritage tourism   91, 98

urban life   170

urban place promotion   76

urban planners   169

urban policy   41, 74, 83, 87, 113

urban regeneration   25, 26, 29, 30, 36, 37, 38, 41, 42, 53, 85, 86, 106, 107, 111, 112, 134, 249, 250

urban renewal   29, 49, 78, 87, 98, 107

urban services class   107

urban studies   1, 37

urban tourism   1-8, 9, 25-38, 41, 53, 71, 74, 79, 84, 86, 87, 103, 110, 111, 112, 169, 170, 171, 179, 182, 219, 236, 240, 241, 245, 246, 248

urban tourism domain   1, 2, 3, 5

urban tourism research   2, 25, 30

urban vacations   28

urban visitor experience   182

V

vacation experience   1, 185

value assumptions   92

value base   214

value components   169

value strategy   171, 172

values   59, 63, 82, 83, 91, 92, 93, 98, 99, 108, 121, 171, 178, 202, 203, 204, 205, 208, 209, 210, 211, 212, 214, 215, 217, 218, 219, 223, 246

Vancouver   27, 29, 31, 32, 33, 37, 38, 39, 57, 59, 60, 78, 81, 87, 97, 113, 126, 129, 149, 166

Vanderbilt, George   157, 158, 159, 162

vision   6, 50, 74, 129, 131, 152, 157, 161, 173, 174, 175, 176, 177, 180, 181, 182, 199-219, 222

vision statement(s)   6, 201-217

visionary planning   215

visioning exercises   199, 210, 212, 214, 217

visiting friends and relatives (VFR)   16

visitor expectations   122, 127

visitor expenditure   31, 46, 47

visitor experience   130, 165, 170, 173, 182

visitor information   126

visitor responses   129

visitor satisfaction   2, 7, 64, 68, 172, 256

W
Walt Disney World   221, 223, 224, 225, 226, 227, 228, 231, 232
waste water   225, 227
water distribution   225
water management   224, 225
Whistler, British Columbia   55, 56, 57, 65
Whistler Resort   57, 58
Winnipeg   29, 32, 33, 37, 38

Y
Yogyakarta 137-148